CCDE In Depth

Orhan Ergun
CCDE #2014:17
CCIE #26567

CISCO CERTIFIED DESIGN EXPERT IN DEPTH

ORHAN ERGUN

www.orhanergun.net

Copyright

Orhan Ergun

WHAT EXPERTS ARE SAYING

I attended the Orhan's training and passed the CCDE Practical exam in August 2016. I highly recommend taking Orhan Ergun's CCDE Bootcamp. I found his resources to be very detailed, thorough and exceptionally the best around.

I am now the first Nigerian CCDE and thanks Orhan.

Hashiru Aminu , Technical Leader at Cisco Systems

I passed the CCDE Practical exam and Orhan's CCDE course was very important contributor to my success.

I definitely recommend his bootcamp to anyone who wants to learn network design and pass the Practical exam.

Daniel Lardeux, Senior Network Consultant at Post Telecom

I passed the CCDE Practical exam after Orhan's bootcamp. I worked from many resources but you cannot even compare Orhan with any other. Don't look around and join his bootcamp if you want to learn network design and pass the CCDE Practical Lab exam.

Muhammad Abubakar Siddique, CCDE & 2XCCIE and JNCIE, Network Architect at VR Networks

I attended Orhan's CCDE Course and I must say the guy has exceeded my expectations in all ways in terms of quality, depth etc.

Deepak Kumar, Senior Network Engineer at HCL

Orhan's Ability to cover the vast technical topics required for the CCDE is tremendous. He is not only technical; he is also an amazing teacher.

Thanks Orhan, you are the best CCDE trainer for sure.

Jason Gooley, System Engineer at Cisco Systems

Cisco Certified Design Expert
Written and Practical Study Guide

Cisco Certified Design Expert Practical

Exam is given every three months at Pearson Professional Center locations (over 275 locations worldwide)

Prerequisite: Students must first pass CCDE written exam

CCDE is vendor neutral network design exam

To my wife Halise and my sweet son Emin Efe and everyone who helped to make this project a success, and not forgetting all those who I worked with and coached to become outstanding Design Experts.

Contents

About the Author

Orhan Ergun,

CCIE # 26567 & CCDE #20140017

Orhan Ergun is a network architect focused on Service Providers, data centers, virtualization, cloud, and network security. Orhan has more than 15 years of networking experience and has been working on many medium and large-scale network design and deployment projects for Enterprise and Service Provider networks.

He provides a Consultancy Services to African, Middle East, and some Turkish Service Providers and Mobile Operators. Orhan has been teaching Cisco Network design concepts such as CCDE and Pre-CCDE for many years, and has created the best CCDE Training Program to share his Network Design experience and knowledge with the networking community.

A good number of his students have successfully passed the CCDE Practical exam so far and Orhan produces 30% of the CCDEs each year. Orhan is sharing his articles and thoughts on his blog www.orhanergun.net. All the training and consultancy services related information can be found from his website.

He is a father, a husband and a networking geek!

Orhan lives in Qatar with his wife, Halise and their son Efe.

Twitter : @OrhanErgunCCDE

Contributing Author

Michael "Zig" Zsiga II, CCIE™ #44883

Zig has been in the networking industry a little over 15 years. He is currently a Lead Technical Architect at ePlus in the New England region of the United States. He holds active CCIE certifications in both Routing and Switching and Service Provider. He also holds a Bachelor's of Science in Computer Science from Park University. Zig has been designing and deploying complex network designs for the US Government and Major Commercial Companies for years. He is a father, a husband, a United States Marine, a gamer, a nerd, a geek and a big soccer fan. He loves all technology and can usually be found in the lab learning and teaching others. Zig lives in New Hampshire, USA with his wife, Julie and their son Gunnar.

R/S

Zig

Twitter: @michael_zsiga

Introduction

Attaining the status of a Design Expert is what a lot of people tend to pursue, but not so many meet success in their pursuit of the CCDE. Becoming a Certified Design Expert is not really a matter of how hard you work, but how smart. You don't have all the time in the world to go making "your" mistakes, just so you could learn from them, or walking the well worn-out path and expecting different results.

In this book, I have poured out my wealth of experience and expertise in the world of network design, this I have done in an easy to understand, non-textbook practical fashion without encapsulating the real thing in a sea of words. This book is written from the inside – out, for those who would like to pass both CCDE Written and Practical exams, or to gain deeper knowledge in network design.

The book contains detailed systematic guide to learning: Many protocols and the technologies which are used in todays Service Provider, Enterprise, Datacenter, and Mobile operator real life network design.

There are a lot of people out there who will try to teach Network Design, they do this haphazardly and at the end of the day they mess up the whole thing. This is not to say that there are no good tutors out there, but they are hard to find. And if you are lucky to find one, it is mostly theoretical and hardly any real-life practical stuff. It is all packed in here.

The knowledge and insight, which I have carefully laid out in this book, will help you bag the CCDE certification and become the star that you deserve to be. Some of the areas that the book covers include: network design principles and all the best practices, tens of network design case studies, design review questions after each chapter, how real life networks look like and insight into how large companies and corporations design their network, techniques to will improve your strategic design thinking, CCDE Practical Lab design scenario, complementary study resources.

Becoming a Design Expert is easy, but you have to work right and most importantly, you have to work smart.

Orhan Ergun

What is the CCDE Practical Exam?

Below are the things, which you should know about CCDE Practical exam.

- Four scenarios in total, over the course of eight hours
- There is no configuration for any vendor equipment
- Vendor-agnostic, but some technologies relevant to Cisco (e.g., HSRP, GLBP, EIGRP, DMVPN) may be asked in the exam
- The CCDE Practical is reading-intensive exam; it will be necessary to skim through some material in the scenario. In the last chapter of the book I will share the hints.
- Analysis, Design, Implementation and Optimization are the four job tasks within the CCDE scenarios.
- Analyzing the design is the most critical and hardest of these four job tasks. Since you need to understand the background information about the company, business and the technical requirements. In the CCDE Practical scenarios, I will show you all the four tasks so different question types will be understood very well.
- Exam score is provided based on these job tasks.
- Passing score is around 75–80%.
- Exam score will be made available immediately after exam. You don't need to wait couple hours or days.

CCDE Task Areas

Generally, there are four task areas that test-takers will encounter in the CCDE exam. One or more tasks can be found in any given scenario.

1. Merge & Divest
2. Add Technologies
3. Replace Technology
4. Scaling

Merge and Divest

When managing corporate mergers or divestments these sorts of questions should be kept in mind:

- What is the best method for the migration? Should a phased approach be taken or migrate everything at once?
- Where will be the first place in the network for migration? Core to the edge, or edge to the core ?
- What happens to the routing, IGP, BGP? Is a "ship in the night" approach suitable or redistribution is better for routing protocol merger?
- Which type of security infrastructure will network support overall?
- What are the Quality of Service Policies of the companies? Will final merged network support Quality of Service or through bandwidth everywhere?
- Will merged network have IPv6?
- Does one of the networks require Multicast? Will merged network support Multicast?
- What is the new capacity requirement of the merged network?
- How will be the merged network monitored? Do exist Network Management tools capable to support all the technologies/protocols of the both network?
- When you divest the network, where will the datacenters be? Can you decommission any datacenter, POP location for cost optimization?

This may not be the entire list but definitely you should at least start asking these questions in your real life design. In the CCDE exam questions will come most of the time from the above considerations.

Adding Technologies

If you are adding new technologies onto an existing network, these sorts of questions should be kept in mind:

* What can be broken? Does this technology affect others technologies/protocols in the network?
* What does this technology provide? Is it really necessary? If you have enough bandwidth in your network, do you really need Quality of Service for example? Or if you would arrange your routing protocol metric well, would you need MPLS Traffic engineering at all?
* What are the alternatives of these technology or protocol? (Throughout the book, you will see a lot of comparison charts which will help you to evaluate alternatives to each technology/ protocol)
* Which additional information do you need to deploy this technology/protocol?
* Every new technology adds some amount of complexity, so consider complexity vs. the benefits of the technology tradeoff! As it is mentioned above, do you really need to deploy MPLS Traffic Engineering for better utilization or with the IGP protocol metric design could you achieve the same goal?

Replacing Technologies

If you are adding new technologies onto an existing network, these sorts of questions should be kept in mind:

* Is this change really needed? Is there a valid business reason behind it?
* What is the potential impact to the overall network?
* What will the migration steps be? Order of operation is very important in network design. If you cannot design the migration process carefully, you might have unplanned down time or planned downtime takes longer than your plan.
* Are there budget constraints?
* Will both of the technology run in the network at the same time?

Are there enough hardware resources on the existing networking equipment?

* Does this new technology require a learning curve? Do your networking team have an experience on the new technology?
* Does your network monitoring tool support new technology?

CCDE Written Exam

This book will help you for the CCDE Written greatly. None of the resources out there covers even the half of the questions in this book. Almost 200 Design Questions and Answers are provided throughout the book and they will help both in CCDE Written and the Practical exams.

Also theory information in this book will provide many real life theory information as well as case studies.

For those who need further study resources, I prepared a CCDE Streamlined Study Resources List with couple other CCDE engineers and the CCDE/CCAr Program Manager Elaine Lopes.

Recommended Reading List

CCDE Streamlined Study Resources prepared by Orhan Ergun, Elaine Lopes, Andre Laurent and Virgilio Spaziani can be found at this link:

https://learningnetwork.cisco.com/community/certifications/ccde/written_exam.study-material

CHAPTER 1
LAYER 2 TECHNOLOGIES

There are many Layer 2 control and data plane technologies in today networks. Ethernet is the main technology, which is used in the Local Area Network, Wide Area Network and in the Datacenters.

In this chapter:

- STP theory and design practices will be explained, as well as VLANs, VTP, and Trunking best practices will be shared.
- Layer 3 first-hop redundancy control mechanisms such as HSRP, VRRP and GLBP will be explained from the network design perspective.
- Campus and datacenter access networks can be built as Layer 2 and Layer 3 access. These two design approaches will be explained in detail and examples will be provided to understand the optimal design for a given business and application requirements.
- Many case studies will be presented as complementary to the theory and the best practice information.
- At the end of this section, you will have many quiz questions and the answers; you will be able to test your layer 2 design knowledge.
- Common network design principles for the availability, scalability, convergence, security, networking topologies, routing protocols, and Layer 2 technologies will be shared

SPANNING TREE

Spanning Tree Protocol (STP) is a control plane mechanism for Ethernet. It is used to create a Layer 2 topology (a tree) by placing the root switch on top of the tree.

Since classical Ethernet works based on data plane learning and Ethernet frames don't have TTL for loop prevention, loops are prevented by the STP blocking the links.

Loop has to be mitigated by blocking some links with the Spanning Tree but blocking links does not allow using all the links actively, nor does it provide for multipathing.

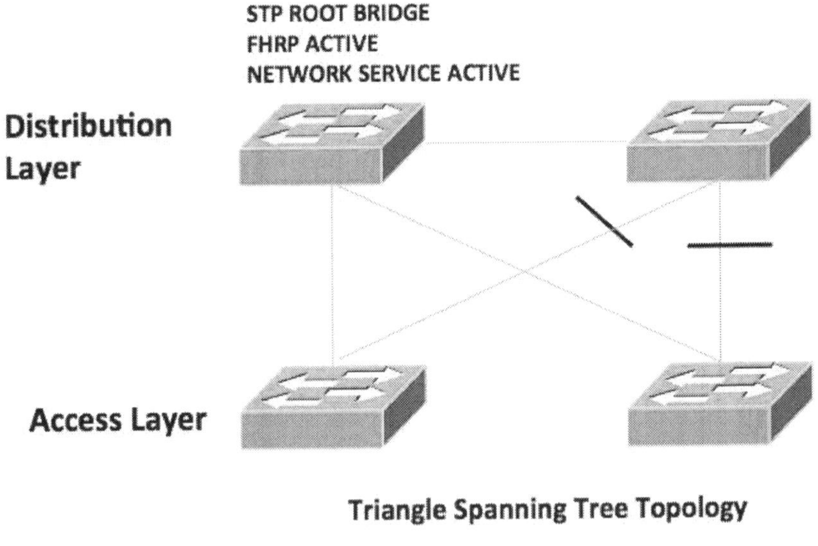

STP ROOT BRIDGE
FHRP ACTIVE
NETWORK SERVICE ACTIVE

Distribution Layer

Access Layer

Triangle Spanning Tree Topology

Access-Distribution Switches and STP

As you can see, in the above topology, Access switches to the right distribution link are blocked to mitigate the Layer 2 forwarding loop.

STP does not allow flow-based load balancing. Two common load balancing techniques are in the Layer 2 networks: VLAN-based and flow-based load balancing.

VLAN BASED LOAD BALANCING

In layer 2 switching, the Ethernet frames should be received from the same port where it was sent, otherwise layer 2 switching or switching loop occurs.

Let me explain this concept with the topology depicted below

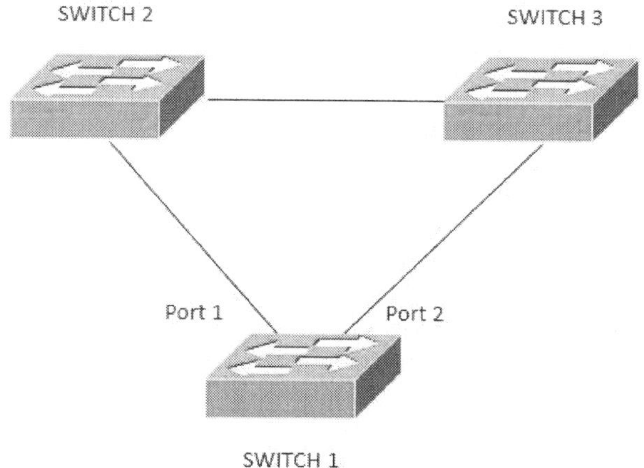

Vlan-based load balancing

In the above figure, either Port 1 or Port2 is used to send the traffic, and the same port should be used to receive the traffic. The switches use MAC addresses to process the Ethernet frames.

The switch cannot see the same MAC address from two different ports. In other words, Switch 1 cannot receive the same MAC address from both Port 1 and Port 2.

In order to resolve this problem, both ports can be placed in a bundle. In standard terms, we can link aggregation group (LAG) with the vendor terms, Etherchannel, or port channel.

Since Switch 1, instead of LAG, in the above topology is connected to two different switches (Switch 2 and Switch3), MLAG (Multi Chassis Link Aggregation Group) or MEC (Multi Chassis Etherchannel) are created between the switches.

On the other hand, spanning tree solves the problem by bringing down one of the ports. If Port 1 sends the frame, Port 2 is disabled.

Spanning tree carries out its full operation by starting to choose the root switch. The rule is that one of the switches is elected as root switch, and all the ports of root switch are always forward. Thus, the ports moving to the root switch or coming from the root switch cannot be blocked.

In the above topology, if Switch 2 is elected as root switch (manually by the administrator or dynamically based on smallest MAC address), Switch 3 is used as the backup-root switch. However, if Switch 2 fails, Switch 3 takes full responsibility of the operation.

When Switch 2 is elected as the root switch, Switch 1 to Switch 3 link is disabled by the spanning tree (So, physically UP but layer 2 down).

If there are multiple VLAN in the network, using Port 1 of the Switch 1 to Switch 2 links for some VLANs and Port 2 of the Switch 1 to Switch 2 for the other VLANs can accommodate all the available links in the network. This process is called VLAN based load balancing.

To say it another way, all the ports of the root switch have to be up from the spanning tree point of view; thus, Switch 1 to Switch 3 is blocked to eliminate loop. So, how would VLANs Switch 1 to Switch 3 link be used?

As you can guess, we would assign a root switch role to different switches in that case.

Switch 2 would be the root switch for some set of VLANs, and Switch 3 would be the root switch for other VLANs. They would also be backup root switch for one another.

There are many spanning tree implementations: namely, CST (Common Spanning Tree), PVST (Per VLAN Spanning Tree), RSTP (Rapid Spanning Tree), RPVST (Rapid Per VLAN Spanning Tree), and MST (Multiple Spanning Tree).

CST is an IEEE standard spanning tree implementation commonly known as 802.1d, and it doesn't allow different root switches for different VLANs. Put simply, it doesn't support more than one instance; thus all the VLANs in the network have to be assigned to the same root switch.

PVST, RPVST, and MST support VLAN based load balancing. So, different VLANs can be assigned to different root switches. RSTP, which is also known as 802.1w doesn't provide VLAN based load balancing.

As you can guess from their names, the difference between RSTP and RPVST is; RPVST (Rapid Per VLAN Spanning Tree) allows VLAN load balancing.

FLOW BASED LOAD BALANCING

Flow-based load balancing is used mostly in layer 2 networks, although in Layer 3 routing, packets can be load balanced per packets or per flow, flow-based load balancing is commonly used with the Local area network, datacenter and datacenter interconnect technologies.

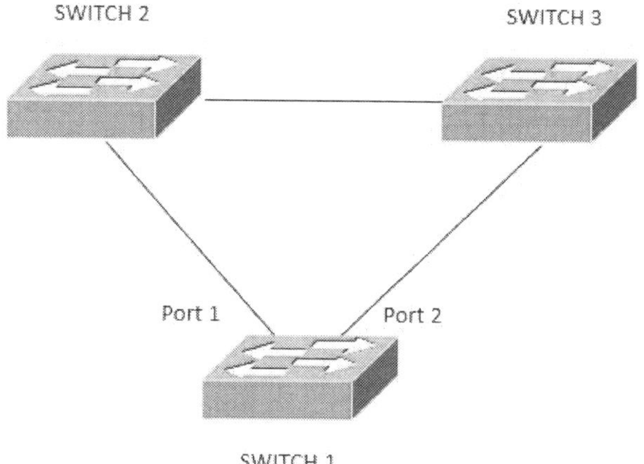

Flow based load balancing

Imagine you have 10 Vlans and the Switch2 is root switch for all 10 Vlans. And in every Vlan you have 10s of hosts.

If the link between switch 2 and switch 3 is Layer 3 link, spanning tree doesn't block any links in this topology. This topology is called then Layer 2 loop-free topology.

Spanning tree deals with the logical layer 2 topology. For the layer 3 part, default gateway purpose; one of the first hop redundancy mechanisms is used. It can be HSRP , VRRP or GLBP.

If HSRP or VRRP is used, one of the switch can be used as a primary for the given Vlan and other switch is used as standby.

Switch 2 for example can be used for Vlan 5 as primary and switch 3 is used as standby for Vlan 5. For another Vlan, for example Vlan 6, switch 3 is used as primary and switch 2 as standby. This allows all the uplinks of switch 1 to be used thus bandwidth is not wasted.

HSRP and VRRP thats why provide Vlan based load balancing. Default gateway for a particular Vlan can be only one of the switches.

If we use GLBP (Gateway Load Balancing Protocol) in this topology, for any given Vlan, both Switch 2 and switch 3 can be used as default gateway. For different host, which come from the same Vlan, Arp replies are sent by different switches.

Switch 2 can be a default gateway of host 1 in Vlan 5 and switch 3 can be a default gateway of host 2 in Vlan 5.

As you can understand, traffic for different set of hosts in the same Vlan can be sent by switch 1 to switch 2 and switch 3 at the same time.

Flow is not described as host of course. For the same host, different destination IP address and port numbers mean different flows. Then, we can say that some of the traffic of host 1 in Vlan 5 can be sent to Switch 2, and some of the traffic of the same host can be sent to switch 3.

SPANNING TREE THEORY

As soon as STP detects a loop, it blocks a link to prevent the loop. CST (Common Spanning Tree) 802.1d which is classic/legacy STP supports only one instance for all VLANs. One instance mean, there is only one topology, thus only one root switch for all the Vlans in the network.

It does not support VLAN based load-balancing. Only Active-Standby topology is supported. One switch can be the root switch for all the Vlans and in case active switch fails, standby become a root switch for all the Vlans.

PVSTP+ is Cisco's 802.1d implementation but supports one-to-one instance to VLAN mapping.

Enhancements to PVSTP provide good optimization for CST, but even PVSTP has slow convergence compared to MST and RSTP.

RSTP (802.1w) is the IEEE standard spanning tree mechanism. Main advantage of RSTP is fast convergence. It provides fast convergence through Proposal Agreement handshake mechanism. A same mechanism and convergence characteristic is enabled in MST as well.

Spanning Tree Toolkit

Some of the spanning tree features are explained below.

- PortFast: Allows the access port bypass the listening and learning phases. Also TCN BPDUs are not sent when port's state changes.
- UplinkFast: Provides three-to-five second convergence after link failure.
- Backbone Fast: Cuts convergence time by MaxAge for indirect failure. Thus provides fast convergence for some topologies.
- Loop Guard: Prevents the alternate or root port from being elected unless Bridge Protocol Data Units (BDPUs) are present. It takes unidirectional link failures if bpdu is not received from the link.
- Root Guard: Prevents external switches from becoming the root. This feature provides optimal switching/forwarding in layer 2 spanning

tree topologies

- BPDU Guard: Disables a PortFast-enabled port if a BPDU is received.
- BPDU Filter: Prevents sending or receiving BPDUs on PortFast enabled ports, but doesn't block the ports. It can be considered as monitoring feature mostly.

In the below diagram, you can see where these features are commonly deployed.

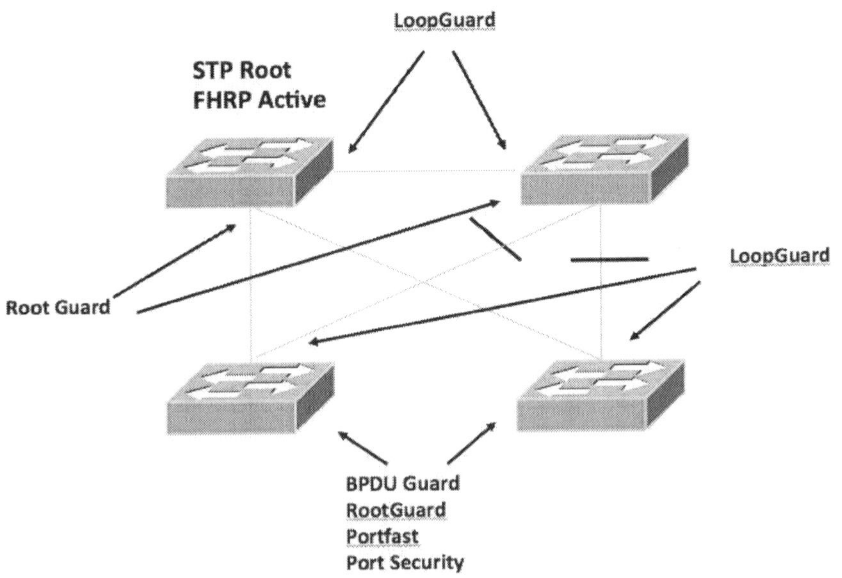

Spanning Tree Features Placement

MST 802.1s is the industry standard. Convergence is like RSTP, proposal, and agreement mechanism. Groups of VLANs are mapped to the STP instances.

If you have 100 VLANs you don't need to have 100 instances as in the case of RPVST+. MST reduces CPU and memory requirements on the switches and provides scalability.

With MST region support, MST can be used between the data centers. However, STP domain is still limited to the local data center. Think of it as an OSPF multi-area. Spanning tree BPDUs are limited to MST region.

MST supports a large number of VLANs; therefore it might be suitable for large data centers or service provider access networks. In the Service Providers access networks MST is used together with QinQ (802.1ah Provider Bridging (PB)) or Mac in Mac(802.1aq Provider Backbone Bridging (PBB)).

- MST in today networks is still used in many datacenters because of its large scale Layer 2 support and its ability to have different MST regions on different datacenters allows STP BPDUs to be limited to an individual data center.

Spanning Tree Best Practices

- Use RSTP or RPVST+ for fast convergence for direct and indirect failures.
- Use MST for scaling. If you have large-scale VLAN deployment and CPU usages is a concern, take advantage of grouping VLANs to MST instance.
- Don't use 802.1d, CST. If you must use standard base, use RSTP or MST.
- Take advantage of VLAN load-balancing, so you can use your uplink capacity.
- VLAN load-balancing can be cumbersome, but it has the advantage of using all uplinks.
- Spanning tree avoids switching loops by blocking some links in the topology. If the requirement is to use all the available links, link can be grouped into a bundle
- LACP and the Cisco preparatory protocol PAGP are used to aggregate multiple physical links into a logical bundle
- LACP is a standard mechanism which can be used only between two switches or between multiple switches
- If LACP is used between multiple switches, solution is called Multi Chassis link aggregation or multichassis etherchannel.
- System ID which is generated by the System Priority and MAC

address of the switches need to be same on two switches if there will be a Multichasis Ether channel.

- For ease of troubleshooting, you can use one distribution switch as primary root switch for odd VLANs and use the other distribution as the primary root switch for even VLANs. This gives better predictability.
- Always enable STP on the access-facing ports to protect the network from intentional or unintentional attacks.
- Port-security is used as a STP loop avoidance mechanism at the edge of Layer 2 campus Ethernet networks.

Spanning Tree Case Study

In the conference room of the company contractors connected a device, which doesn't generate STP BPDU, with two ports to the existing switch environment.

Question 1:

What would be the implication of this?

Question 2:

How can future problems be mitigated?

Answer

This problem happened in the early days of networking. Hubs don't generate STP BPDUs. If you connect a hub with two ports to a switch, forwarding loop occurs.

In order to stop it you can remove one of the cables. However, had the contractor known the complication from the start they most likely would have chosen a different configuration.

That's why a feature that can prevent a loop should be in place in advance.

- BPDU Guard and BPDU Filter are the two features, which react based on Spanning Tree BPDU.

- BPDU Guard shuts down the switch port if STP BPDU is received from the port.
- BPDU Filter doesn't shut down the port but can give some information about the BPDU.

According to this case study, BPDU is not generated. In this case; port-security helps.

Port-security doesn't allow two MAC addresses to be shown on the two ports of a given switch. If this happens, port-security feature shutdown the ports.

This is why it is one of the best practices to enable port-security not only as a security feature, but as an STP feature as well.

VLAN, VTP, and the Trunking Best Practices

- VTP is generally not recommended anymore because of configuration complexity and the potential for catastrophic failure. In other words, a small mistake on the VTP configuration can take whole network down.
- If VTP must be used, VTP Transparent mode is best practice because it decreases the potential for operational error.
- Always configure VTP Domain name and password.
- Manually prune unused VLANs from trunked interfaces to avoid broadcast propagation.
- Don't keep default VLAN as native VLAN, it protects from VLAN hopping attacks.
- Disable trunks on host ports.
- Don't put too many host in one VLAN; keep it small to provide manageable fault domain. In the same VLAN all broadcast unknown unicast packets have to be processed by all the nodes.
- If fast convergence is required, don't use Dynamic Trunking Protocol (DTP). DTP slows down the convergence because switches negotiate the trunking mode.

FIRST HOP REDUNDANCY PROTOCOLS

Three commonly used First Hop Redundancy Protocols (FHRP) are; HSRP, VRRP and GLBP.

HRSP and GLBP are the Cisco-specific protocols, but VRRP is IETF standard, so using VRRP if you need multivendor interoperability is important design constraint.

HSRP and VRRP use one virtual IP and one virtual MAC address for gateway functionality.

HSRP

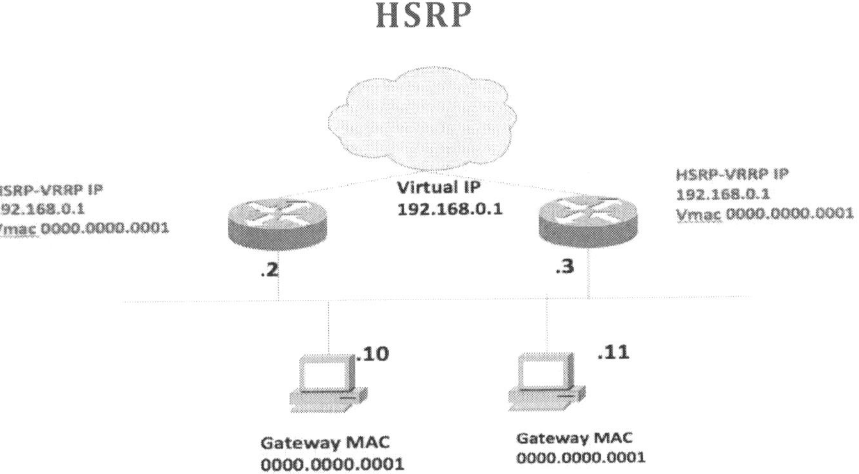

HSRP VIP-VMAC

In the above figure only HSRP protocol is shown but VRRP works in exactly the same way. One Virtual MAC address is mapped to one virtual IP address. Switches have their own physical IP address as well.

Only one switch can be HSRP active switch in any given time. If Active switch fails, standby takes the gateway responsibility by responding the ARP requests with the common Virtual MAC address.

Host's gateway IP address doesn't change. On the hosts, virtual IP address is configured.

GLBP

GLBP uses one virtual IP and several virtual MAC addresses. For the client's ARP requests, the Active Virtual Gateway (AVG) responds different virtual MAC addresses, thus network-based load balancing can be achieved.

Multiple switches can be actively forwarding the network traffic. GLBP is Cisco preparatory protocol and may not work with the different vendor equipment together.

Different clients use different devices as their default gateway. But on all the clients same IP address is configured as default gateway IP address. This IP address is the Virtual GLBP IP.

GLBP might be suitable for a campus but not for Internet Edge since the firewall uses the same IGW as its default gateway by using the same IP address. In order to explain Why GLBP is not suitable on the Internet Edge in detail, at the end of this chapter, case study will be presented.

HSRP, VRRP and GLBP First Hop Redundancy Protocols Technical Comparison

Below table summarizes the similarities and the differences of all the first hop redundancy protocols in great detail. Network designers should know the pros and cons of the technologies, protocol alternatives and their capabilities from the design point of view.

Design Requirement	HRSP	VRRP	GLBP
Suitable on LAN	YES	YES	YES
Suitable on Datacenter	YES, if layer 3 access is not used	YES, if layer 3 access is not used	YES, if layer 3 access is not used
Suitable on Internet Edge	YES, but theremight be better options, such as routing with the firewall or Router behind the firewall	YES, but theremight be better options, such as routing with the firewall or Router behind the firewall	NO, it creates polarization issues. This is explained in detail in Orhan Ergun's CCDE Course
Standard Protocol	NO, Cisco Propriety	YES, IETF Standard	NO, Cisco Propriety
Preemption Support by default	No, you need to configure it manually, and preemption is important to prevent suboptimal trafic flow	YES, it is Enabled by default, and you can disable it on any vendor implementation	NO, you need to configure it manually, and preemption is important to avoid suboptimal traffic flow
Virtual IP and MAC	1 Virtual IP and 1 Virtual MAC	1 Virtual IP and 1 Virtual MAC	1 virtual IP and Multiple Virtual MACs
Stuff Experience	Very well known	Well known	Not well known
Flow Based Load Balancing	NO	NO	YES, Active Virtual Gateway responds to ARP requests with ddifferent Active Virtual Forwarder in an individual Vlan
Vlan baseed Load Balancing	YES, with HSRP groups	YES, with HSRP groups	YES, with GLBP Groups
Transport Protocol	Multicast	Multicast	Multicast
Default Convergence	Slow - 10 seconds	Fastest, but still slow for some applications - 3 seconds	Slow - 10 seconds
Security	MD5 Autentication	MD5 Autentication	MD5 Autentication
More than 2 device Support	YES	YES	YES
IPv6 Support	YES	YES, with VRRP v3	YES
Active Node Support	YES, with Anycast HSRP	YES	YES

HSRP-VRRP-GLBP Technical Comparison

First Hop Redundancy Protocol Case Study 1

Requirements:

An Enterprise company will implement FHRP on their distribution switches.

The requirement is; if the failure happens at the distribution switches, they don't want all the users in a given VLAN to be affected by the failure.

Some users in a given VLAN should still be able to operate.

Question:

Which FRHP should the company use? Why?

Answer:

As previously indicated in this chapter, only one device is used as an active gateway with HSRP and VRRP.

If failure happens, standby device takes responsibility and even with fast hellos and BFD there will still be downtime. During network convergence client's traffic will be affected.

With GLBP, in any given VLAN, there can be more than two active gateways, thus allowing client traffic to be divided among the active gateways.

If failure occours in a GLBP enabled network, only some of the client's traffic in a given VLAN is affected. If there are two active gateways, only half of them will be affected in a given Vlan.

Thus, for the purposes of this question, GLBP is the best choice.

First Hop Redundancy Protocol
Case Study 2

Which one is more suitable for the Internet edge, HRSP or GLBP? Let's look at the images below.

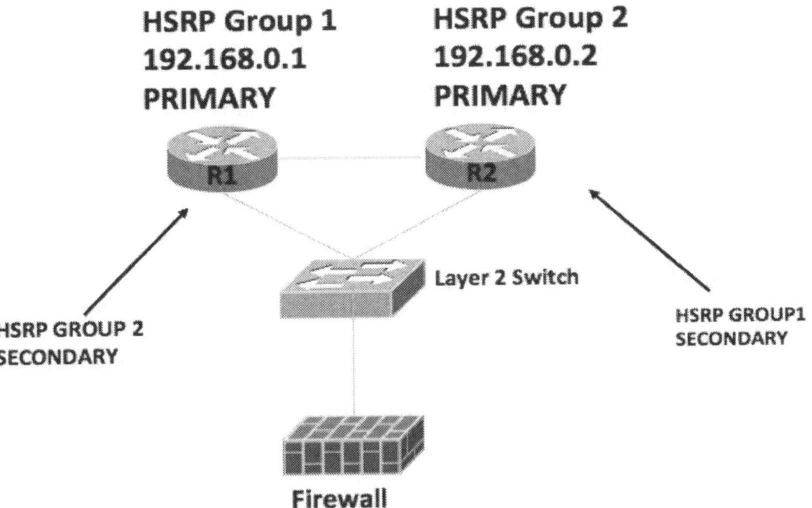

Let's first examine HSRP:

For the HSRP redundancy, two HSRP Groups can be created on both routers; each router is active for one of the HSRP group's. Egress traffic from the firewall is load balanced between the R1 and R2. Static routes are configured on the Firewall to each HRSP group. When the traffic arrives to the Routers, BGP handles outbound forwarding.

On the firewall, the default route is pointed to the both Internet gateways. (We divide the default route to the half actually.)

- First half of the default route is sent to the HRSP Group 1 address route outside 0.0.0.0 128.0.0.0 192.168.0.1
- Second half of the default route is sent to the HRSP Group 2 address route outside 128.0.0.0 128.0.0.0 192.168.0.2

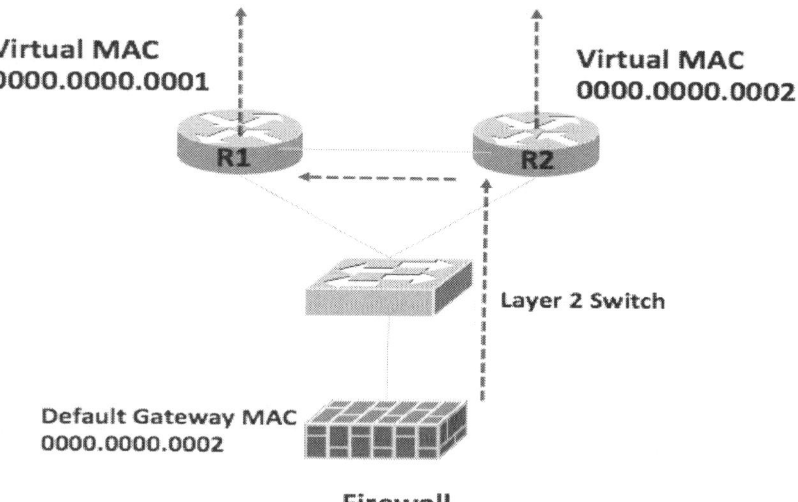

What about Gateway Load Balancing Protocol (GLBP)?

The firewall sends an ARP request and the AVG (Active Virtual Gateway) will respond with virtual MAC of either R1 or R2. Traffic is now polarized to a single link from the Firewall.

If Router 2 is responded as the Active Virtual Forwarder, traffic goes from the firewall to the Router 2 only.

There might be an issue with this design because, if there is Local Preference setting on the Routers and the higher local reference on the R1, all the traffic from the Firewall first go to the R2 and then over the R1-R2 link to the R1 for outbound traffic forwarding.

From the case study above, we can see that although HSRP might seem more complex configuration-wise, traffic will not be polarized to only one exit point, as in the case of GLBP.

In the GLBP case, one of the links from firewall to Internet Gateway is not used.

STP/HSRP Interaction

In the networks, all protocols interact with each other. Whenever you add, replace or change the protocol, as a network designer you should consider the overall impact. Throughout the book many interactions will be shown and the best practices will be shown to find an optimal design.

First interaction is between layer 2 protocols and the gateway protocols. Spanning tree and the HSRP interaction is explained in the below example.

One important factor to take into account when tuning HRSP is its preemptive behavior.

Preemption causes the primary HSRP peer to re-assume the primary role when it comes back online after a failure or maintenance event.

Preemption is the desired behavior because the STP/RSTP root should be the same device as the HSRP primary for a given subnet or VLAN. If HSRP and STP/RSTP are not synchronized, the interconnection between the distribution switches can become a transit link, and traffic takes a multi- hop L2 path to its default gateway.

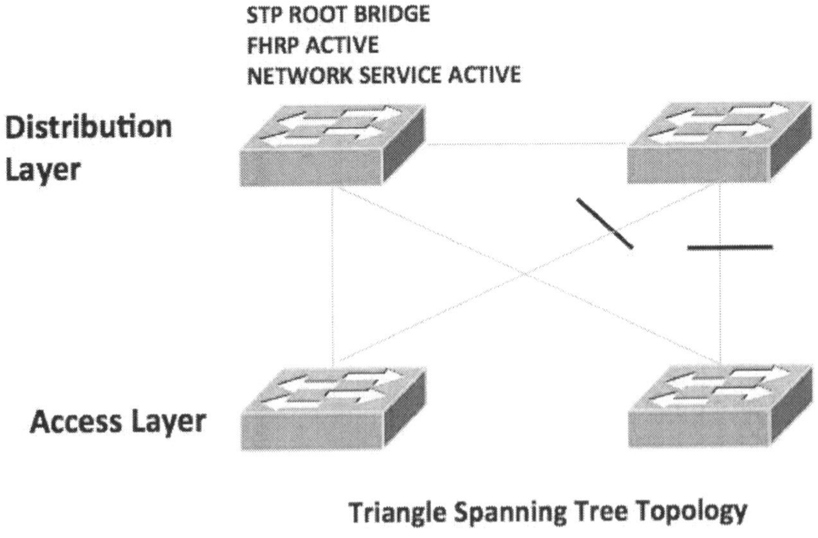

Spanning Tree- FHRP Interaction

In the topology above, Spanning Tree root, First Hop Redundancy (HSRP, VRRP) functionality is on the same device. If there is a network services devices such as Firewall, active firewall context should be also on the same device.

Imagine, left distribution switch (STP Root, FHRP Active) device fails in the above topology. Right distribution device become STP root and the FHRP active.

When the failed left distribution device comes back, since by default STP is preemptive, left distribution device become STP root again. But if HSRP is used in the above topology as First Hop Redundancy Protocol, since HSRP preemption is not enabled by default, right distribution device stays as HSRP active.

When the Spanning tree root and the HSRP active functionality is on the different devices for the same Vlan, traffic has to pass through the Inter distribution link.

Which mean, when the access switches send the packet, network traffic goes through first, left distribution switch and then right distribution switch on the above topology, because the right distribution switch is the default gateway.

HSRP preemption needs to be aware of switch boot time and connectivity to the rest of the network. It is possible for HSRP neighbor relationships to form and preemption to occur before the primary switch has L3 connectivity to the core. If this happens, traffic can be dropped until full connectivity is established.

The recommended best practice is to measure the system boot time, and set the HSRP preempt delay statement to a greater than this value.

ACCESS NETWORK DESIGN

Local Area and the Datacenter access networks can be based on Layer 2 or Layer 3. There are pros and cons of both approaches. In this section, first Layer 2 Access design and the deployment models;

- Loop Free Access Design
- Looped design
- Layer 3 Access design that is also known as Routed Access design will be explained.

Layer 2 Access Design

If access and distribution layer connection is based on Layer 2, then this topology is known as Layer 2 access design.

Layer 2 access topologies can be implemented as looped or loop-free model.

There should be FHRP (HSRP, VRRP or GLBP) since we want to have more than one distribution switch for redundancy.

Spanning tree runs in this design model between the access and the distribution layer devices.

This design model is more common in real life deployments compare to layer 3 access design, which will be explained later in this chapter.

Layer 2 Loop-Free Topology

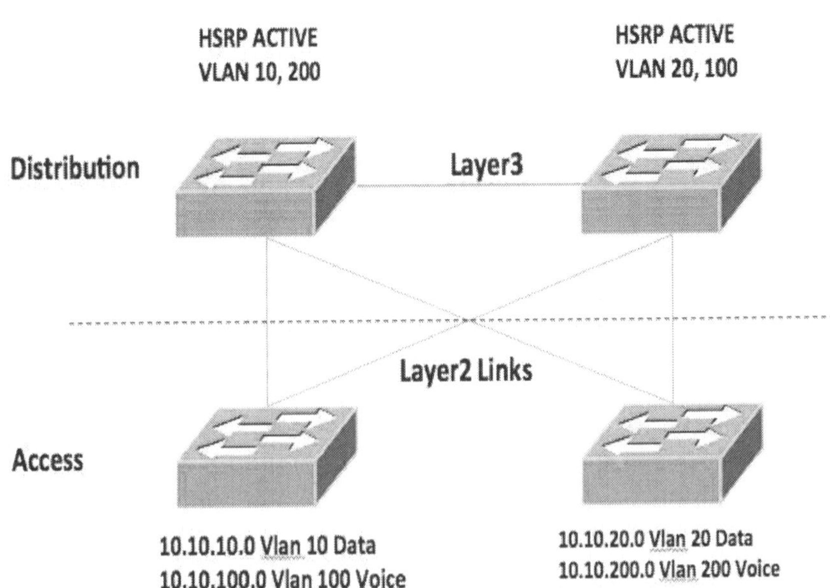

In loop-free design, the link between distribution layer switches is Layer 3, thus there is no loop in the topology and the STP does not block any link.

For loop-free topology, first hop redundancy protocol still runs on the distribution layer switches and the FHRP BPDUs travel through access switch links.

In layer 2 loop free topologies same Vlan is not used on every access switches. As you can see from the above topology, different Data and the Voice Vlans are used on different access switches. And for the Vlan based load balancing, different distribution switches are arranged as STP root and FHRP active for different Vlans.

Layer 2 Looped Topology

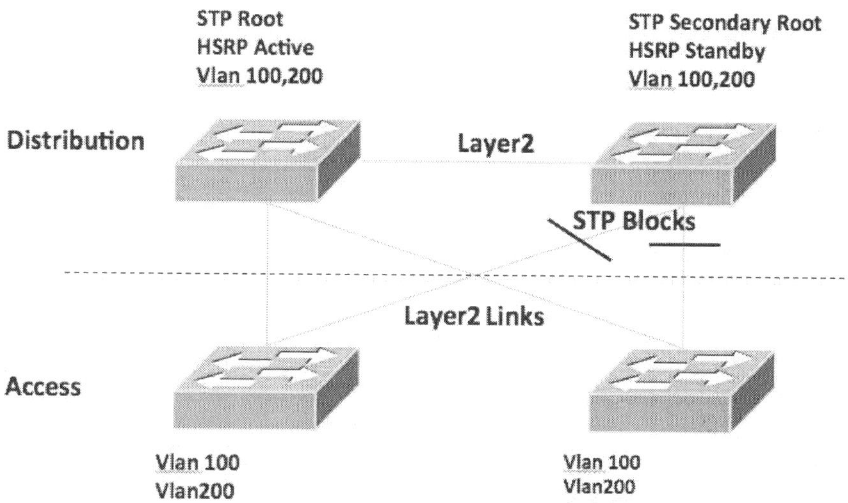

In looped design, the link between distribution layer switches is Layer 2, so STP will block one of the links to prevent loop.

Same VLAN can be used on every access switch.

As a best practice, STP Root switch should be aligned with FHRP active and if we have network services devices such as firewalls, we want to align active firewalls with STP and FHRP.

Layer 3 Access Design/Routed Access Design

Also known as routed access design.

- The connections between access and distribution layer switches are Layer 3, so client's first hop gateway is access layer switch.

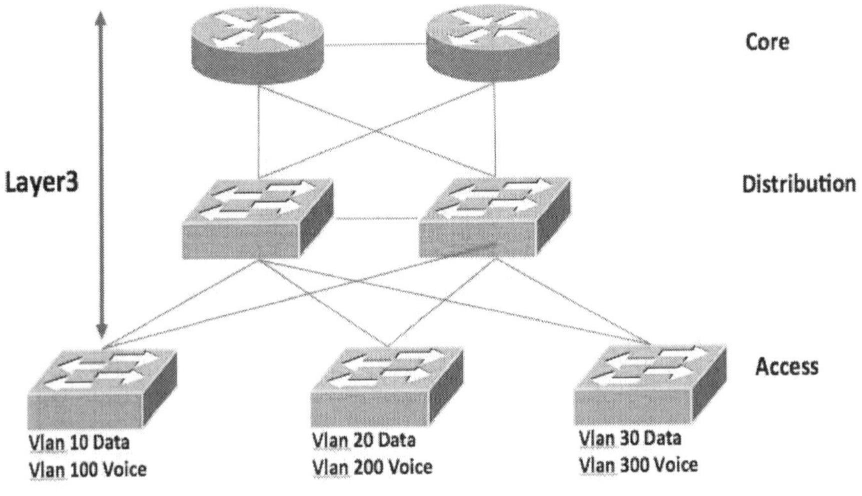

Unique Voice and Data VLANs

In Layer 3 Access/Routed Access design there is no need to have FHRP since the access layer switch is the first hop gateway. We can take advantage of fast convergence since we can use and tune any IGP protocols between access and distribution layer. Note that tuning protocol convergence time comes with it's own complications.

Tuning routing protocol for faster convergence may affect overall stability of the network.

You might have false positives. Configuration will also be much more complex.

There is no STP anymore in layer 3 access design , at least between access and distribution layer, but still you may want to protect user site loop by enabling STP at the edge.

The drawback of this design is that the same VLAN cannot be used on different access layer switches for the sake of campus network usage.

Layer 2 vs. Layer 3 Access Design Models Comparison

Below table summarizes the similarities and the differences of these two access layer design models in great detail. Network designers should know the pros and cons of the technologies, protocol alternatives and their capabilities from the design point of view.

Design Concern	Layer 2 Access	Layer 3/ Routed Access
Multiple path from the access to the distribution	YES, if there is Link Aggregation Group (LAG) or Fabric technologies. NO, if there is spanning tree	YES, Access to Distribution is layer 3, ECMP might work
Default Gateway Node	Distribution switch in 2 and 3 tier hierarchy	Access switch
Spanning Tree Requirement	If there is no Fabric Based Protocols (TRILL, SPB, Fabricpath) or LAG, otherwise, spanning tree is required	No spanning tree
Default Gateway Protocols	HRSP, VRRP, GLBP	No default gateway protocol is required, since there is no HSRP, VRRP, or GLBP between Access Switches
VLAN can be spanned between access switches	YES	NO
Convergence	If there is Spanning Tree, it is slow, but if there is LAG, it is very fast	Fast, compared to Spannning Tree, can be a sub-second with fast convergence and sub 50ms with Fast Reroute Mechanisms. ECMP also provides software based failover between the paths
Stuff Experience	Well known	Well known
Possible network meltdown	If there is Spanning Tree, Spanning Tree bug can take down the network	no Layer 2 Loop,Layer 3 Ip header has TTL field, even if there is a loop, it is a microloop. when topology converges, it stops
Required Protocols	Spanning Tree or LAG and Fast Hop Redundancy Protocols (HSRP, VRRP, GLBP)	Any Layer 3 routing protocol, including Static Routing, can run
QoS Support	Good	Good
Multicast Support	Layer 2 based	Layer 3 based PIM, ASM, SSM and Bidir
Security	Many first hop security technologies, Dynamic ARP Inspection, DHCP Snooping, Port- Security and so on	Same as layer 2 Access

Design Concern	Layer 2 Access	Layer 3/ Routed Access
IPv6 Support	YES	YES
Default Convergence	Slow	Fast
Places in the network	LAN and Datacenter, but mainly LAN	LAN and Datacenter, but mainly Datacenter. This is because of the requirement of large scale Datacenter to keep Layer 2 domain as minimum as possible. So starting Layer 3 from the edge of the network

Layer 2 vs. Layer 3 Access Design Models Comparison

Access Network Design Case Study 1

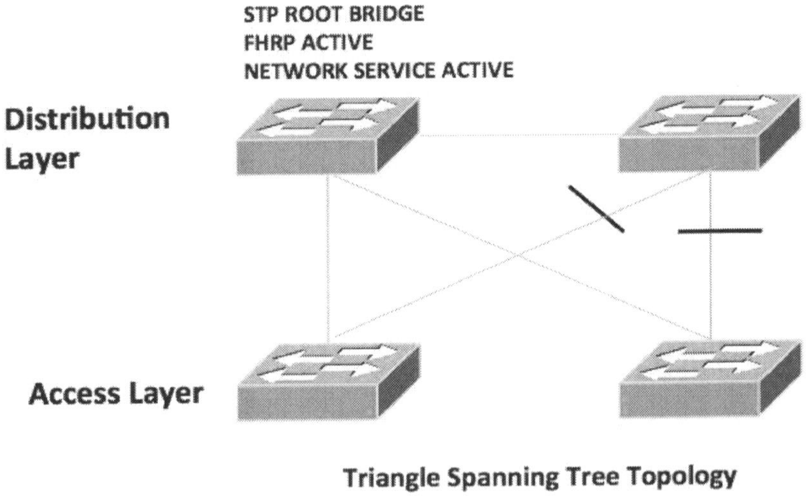

Triangle Spanning Tree Topology

In the figure above, Access and Distribution layer switches are shown.

Question 1.:

Why do we always place STP root switch and FHRP gateway at the distribution layer in the campus networks?

What is the design implication if it were placed in the access layer instead?

Answer 1:

A traffic pattern in campus networks is mostly in North/South direction.

In two or three layer hierarchical designs (Access-Distribution or Access-Distribution-Core) , Layer 2 and Layer 3 are placed on the distribution layer.

Distribution layer is used for scalability, modularity, and hierarchy.

When the network has distribution layer, any access layer switches can be upgraded smoothly. Also, some functions are shared between the access and distribution layer devices.

Access layer provides edge functions such as filtering, client access, QoS, and first hop security features such as Dynamic ARP inspection, DHCP Snooping, Port-Security and so on.

Distribution layer is responsible for the route and traffic/speed aggregation.

Layer 3 starts at the distribution layer. Thus, FHRPs are enabled at the distribution layer.

Thus, it is logical to place STP root and FHRP gateway at the top position at the network.

Question 2:

If there is a three-layer hierarchy, can the root switch functionality be put into the Core layer?

Answer 2:

No. The Layer 2 domain would be much larger in that case and we always want to keep Layer 2 domain small unless the application requires it to be much larger such as with VMotion or Layer 2 extension.

With Layer 3 access design, since the default gateway is access layer switches and there is no First Hop redundancy protocol on the switches, layer 2 domain size is the smallest compare to the other local area network design options (Layer 2 looped or loop-free access designs).

Access Network Design Case Study 2

Question

Where would Layer 2 looped design is better from the Layer 2 campus network design point of view?

Answer:

In an environment where Layer 2 VLAN needs to be spanned on many access switches. Classic example is the datacenter.

In the datacenter's hosts (specifically, virtual machines) can move between access switches. VLANs should be spread on those switches.

It is also very common in campus environments where WLAN is used commonly on every access switch.

In environments where Layer 2 needs to be extended on many access switches, Layer 2 looped design is the only design option with Spanning Tree.

There are many Virtual Overlay technologies, which works based on Layer 3 access design. VXLAN, NVGRE, STT and GENEVE are the virtual overlay protocols, which provide Layer2 over Layer 3 tunneling, and they are mainly used in the datacenter environment.

LAYER 2 TECHNOLOGIES REVIEW QUESTIONS

Question 1:

What is the name of below topology?

A. Layer 2 loop free access design
B. Layer 2 looped access design
C. Layer 3 routed access design
D. Layer 2 routed access design

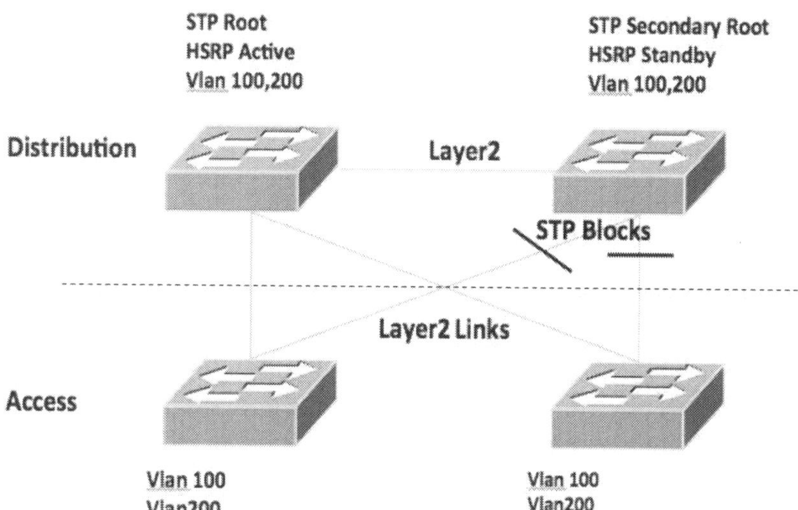

Answer 1:

The topology is called Layer 2 looped topology since the connection between the two distribution layer switches is Layer 2. Once it is Layer 2, STP has to block one link, which is far from the root switch to prevent a forwarding loop.

Question 2:

Spanning tree blocks some link to prevent forwarding loop in layer

2 Ethernet topologies. With which below technologies the spanning tree does not block any link? (Choose Two)

A. MST

B. LACP

C. PAGP

D. DTP

Answer 2:

MST is the standard spanning tree protocol.

DTP is dynamic trunking protocol and it is not used for link aggregation purposes. Two protocols are used to aggregate multiple links in a bundle. Spanning tree doesn't block those aggregated links.

These protocols are LACP and Cisco preparatory protocol; PAGP.

That's why the correct answer of this question is B and C.

Question 3:

Which below option is true for the LACP?

A. LACP system ID is generated with System Priority and switch MAC address

B. LACP is a layer 3 mechanism which is used for Layer 3 load balancing

C. LACP is a first hop redundancy mechanism

D. LACP is a Cisco proprietary link aggregation protocol

Answer 3:

Although it is a link aggregation protocol, LACP is not a Cisco proprietary protocol.

That's why Option D is incorrect. It is not a layer 3 load balancing mechanism. It is not a first hop redundancy mechanism either. Thus Option B and C are incorrect too.

System ID, which is an important component of LACP, is created with System Priority and switch mac address. Answer of this question is A.

Question 4:

Which below technologies can be used as First Hop redundancy gateway protocol? (Choose Three)

A. HSRP

B. VRRP

C. Spanning Tree

D. OSPF

E. GLBP

Answer 4:

HSRP, VRRP and GLBP can be used as first hop redundancy gateway protocols. First hop redundancy means if the gateway of the users/hosts fail, secondary device take the gateway responsibility.

That's why the answer of this question is A, B and E.

Question 5:

Fictitious Company has two datacenters and two interconnect links between the datacenters. Company is extending a specific Vlan between the datacenters. Which below protocols allow this Vlan traffic to be used over the both interconnect links? (Choose Two)

A. RPVST

B. MST

C. Etherchannel

D. Multi Chassis Etherchannel

Answer 5:

If any spanning tree mode is used for those two links, as it was explained in the Layer 2 technologies chapter of the book, one of the link is blocked for any particular Vlan as Spanning tree doesn't support flow based load balancing.

Etherchannel between the datacenter can provide flow based load balancing for those two datacenter interconnect links, if both links are terminated on the same devices.

If links are terminated on the different devices in each datacenter then Multi Chassis Etherchannel provide flow based load balancing. Since in the question is not told whether they are terminated on the same or different devices, both are the options are true.

That's why answer of this question is C and D.

Question 6:

Which first hop redundancy protocol is more suitable for the below topology?

A. HSRP

B. GLBP

C. Spanning Tree

D. MLD

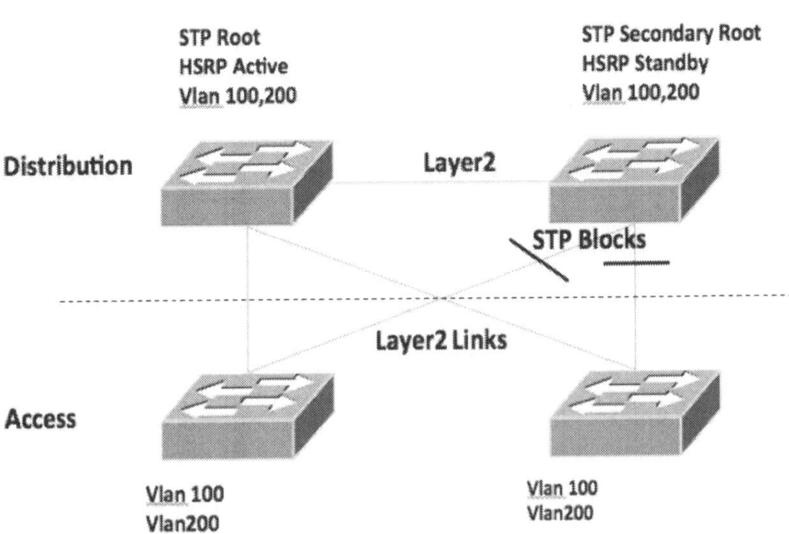

Answer 6:

Spanning Tree and MLD (Multicast Listener Discovery) are not the first hop redundancy protocols. Before starting to explain whether HSRP or GLBP is more suitable let me explain some concepts on GLBP and HSRP.

GLBP provides flow-based load balancing. Two common load-balancing techniques are in the Layer 2 networks; VLAN-based and Flow-based load balancing.

VLAN-based load balancing allows the switch to be an active Layer 3 gateway for only some set of VLANs and the other distribution stays as standby. For the other set of VLANs the standby switch acts as an active switch and the active switch acts as standby. HSRP and VRRP work in this way.

VLAN 100 HSRP active gateway can be the left distribution switch, and VLAN 101 can be the right distribution switch. Flow-based load balancing is meant to allow both distribution switches to be used as an active-active for the same VLAN.

Some users from the particular VLAN use one distribution switch as an active default gateway and other users from the same VLAN use what was a previously standby switch as an active switch.

In this way you can use both distribution switches as active-active and you can utilize all the links in the Layer 2 networks. However, supporting this configuration instead of using GLBP is more complex from a design point of view.

If you want both right and left distribution switches to be used active-active for the same VLAN, e.g., VLAN 100, then you need to use GLBP. However, STP should not block the Layer 2 links. How can this be achieved?

One way is to change the inter-distribution link to Layer 3. In that way none of the access layer links between access and distribution layer switches will be blocked, thus you can use all the uplinks.

If you use GLBP with the above topology, since the right access to distribution link will be blocked, all the user traffic from the right access switch will go first to the left distribution switch then through the interconnect link traffic will go to the right distribution switch since right distribution switch as an Active GLBP virtual forwarder replies to the ARP packets. That's why in this way always sub optimal path is used.

That's why answer of this question is HSRP.

Question 7:

Which below technology provide a Spanning Tree unidirectional failure detection if BPDU is not received?

A. Spanning Tree Rootguard
B. HSRP
C. Loop Guard
D. BPDU filter
E. Bpdu guard

Answer 7:

As it was mentioned in the Spanning Tree section of the layer 2 technologies chapter of the book, Loop guard protects spanning tree unidirectional link failure scenarios if BPDU is lost. That's why the correct answer of this question is C.

Question 8:

How fast convergence is achieved in RSTP (802.1w)?

A. Fast hello timers
B. Proposal and agreement handshake mechanism
C. Fast convergence cannot be achieved in RSTP
D. Spanning tree backbone fast

Answer 8:

Fast convergence in RSTP (802.1w) and MST (802.1s) is achieved with Proposal and Agreement Handshake mechanism as it was explained in the Layer 2 technologies chapter.

Question 9:

Which below spanning tree mode provides maximum scaling?

A. CST
B. RSTP
C. MST
D. PVSTP+

Answer 9:

As a spanning tree mode, MST provides maximum scaling. If the requirement is to provide scaling in Spanning Tree topologies, for example in the datacenter, then MST is the best choice.

Question 10:

What is the main function of Access Layer in hierarchical campus network design?

A. Provides aggregation points for the network services such as Firewalls, load balancers

B. Provides user access, first hop security and QoS functions

C. Provides layer 3 routing to the wide area network

D. Provides layer 3 virtualization in the campus network

Answer 10:

Main function of access layer in campus network is providing user access, first hop security mechanisms, QoS functions such as Classification and markings and so on.

Layer 3 virtualization can be provided if there is routed access design and VRF configured on the access layer devices but it is specific design and not the main function.

Layer 3 routing is also the same; it can be done on the access layer devices if the routed access design is used but not the main function.

That's why the correct answer is B.

Question 11:

Which below mechanism provides flow based load balancing?

A. HSRP

B. VRRP

C. GLBP

D. Spanning Tree

Answer 11:

Out of given options, only GLBP supports flow based load balancing as it was explained in detail in the Layer 2 technologies chapter.

Question 12:

Which below mechanism provide optimal layer 2 switching in a campus network design?

A. BPDU Guard

B. Spanning Tree Portfast

C. Root Guard

D. BPDU filter

E. ECMP

Answer 12:

Since the question is asking optimal layer 2 forwarding/switching, ECMP is not an option.

Portfast is used to reduce the convergence time on the edge/user ports and preventing TCN on those ports. BPDU Guard and BPDU filter are used to prevent the ports to be connected to another switch in the campus.

Root Guard is used for determinism and identification of the root switch placement. When root guard is enabled on the root switch, even if new switch is added onto the network, traffic flow doesn't change.

But assumption is choosing the root switch placement accordingly.

In a campus network, since the most of the traffic is north south, root switch is always place on the distribution layer devices in layer 2 access design as it was explained in a case study earlier in the Layer 2 technologies chapter.

The correct answer of this question is C.

Question 13:

Which below statements are true for Vlan based Load Balancing? (Choose Two)

A. Hosts in different Vlans can use different default gateways

B. Hosts in the same Vlan can use different default gateways

C. Odd and Even Vlan numbers traffic can be sent through different default gateways for load balancing
D. Maximum 100 Vlans can use an individual default gateway

Answer 13:

Odd and Vlan number separation is common method in Vlad based load balancing. That's why Option D is one of the correct options.

Hosts in different Vlans can use different default gateways. Whole idea of Vlan based load balancing is this.

There is no Vlan limitation per default gateway.

That's why answer of this question is A and C.

Question 14:

Why Spanning Tree and FHRP synchronization/interaction is necessary?

A. To prevent blackholing
B. To prevent sub optimal forwarding
C. To provide fast convergence
D. To provide better security

Answer 14:

As it was explained in the Spanning Tree/FHTP part of the Layer 2 technologies chapter, it is necessary to provide optimal forwarding.

Question 15:

Which below statements are true for the Layer 3 routed access design? (Choose Three)

A. There is no spanning tree between access and distribution layers
B. Spanning Tree should be enabled on the user facing ports
C. ECMP routing can be done between access and distribution layer devices

D. Maximum 4 links can be used between access and distribution layer devices

E. Any given vlan can be spanned between access layer devices

Answer 15:

There is no spanning tree in layer 3-access design/routed access design between the access and distribution layer switches.

Spanning tree should be enabled on the user facing ports to prevent intentional and unintentional layer 2 attacks and loop issues.

ECMP (Equal Cost Multipath) routing can be done between access and distribution layer devices.

You can use 8 or more links between the access and distribution layer devices depends on hardware and vendor capabilities.

Vlans cannot be spanned between access switches in layer 3-access design.

That's why the correct answer of this question is A, B and C.

LAYER 2 FURTHER STUDY RESOURCES

Books

Tiso, J. (2011) Designing Cisco Network Service Architecture (ARCH) Foundation Learning Guide: (CCDP ARCH 642-874) (Third Edition), Cisco Press.

Videos

Ciscolive Session-BRKCRS-2031 Ciscolive Session – BRKRST – 3363 Ciscolive Session-BRKCRS-2468

https://www.youtube.c om/watch?v=R75vN-frPhE

Articles

http://www.pitt.edu/~dtipper/2011/COE.pdf
http://orhanergun.net/2015/05/common-networking-protocols-in-lan-wan-and-datacenter/
http://www.cisco.com/c/en/us/td/docs/solutions/Enterprise/Data_Center/DC_Infra2_5/DCInfra_6.pdf
https://www.cisco.com/web/ME/exposaudi2009/assets/docs/layer2_attacks_and_mitigation_t.pdf

CHAPTER 2

NETWORK DESIGN TOOLS AND THE BEST PRACTICES

There are design tools, which we should consider for every design. LAN, WAN and the data center where this common design tolls and attributes should be considered.

Many of the principles in this chapter is not only for the networking technologies and the protocols but also applicable to compute, virtualization and storage technologies as well.

First 'reliability' will be explained; Components of the reliable network design and the resiliency concept will be explained.

RELIABILITY

Reliability is within the reasonable amount of time, which depends on the application type and architecture, delivering the legitimate packets from source to destination.

This time is known as delay or latency and it is one of the packet delivery parameters. Consistency of delay known as jitter and it is very important for some type of applications such as voice and video, jitter is our second delivery parameters.

Third packet delivery parameter is packet loss or drop; especially voice and video traffic is more sensitive to packet loss compare to data traffic.

Packet loss is application dependent and some applications are very drop/packet loss sensitive. General accepted best practices for the delay, jitter and packet loss ratio has been defined and knowing and considering them is important from the network design point of view. For example for the voice packets one way delay which is also known as 'mouth to ear' delay should be less than 150ms.

Reliability should not be considered only at the link level. Network links, devices such as switches, routers, firewalls, application delivery controllers, servers, storage systems and others should be reliable; also component of these devices needs to be reliable.

For example, if you will carry the voice traffic over unreliable serial links, you may likely encounter packet drops because of link flaps. Best practice is to carry voice traffic over the low latency links, which don't have packet loss and the latency. If you have to utilize those cheaper unreliable links such as Internet, you should carry the Data traffic over them.

But actually whichever device, link or component you choose, essentially they will fail.

Vendors share their MTBF (Meantime between failure) numbers. You can choose the best reliable devices, links, component, protocols and architecture; you need to consider unavoidable failure. This brings us the resiliency.

RESILIENCE

Resiliency is how the network behaves once the failure happen. Is that highly available, will it convergence and when?

Resilience can be considered as combination of high availability and convergence. In order any network design to be resilient, it should be redundant and converge fast enough to avoid application timeout.

Thus, resiliency is interrelated with redundancy and the fast convergence/fast reroute mechanisms.

Every component and every device can and eventually will fail, thus system should be resilient enough to re converge/recover to a previous state. As it is stated above; Resiliency can be achieved with redundancy.

But how much redundancy is best for the resiliency is another consideration to be taken into an account by the network designers.

Many tests has been performed for routing convergence based on link number for different routing systems and it seems two or three links are the best optimum for the routing re convergence.

For the routing systems, there are two approaches for faster convergence than their default convergence time. Fast convergence is achieved with protocol parameter tuning, failure detection time reduction, propagation of failure to the routing system, processing the new information to find a new path and routing and forwarding table updates of the routers.

For the fast reroute, backup-forwarding entry should be in the devices forwarding table, pre-computation of the alternate path is necessary.

Understanding different Fast Reroute mechanisms and their design characteristics are important for the network engineers.

FAST CONVERGENCE AND FAST REROUTE

Network reliability is an important measure for deployability of sensitive applications. When a link, node or SRLG failure occurs in a routed network, there is inevitably a period of disruption to the delivery of traffic until the network reconverges on the new topology.

Fast reaction is essential for the failed element. There are two approaches for the fast reaction:

Fast convergence and fast reroute. When a local failure occur four steps are necessary for the convergence.

1. Failure detection
2. Failure propagation
3. New information process
4. Update new route into RIB/FIB

For fast convergence, these steps may need to be tuned. Although the RIB/FIB update is hardware dependent, the network operator can configure all other steps.

One thing always needs to be kept in mind; Fast convergence and fast reroute can affect network stability.

Unlike fast convergence, for the fast reroute, routes are pre-computed and pre-programmed into the router RIB/FIB.

There are many Fast Reroute mechanisms available today. Most known ones are; Loop Free Alternate (LFA), Remote Loop Free Alternate (rLFA), MPLS Traffic Engineering Fast Reroute and Segment Routing Fast Reroute.

Loop Free Alternate and the Remote Loop Free Alternate if also known as IP or IGP Fast Reroute Mechanisms. Main difference between MPLS Traffic Engineering Fast Reroute and the IP Fast Reroute mechanisms are the coverage.

MPLS TE FRR can protect the any tunnel in any topology. IP FRR mechanisms need the physical topology of the networks to be highly connected. Ring and square topologies are hard for the IP FRR topologies but not a problem for MPLS TE FRR at all.

But if MPLS is not enabled on the network, adding MPLS and RSVP-TE for just MPLS TE FRR functionality can be too complicated. In that case network designers may want to evaluate their existing physical structure and try to alternate/backup path by adding or removing some circuit in the network. IGP metric tuning also helps router to find alternate loop free paths.

IGP, BGP and MPLS Traffic Engineering Fast Reroute details will be covered in the later chapters in detail.

SCALABILITY

Scalability is the ability to change, modify or remove the part of entire system without having a huge impact on the overall design. There are two scalability approaches for the IT systems. These approaches are scale up or scale out and implies for the Network, Compute, Storage, Application, Database and many other systems.

Scalability through scaling up the system can be defined as to increase the existing system resources without adding a new system.

Consider scale out application architecture, if application can be run over the two different servers, we can do some maintenance on the one of the servers without affecting the user experience.

Consider we have only one router as a network device and we need to plan software upgrade. If we have a two supervisor engines for control plane activities on that router, we can upgrade the software without having a downtime and maintenance will not be an issue. We don't have to have Flag Day for upgrade activity.

Although the benefit of having scale up approach for high availability is limited, obviously in this case it helps.

Scaling with the scale out approach provides better high availability. Secondary system might be processing the load or worst case; it waits as an idle to take responsibility in case of a primary system failure.

Once we modify, remove or add additional component into a system we don't expect to have an impact on the running system. As an example, let's examine scalability of routing protocols. If we have many router and many links in the single area OSPF deployment, even small link flap can trigger the all routers to calculate a new topology.

Up to some limit it might be acceptable but after that limit it affects the overall routing domain a lot. For the OSPF case, limit is defined generally with the Routing LSA size.

For having scalability, choosing the correct technology is important. Consider you need additional ports in your data center aggregation layer switch to support more compute resources. Of course you can create additional access-aggregation POD and connect to your core if you have three-tier architecture But rather, two tier leaf and spine architecture for the physical design could be considered since it doesn't not only provide scalability but also better east-west application performance and would be simpler architecture than the POD based design.

Lastly, scalable systems also should be manageable. While growing in size, if system starts to become non manageable, it will affect inversely the scalability of the system. In order to perform any change, network shouldn't need flag days, long and frequent maintenance windows because of operationally complex environment. (OPEX)

This brings us to the next design tools, which is COST

COST

Cost is generally afterthought in network design. But most of the time it is very important constraint in the projects. If we breakdown the components of cost:

OPEX:

OpEx refers to operational expenses such as support, maintenance, labor, bandwidth and utilities. Creating a complex network design may show off your technical knowledge but it can also cause unnecessary complexity making it harder to build, maintain, operate and manage the network.

A well- designed network reduces OpEx through improved network uptime (which in turn can avoid or reduce penalties related to outages), higher user productivity, ease of operations, and energy savings. Consider creating the simplest solution that meets the business requirements.

CAPEX:

CapEx refers to the upfront costs such as purchasing equipment, inventory, acquiring intellectual property or real estate. A well-thought design provides longer deployment lifespan, investment protection, network consolidation and virtualization, producing non-measurable benefits such as business agility and business transformation and innovation, thus reducing risk and lowering costs in the long run.

Last metric in the COST constraint is TCO (Total cost of ownership).

TCO is a better metric than pure CapEx to evaluate network cost, as it considers CapEx plus OpEx. Make your network designs cost-effective in the long run and do more with less by optimizing both CapEx and OpEx.

There are certainly other network design attributes such as Flexibility, security, modularity and hierarchical design. These design tools or goals will be covered throughout the book.

But very briefly flexibility and the modularity can be described as below.

FLEXIBILITY

Flexibility refers to the ability of a network design to adapt to business changes, which can come in a planned or unplanned way. There are a few constants in life: death, taxes and change – not much we can do about the first two, but certainly we can influence how to adapt to change. Merger, acquisition, divesture can happen anytime in any business. How your network will react to these rapid changes?

You can make network design more flexible by making it more modular.

MODULARITY

Modularity means to divide the network by functions or policy boundaries, making it replicable (for example on branches) and thus easier to scale and operate, and enabling business continuity. How do you make a design modular?

1. Choose the physical topology: Some topologies such as hierarchical or leaf&spine are more conducive to allow for modules than others (fully meshed, for example).
2. Split functions or geographies: Separate campus, branches, data center and applications, Internet, network management systems, and security policy boundaries to make each function easier to expand, upgrade, enhance or change. Make them small enough to ease replication.
3. Break it into smaller pieces: Create smaller fault domains so that a failure on a part of the network doesn't propagate to other parts, by subdividing the functions as appropriate.

DESIGN CONSIDERATIONS FOR NETWORK MERGERS AND ACQUISITIONS

Network mergers and acquisitions are the processes, which can be seen in any type of businesses. As a network designer, our job to identify the business requirements of both existing networks and the merged network and finding best possible technical solutions for the business.

There are many different areas that need to be analyzed carefully. Wrong business requirement gathering and design analyze, definitely lead to catastrophic failures.

Business and network analysis and technical information gathering are the key steps and there are many questions which need to be asked and answered should be well understood.

Network mergers and acquisitions are also called as Network integration.

Below are the key points for any type of network mergers and acquisitions projects.

- Business analysis and information gathering
- Applications of the company, at least the business critical applications should be understood and analyze very well.
- What are the capabilities of these applications and what are the requirements from the existing network.(Packet loss, jitter, delay, application traffic flow, security and QoS requirements and so on). Basically in this step, we analyze the current infrastructure of the companies. IP addressing scheme, Application requirement, physical topology gathering, business future growth forecast analysis, security, QoS, Multicast, OAM and management infrastructure capabilities and information should be gathered.
- What type of WAN, LAN and DC infrastructure each network is using, Is any VPN solution deployed on the WAN, is there a traffic engineering requirement on WAN or DC, Is IPv6 supported on any of the companies? Is there any single point of failure and what will be the high availability requirement of merged network?
- What is the convergence time of the network and what is the required convergence time of any single component failure? (You shouldn't design the network for multiple failures)

As you can see there are so many questions, which should be asked and noted during the business analysis. This is most time consuming step of any network design but definitely worth to do it properly to avoid any future problem and having best network design.

Analyzing the design for network mergers and acquisitions is not different analyzing the design for the greenfield network. Application and business requirements are always the most important, technology is second. Alternative technologies always can be found.

- Where will be the first place in the network for the merger ?

When two network merge, generally two networks are connected through their core network component. If there is any overlapping issue, for example IP Address, these should be fixed. Traditionally IP address overlap issue is fixed via NAT (Network Address Translation).

Physical location selection is very important. As you will see later in the post, some of the sites can be decommissioned for the operational cost savings. After deciding the locations, which will be used, by extending the current WAN connections companies can start to reach each other.

- What happens to the routing, IGP, BGP? Is a "ship in the night" approach suitable or redistribution is better for routing protocol merger?

One common routing protocol can run through both network or if there are two different IGPs, redistribution can take place. If there is MPLS on the networks, any type of Inter-AS VPN solution can be deployed. In some Inter-AS MPLS solutions redistribution is not required.

Running common IGP is always better compare to dealing with redistribution. It is better for management, troubleshooting, convergence, availability and for many other design objectives.

- Which type of security infrastructure will merged network support?

What are the existing security policy and parameters of each individual network. You should deploy common security policy for the merged network. You should make sure edge of the network as secure as possible and core of the network just should transport the packets.

- What is the Quality of Service Policies of the companies? Will final merged network support Quality of Service or through bandwidth everywhere?

- Quality of service policy of end-to-end network should be deployed by understanding the applications of the each individual company.

That's why understanding the applications which was the analyzing the network task, is crucial. You should follow best current practices for QoS design.

Some businesses don't use QoS, especially on their core network. They generally have their DWDM infrastructure, so when they need extra capacity, they can provision quickly and start using it.

The reason why they don't use QoS is simplicity. They want to keep their core network as simple as possible. This approach is seen generally in the Service Provider business.

- Will merged network have IPv6?

IPv6 is unavoidable. There are many IPv6 business drivers for any type of business. If IPv6 only design is not possible for the merged company, at least IPv6 transition mechanisms should be understood very well and considered for the merged network.

- Does one of the networks require Multicast? Will merged network support Multicast?

If Multicast is running on any of the companies, most probably merged network will require and benefit from the multicast deployment as well. PIM (Protocol Independent Multicast) and current multicast best practices should be understood and deploy based on the company requirements. Some applications of the company may benefit from the special Multicast routing protocol deployment model such as PIM ASM (Any source multicast), PIM SSM (Source Specific Multicast) or PIM Bidir (Bidirectional Multicast).

- What is the new capacity requirement of the merged network?

When two networks merge overall capacity requirement for edge and core network generally changes. Understanding network capacity planning is key and network designers should understand the available methods for backbone and overall network capacity planning tools and best practices.

- How will be the merged network monitored? Do exist Network Management tools capable to support all the technologies/protocols of the both network? Both companies may have different monitoring tool, application support might be different of their tools as well. Monitoring and management tools should be considered before the merger because tools should be able to support all applications, protocols and technologies of the merged network.

- When you divest the network, where will the datacenters be? Can you decommission any datacenter, POP location for cost optimization?

Some of the locations of the companies may overlap and some POP locations and/or datacenters, even Head Quarters can be decommissioned to reduce operational expenses.

Physical topology of the companies should be understood well and if there is cost of advantage of choosing particular location, definitely needs to be considered.

This is definitely not be the entire list for network mergers and acquisitions, but you should at least start your design with these questions in your real life design as well as in the design certification exams. In the CCDE exam, questions will be based on above considerations mostly.

DESIGN BEST PRACTICES FOR HIGH AVAILABILITY, SCALABILITY, CONVERGENCE AND OTHER DESIGN TOOLS

The section below lists design recommendations and practical knowledge will be provided for the network design tools.

These are protocol independent. For the protocols such as OSPF, IS-IS, EIGRP, BGP, MPLS, Multicast, QoS and IPv6, design recommendations and the best practices will be provided in the related chapters accordingly.

High Availability:

- Availability of a system is mainly measured with two parameters. Mean time between failure (MTBF) and Mean time to repair (MTTR). MTBF is calculated as average time between failures of a system. MTTR is the average time required to repair a failed component (link, node, device in networking terms)

- Too much redundancy increases the MTTR of the system (Router, Switch or overall network) thus inversely effect the availability.

- Most failures are caused by human error. In fact, the estimated range is between 70 and 80%. How can so many people be incompetent? Actually, they are not! It's actually a design problem. In hub and spoke deployment for example, if adding spoke sites causes an entire network meltdown, this is a design problem and not the operator's mistake. You should increase the hub capacity.

- Due to BGP path vector behavior, BGP route reflector selects and advertise only one best path to all BGP route reflector clients, but some applications such as BGP PIC or BGP Multipath require more than one best path.

- Not every network needs 5x9 or 6x9 availability. Before deciding upon the availability level of a network design, understand the application requirements and the place where the design will be applied on the network.

  For example, availability requirements for a company's centralized datacenter will be very different than one of its retail stores.

Convergence:

- Don't use Routing Protocol hellos for the Layer 3 routing failure detection, at least don't tune them aggressively, instead leave with the default. Use BFD whenever possible for failure detection in Layer 3.

- BFD supports all routing protocols except RIP. It supports LDP and MPLS Traffic Engineering as well.
- If you can detect the failure in Layer 1, then don't enable BFD (Bidirectional Forwarding Detection) as well.
- Pooling-based mechanisms are always slower than event-driven mechanisms. For example, Layer 1 loss of signal will be much faster than BFD hellos; Automatic Protection Switching (APS) on SDH links are always faster than BFD hellos for failure detection.
- Distance Vector Protocol converge time is the same as Link-State Routing Protocols. If there is a feasible successor in the EIGRP topology, EIGRP by default converges faster than other routing protocols.
- BGP doesn't have to converge slowly. Understanding the data plane and control plane convergence difference is important for network designers. BGP control plane and data plane convergence is explained in detail in the BGP chapter.
- BGP route reflector is not always the best solution. It hides the available alternate next-hops, slows down the network convergence, and requires route reflector engineering thus requires stuff experience.

SCALABILITY:

- In modern platforms there are software and hardware forwarding information tables. Software forwarding is a very resource-intensive task; utilize hardware forwarding if you need better performance.
- Multi-area OSPF or multi-level IS-IS design is not always necessary but you should know what business problem you are trying to solve. Resiliency? Opex? Security? Reliability? Scalability? In general Scalability is considered as a reason to deploy Multi Area OSPF or Multi Level IS-IS. These two topics will be covered in great detail in the related chapters.
- Try to find a way to deploy any technology, feature, or protocol with the least amount of configuration possible. If you can achieve the same result with lesser configuration steps, prefer that one.

Load Balancing:

- Load balancing and load sharing is not the same thing. Load sharing terminology should be used for the routers or switches but load balancing requires more intelligence such as Load balancer. If the downstream device is busy, routers or switches cannot take this information into an account. But Load Balancers can!

- Load balancing is any intelligence feature that devices need to support, such as destination health check, considering destination device resource utilization, the number of connections, etc. The load balancers do this. Routers perform load sharing. Routers only take the routing metric into account to send the packet to the destination. Traffic Sharing can be over equal or unequal cost paths.

- OSPF and IS-IS can do the unequal cost load sharing with the help of MPLS-Traffic Engineering only. By default they don't support unequal cost multipath routing. EIGRP by default can route the packets over unequal cost paths.

Redistribution:

- You may need to redistribute routing protocols. You may have a partner networks or BGP into IGP for default route advertisement.

- Redistribution should be used in conjunction with the filtering mechanisms such as route tags.

- Keep in mind that these mechanisms increase overall complexity of the network. Also be aware of routing loops during redistribution operation. Two-way redistribution is the place where routing loops are most likely to occur. And most common prevention for routing loop in this case is to use route tags.

- Redistribution between routing protocols does not happen directly; routes are installed in RIB and pull from the RIB to other protocol. So route should be in the RIB to be redistributed. A classic example of this is BGP. If the network is not in the routing table of the router, which is RIB, it cannot be taken to the BGP RIB. This is why those routes cannot be sent to another BGP neighbor.

- If avoidable, don't use redistribution. Managing redistribution can be very complex.

Optimal Routing:

- Overlay protocols should follow the underlay protocol to avoid sub optimal routing and traffic blackholing. In other word, they should synchronize. For example FHRP (HSRP, VRRP, GLBP) should synchronize with STP to avoid sub optimal forwarding. IGP/BGP and IGP/LDP synchronization are the other examples and will be explain on the topologies, later in the book.

- Control plane state is the aggregate amount of information carried by the control plane through the network in order to produce the forwarding table at each device. Each piece of additional information added to the control plane such as more specific reachability information, policy information, security configuration, or more precise topology information adds to the complexity of the control plane.

- This added complexity, in turn, adds to the burden of monitoring, understanding, troubleshooting, and managing the network. Removing control plane state almost always results in decreased optimality in the forwarding and handling of packets travelling through the network, which creates sub-optimality.

- We don't configure the networks; we configure the networking devices (Routers, Switches etc.) Understanding the overall impact of configuring one router on the network holistically is very important. We try to configure the many routers, switches etc. and wait the result to be a coherent. But at the end we face all kinds of loops, micro loops, broadcast storms, routing churns, and policy violations.

- It is a good idea to create a small failure domain in Layer 2 and Layer 3, but you must be aware of suboptimal routing and black holes. There is an important design tradeoff: Whenever summarization is done, chance of Sub-optimal routing increases!

- Summarization is done at the aggregation layer in three-tier hierarchy. Doing it at the aggregation simplifies the core network since there will be less amount of routing table entry in the core and access network changes don't impact the network core. Core should remain as simple.

Network Topologies:

- Intelligence should be at the edge of the networks and the network core should be as simple as possible. The responsibility of the network core is fast packet forwarding, not the traffic aggregation, policy insertion, or user termination.

- Try to create triangle physical topology instead of a square. In the case of link failure, triangle topologies converge faster than squares.
- Ring topology is the most difficult of all the routing protocols from the viewpoint of convergence and optimality. Simply adding some links and creating partial-mesh topology instead of ring provides a more optimal path, better resource usage, and faster convergence time in case of link or node failure.
- Full mesh topologies are the most expensive topologies since every device needs to be connected to each other.
- When there is a big traffic demand between any two location in a ring topology based network, direct link is added between the two locations. Then topology becomes partial mesh.

MODULARITY:

- Modular network design allows each module to be managed independently.
- Common security policy should be deployed across entire network
- Modular design allows different modules to be managed by different teams. In the Service Provider networks this is common. Access, Aggregation and Core networks are modular and they generally managed by individual teams.
- Modular design reduces deployment time since the same configuration is used for the new module, same physical topologies are used and so on.
- Hierarchical design is an example of modular design. Hierarchy helps for flexibility. Also it helps for scalability.

SECURITY:

- Enabling a new feature such as IPv6 or Multicast on part of the network can open the rest of the network to security attacks.
- Network Address Translation is not a security mechanism.
- MPLS VPNs is equally secure with ATM and TDM based networks.

- Predictable network design is good for security. Removing unnecessary complexity from the design makes network more predictable thus more secure.
- Don't enable the routing protocols on the user/customers ports; otherwise bad routing entries can be injected into the routing system.
- Always use BGP hardening features on the Internet Gateways
- More security devices is not necessarily mean more secure network
- Stateful security devices such as Firewall, IPS/IDS, Load Balancer requires symmetric routing. This makes network design harder.
- Stateful devices in the datapath can be a bottleneck. Putting a big datacenter firewall vs. smaller virtual firewalls per host or VM is a good example for this.

SIMPLICITY AND COMPLEXITY:

- There are two types of reachability information (MAC or IP) learning mechanisms: control plane learning and data plane learning. Classical Ethernet and VPLS are examples of data plane learning. Routing protocols, LISP, DMVPN are the technologies that use control plane to build reachability information.
- There are generally two types of control plane learning: push based and pull based. Routing protocols are the example of a push based control plane, since routing neighbors send reachability information to each other by default when the adjacency is set up. LISP and DMVPN are pull based control plane mechanisms since devices don't by default send reachability information to each other. Instead, they send to this information to a centralized node. In LISP terminology it is the Map Server and in DMVPN it is a DMVPN hub.
- If you need a robust network some complexity is necessary.
- You should separate necessary complexity from unnecessary complexity. If you need redundancy, dual redundancy is generally good enough. You add unnecessary complexity by adding a third level of redundancy.
- In your design, the motto should be "two's company, three's a crowd". Complexity is inescapable, but unnecessary complexity should be avoided.

- Network design is about managing the tradeoffs between different design goals. Not all network design has to have fast convergence, maximum resiliency characteristics, or be scalable. Complexity can be shifted between the physical network, operators, and network management systems; overall complexity of the network is reduced by taking the human factor away
- SDN helps to reduce overall network complexity by shifting some responsibility from the human operators.
- Don't use cutting-edge technologies just to show off your skills! Remember, things that may seem simple in actuality might be very complex.

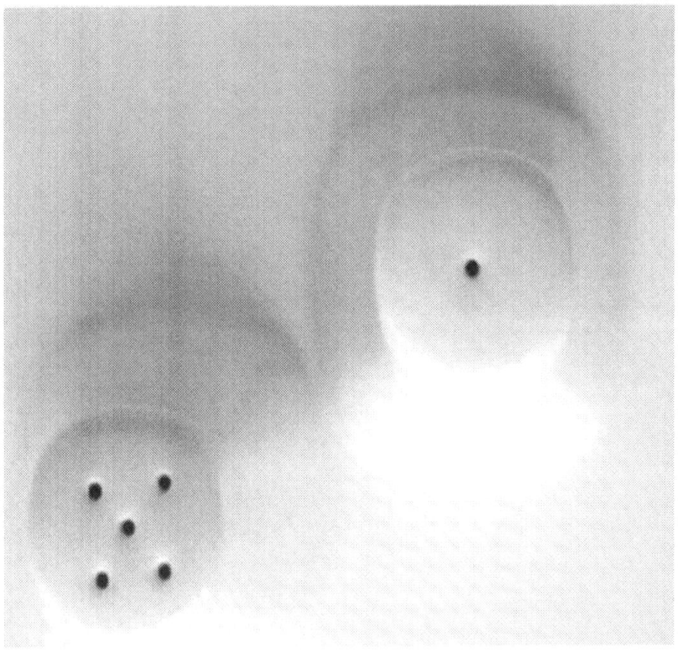

Which one is salt and which one is pepper? It must be simple to understand!

- Your design shouldn't be confusing. Can you understand in above picture; which one is salt and which one is pepper without testing? When the complexity of your network increases, you cannot simply operate it without testing and very careful planning.
- Features can be intended for robustness, but instead create fragility. The impact may not be seen immediately, but it can be huge. In design this is known as the Butterfly Effect.

" A butterfly flapping its wings in South America can affect the weather in Central Park."

Last but not least:

KNOW THE PURPOSE OF YOUR DESIGN!

Imagine that you designed this teapot. Is it functional as a teapot?

NETWORK DESIGN TOOLS AND THE BEST PRACTICES REVIEW QUESTIONS

Question 1:

In the below figure, two routers are connected through two links. OSPF routing protocol is running over the links.

Which below statement is true for the below figure?

A. Adding more links between the routers increase routing table size

B. IS-IS would be a better option

C. More links provide better resiliency

D. More links provide faster convergence

E. More links provide better security

Answer 1:

Adding more links don't provide better security. Resiliency depends on redundancy, convergence and reliable packet delivery. More links don't necessarily provide better resiliency. General rule of thumb, 2 links is best for resiliency.

We cannot know whether IS-IS would be better since there is no other requirement.

Option A is definitely correct. More links increase routing table size since OSPF is running on individual links and more links means more routing table entry.

If there would be an etherchannel between the routers and OSPF would run on top of that link, adding more link wouldn't increase the routing table size.

That's why; answer of this question is A.

Question 2:

Which below technologies provide fast failure detection? (Choose two)

A. BFD

B. Routing fast hellos

C. Loopguard

D. SPF Timers

E. BGP Scanner time

Answer 2:

Loopguard, SPF timers and BGP Scanner Timers are not used for fast failure detection. BGP Scanner time for example is 60seconds and reducing can create 100% CPU utilization. Thus better and newer approach Next Hop Tracking is used in BGP, as it will be explained in the BGP Chapter.

Routing Protocols hellos can be tuned to provide fast failure detection and the purpose of BFD is to provide fast failure detection.

Thus the correct answer of this question is A and B.

Question 3:

Which of the below protocols support BFD for fast failure detection? (Choose all that apply)

A. Static Routing

B. OSPF

C. IS-IS

D. EIGRP

E. BGP

F. RIP

Answer 3:

All the routing protocols above except RIP support BFD as it was mentioned in this chapter. They can register to BFD process for fast failure detection. In case of failure BFD inform these protocols to tear down the routing session.

RIPv2 on the other hand supports BFD.

Question 4:

What are the benefits of having modular network design? (Choose Two)

A. Each module can be designed independently from each other

B. Each module can be managed by different team in the organization

C. Each module can have a separate routing protocol

D. Each module can have different security policy

Answer 4:

If the design supports modularity, then each module can be designed independently, In access, aggregation, core module for example, access network can be hub and spoke, distribution can be full mesh and core network can be partial mesh.

Also commonly in the service provider networks, access and core team are the separate business units and modularity provides this opportunity. Or in large Enterprises, different team can managed the different geographical areas of the network, which has been designed by considering modularity.

Modularity is not done to have different routing protocols and companies should deploy common security policies across all domains.

That's why the correct answer of this question is A and B.

Question 4:

Which below statements are true for the network design? (Choose Two)

A. Predictability increases security

B. Every networks need 5x9 or 6x9 High Availability

C. Using more than routing protocol in the network increases availability

D. Modular network design reduces deployment time

Answer 4:

As it was explained in this chapter, modular network design reduces deployment time. And predictability increases security. Predictable networks also reduces troubleshooting time thus increases high availability.

Not every networks need 5x9 or 6x9 high availability. Using more than one routing protocol in the network, if there is mandatory reason such as partner network requirement, is not a good design.

That's why the answer of this question is A and D.

Question 5:

If there is two-way redistribution between routing protocols, how can routing loop is avoided?

A. Deploying Spanning Tree

B. Deploying Fast Reroute

C. Implementing Route tags

D. Only one way redistribution is enough

Answer 5:

As it was explained in the redistribution part of the Best Practices chapter of the book, route tags are the common method to prevent routing loops if redistribution is done at multiple locations between the protocols

That's why the answer of this question is C.

Question 6:

Which below statements are true for the network design? (Choose Three)

A. Using triangle topology instead of square reduces

convergence time that's why it is recommended

B. Full mesh topology is the most expensive topology to create

C. Using longer and complex configurations always better so people can understand how good network designer you are

D. Sub optimal routing is always bad so avoid route summarization whenever you can since it can create sub optimal routing

E. Network complexity can be reduced by utilizing SDN technologies

Answer 6:

Network complexity can be reduced by utilizing SDN technologies as it was explained in this chapter. It helps to shift the configuration task from the human to the software. That's why Option E is one of the correct answers.

Route summarization can create sub optimal routing but sub optimal routing is not always bad. For some type of traffic in the network, optimal routing may not be required at all. And just because we might have sub optimal routing, we shouldn't avoid doing summarization. That's why Option D is incorrect.

It should be obvious that Option C doesn't make sense.

Option A and B are also correct. Triangle topology reduces convergence time and full mesh topologies are the most expensive topologies.

Correct answers of this question are; A, B and E.

Question 7:

What is the key benefit of hierarchical network design?

A. Less Broadcast traffic

B. Increased flexibility and modularity

C. Increased security

D. Increased availability

Answer 7:

Hierarchical design may not be redundant and highly available. Also it doesn't bring additional security but key benefit of it is flexibility and modularity as it was explained in the Best Practices chapter.

That's why the answer of this question is B.

Question 8:

If routing summarization is done which below statements are valid for the link state protocols? (Choose Two)

A. Convergence will be slower
B. Sub optimal routing may occur
C. Traffic blackholing may occur
D. Routing table size grows

Answer 8:

As it was explained in the chapter, when route summarization is done routing table size gets smaller which makes converges faster. It can create sub optimal routing and traffic might be blackholed in some failure scenarios.

That's why the answer of this question is B and C.

Question 9:

What would be the impact of doing summarization at the aggregation layer in three-tier hierarchy? (Choose Two)

A. Core network can be simplified, it doesn't have to keep all Access network routes
B. If you have summary in the aggregation layer, core can be collapsed with aggregation layer
C. Access network changes don't affect the core network
D. Aggregation is the user termination point and summarization shouldn't be made at aggregation layer

Answer 9:

In three-layer hierarchy aggregation layer is the natural summarization point. When the summarization is done at the aggregation layer, core layer is simplified and the access network changes don't affect the core layer.

Collapsing the core is not the result of summarization since the main reason of using core layer is physical scaling requirement. With summarization physical requirements don't go away.

Aggregation layer is not the user termination point. User termination is the access layer responsibility, thus Option D is incorrect.

Answer of this question is A and C.

Question 10:

Which routing protocol supports unequal cost multi path routing?

A. OSPF

B. IS-IS

C. EIGRP

D. RIPv2

Answer 10:

In the above question, all the routing protocols are dynamic routing protocols and among them only EIGRP supports unequal cost multi path routing. And as it was explained in the chapter, with MPLS Traffic engineering tunnels only, OSPF and IS-IS can support unequal cost multipath.

That's why the correct answer of this question is C.

NETWORK DESIGN TOOLS AND THE BEST PRACTICES FURTHER STUDY RESOURCES

VIDEOS

http://ripe61.ripe.net/archives/video/19/

ARTICLES

http://orhanergun.net/2015/01/route-redistribution-best-practices/
https://tools.ietf.org/html/draft-ietf-ospf-omp-02
https://www.ietf.org/rfc/rfc3439.txt
http://orhanergun.net/2015/01/load-balancing-vs-load-sharing/

Chapter 3
OSPF

If the requirement is to have MPLS Traffic Engineering, standard-based, and Enterprise-level protocol, then the only choice is OSPF. IS-IS can support MPLS Traffic Engineering as well, IS-IS is also a standard protocol, but it is not an Enterprise-level. Especially once it is considered that most of the Enterprise network may require IPSEC, IS-IS cannot run over IPSEC.

Also IS-IS is not known widely by the Enterprise network engineers.

OSPF as a link-state protocol shares many similarities with IS-IS, however OSPF can be used with IPSEC, but since IS-IS does not work over IPSEC, making IS-IS unsuitable for an Enterprise environment.

- In this chapter, OSPF theory, design best practices, and case studies will be covered.

OSPF THEORY

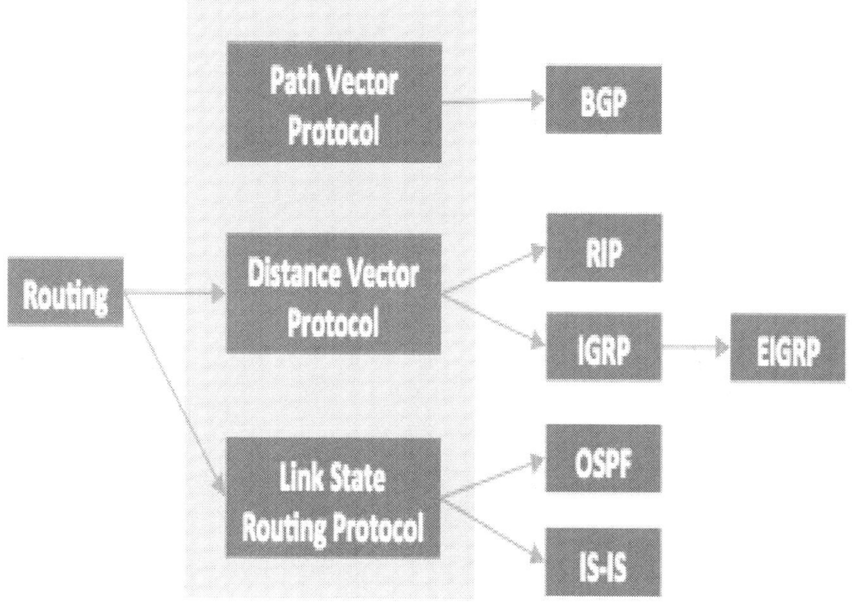

As you can see from the above picture, OSPF is a Link-State Routing protocol. But Why OSPF is link state and what is Link State Routing?

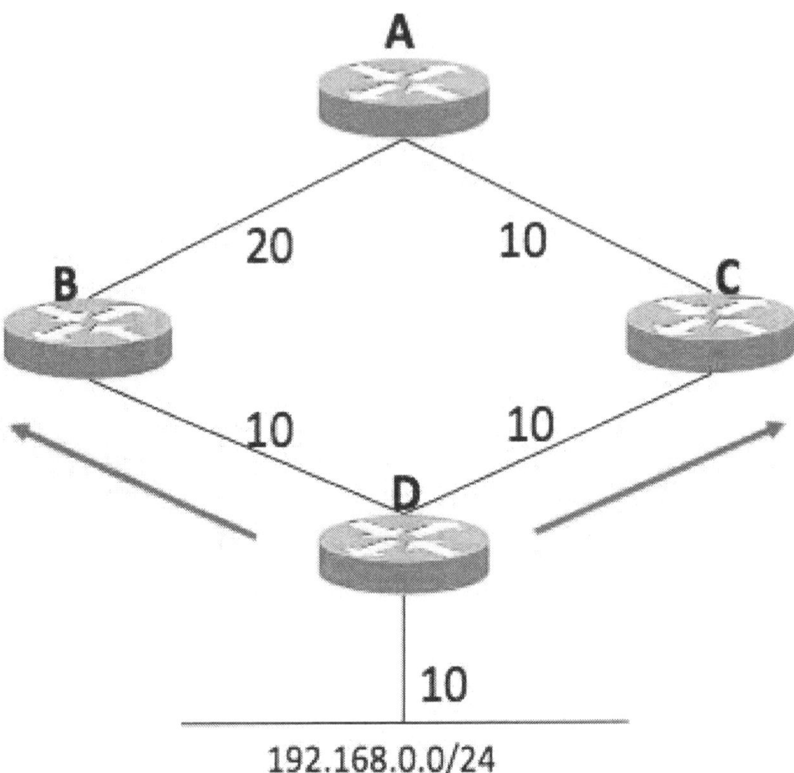

In the link state protocols, each router advertises the state of its link to every other router in the network.

D determines that it is connected to 192.168.0.0/24 with metric 10. Connected to B with metric 10 and Connected to C with metric 10 as well. In turn, Router B and Router C advertise this information to Router A.

In OSPF (Similar in IS-IS) all the connections and their associated metric is known by all the routers. In above topology, Router A knows that 192.168.0.0/24 network is connected to Router D.

In Distance Vector Protocols (EIGRP, RIP) Router A would only know that 192.168.0.0/24 network is reachable through Router B or Router C. Router A wouldn't know that the network is connected to Router D. This is called as OSPF's distance vector behavior.

This information is called topology information. Since they are Link State Routing Protocols, in OSPF and IS-IS networks, every router knows the topology information. (Who is connected to who and how)

OSPF Link-State Advertisement

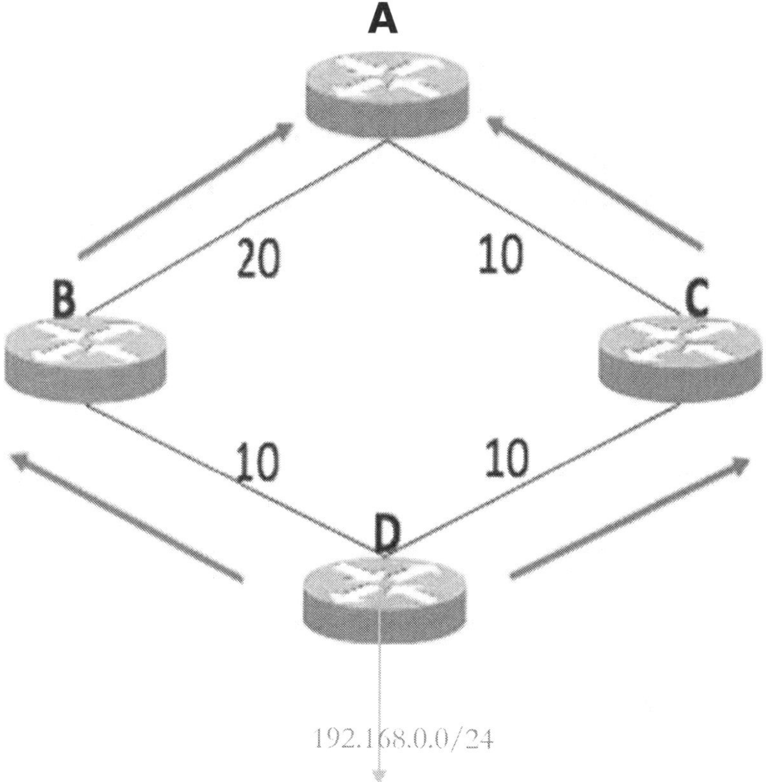

Since information is flooded within a link-state network, In OSPF, every router should have the same information about the network.

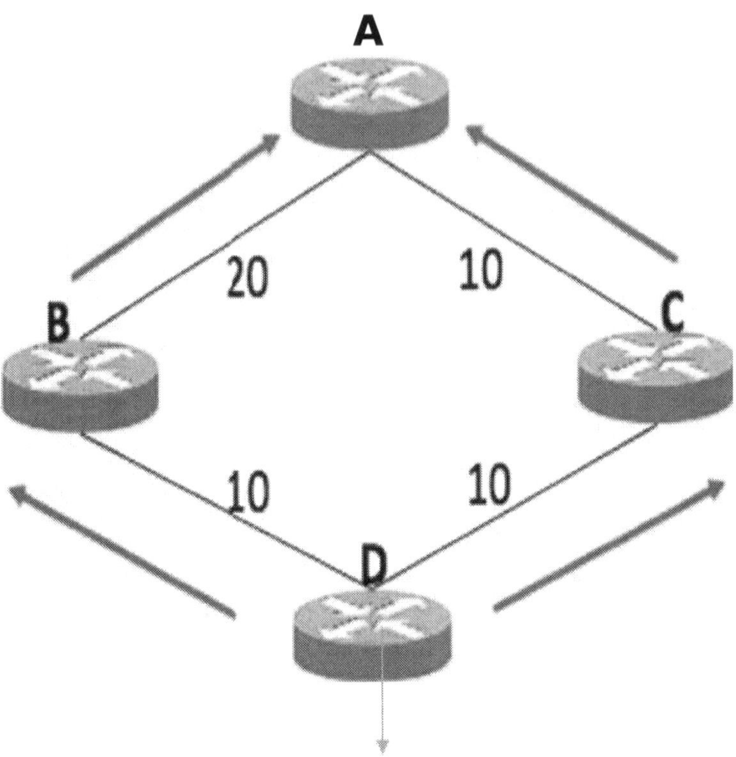

192.168.0.0/24

Each router in the network uses this Information (Topology information) to build shortest path tree to each destination in the network. The shortest path first (SPF) algorithm is used to build this tree.

Reachability information mean is the Subnets (IP addresses). Knowing 192.168.0.0/24 is reachability, knowing that subnet is connected to Router D is the Topology information.

Flooding of topology and reachability information throughout the network seriously impacts the scaling of a network. When scaling becomes an issue the network is broken into separate flooding domains, which are called Areas in OSPF.

The router connecting the two OSPF Areas is called an Area Border Router (ABR). In a particular area every router has identical topology information. Every router knows which network is behind which router and it's metrics.

OSPF, unlike EIGRP and IS-IS, works differently on different media. On broadcast network DR (Designated Router) creates a pseudo-node to avoid unnecessary flooding. DR creates Type 2 LSA (Network LSA) to inform the connected routers on the broadcast network.

Highest priority OSPF router on the broadcast segment wins the designated router (DR) election. If priorities are the same then highest router ID wins the DR election. On every broadcast segment there can be only one DR.

Unlike IS-IS, there is a Backup Designated Router (BDR) in OSPF.

There are eleven types of LSAs in OSPF; six of them are important for the OSPF routing protocol design. We can only have scalable, resilient, fast-converged OSPF design when we understand OSPF LSAs and area types and their restrictions.

OSPF LSA Types

LSA Type	Description
1	Router LSA
2	Network LSA
3 and 4	Summary LSAs
5	As External LSA
6	Multicast OSPF LSA
7	Defined for NSSAs
8	External attribute LSA for Border Gateway Protocol (BGP)
9, 10, 11	Opaque LSAs

Above table lists all the OSPF LSAs, Type 6 and Type 8 is never implemented. Type 9 through Type 11 is used in specific applications such as MPLS Traffic Engineering, Segment Routing, OSPF Graceful Restart and so on.

6 Critical LSAs for OSPF Design

OSPF Router LSA

Also called as OSPF type 1 LSA.

Every router within a single area generates a router LSA to advertise link and prefix information.

In an area every router has to have same routing information, otherwise routing loop might occur.

Important network design best practice is for the OSPF Router LSA is not to exceed the Interface MTU.

If Router LSA size exceeds the interface MTU value, routers fragment and reassemble the fragmented packets. Fragmentation is always bad! Especially if it is done by the routers. In IPv6, Routers don't fragment or reassemble the packets though. Hosts handle the fragmentation.

OSPF Network LSA

Also called as OSPF type 2 LSA.

Type 2 LSA is used to advertise connected routers to multi access network by the DR (Designated Router).

OSPF uses DR (Designated Router) and BDR (Backup Designated Router) on multi access network such as Ethernet. DR and BDR reduce the number of flooding in multi access network thus help in scalability. But on point-to-point link, if OSPF is enabled, it is best practice to set OSPF network type as ' Point to Point'. Otherwise unnecessary Type 2 LSA is created by DR.

If point-to-point OSPF network type is set there is no DR or BDR.

DR and BDR election takes time, that's why from design best practice point of view, if the requirement is fast convergence, it is good to change the OSPF network type to point to point, even if the physical connection is Ethernet. (When two routers are connected back to back via Ethernet, even though there are only two routers, still there will be DR/BDR election)

OSPF Summary LSA

Also called as OSPF type 3 LSA.

Generated by the OSPF ABR (Area Border Router) in multi area OSPF environment.

OSPF ABR doesn't send topology information between the OSPF areas.

Instability in one area doesn't affect the other areas.

OSPF Type 3 LSA is generated by the OSPF ABR. Important design question for the OSPF summary LSA is, how many ABR should be between two areas. The answer is two. One would be bad for the high availability and more than two ABR create unnecessary complexity since there would be 3x amount of Summary LSA for each prefix.

OSPF ABR has too much work in Multi Area OSPF design. On Multi access network OSPF DR also has more work than DR Other routers. That's why it is good practice to have OSPF DR and OSPF ABR function on different routers whenever it is possible.

OSPF ASBR Summary LSA

Also called as OSPF Type 4 LSA.

In order to reach to an ASBR (Autonomous System Boundary Router) from different area, ABR creates a Type 4 LSA.

It is important to understand that ASBR doesn't generate Type 4 LSA. ASBR generates Type 5 LSA for the external prefixes. Also ASBR generates Type 1 LSA for its own reachability information. When an ABR receives Type 1 LSA advertisement of ASBR, it generates Type 4 LSA and floods Type 4 LSA to the other areas.

If there is no Type 5 LSA, Type 4 LSA is not generated.

There are some special type of Areas which has been explained in different article on the website such as Stub, NSSA areas which don't allow Type 5 LSA, in those areas, there is no Type 4 lsa as well.

OSPF External LSA

Also called as OSPF Type 5 LSA.

External LSA is used to advertise external reachability information.

External LSA is flooded to every router in the domain. ABR don't regenerate it. ABR just passes that information as is.

From different routing domain such as BGP or EIGRP, routes might be redistributed for many reasons.

In that case, for those routes, type 5 OSPF external LSA is created by the router, which does the redistribution. That router is called an ASBR (Autonomous System Boundary Router).

OSPF NSSA External LSA

Also called as OSPF Type 7 LSA.

Used in NSSA (Not-so-stubby) area to allow redistribution external routing information.

This is a special type of LSA, which is only used in NSSA area. This LSA type is translated (converted) to Type 5 External LSA by the ABR (Area Border Router) and send to the other areas as Type 5.

In NSSA area, Type 4 or Type 5 LSA is not allowed. So type 7 can go to other areas Type 5 but Type 5 LSA cannot go to the NSSA areas as Type 7 or any other LSA type. It is not allowed at all!

OSPF Opaque LSAs: Type 9,10 and 11 are the opaque LSAs.

RFC 5250 ' The OSPF Opaque LSA Option ' explains these LSAs in great detail.

Type 9 LSA is used for OSPF Graceful Restart operation.

Type 10 LSA is used for MPLS Traffic Engineering.

Using different LSAs and having different Area types in OSPF provides flexibility and scalability.

OSPF LSAs is similar to IS-IS TLVs, although there are some differences and will be explained in IS-IS chapter.

OSPF Area Types

OSPF Area Types – Different Areas in OSPF are used to create smaller fault domains. There are two OSPF area types in total.

OSPF Backbone and non-backbone area.

Backbone area in OSPF is Area 0. OSPF prevents loop by using backbone area concept. All the non-backbone areas should be connected to the Backbone area.

There are many Non-Backbone OSPF Area types. These are; Normal Area, Stub, Totally Stub, NSSA and Totally NSSA Areas.

Regular OSPF Non-Backbone Area If the OSPF Area is not an Area 0 (OSPF Backbone Area) and not also OSPF Stub, Totally Stub, NSSA or Totally NSSA Area, then it is regular OSPF non-backbone area.

If you have two areas in your network one has to be Area 0 and other area can be any other number.

Topology information, which is the connection information among the routers, is not sent between the OSPF Areas.

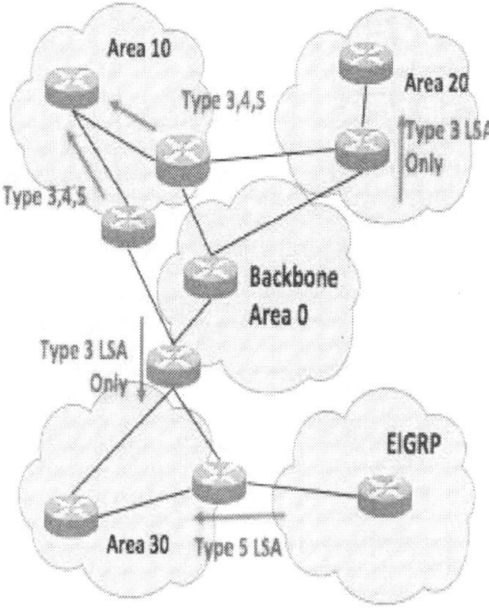

Area 10 is regular area thus all the LSA types Including type 3 and 5 are allowed

ABRs create Type 4 LSA into an Area 10

Area 20 is Stub Area. That's why only Type 3 LSA Is allowed

Type 5 LSA is not allowed in Stub Area Thus type 4 is not generated as well.

In the topology above Area 10 is a regular non-backbone area. Regular OSPF areas allow all the LSA Types into the Area.

There is no auto summarization in OSPF between the areas that's why reachability information by default is sent between OSPF backbone area and the regular OSPF non-backbone areas.

In the above topology, Area 30 has an ABR connected to the EIGRP domain. The external subnets are sent into Area 10 since it is a regular OSPF area. (Not Stub, Totally Stub, NSSA or Totally NSSA).

We will see that this will be not the case with other OSPF non-backbone areas.

OSPF Stub Area

In the topology above Area 20 is OSPF Stub Area. Stub Area as you can see from the above figure, doesn't allow Type 4 and Type 5 LSAs. Only Type 3 LSA is allowed into OSPF Stub Area.

Type 4 LSA is known as ASBR Summary, Type 5 LSA is known as OSPF External LSA and both are not allowed into the OSPF Stub Area.

That's why the Area 20 routers cannot learn external subnets, which come from the EIGRP domain.

Instead those networks are reached via default route. Default route is sent into the OSPF stub area as OSPF Type 3 LSA, which is Inter-Area OSPF LSA.

OSPF Totally Stub Area

Imagine that Area 20 is an OSPF Totally Stub Area. Then it wouldn't allow Type 3 LSA in addition to Type 4 and Type 5 LSA as well.

If the requirement is higher scalability then OSPF Totally Stub Area provides better scalability compare to OSPF Stub Area.

One thing you should keep in mind that, when the OSPF area becomes Stub, Totally Stub, NSSA and totally NSSA area, chance of the sub optimal routing in the network increases. Network designers should be aware on this.

OSPF NSSA Area

Redistribution into the OSPF Stub area is not allowed. But if the requirement is to redistribute into the OSPF Stub area, then OSPF Not-So-Stubby Area is used.

OSPF NSSA area allows route to be redistributed.

Redistributed routes appear in the OSPF NSSA area as Type 7 LSA.

Type 7 LSA is translated by the OSPF ABR to the OSPF Type 5 LSA. If there are more than one OSPF NSSA ABRs, the router, which has higher Router ID, does the translation only.

Default route is not sent by default to the OSPF NSSA area. You may manually send it into the OSPF NSSA area on the ABR though.

Type 7 LSA is translated to the Type 5 LSA and sent to all routers in the OSPF domain. But Type 5 LSA is not sent to the OSPF NSSA Area. It is not allowed. Since Type 5 LSA is not allowed, Type 4 LSA is not allowed too.

OSPF Totally NSSA Area

If the requirement is redistribution into the OSPF Stub area with a better scalability than the OSPF NSSA area then the solution is OSPF Totally NSSA Area.

In OSPF Totally NSSA Area, in addition to Type 4 and Type 5 LSA, Type 3 LSA is not allowed as well.

Default route is sent by the NSSA ABR into Totally NSSA area, which is different than OSPF NSSA Area.

If you are familiar with IS-IS routing protocol, Totally NSSA area is similar to IS-IS Level 1 domain.

In IS-IS level 1 domain, IS-IS LSPs are not allowed but only ATT bit of L1 LSP is allowed in Level 1 sub domain.

Since IS-IS Level 1 domain allows redistribution in IS-IS, all these behavior can be considered the same with OSPF Totally NSSA area.

In the below table, Backbone and Non-backbone OSPF areas and the allowed LSA types in each area is shared.

LSA Type	Description
Backbone	1, 2, 3, 4, 5
Regular	1, 2, 3, 4, 5
Stub	1, 2, 3
Totally Stubby	1, 2, Default 3
Not So Stubby	1, 2, 3, 4, 7

OSPF Multi-Area Design

To reduce the impact of flooding, Multi-Area OSPF design may be used. With today's hardware, hundreds of OSPF routers can be placed in an OSPF area.

The problem with the number of routers in an area is the router LSAs. Every OSPF router has to generate Router (Type 1) LSA. Each additional link and subnet makes the router LSA bigger and when the Router LSA exceeds the interface MTU, the packet is fragmented. Fragmentation should always be avoided.

Special areas such as Stub and NSSA in OSPF provide fault isolation. These OSPF area types are explained earlier in this chapter.

There is a special node in Multi Area Design; Area Border Router (ABR).

ABR must have a connection to more than one area; at least one area should be in Area 0 (Backbone Area) but even creating a loopback interface and placing it into Area 0 makes that router an ABR.

There are some questions designer should ask when they deal with OSPF design. At least as a designer you should know the answer so your design can be scalable, resilient, faster converge and optimal.

- How many routers should be placed in one OSPF area?
- How many ABR should we have per OSPF area?
- How many OSPF area ABR should have?

Let's look at each of these questions in detail.

How many routers should be in one OSPF area?

Number of neighbor is more important question which we should ask

Always try to keep router LSA under the MTU size to avoid fragmentation

Routers cannot deal with fragmentation and reassembly well

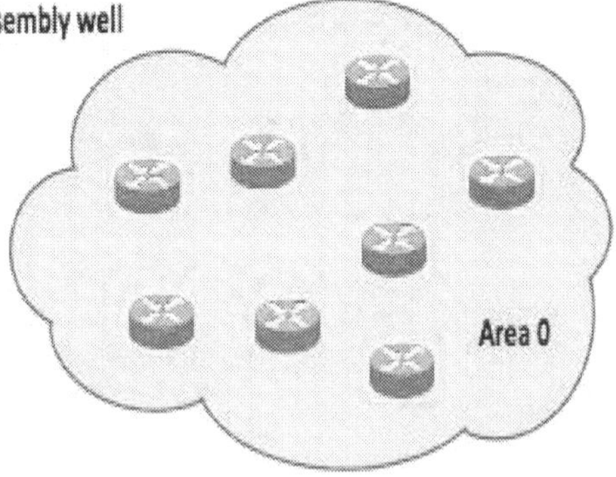

There is no numeric answer of this question. It depends on how many links each router have, stability of the links, hardware resources such as CPU and Memory of the routers and physical topology of the network.

For example in full mesh topology, every router is connected to each other and number of links are too much compare to ring or partial topologies.

Thus, in one OSPF network you may place 50 routers in one OSPF area, but other OSPF network can have 100s of routers in one area.

Also, every link and node fails, doesn't matter how much redundancy you have. That is unavoidable. Rate of failure impacts the number of routers in an OSPF area. Stabile links and nodes are the key for large scale OSPF design.

How many ABR (Area Border Router) per OSPF Area?

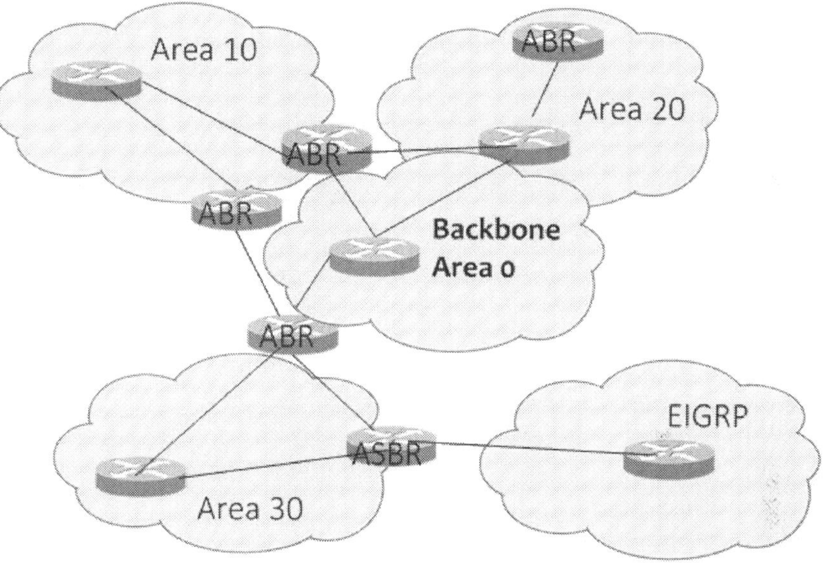

In the previous diagram, there are two ABRs in Area 10. For redundancy and optimal traffic flow, two is always enough. More ABRs will create more Type 3 LSA replications within the backbone and non-backbone areas.

In large-scale OSPF design, the number of ABRs will have a huge impact on the number of prefixes. Thus having two ABR is good for redundancy for the critical sites.

For example some of the remote offices or POP locations may not be critical as others and having only one ABR can be tolerated by the company. In this case that specific location may have only one ABR as well.

Keep in mind that, two is company, three is crowded in design.

How many OSPF areas are suitable per OSPF ABR?

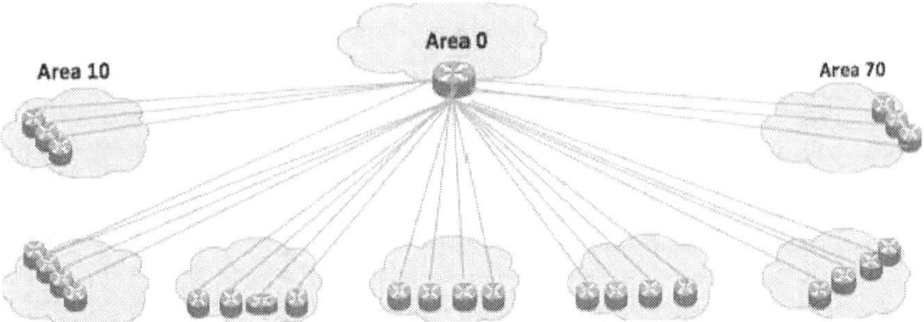

- More areas per ABR might create a resource problem on the ABR.
- Much more Type 3 LSA will be generated by the ABR. Also, when the failure happens ABR slows down the convergence (Similar to BGP Route Reflector and will be explain in the BGP chapter).
- Thus having maximum amount of routers in a given area without creating fragmentation issue and having two ABR per OSPF areas is the best practice. If you have 100 sites, you don't want to place if site in different Area. Having one or two OSPF area is always enough in today networks.

Best Practices on OSPF Areas:

- Topology information is not sent between different OSPF areas, this reduces the flooding domain and allows large scale OSPF deployment. If you have 100s of routers in your network, you can consider splitting the OSPF domain into Multiple OSPF areas. But there are other considerations for Multi Area design and will be explained in this chapter.
- Stub, Totally Stub, NSSA and Totally NSSA Areas can create sub optimal routing in the network.
- OSPF Areas are used for scalability. If you don't have valid reason such as 100s of routers, or resource problems on the routers, don't use multiple areas.
- OSPF Multi area design just increases the complexity.
- Two is company, three is crowded in design. Having two OSPF ABR provides high availability but three ABR is not a good idea.
- Having single OSPF area per OSPF ABR is very bad and there is no use case for that. You should monitor the routers resources carefully and placed as much router as you can in one OSPF area.
- Not every router has powerful CPU and Memory, you can split up the router based on their resource availability. Low end devices can be placed in a separate OSPF area and that area type can be changed as Stub, Totally Stub, NSSA or Totally NSSA.
- Always look for the summarization opportunity, but know that summarization can create sub optimal routing. (OSPF summarization and sub optimal routing will be explained in this chapter).
- Good IP addressing plan is important for OSPF Multi Area design. It allows OSPF summarization (Reachability) thus faster convergence and smaller routing table.
- Having smaller routing table provides easier troubleshooting.
- OSPF NSSA area in general is used at the Internet Edge of the network since on the Internet routers where you don't need to have all the OSPF LSAs yet still redistribution of selected BGP prefixes are common.

OSPF Single vs. Multi Area Design Comparison

Below table summarizes the similarities and the differences of these two OSPF design models in great detail. Network designers should know the pros and cons of the technologies, protocol alternatives and their capabilities from the design point of view.

Design requirement	Flat OSPF/ Single Area	Multi Area OSPF Design
Scalability	NO, it is not scalable. In large scale OSPF design, any change on the Ruters triggers Full SPF run	YES, Change in one OSPF Area triggers Partial SPF run in another Area. Topology information is not sent between the OSPF Areas
Working on Full Mesh Topology	YES, but not sclable	YES
Working on Hub and Spoke	YES	YES
Convergence	Better than Multi Area Design	ABR adds additional latency (Processing delay) during convergence
Reachability Information	YES, Inside an Area, all routers have the same Likk State Database	YES, by default all the prefixws are learnt by every router in any OSPF Area. there is no automatic summmarization
Topology Information	YES, Inside an Area, all routers have the same Likk State Database	NO, ABR stops topolgy information, one Area topology is not known by the other OSPF Area
Which LSAs are shown in the Link State Database	Type 1 and Type 2 (If there is external, then Type and Type 7 as well)	Type 1 and Type 2 (If there is external, then Type and Type 7 as well)
MPLS traffic Engineering	Good, every router has same topology information: which router is connected to which, and the metric between them, and so on	Hard, it requires MPLS TE extension or Path Computation Element
Troubleshooting	Easier than Multi Area OSPF design	More nodes, more LSAs makes it harder to troubleshoot, compared to Single Area/Flat OSPF design
Stuff Experience	Welll known	Well known

Design requirement	Flat OSPF/ Single Area	Multi Area OSPF Design
IPv6 Support	YES, with OSPFv3	YES, with OSPFv3
Additional Nodes	None	ABR (Area Border Router)
QoS Support	Good, no difference	Good, no difference
Multicast Support	Good, no difference	Good, no difference
Resource requirement	More, every router needs to keep both reachability and the topllogy information inside OSPF domain	Less, routers only keep topology information of their Area, but reachability information of the entire OSPF domain
IPv6 Support	YES, it can be set up over IPv6 payload. So IPv6 over DMVPN and DMVPN over IPv6 are both possible	YES
Can it run over other VPN?	YES, it can run over GRE, MGRE, and DMVPN	YES, can be designed over GRE, Mgre, DMVPN. In Hub and Spoke technologies such as DMVPN, Spokes can be placed in non-Backbone areas

OSPF Flat/Single Area vs. Multi Area Design Models Comparison

INTERACTION BETWEEN OSPF AND OTHER PROTOCOLS

OSPF interacts with many protocols in the network such as STP, BGP, and MPLS. Understanding the impact of interactions is the first step for robust network design.

OSPF interacts with the other protocols in the network sometimes as an overlay, in some cases as an underlay protocol. If BGP is running in the network, OSPF provides underlay routing for the BGP neighbors.

BGP convergence should be synchronized with the OSPF convergence, otherwise black hole occurs.

Or when it is used in the Campus or datacenter networks in cooperation with the first hop redundancy protocols, convergence of OSPF should be tracked by the first hop redundancy protocols, otherwise black hole occurs.

These are not only the interactions, which need to be considered in OSPF. MPLS, Multicast, QoS interactions are important as well.

Let's take a look at a case study regarding OSPF interaction with BGP to understand why they should synchronized.

OSPF-BGP Interaction Case Study

- OSPF is running as an IGP protocol in the below network. There is no MPLS in the core and all routers run BGP. (This is called BGP Free core and will be explained in BGP chapter in detail).
- For scaling purposes, the company decided to use BGP Route Reflector design.
- Routers B and C are the Route Reflectors and Routers A and D are the Route Reflector clients.
- The company wants to perform maintenance on Router B, but they don't want to have any downtime.
- What would be your design recommendations for the company?
-

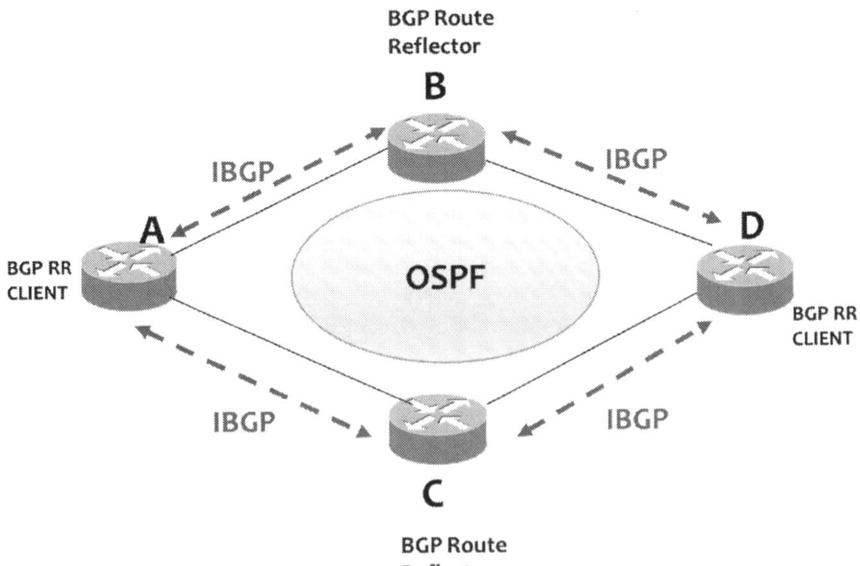

BGP as an overlay protocol needs next-hop reachability. Static routing or the dynamic routing protocol is used to create an underlay network infrastructure for the overlay protocols such as BGP, LDP, and PIM.

In this case study, one of the routers in the path towards BGP next-hop will be reloaded (Router B). So there might be two problems here.

First problem: When Router B is reloaded, traffic going through Router B shouldn't be dropped. Router B should signal the other OSPF routers and inform that it should be going down. Traffic shouldn't be sent to Router B during reload.

This signaling is done with the OSPF Stub Router Advertisement feature.

"Max-metric router-lsa" configuration knob is used by OSPF for graceful restart purpose.

With this feature, OSPF routers are not used as Transit node anymore.

Important note is, routers loopback is still sent with the regular metric, not with the max-metric. Otherwise BGP neighborship with the reloaded router wouldn't come up.

IGP always converges faster than BGP.

Second problem: when Router B comes back, BGP traffic towards Router B will be black holed, because the IGP process of Router B will converge faster than its BGP process.

IGP should wait until BGP to converge. Router B should take the BGP traffic once BGP prefixes are installed in the routing table.

This is done with the OSPF Stub Router Advertisement feature as well. "Max-metric router-lsa on-startup wait-for-bgp" is used by OSPF, so until BGP process is converged; OSPF process doesn't use the Router B as its path towards any destination.

These two features are known as OSPF Stub Router Advertisement.

In this case study, with the OSPF Stub Router Advertisement feature, other OSPF routers are signaled for graceful restart and OSPF convergence is synchronized with BGP convergence. (Router doesn't receive traffic until BGP converge).

OSPFv2 vs. OSPF v3 Comparison

There are some new LSA types in OSPFv3. These LSAs bring scalability for the OSPFv3.

OSPFv3 actually very different from the LSA and network design point of view, although configurations of the two protocols are similar.

Below table summarizes the similarities and the differences of these two protocols in detail. Network designers should know the pros and cons of the technologies, protocol alternatives and their capabilities from the design point of view.

Design Requirement	OSPFv2	OSPFv3
Scalability	Good	Better, since router and Network LSA doesn't contain prefix information, but only topology information
Working on Full Mesh	Works well with mesh group	Works well with mesh group
Working on Hub and Spoke	Works poorly, requires a lot of tuning	Doesn't work well, requires tuning
Fast Reroute Support	YES, IP FRR	YES, IP FRR, but limited platform support
Suitable on WAN	YES	YES
Suitable on Datacenter	DCs are full mesh, therefore, not well	DCs are full mesh not so well
Suitable on Internet Edge	NO, it is designed as an IGP	NO, it is designed as an IGP
Standard Protocol	YES, IETF Standard	YES, IETF Standard
New LSAs	None	Links LSA (Type 8) is used for adjacency formation, and link local scope only, Inter-Area-prefix LSA (Type 9)which is one of the biggest enhancement since it is used to carry prefix information only, inside an area
LSA Types	Router (Type 1), Network (Type 2), Summary (Type 3) ASBR, External (Type 4), AS External (Type 5), NSSA (Type 7)	Router (Type 1), Network (Type 2) Inter-Area Prefix (Type 3), Inter-Area Router (Type 4), AS External, (Type 5), NSSA (Type 7), Link LSA (Type 8) Intra-Area Prefix LSA (Type 9)

Design Requirement	OSPFv2	OSPFv3
Transport	Multicast, 224.0.0.5 and 224.0.0.6	Same, but with IPv6 addresses. Multicast FF02::5 and FF02::6
Reachability info handling	Inside an Area and Network LSA carriess the reachability information between areas reachability info is carried in Summary(Type 3) LSA	Inside an area, reachability information is carried in Intra-area Prefix LSA (Type 9), which is a new LSA type. Inter-Area Prefixes are still carried in type 3 LSA, but the name is changed as Inter-Area Prefix LSA
Topology info handling	Inside an Area Router and Network LSA, carries the topology information. Topology info is not carried beyond an area	Same. Inside an Area Router, and Network LSA carries the topology information, and this is not carried beyond an area
Stuff experience	Very well known	Not well known, especially topology and reachability information handling, Multi Area Adjacency and new LSA types should be understood better
Overlay Tunnel Support	YES, it supports	YES, it supports
MPLS Traffic Engineering Support	YES, with CSPF or external controllee	YES, with CSPF or external controller
Security	MDS Authentication	Authentication is removed, since it runs on IPv6. IPv6 supports IPSEC and Authentication, this simplifies OSPF header
Suitable as Interprise IGP	YES	YES
Suitable as Service Provider IGP	YES	Definitely
Complexity	Easy	Moderate
Resource requirement	Full SPF runs on prefix or topology change as it is worsee than OSPFv3	If topology doesn't change, full SPF is not needed. Prefix information is carried in new LSA, not in Router LSA any longer
Ipv6 Support	NO	YES
IPv4 Support	YES	YES
Default Convergence	Slow	Even Slower, if multiple address families are used

Design Requirement	OSPFv2	OSPFv3
Troubleshooting	Easy	Harder, requires understanding of IPv6 addressing, after that, it is the same packet types, LSA, LSU, DBD
Routing Loop	Inter area prefixes Should be recieved from ABR. All non-backbone areas should be connected to the backbone area	Same as OSPFv2. Inter area prefixes should be recieved from ABR, all non-backbone areas should be connected to the backbone area

OSPFv2 vs. OSPFv3 Comparison

OSPF Route Summarization

OSPF does not support auto summarization, only manual. OSPF route summarization can be of two types:

- Internal route summarization;
- External route summarization.

In OSPF you can do internal route summarization only on the OSPF ABR. The reason for this is that Link State Database for all routers in an OSPF area must be the same for that area. External routes can be summarized only on the ASBR. This will be different in IS-IS.

As with all the features in the networks, Summarization has pros and cons and understanding those is very important for the network designers.

Benefits of OSPF Route Summarization:

- Smaller routing table
- Localizes the impact of topology change
- Less CPU, memory and bandwidth utilization
- Less LSA flooding in the network
- Overall scalability of the network increases
- Convergence time in case of failure (Link or Node) is reduced, network converges faster

- Troubleshooting become easier

  OSPF route summarization removes reachability information.

  Drawbacks of OSPF Route Summarization

- Less specific routing information can create suboptimal routing
- MPLS end-to-end LSP is broken if the Router Loopback interfaces are summarized. (This will be explained in the MPLS chapter in detail).

OSPF route summarization breaks the MPLS LSP, since LDP cannot have aggregated FEC unless the RFC 5283-LDP Extension to Inter-Area LSP is in use.

So LDP should see the /32 IP address in the routing table to assign a label for the prefixes. That's why Loopback interfaces are configured as /32.

Let's look at how OSPF route summarization can create sub optimal routing with the below case study.

OSPF Sub Optimal Routing with Route Summarization Case Study:

In the topology below, Router C and D are summarizing 192.168.0.0/24 and 192.168.0.0/24 as 192.168.0.0/23.

They both send the summary route with metric 100.

Same thing happens for the Router E to 192.168.0.0/24 traffic. It follows the yellow path for the half of the traffic.

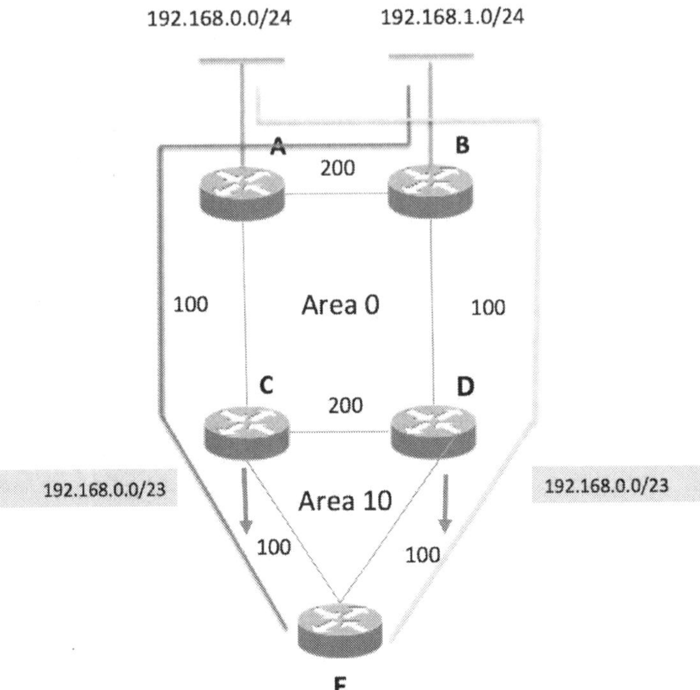

Inside the Area 10, Router E chooses the closest ABR to go out from the area. Since both ABR sends with the same metric, Router E, for both 192.168.0.0/24 and 192.168.1.0/24 destined traffic, does ECMP (Equal cost multipath).

- Half of the traffic from Router E to 192.168.0.0/24 and 192.168.1.0/24 always goes through sub optimal path.

If the Router C – D link is in Area 10, Router E to 192.168.1.0/24 traffic follows the green path (E-C-A-B). The reason is, when the traffic arrives from Router E to Router C, Router C receives 192.168.1.0/24 traffic from the Router C-D link as Inter area route (Type 3). But Router C sees 192.168.1.0/24 traffic from the Router A as Intra Area route (Type 1). Since Intra are route is preferred over Inter area route in OSPF, if the Router C-D link is in Area 10, longer path is chosen.

OSPF Fast Convergence

Netwok convergence is between the failure event and the recovery.

treough the path, all the routers process the event and update their routing and forwarding table. Thus, there are four convergence in general:

1. Failure Detection
2. Failure Propagation
3. Processing the new information
4. Routing and Forwarding table update

Convergence is a control plane event, and for IGPs, it can take seconds; BGP routers which have full internet routing table, control plane convergence can take minutes.

Protection is a data plane recovery mechanism. As soon as failure is detectted and propagated to the nodes, data plane can react and a backup path can be used. A backup path should be calculated and installed in routing and forwarding table before the failure event.

Network reliability is an important measure for deployability of sensitive applications.

When a link, node or SRLG (Shared Risk Ling Group) failure occurs in a routed network, there is inevitably a period of disruption to the delivery of traffic until the network reconverges on the new topology.

Fast reaction is essential for the failed element. There are two approaches for the fast reaction:

Fast convergence and fast reroute.

When a local failure occur four steps are necessary for the convergence.

Four necessary steps in fast convergence

1. Failure detection

Layer 1 Failure detection mechanisms:

- Carrier delay
- Debounce Timer
- Sonet/SDH APS timers

Layer 3 Failure detection mechanisms:

- Protocol timers (Hello/Dead)
- BFD (Bidirectional Forwarding Detection)

For the failure detection, best practice is always use Physical down detection mechanism first. Even BFD cannot detect the failure faster than physical failure detection mechanism.

Because BFD messages is pull based detection mechanism which is sent and receive periodically, but physical layer detection mechanism is event driven and always faster than BFD and Protocol hellos.

If physical layer detection mechanisms cannot be used (Maybe because there is a transport element in the path), then instead of tuning protocol hello timers aggressively, BFD should be used. . Common example to this is if there are two routers and connected through an Ethernet switch, best method is to use BFD.

Compare to protocol hello timers, BFD is much ligher in size, thus consumes less resource and bandwidth.

2. Failure propagation

Propagation of failure throughout the network.

Here LSA throttling timers come into play. You can tune LSA throttling for faster information propagation. It can be used to slow down the information processing as well.

Also LSA pacing timers can be tuned for sending update much faster.

3. New information process

Processing of newly arrived LSA to find the next best path. SPF throttling timers can be tuned for faster information process for fast convergence.

4. Update new route into RIB/FIB

For fast convergence, these steps may need to be tuned.

Although the RIB/FIB update is hardware dependent, the network operator can configure all other steps.

One thing always needs to be kept in mind; Fast convergence and fast reroute can affect network stability.

Unlike fast convergence, for the fast reroute, routes are precomputed and preprogrammed into the router RIB/FIB.

Additional, an alternate is found, if possible, and pre-installed into the RIB/FIB. As soon as the local failure is detected, the PLR (Point of Local Repair) switches the routes to use the alternate path. This preserves the traffic while the normal convergence process of failure propagation and SPF recomputation occurs. Fast reroute mechanisms and the comparison charts of common fast reroute mechanisms are going to be explained in the MPLS Traffic Engineering section of MPLS chapter.

OSPF Full-Mesh Topology Design

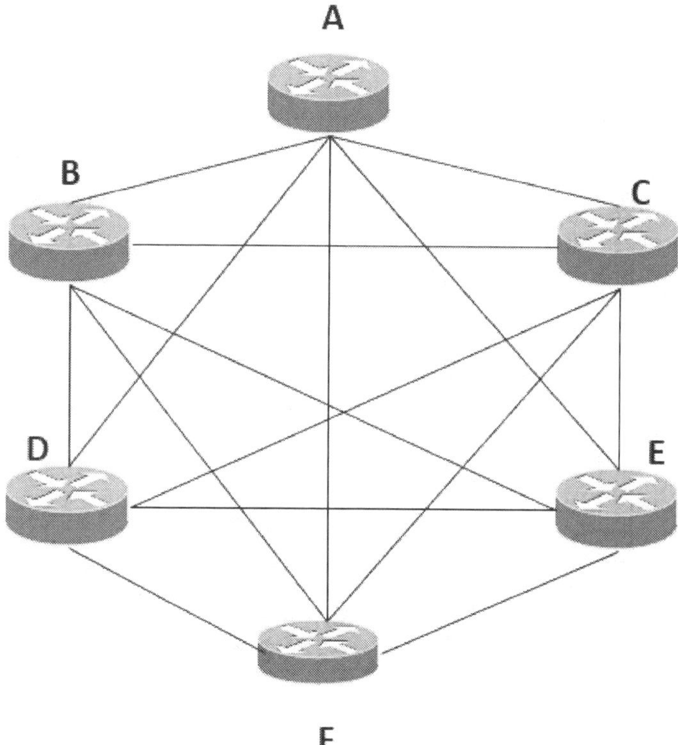

Mesh group is a mechanism that reduces the amount of flooding in a OSPF full-mesh topology. With mesh group, we can designate couple routers in the topology to flood. Those routers will be responsible for a flooding event. In this topology, Routers A and B can be assigned as the flooders. It is important to select powerful devices as flooders in the mesh group since their duty is to flood the LSAs in all the networks.

- This is the formula: for N routers, there are (N) (N-1)/2 links. If there are only two routers in the topology, the total number of links between them is one; if there are three routers, there are three links; if there are four routers, there are six links; and if there are five routers, there are ten links.

In the above topology there are six routers, so there are fifteen links. Even if one loopback is added to any one of these routers, that loopback information is flooded in all of the routers over all of the links.

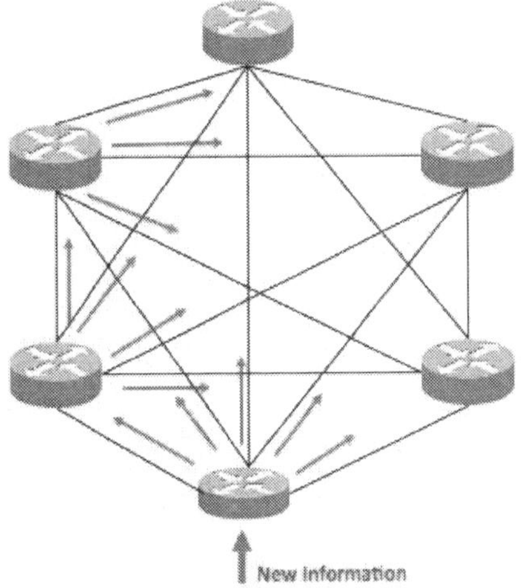

Flooding in full mesh is a big concern, especially in large scale OSPF deployment

Each router receives at least one copy of the new information from each neighbor

Mesh Group is one mechanism which we can use to reduce the amount of flooding in a full mesh

With Mesh Group, we designate couple routers in the topology to flood. Those routers will responsible from flooding event

Any topology poses a challenge for OSPF. OSPF needs to be adjusted to work in a topology that can create configuration complexity. OSPF can deal with ring topology better than EIGRP can, although ring topology is hardest topology for all the routing protocols from the fast reroute, optimal routing and capacity planning point of view.

OSPF Hub and Spoke Topology Design

We need to be careful about Designated Router (DR) in Hub and Spoke topology.

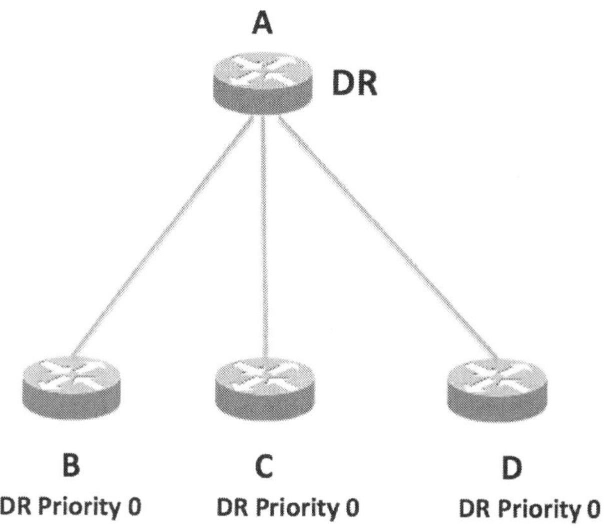

In the above picture, A is Hub router; B, C and D are the spoke routers. In Hub and Spoke topologies, Hub router should be the OSPF DR. Otherwise flooding fails. In the above topology, if any of the spokes consider itself as DR and Hub also believes that spoke is the DR (Because higher DR priority), remote sites cannot reach each other.

Thus the best practice in Hub and Spoke network, configure Hub router as DR and set the priority as ' 0 ' on all the spoke routers. With Priority 0, spoke routers don't even participate DR/BDR election.

In large scale Hub and Spoke deployment, other design recommendation is; spoke sites should be placed in Stub, Totally Stub, NSSA or Totally NSSA areas if the optimal routing is not a concern from the spokes sites.

If redistribution is required, then NSSA and Totally NSSA area should be chosen for the spoke sites.

OSPF: Case Study – ABR Placement

Where should we place an ABR in the below topology? Why?

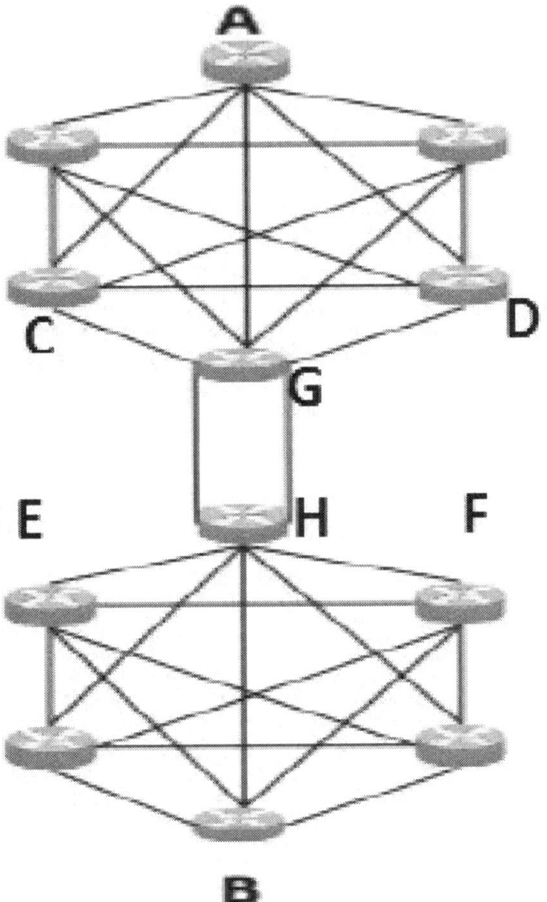

Between Router A and Router B there are 1800 different paths. (5x6) x 2 (5x6). If we put all of them in the same area there would be flooding, convergence, resource utilization, and troubleshooting problems. If we use Router G, or if Router H as an ABR, we will have only 32 paths max (5x6) +2 between Routers A and B. This will greatly reduce the load on the resources, reduce the overall complexity, and make troubleshooting easier.

Always put an ABR where you can separate the complex topologies from each other.

OSPF: Case Study – OSPF Multi Area Adjacency

Question:

What is the path from Router C to 192.168.10.0/24 and from Router D to 192.168.0.0/24 networks? Is there a problem with the path? Why? What is a possible solution?

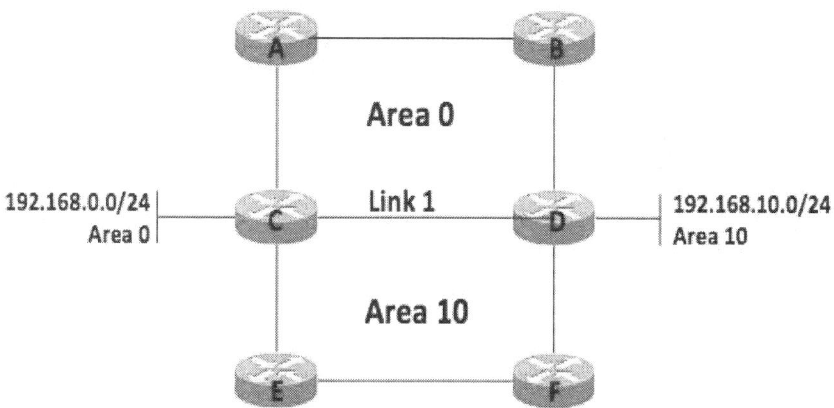

- If Link 1 is in Area 0, Router C will choose a path through E, F, and D to 192.168.10.0/24 rather than Link 1. This is because OSPF always prefers intra-area routes over inter-area routes.
- If Link 1 is placed in Area 10, Router D will choose a path through B, A, and C to 192.168.0.0/24 for the same reason. This is suboptimal.
- Placing link into Area 1 and creating virtual link is a temporary solution. New OSPF adjacency is also required for each additional non-backbone.

  Best solution: RFC 5185 -OSPF Multi-Area Adjacency.

  More than one OSPF adjacency multiple-area can be allowed with the RFC 5185

- Below is a sample configuration from the Cisco device which supports RFC 5185:
- rtr-C(config)# interface Ethernet 0/0
- rtr-C(config-if)# ip address 192.168.12.1 255.255.255.0

- rtr-C(config-if)# ip ospf 1 area 0
  rtr-C(config-if)# ip ospf network point-to-point
  rtr-C(config-if)# ip ospf multi-area 2

OSPF: Case Study – OSPF at the Internet Edge

Enterprise Company wants to run OSPF at the Internet edge between their Internet Gateway routers and the firewalls. Which type of OSPF area is most suitable in this design and why?

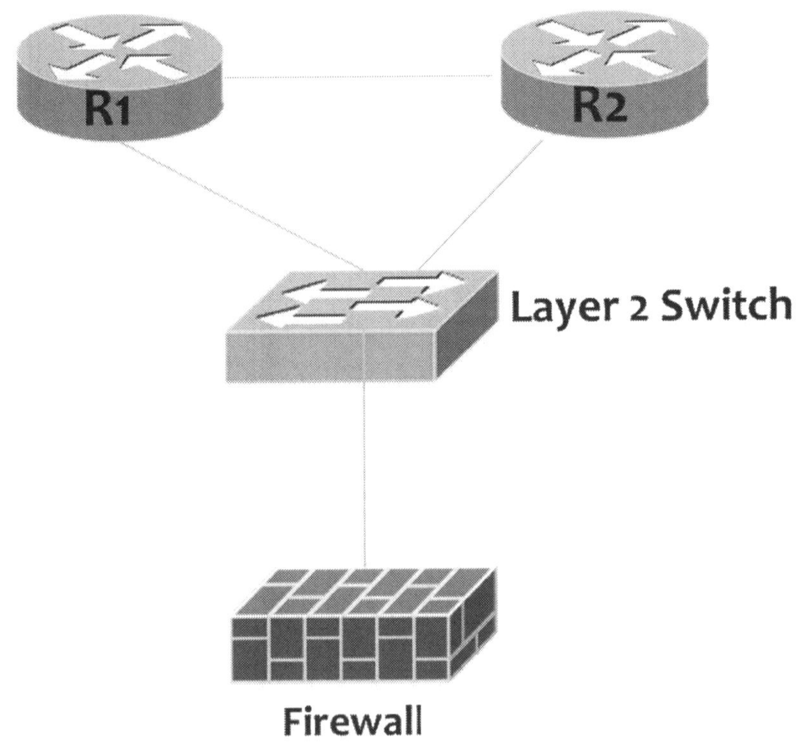

Solution:

If OSPF is used at the Internet edge, IGWs (Internet Gateways) don't need to have full OSPF routing table.

Using Stub or NSSA areas is most suitable. Firewalls only need a default route from the Internet gateways. Because traffic engineering is done with BGP and running BGP on the Firewalls instead of Routers is not a good practice.

Default route, partial route, or even a full route can be received from the BGP neighbor, but only default route is needed by the firewalls. It is a good practice to redistribute the default route from BGP to OSPF. If the link fails between the customer and the service provider, BGP goes down and the default route is removed from OSPF as well.

Only NSSA allows redistribution into OSPF Stub areas.

If OSPF is implemented, NSSA is the most suitable area on the Internet edge.

OSPF QUIZ QUESTIONS

Question 1:

How many routers can be placed in any given OSPF area?

- A. 50
- B. 100
- C. 250
- D. Less than 50
- E. It depends

Answer 1:

As it is explained in the OSPF chapter, you cannot have a numeric answer for this question.

There is no numeric answer of this question. It depends on how many links each router have, stability of the links, hardware resources such as CPU and Memory of the routers and physical topology of the network.

For example in full mesh topology, every router is connected to each other and number of links is too much compare to ring or partial topologies.

Thus, in one OSPF network you may place 50 routers in one OSPF area, but other OSPF network can have 100s of routers in one area.

Question 2:

Why there are many different types of LSAs are used in OSPF? (Chose all that apply)

A. Provides Scalability

B. Allow Multi-Area OSPF design

C. Provides fast convergence

D. Provides High Availability

E. Better Traffic Engineering

Answer 2:

Question here is asking the reason of having multiple different types of OSPF LSAs. As you have seen in the OSPF chapter there are 11 different types of OSPF LSAs.

Although there are other reasons to use OSPF LSAs, two important ones are scalability and Multi-Area design. They don't help for fast convergence or high availability LSAs are not related with High Availability or Fast convergence. Although MPLS Traffic engineering can use OSPF Opaque LSAs for the distributed CSPF calculation, CSPF is not mandatory and many networks which have MPLS Traffic engineering uses Offline Path calculation tool such as Cariden Mate.

Question 3:

What does topology information mean in OSPF?

A. IP addresses of the directly connected interface

B. IP addresses of the loopback interfaces of all the routers

C. Provides an IP reachability information and the metric of all the physical and logical interfaces

D. Provides a graph of the OSPF network by advertising connection information such as which router is connected to which one and the metric of the connections

Answer 3:

There are two type of information is provided in link state protocols: Topology and reachability information.

Reachability information means IP addresses of the physical or logical interfaces of the routers. Topology information explains, which router is connected to which one, what is the OSPF metric value between them, thus provide a graph of the OSPF network.

Based on this information every router runs SPF algorithm to find a shortest path to each and every destination in the network.

Question 4:

Why more than one Area is used in an OSPF network?

A. They are used for high availability

B. They are used for easier troubleshooting

C. They are used to provide scalability by having smaller flooding domains

D. Since topology information is not shared between OSPF areas, they provide better security

Answer 4:

OSPF areas are used mainly for scalability. Having smaller domain means, keeping topology information in an area and not sending between the areas. More than one area doesn't provide high availability and doesn't make troubleshooting easier.

Also in OSPF having more than one area doesn't prevent a route to be propagated to other areas by default, it requires manual configuration and even in that case it doesn't bring extra security.

Question 5:

Which router in the below topology should be an ABR?

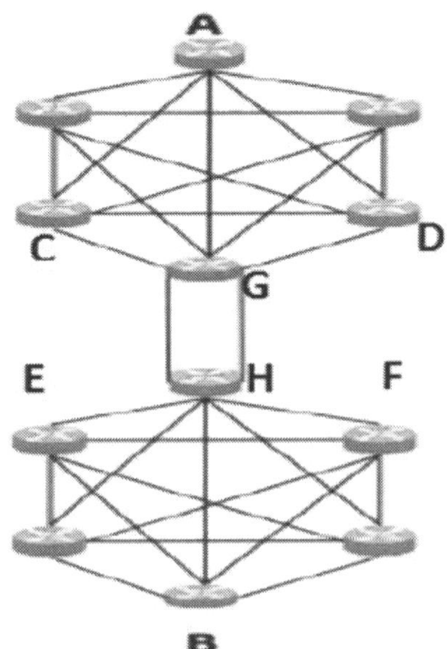

A. G or H
B. A or B
C. C or D
D. E or F
E. G

Answer 5:

Router G or H should be an ABR to separate two full mesh topology from each other. Otherwise each router in the top full mesh network would run full SPF algorithm for each other router in the below full mesh network in case link failure, metric change or when new link or prefix is added.

Question 6:

In the below topology, Router B needs to be reloaded. Network operator doesn't want any traffic loss during and after Router B's maintenance operation. Which feature should be enabled on the Router B?

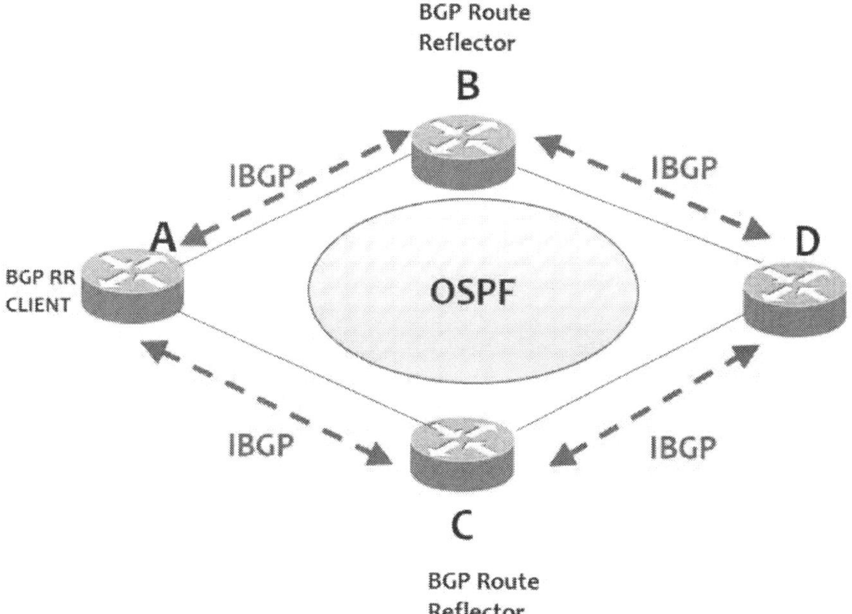

A. Max-metric router-lsa on startup wait-for-bgp

B. OSPF prefix-list

C. Type2-lsa on-startup wait-for-bgp

D. IGP LDP synchronization

Answer 6:

BGP as an overlay protocol needs next hop reachability. Static routing or the dynamic routing protocol is used to create an underlay network infrastructure for the overlay protocols such as BGP, LDP, PIM and so on.

One of the routers in the forwarding path towards BGP next hop will be reloaded. We might have two problems here

When Router B is reloaded, traffic is going to Router B shouldn't be dropped. Router B should signal the other OSPF routers.

This signaling is done with OSPF Stub Router advertisement feature. ' Max-metric router-lsa ' is used by OSPF for graceful restart. Second problem is when the Router B comes back; BGP traffic towards Router B will be black holed, because IGP process of Router B will converge faster than its BGP.

IGP should wait to BGP. Router B should take the BGP traffic once BGP prefixes installed in the routing table.

This is done with the OSPF Stub router advertisement feature as well.

' MAX-METRIC ROUTER-LSA ON-STARTUP WAIT-FOR-BGP ' IS USED BY OSPF, SO UNTIL BGP PROCESS IS CONVERGED, OSPF DOESN'T TAKE TRAFFIC.

Question 7:

How many level of hierarchy is supported by OSPF?

A. One

B. Two

C. Three

D. As many as possible

Answer 7:

OSPF supports two level of hierarchy. Hierarchy is common network design term, which is used to identify the logical boundaries. Backbone area and Non-Backbone areas are the only two areas, which are supported by OSPF, thus it supports only two level of hierarchy.

Question 8:

Which below options are correct for OSPF ABR? (Choose all that apply)

A. It slows down the convergence

B. It generates Type 4 LSA in Multi Area OSPF design

C. It does translation between Type7 to Type 5 in NSSA area

D. It does translation between Type 5 to Type 7 in NSSA area

E. It prevents topology information between OSPF areas

Answer 8:

OSPF ABR slows down the network convergence. Because it needs to calculate for each Type 1 and Type 2 LSAs, corresponding Type 3 LSAs and send its connected OSPF areas.

OSPF ABR generates Type 4 LSAs in Multi Area OSPF Design. When ABR receives the external prefixes in an Area, it translates Type 1 LSAs of the ASBR to Type 4 LSA and sends it to the other areas.

In NSSA Area, ABR translates Type 7 LSA to Type 5 LSA, but there is no Type 5 to Type 7 LSA translation. It is not allowed.

Topology information is not sent between the OSPF Areas, ABR stops topology information.

Thus the answer of this question is A- B – C- E.

Question 9:

Why Designated Router is used in OSPF network?

A. It is used to have an ABR in the network

B. It is used to create topology information

C. It is used to centralize the database, instead of keeping distributed OSPF link state database in every node

D. It is used to avoid flooding information between each device in multi access OSPF network

Answer 9:

Designated Router (DR) is used to avoid flooding information between each OSPF device in Multi-Access networks such as Ethernet or Frame Relay.

Routers only send their update to DR and DR floods this information to the every router in the segment. Multicast Group addresses 2224.0.0.5 and 224.0.0.6 is used for communication in IPv4.

Question 10:

Which below feature is used to avoid blackholing when OSPF and LDP are used together?

A. OSPF Fast Reroute

B. OSPF Multi Area Design

C. IGP LDP Synchronization

D. Converging OSPF faster than LDP in case of failure

Answer 10:

The problem occurs when link or node fails when OSPF and LDP is used together. It also occurs when IS-IS and LDP is together and the IG-LDP synchronization provides a label for the IGP prefixes in the Label database, otherwise since IGP converge first and then LDP, packets would be blackholed.

Chicken and egg problem is solved and blackholing is avoided.

Question 11:

Which below option is correct for the given topology?

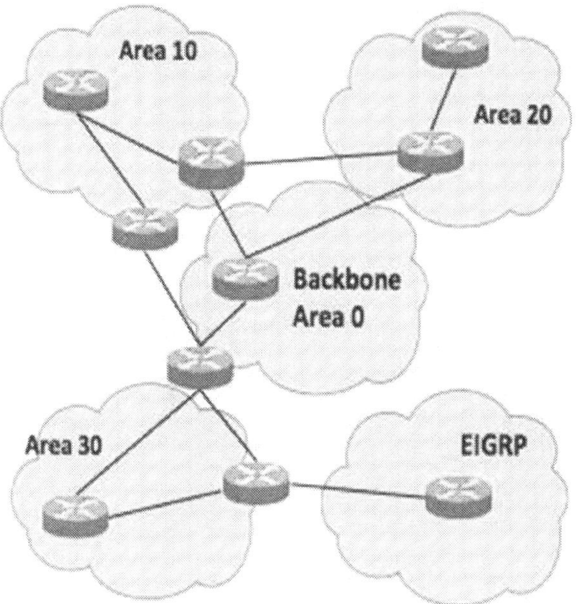

A. Area 20 has to be Stub area

B. Sending default route might create suboptimal routing for internal Area 20 routers

C. ABR of Area 20 has to be Designated Router

D. Area 20 doesn't receive Type 1 and Type 2 LSAs from the other areas

Answer 11:

Area 20 can be any type of OSPF area since there is no given requirement.

Sending default route cannot create suboptimal routing because there is only one exit point from the Area 20. Sub optimal routing can only be created if there is more than one exit from the Area.

ABR of Area 20 doesn't have to DR. In fact, DR and ABR shouldn't be the same router. Since both operations are resource intensive and separating these two ask is a best practice.

Type 1 and Type 2 LSAs cannot be received from the other Areas because topology information is not allowed between the OSPF areas and in OSPFv2 Type 1 and Type 2 LSAs carry topology information in addition to reachability information. Thus correct answer of this question is D.

Question 12:

In the below topology Area 30 is an NSSA area. Which below option is true?

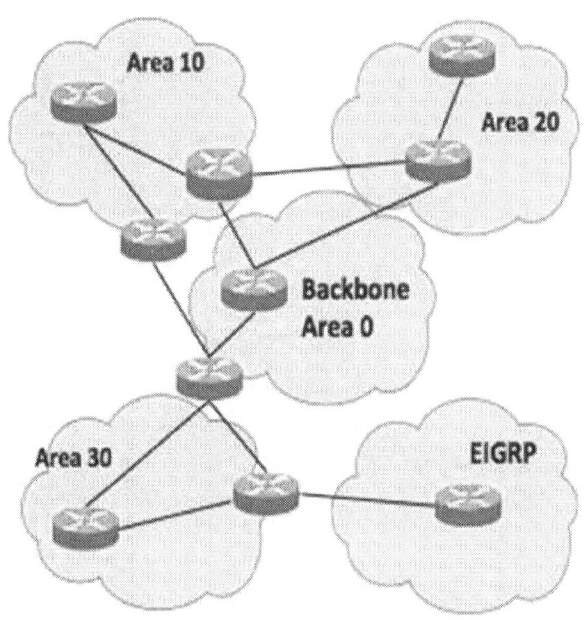

A. There will not be any Type 3 LSA in Area 30
B. ABR of Area 30 will translate Type 7 LSA to Type 5 LSA
C. There will not be any Type 1 or Type 2 LSA
D. EIGRP prefixes will not be allowed in Area 30

Answer 12:

Since Area 30 is an NSSA area; there will be Type 3 LSA, that's why Option A is incorrect. There will be Type 1 and Type 2 LSA, but not from the other Areas.

In Are 30, every router generates Type 1 LSAs, and of there is multi-access network, the DR will generate Type 2 LSA as well.

EIGRP prefixes will be allowed and they will be seen as Type 7 LSA in the Area 30.

Only Option B is correct, because ABR of Area 30 translate Type 7 LSA which is the EIGRP prefixes to Type 5 LSA send them to the network.

Question 13:

In the below topology Area 10 is Totally NSSA Area. Which below option is true?

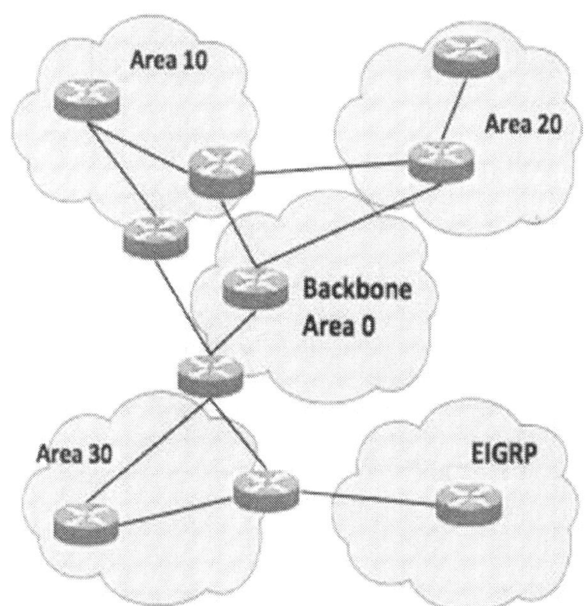

A. Area 10 will not have any Type 1 or Type 2 LSA

B. Area 10 will not have EIGRP prefixes

C. Area 10 cannot reach to EIGRP prefixes

D. Both ABRs of Area 10 will do the Type 7 to Type 5 translation

Answer 13:

Area 10 will be able to reach EIGRP network through default route even if it is Totally NSSA. But Area 10 devices cannot have specific EIGRP prefixes because Type 3, 4, 5 LSAs are not allowed in Totally NSSA Area. Answer of this question is B.

Question 14:

Which below topology OSPF is worse than EIGRP in large-scale implementation?

A. Full Mesh

B. Partial Mesh

C. Hub and Spoke

D. Ring

Answer 14:

In Full Mesh physical topology, Mesh Group feature allows only two routers to flood LSAs into the area. Mesh Group is supported by both OSPF and IS-IS.

This brings scalability into OSPF.

Ring and Partial mesh topologies are hard for all the routing protocols. Ring and Partial mesh are cheaper to build but convergence, optimal routing and fast reroute is very hard in Ring and Partial mesh.

EIGRP is best in Hub and Spoke topology from the scalability point of view, because it doesn't require so many configurations for its operation. OSPF on the other hand, requires a lot of tuning for its operation in Large scale Hub and spoke topology.

Question 15:

Why OSPF is used as an Infrastructure IGP in an MPLS VPN environment?

A. To carry the customer prefixes

B. Reachability between the MPLS VPN endpoints

C. OSPF is not used in MPLS VPN environment as an Infrastructure IGP protocol but BGP is used

D. LDP required IGP

Answer 15:

LDP requires IGP yes but it is not relevant. It could be EIGRP or IS-IS as well.

And the purpose of OSPF or any other IGP.as an Infrastructure protocol is to carry the loopback interface addresses of the MPLS VPN endpoints.

So the OSPF is used for reachability between the VPN endpoints (PE devices) in SP networks. OSPF is not used to carry the customer prefixes as an Infrastructure IGP.

Knowing the difference between the Infrastructure IGP and the PE-CE IGP protocol in MPLS VPN is important. This will be explained in detail in the MPLS chapter.

Question 16:

Which OSPF feature in MPLS VPN PE-CE is used to ensure MPLS service is always chosen as primary link?

A. OSPF max-metric

B. OSPF prefer-primary path

C. OSPF sham-link

D. Passive-interface

E. Virtual link

Answer 16:

Even domain IDs are the same in both site of the MPLS VPN, without sham-link feature only Type 3 LSA can be received from the PE by CE.

Sham-link is used to receive Type 1 LSA and even if there is a backup connection between the CEs, only changing cost on either PE-CE or CE-CE link make MPLS link as primary.

OSPF as a PE-CE protocol will be explained in detail in the MPLS chapter.

Question 17:

Which below options are correct for OSPF? (Choose all that apply)

A. OSPFv2 doesn't support IPv6 so when IPv6 is needed, OSPFv3 is necessary

B. OSPF virtual link shouldn't be used as permanent solution is OSPF design

C. OSPF and BGP are the two separate protocols so when OSPF cost changes, it doesn't affect BGP path selection

D. OSPF can carry the label information in Segment Routing so LDP wouldn't be necessary

E. OSPF unlike EIGRP, supports MPLS Traffic Engineering with dynamic path calculation

Answer 17:

Only incorrect option of this question is C. although they are two separate protocols; changing the OSPF metric can affect the best BGP exit point.

Taking IGP cost into consideration to calculate best path for the BGP prefixes is called Hot Potato Routing.

Changing IGP metric can affect BGP best path.

Question 18:

What is the reason to place all routers in Area 0/Backbone Area, even in flat OSPF design?

A. You cannot place routers in non-backbone area without backbone area

B. Type 3 LSAs should be received from the ABR

C. Future Multi Area design migration can be easier

D. It is not a best practice to place all the routers in Area 0 in Flat/Single OSPF area design

Answer 18:

In OSPF design, all the routers can be placed in any Non-Backbone area. If you have 50 routers in your network, you can place all of them in Area 100 for example.

But having the routers in OSPF Backbone area (Area 0) from the early stage of network design provides easier migration to Multi Area OSPF design.

This is true for the IS-IS as well. In IS-IS you can have all the routers in the network in Level 1 domain. But having them in Level 2 allows easier Multi-Level IS-IS design if it is required in the future. This will be explained in the IS-IS chapter with the case study.

Question 19:

In OSPFv2 which LSA types cause Partial SPF run? (Choose Three)

A. Type 1

B. Type 2

C. Type 3

D. Type 4

E. Type 5

Answer 19:

In OSPFv2, Type 3, 4 and 5 causes Partial SPF run. Not full SPF. Partial SPF is less CPU intensive process compare to Full SPF run.

Thus the correct answer of this question is C, D and E.

Question 20:

Based on which design attributes, number of maximum routers change in OSPF area?

A. It depends on how many area is in the OSPF domain

B. Maximum number of routers in OSPF area should be around 50

C. Depends on link stability, physical topology, number of links, hardware resources, rate of change in the network

D. If there are two or more ABRs, number can be much more

Answer 20:

Depends on link stability, physical topology, number of links on the routers, hardware resources and rate of change in the network. If some links flap all the time, this affects the routers resources and the scalability of the network.

Question 21:

How many OSPF ABR routers should be in place in OSPF by keeping also redundancy in mind?

A. One

B. Two

C. Three

D. If the number of routers in an area is too much, it can be up to 8 ABRs

Answer 21:

In large-scale OSPF design, the number of ABRs will have a huge impact on the number of prefixes. Thus having two ABRs is good for redundancy for the critical sites.

For example some of the remote offices or POP locations may not be critical as other locations and having only one ABR in those locations, can be tolerated by the company.

In this case that specific location may have only one ABR as well.

Keep in mind that; two is company, three is crowded in design.

Question 22:

What are the most important reasons of route summarization in OSPF (Choose Two)

A. In order to reduce the routing table size so routers have to store and process less information

B. In order to increase the availability of the network

C. Increase the security of the routing domain
D. In order to reduce the impact of topology changes
E. In order to provide an optimal routing in the network

Answer 22:

If there is route summarization, sub optimal routing might occur as it was explained in the OSPF chapter. Thus Option E is incorrect.

Availability and security doesn't increase with route summarization. But topology change affects is definitely reduced.

Also the routing table size is reduced and this provides better memory and CPU utilization, fast convergence and better troubleshooting.

That's why the answer of this question A and D.

OSPF Further Study Resources

Books

Doyle, J. (2005). *Choosing an IGP for Large-Scale Networks*, Addison-Wesley Professional.

Videos

Ciscolive Session-BRKRST-2337

Articles

http://www.cisco.com/web/about/ac123/ac147/archived_issues/ipj_16-2/162_lsp.html
http://orhanergun.net/2015/02/ospf-design-challenge/
https://tools.ietf.org/html/rfc4577

CHAPTER 4
IS-IS

IS-IS is a link-state routing protocol, similar to OSPF. If you are looking for service provider grade, MPLS Traffic Engineering support, and extendable protocol for easier future migration then the only choice is IS-IS. Commonly used in service providers and sometimes in the large Enterprise networks. Flexibility in terms of tuning: TLV-based protocols allow many parameters to be tuned.

Good scalability: IS-IS multi-level design allows very large-scale IS-IS networks

L1 domain is similar to OSPF Totally NSSA since the L1 domain doesn't accept anything other than default route from the Level 2 domain and redistribution is allowed into the L1 domain.

IS-IS shares similar convergence characteristics with OSPF. SPF, LSA Throttling timers, LSA Pacing, and Processing and Propagation timers are tunable in IS-IS as well.

IS-IS, like OSPF supports MPLS Traffic Engineering, IP Traffic Engineering (LFA, Remote LFA) and also supports Segment Routing. Totally different protocols are not necessary to support new extensions. With IS- IS IPv6, MTR, and many other protocols just can be used with additional TLVs.

- IPv6 Address Family support (RFC 2308)
- Multi-Topology support (RFC 5120)
- MPLS Traffic Engineering (RFC 3316)

IS-IS is a Layer 2 protocol and is not encapsulated in IP, because it is difficult, if not impossible, to attack Layer 2 networks remotely. IS-IS is accepted as being more secure than OSPF.

IS-IS uses NET (Network Entity Title) addresses similar to OSPF Router ID. IP support to IS-IS is added by the IETF after ISO invented it for the CLNS. If IS-IS is used together with IP, it is called Integrated

IS-IS.

ISPs commonly choose addresses as follows:

- First 8 bits: pick a number (49 used in these examples) Next 16 bits=area ID
- Next 48 bits: router loopback address (6 bytes, every 4 numbers is 2 bytes)
- Final 8 bits (2 Numbers) is 00 on the routers

EXAMPLE:

- NET: 49.0001.1921.6800.1001.00 49.0001 is the IS-IS Area ID
- 192.168.1.1 (Router loopback) in Area 1
- 00 is the NSEL

OSPF vs. IS-IS Terminology

OSPF	IS-IS
Host	End System (ES)
Router	Intermediate System (IS)
Link	Circuit
Packet	Protocol Data Unit (PDU)
Designated Router (DR)	Designated IS (DIS)
Backup Designated Router (BDR)	N/A (No backup DIS is used)
Link-State Advertisement (LSA)	Link-State PDU (LSP)
Hello Packet	IIH PDU
Complete Sequence Number PDU (CSNP)	Database Description (DBP)
Sub-Domain (Area)	Area
Level-1 Area	Non-backbone Area
Level-2 Subdomain (backbone)	Backbone Area
L1L2 Router	Area Border Router (ABR)
Any IS	Autonomous System Boundary Router (ASBR)

IS-IS Fast Convergence

IS-IS fast convergence steps are very similar to OSPF fast convergence.

Four necessary steps in fast convergence

1. Failure detection

Layer 1 Failure detection mechanisms:

- Carrier delay
- Debounce Timer
- Sonet/SDH APS timers
- Layer 3 Failure detection mechanisms:
- Protocol timers (Hello/Dead)
- BFD (Bidirectional Forwarding Detection)

For the failure detection, best practice is always use Physical down detection mechanism first. Even BFD cannot detect the failure faster than physical failure detection mechanism.

Because BFD messages is pull based detection mechanism which is sent and receive periodically, but physical layer detection mechanism is event driven and always faster than BFD and Protocol hellos.

If physical layer detection mechanisms cannot be used (Maybe because there is a transport element in the path), then instead of tuning protocol hello timers aggressively, BFD should be used. Common example to this is if there are two routers and connected through an Ethernet switch, best method is to use BFD.

Compare to protocol hello timers, BFD is much ligher in size, thus consumes less resource and bandwidth.

2. Failure propagation

Propagation of failure throughout the network.

Here LSP throttling timers come into play. You can tune LSA throttling for faster information propagation. It can be used to slow down the information processing as well. Also LSP pacing timers can be tuned for sending update much faster.

3. New information process

Processing of newly arrived LSP to find the next best path. SPF throttling timers can be tuned for faster information process for fast convergence.

4. Update new route into RIB/FIB

For fast convergence, these steps may need to be tuned. Although the RIB/FIB update is hardware dependent, the network operator can configure all other steps. One thing always needs to be kept in mind; Fast convergence and fast reroute can affect network stability.

In both OSPF and IS-IS Exponential backoff mechanism is used to protect the routing domain from the rapid flapping events. It slows down the convergence by penalizing the unstable prefixes. Very similar mechanism to IP and BGP dampening.

IS-IS Router Types

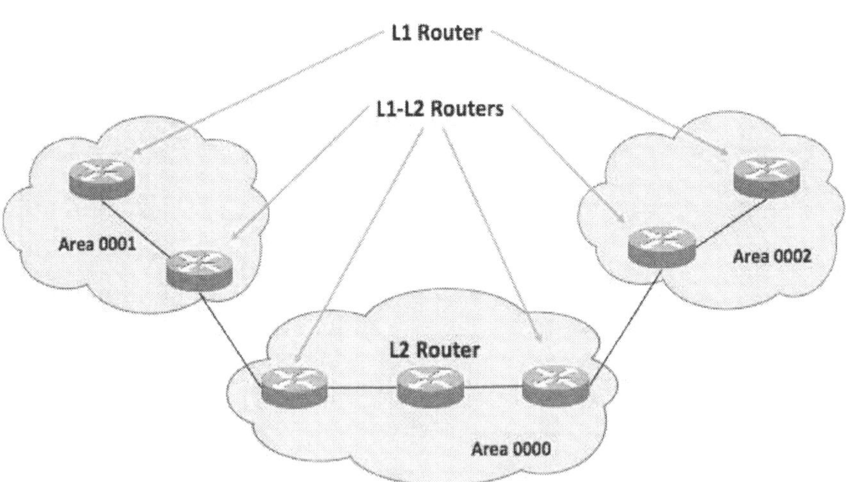

- If the area ID is the same on both routers, both L1 and L2 adjacency can be set up.
- If the area IDs are different, only an L2 adjacency can be set up.
- There is no backbone area in IS-IS as there is in OSPF. There are only contiguous Level 2 routers. Level 2 domains must be contiguous.

- IS-IS Level 2 domain can be considered as similar to the OSPF backbone area.

THERE ARE THREE TYPE OF ROUTERS IN IS-IS:

Level 1 Router

- Can only form adjacencies with Level 1 routers within the same area
- LSDB only carries intra-area information

Level 2 Router

- Can form adjacencies in multiple areas
- Exchanges information about the entire network

LEVEL 1-2 IS-IS ROUTERS

These routers keep separate LSDB for each level, one for Level 1 databases and one for Level 2 databases.

These routers allow L1 routers to reach other L1 routers in different areas via L2 topology.

Level 1 routers look at the ATT bit in L1 LSP of L1-L2 routers and use it as a default route to reach the closest Level 1-2 router in the area. This can create suboptimal routing.

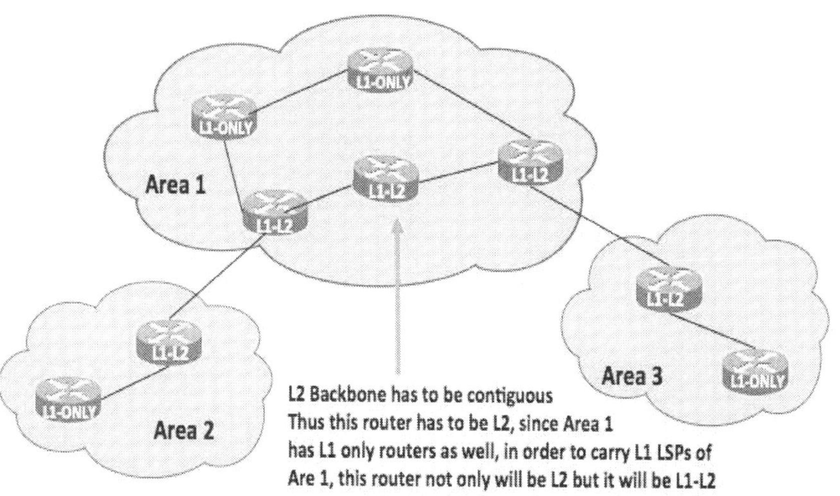
Hierarchy Levels
Level 1, Level 2 and Level 1-2 Routers
L1-ONLY
L1-ONLY
L1-L2
L1-L2
L1-L2
Area 1
L1-L2
L1-L2
L1-ONLY
Area 2
L1-ONLY
Area 3
L2 Backbone has to be contiguous
Thus this router has to be L2, since Area 1
has L1 only routers as well, in order to carry L1 LSPs of
Are 1, this router not only will be L2 but it will be L1-L2

IS-IS Design

In new IS-IS design, starting with L2-only is the best option; migration to multi-level design is easier when starting with L2. Domain migration will be harder if design is started with L1.

If you start with L1-L2 then all the routers have to keep two databases for every prefix. This is resource-intensive without additional benefit.

When designing multi-level IS-IS with more than one exit (L1-L2 routers), you will more likely create suboptimal routing. Suboptimal routing is not always bad, just know the application requirements. Some applications can tolerate suboptimal routing and you can have low-end devices in L1 areas; edge and core can be placed in L1.

IS-IS Area and Levels Design

Edge and core can be placed in the same Level 2 area.

Edge and core can be placed in different Level 2 areas; this can make future multi-level migration easier. POPs can be placed in Level 1 areas and core in Level 2, as illustrated. This can create suboptimal routing, but provides excellent scalability.

In the below pictures you will see different POP and Core design models and their characteristics.

L1 in the POP and Core

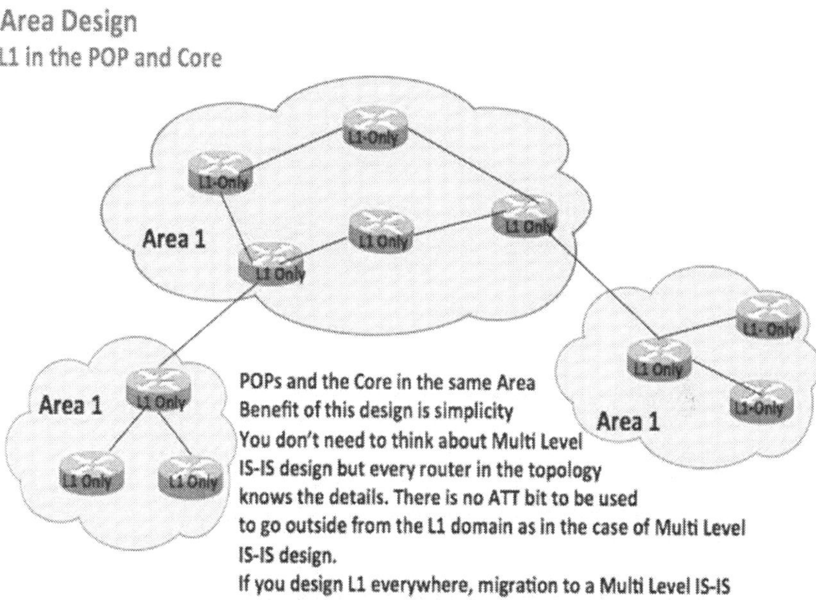

L2 in the POP and the Core

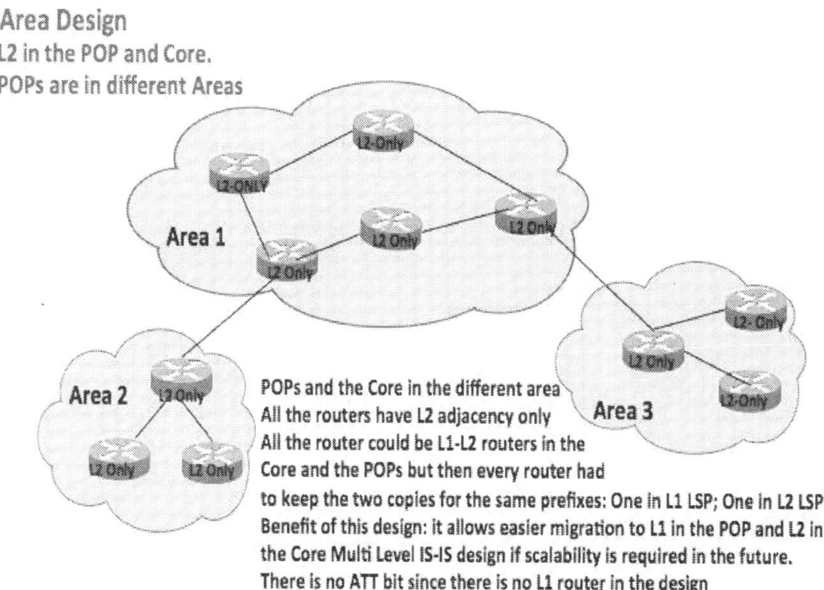

Area Design
L2 in the POP and Core.
POPs are in different Areas
L2-Only
L2-ONLY
Area 1
L2 Only
L2 Only
L2 Only
L2- Only
L2 Only
L2-Only
Area 3
Area 2
L2 Only
L2 Only
L2 Only
POPs and the Core in the different area
All the routers have L2 adjacency only
All the router could be L1-L2 routers in the
Core and the POPs but then every router had
to keep the two copies for the same prefixes: One in L1 LSP; One in L2 LSP
Benefit of this design: it allows easier migration to L1 in the POP and L2 in
the Core Multi Level IS-IS design if scalability is required in the future.
There is no ATT bit since there is no L1 router in the design

L1 only POPs L2 Only Core

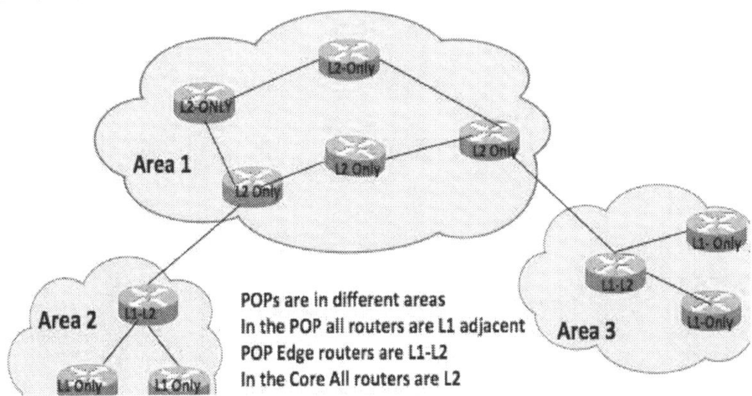

In the POP all routers are L1 adjacent
POP Edge routers are L1-L2
In the Core All routers are L2

Network design, especially large-scale network design is all about managing interaction and understand the tradeoffs. IS-IS as an IGP provides an underlying infrastructure for BGP and MPLS overlays.

IS-IS BGP Interaction

Below is the interaction of IS-IS with BGP. The overload bit is used to signal the other routers, so the router is not used as transit router.

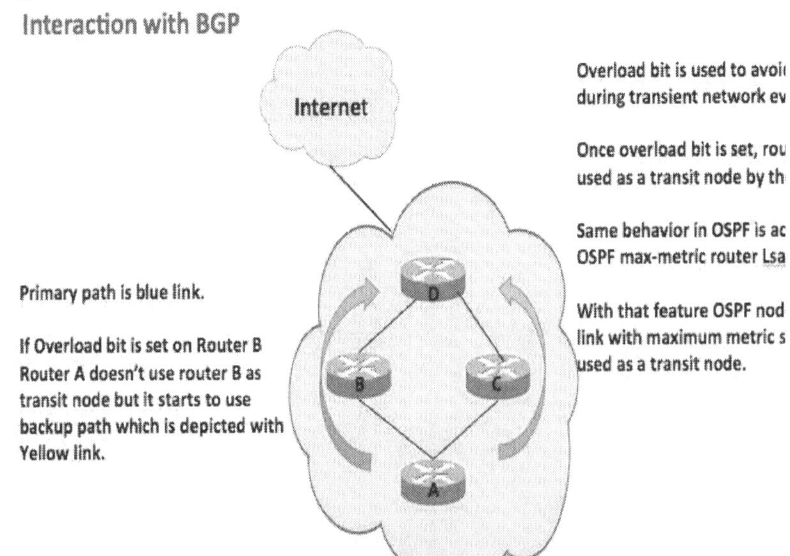

Interaction with BGP
Internet
Primary path is blue link.
If Overload bit is set on Router B
Router A doesn't use router B as
transit node but it starts to use
backup path which is depicted with
Yellow link.
D
B
C
A
Overload bit is used to avoi
during transient network ev
Once overload bit is set, rou
used as a transit node by th
Same behavior in OSPF is ac
OSPF max-metric router Lsa
With that feature OSPF nod
link with maximum metric s
used as a transit node.

Flat/Single Level vs. Multi Level IS-IS Design Comparison

Below table summarizes the similarities and the differences of these two design models in great detail. Network designers should know the pros and cons of the technologies, protocol alternatives and their capabilities from the design point of view.

Design Requirement	Flat IS-IS/Single Level Design	MultiLevel IS-IS Design
Scalability	It is scalable, but not to Multi-Level.	YES, better than Flat IS-IS/ Single Level Design
Working on Full Mesh topology	YES, but not scalable. Mesh Group provides scalability.	YES, more scalable and Mesh group feature is available as well
Working on Hub and Spoke	YES	YES
Convergence	Better than Multi Level IS-IS	L1-L2 routersadd additional latency (Processing Delay) during convergence
Reachability Information	YES, inside a level (Sub-domain), all the routers have same Link State Database.	NO, reachability information is not sent between IS-IS level (Sub-domain) Only default route is sent from the Level 2 to Level 1 with ATT bit
Topology Information	YES, inside a level (Sub-domain), all the routers have same Link State Database.	NO, L1-L2 routers stops topology information, one level (Sub-domain) topology is not known by the other level
MPLS Traffic Engineering	Good. Every router has the same topology information: Which router is connected to which, and the metric between them and so on	Hard, it requires MPLS TE extension or Path Computation Element
Troubleshooting	Easier than Multi Level IS-IS design	More nodes, more LSPs makes it harder to troubleshoot, compared to Single Level/Flat IS-IS design
Stuff Experience	Not well known	Not well Known
IPv6 Support	YES	YES
Additional Nodes	None	L1-L2 router (similar to OSPF ABR)
QoS Support	Good, no difference	Good, no difference
Multicast Support	Good, no difference	Good, no difference
Resource Requiremnent	More, every router needs to keep both reachability and topology informationn inside IS-IS domain	Less, routers only keep topology information of their Level (Sub-domain), but not the reachability information of the entire IS-IS domain

Design Requirement	Flat IS-IS/Single Level Design	MultiLevel IS-IS Design
DMVPN Support	NO, IS-IS cannot run over DMVPN	NO, IS-IS cannot run over DMVPN
Can Run Over VPN	YES, it can run over GRE and Multipoint GRE	YES, it can be designed over GRE and Multipoint GRE

Single vs. Multi Level IS-IS Design Comparison

IS-IS and MPLS Interaction

When IS-IS multi level design is used in MPLS enabled networks, MPLS LSP is broken since LDP does not have capability of aggregated FECS. In other words, if LDP is used for label distribution, all the routers in the IS-IS network have to have /32 loopback address of the PE devices in their routing table. Otherwise, a label is not assigned.

Fortunately, there are three ways to solve this problem:

- You can leak the loopback of PEs into L1 domain.
- RFC 5185 (LDP extensions) allows aggregated FECs. So you don't need /32 in the routing table to assign a label for the MPLS FEC (Forwarding Equivalence Class)
- RFC 3107 is also known as BGP+Label or BGP LU (Labeled Unicast). IPv4 Label is assigned by the BGP. It is not a label for the VPN prefixes, it is a label for the IP prefixes.

Seamless MPLS uses this concept. Inter-domain Hierarchical MPLS LSP is created and all the PE loopbacks are carried through Multi Protocol BGP. Seamless MPLS will be explained in the MPLS chapter.

IS-IS – MPLS Interaction Case Study

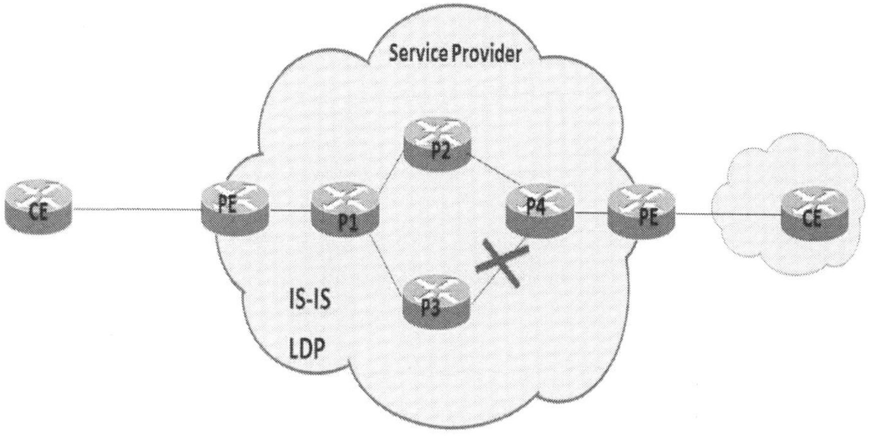

In the topology above, IS-IS is running in the network of the service provider. For the transport label distribution or topmost label/tunnel label, LDP is used even though RSVP or segment routing could be used as well.

Question 1:

What happens if P3-P4 link fails?

Question 2:

Do you need to know the level of IS-IS network to provide a solution?

Question 3:

What would be your design recommendation to ensure high-availability on this network?

Answer 1:

If any link fails in the MPLS networks, IGP will not converge on the failed link before getting green light from the LDP.

Also, if P3-P4 link fails in the topology shown above, P1-P2-P4 link is used. If the link returns and if IGP converges before LDP comes together, P3 cannot create a label for the prefixes; it sends the regular IP packet to P4. In fact, P4 drops the packets because it cannot recognize the CE (customer).

ANSWER 2:

It doesn't matter which IS-IS Level (L1 or L2) is used to provide a solution for this problem.

Here the question is see if you know the solution already.

This type of question will be asked in the CCDE Practical exam and the task domain will be analyzing the design.

ANSWER 3:

If IGP-LDP synchronization feature is enables, P3 and P4 signal their neighbor not to P3-P4 link unless LDP converges. IGP signals the other nodes in the routing domain for BGP convergence in exactly the same way. OSPF Case Study 5 showed IGP-BGP synchronization.

With OSPF max-metric router-lsa and IS-IS overload bit, OSPF and IS-IS signals the other node in the IGP domain for BGP converge. Protocol interaction is for optimal routing design. If overlay protocols do not follow the underlay protocols or physical topology suboptimal routing, blackholes, or routing or forwarding loops can occur.

In order to avoid issues, synchronization should be enabled.

So far in this class you have seen, STP-FHRP, IGP–BGP, and IGP-MPLS interactions within the case studies.

More case studies regarding interactions for different technologies will be provided in later sessions.

OSPF vs. IS-IS Design Comparison

Below table summarizes the similarities and the differences of these two link state Interior Gateway Protocols in great detail. Network designers should know the pros and cons of the technologies, protocol alternatives and their capabilities from the design point of view.

Design Requirement	OSPF	IS-IS
Scalability	2 tier hierarchy, less scalable	2 tier hierarchy, less scalable
Working on Full Mesh	works well with Mesh Group	Works well with Mesh Group
Working on Ring Topology	Ring is hard for the routing protocols, in the case of a failure, micro loop occurs	Same as OSPF
Working on Hub and Spoke	Works poorly, it requires a lot of tuning	Same as OSPF
Fast Reroute Support	YES, IP FRR	YES, IP FRR
Suitable on WAN	YES	YES
Suitable on Datacenter	DCs are full mesh, and full mesh operation requires a lot of tuning. Instead, in large scale data centers, Layer 2 protocols os BGP is used	Same as OSPF, but since IS-IS runs on layer 2, it is used as the controlpoint for many overlay technologies such as OTV, Fabricpath, TRILL, SPB, in the datacenter
Suitable on the Internet Edge between two AS	NO, it is designed as an IGP	NO, it is designed as an IGP
Standard Protocol	YES, IETF Standard	YES, IETF Standard
Stuff Experience	Very well Known	Not well known, although it is common in the Service Provider Network, it is not used in the Enterprise Networks
Overlay tunnel Support	YES	Doesn't support IP tunnels
MPLS Traffic Engineering Support	YES, with CSPF	YES, with CSPF
Security	Less secure	More secure since it is on layer 2
Suitable as Enterprise IGP	YES	NO, it lacks IPSEC, it could still be implemented as GRE over IPSEC, since GRE supports IP, and non-IP protocols
Suitable as Service Provider IGP	YES	Definitely, IS-IS was actually invented to be used in large scale service provider networks
Complexity	Complex, it has 11 types of LSAs	Easy, there are only two levels
Policy Support	Good	Good
Resource Requirement	SPF requires more processing power compared to DUAL algorithm, but in 2016, it is not an issue for most routers.	SPF requires more processing power, compared to DUAL algorithm, but in 2016, it iis not an issue for most of the routers
Extendibility	Not good	Good, thanks to TLV support
IPv6 Support	YES, but it requires new protocol, OSPFv3	YES, it doesn't require a new protocol, IPv6 is implemented with the new TLVs only
Default Convergence	Slow	Slow
Training Cost	Cheap	Cheap
Troubleshooting	Easy	Very Easy

Design Requirement	OSPF	IS-IS
Routing Loop	Good protection,LSA Sequence numbers inside an area and for the multi area design, all non-backbone areas have to be connected to the backbone area	Good protection, LSP sequence numbers inside of a level, and Up/Down bit between two levels in the multi-level IS-IS design

OSPF vs. IS-IS Design Comparison

IS-IS: Case Study – OSPF to IS-IS Migration

Fastnet is a fictitious service provider, which has had some security problems with their internal IGP routing recently. They want to deploy IPv6 on their network very soon but they don't want to run two different routing protocol (one for existing IPv4 and new IPv6 architecture).

They currently have OSPF routing protocol deployed in their network. Fastnet knows that adding a new feature in IS-IS by the vendors is faster than OSPF in general. Also thanks to the TLV structure of IS-IS, when additional features are needed, IS-IS is easily extendable.

Since the majority of service providers historically use IS-IS for their core IGP routing protocol, Fastnet decided to migrate their IGP from OSPF to IS-IS.

Please provide a migration plan for Fastnet for smooth transition. Fastnet will plan all of their activity during a maintenance window. Fastnet has been using flat OSPF design, but they want flexible IS-IS design which will allow Fastnet to migrate to multi-level IS-IS in the future.

High-Level Migration Plan from OSPF to IS-IS for FASTNENT

Below are the steps for the migration. A "ship in the night" approach will be used. Both routing protocols will be running on the network at the same time during migration.

1. Verify OSPF configuration and operation

2. Deploy IS-IS over entire network

3. Set OSPF admin distance to be higher than IS-IS

4. Check for leftovers in OSPF

5. Remove OSPF from entire network

6. Verify IGP and related (BGP) operation

Detailed OSPF to IS-IS Migration Steps

1. Verify OSPF configuration and operation.
    - Check if there are any routing table instabilities.
    - Ensure that next-hop values for the BGP are valid and reachable.
    - Check OSPF routing table and record the number of prefixes.
2. Deploy IS-IS over entire network.
    - IS-IS admin distance is higher than OSPF in many platforms, leave as-is in this step.
    - Use wide metrics for IS-IS. This will allow IPv6, MPLS Traffic Engineering, and new extensions.
    - Deploy L2-only IS-IS since flexibility is desired. L2-only reduces the resource requirements on the routers and allows easier migration to multi-level IS-IS.
    - Deploy both IPv4 and IPv6.
    - Deploy IS-IS passive interface at the edge links; these links should be carried in IBGP. Prefix suppression can be used to carry infrastructure links in IBGP, but these are not a requirement of Fastnet.
    - Make sure the IS-IS LSDB is consistent with OSPF routing table.
3. Set OSPF admin distance to be higher than IS-IS.
    - Increase the AD of OSPF across the entire network.
4. Check OSPF leftovers.
    - In this step all the prefixes in the routing table should be learned by IS-IS. If there are any OSPF prefixes, we should find out why they are there. You can compare the "show IP OSPF neighbor" with "show IS-IS neighbor"; should be the same number of neighbors for both.
    - If the number is not the same, fix the problem

5. Remove OSPF from entire network.

   - All the OSPF processes can be removed.

   - If there is interface-specific configuration such as Traffic Engineering (metric/cost), authentication should be removed a well.

6. Verify IGP and related operations.

   - Entire network should be functioning over IS-IS. Verify IGBP sessions.

   - Verify MPLS sessions

   - Verify customer and edge link prefixes.

IS-IS Sub Optimal Routing Case Study

In the below topology metrics are shown and the traffic between Router A and the Router B will be analyzed.

There are three IS-IS areas in the topology. Router levels are shown as well. Router A and B are the internal IS-IS L1 routers.

Internal routers always chooses the smallest metric which is advertised by their L1L2 router in Multi Level/Multi Area IS-IS design.

In the below topology since Router A only knows the topology information for its area, and the left L1L2 router advertises the Router B with the smaller metric, blue path is chosen for Router A to B traffic.

Obviously total metric of blue path is smaller (10+5+5) than blue one (5+5+5+5+5+5) but still blue path is used for the Router A to B traffic.

One solution to this problem is to leaked the Router B information on both L1L2 routers of the Router A's area.

SUB OPTIMAL ROUTING with IS-IS

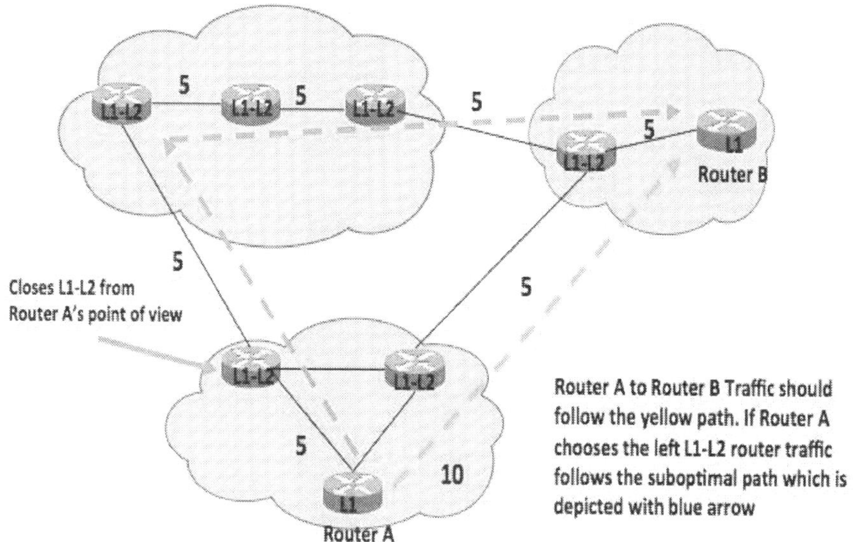
5
L1-L2
L1-L2
5
L1-L2
5
5
L1-L2
L1
Router B
5
Closes L1-L2 from
Router A's point of view
5
L1-L2
L1-L2
Router A to Router B Traffic should
follow the yellow path. If Router A
chooses the left L1-L2 router traffic
follows the suboptimal path which is
depicted with blue arrow
5
10
L1
Router A

IS-IS Blackholing and Link Level Placement Case Study

In the illustrated topology for simplicity only one of the regions of the company is shown.

Level 1 routers use L1L2 routers to reach to the rest of the network. What would happen if the link between Router A and Router C fails?

Area 49.0002

L1

L1L2

L1L2

Router C

L1L2

Router D

L1L2

L1

Router A

L1

Router B

Area 49.0001

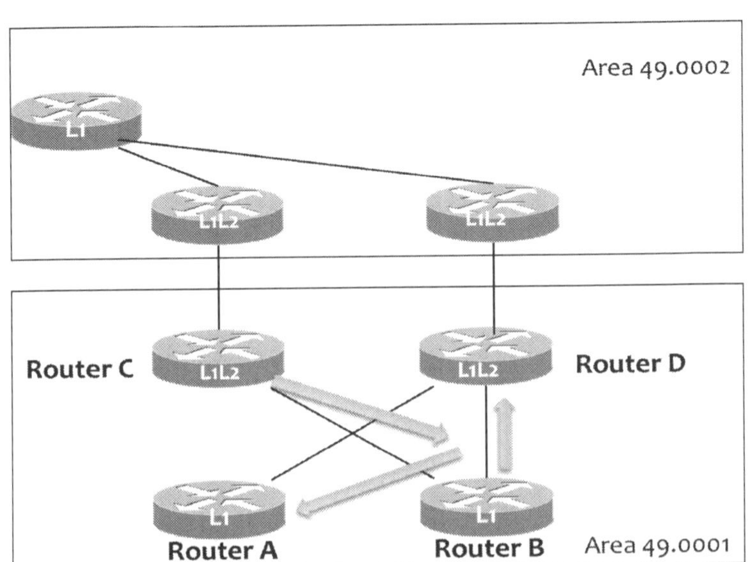

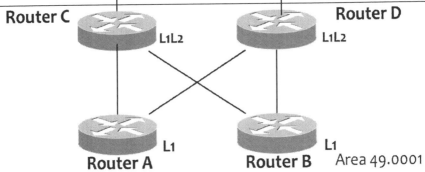

When Router A to Router C link fails, the traffic from L1L2 router flows through the other L1 router. This creates suboptimal traffic flow, but it is tolerated since the faulty link is repaired after some time.

The L1 router (Router B in this topology) might have performance and bandwidth issues since it was handling half of the traffic before the failure. The solution is to connect a direct link between the L1L2 routers as shown in the below topology.

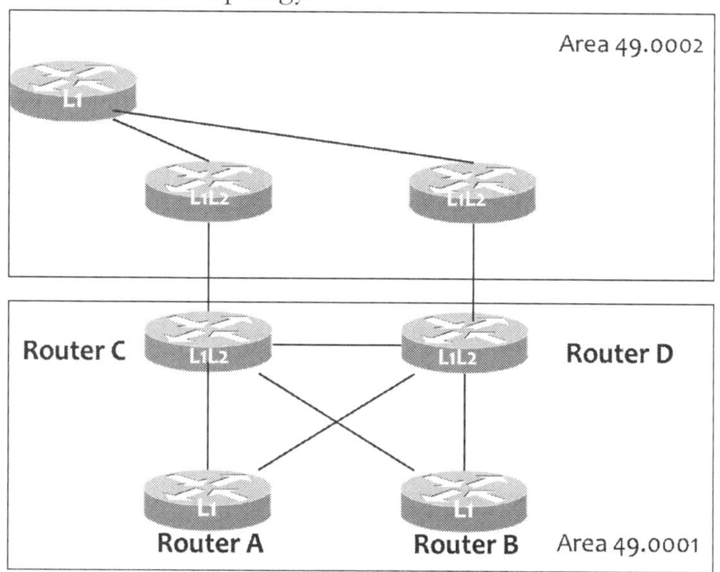

Question

Which IS-IS level new link between L1L2 should the L1L2 routers be placed into?

It should be the L1L2 link. If it was only L2, Router C would learn all the prefixes of Router A from Router B as L1 LSP and from direct link as L2 LSP. Since L1 is preferred over L2, a suboptimal path is still used.

The best solution is to place the direct inter-L1L2 link into L1L2.

- If Level 1 domain is partitioned in the IS-IS network, it can be connected over the Level 2 backbone.
- This concept is known as Virtual Link. Virtual Link is used in OSPF as well.
- In our case study, Area 20 is partitioned. In order to connect the Level 1 domain and provide full reachability between L1 routers of Area 20, virtual link/adjacency is created over Level 2 backbone.

- Please know that this feature in the RFC is defined as optional so implementation may ignore it. Cisco routers don't support Partitioned Level 1 domain repair.

IS-IS REVIEW QUESTIONS

Quesiton 1:

Which OSPF Area is similar to IS-IS Level 1 sub domain?

A. Backbone area

B. Stub Area

C. Totally Stub Area

D. Totally NSSA Area

Answer 1:

Answer of this question is D. Because IS-IS level 1 domain allows route redistribution and only the default route is sent from the L2 domain. This was explained in the IS-IS chapter.

Question 2:

If two IS-IS devices are connected to an Ethernet switch. Which below option provides fastest down detection to the IGP process?

A. Tuned IS-IS LSP timers

B. BFD

C. Tuned IS-IS SPF Timers

D. IS-IS Hello timers

Answer 2:

Tuning LSP and SPF timers can improve the convergence of IS-IS in case of a failure but they don't provide fast failure detection.

Reducing the hello timers can provide shorter failure detection time but cannot be tuned as much as BFD. Also since there is an Ethernet switch in between, port-failure event cannot trigger remote port interface down event. BFD is a best solution, especially if there is a node, which prevents end-to-end failure signaling between two devices.

Question 3:

Why IS-IS overload bit is set in IGP – BGP synchronization?

A. In order to prevent routing loop

B. In order to prevent traffic loss which can be caused by blackholing

C. In order to prevent routing oscillation

D. For fast convergence

Answer 3:

As it was explained in the IS-IS chapter, it uses to signal the other routers so the node is not used as transit. If node would be eligible to be used as primary path, blackhole would occur since BGP and IGP converges times are not the same.

IGP should wait BGP before staring to accept network traffic.

That's why; answer of this question is B.

Question 4:

Which of the below mechanisms are used to slow down the distribution of topology information caused by a rapid link flaps in IS-IS? (Choose Two)

A. ISPF

B. Partial SPF

C. Exponential Back Off

D. LSA Throttling

E. SPF Throttling

Answer 4:

Exponential back off mechanism is used in OSPF and IS-IS to protect the routing system from the rapid link flaps. Also LSA throttling timers can be tuned to protect the routing system from these types of failures.

But LSA throttling timers tuning also will affect on convergence so careful monitoring is necessary if there is IS-IS fast convergence requirement in design.

That's why the correct answer of this question is C and D.

Question 5:

When would it be required to leak the prefixes from Level 2 to Level 1 subdomain? (Choose Two)

A. When optimal routing is necessary from the Level 1 routers towards the rest of the network

B. When MPLS PE devices are configured in Level 1 domain

C. When ECMP is required from Level 1 domain to the rest of the network

D. When unequal cost load balancing is required between L1 internal routers and the L1-L2 routers

Answer 5:

Unequal cost load balancing is not supported in IS-IS. Even if you leak the prefixes it won't work. ECMP is done by hop by hop. Even L2 prefixes are not leaked into the L1 domain; still internal L1 domain routers can do the ECMP towards L1-L2 routers if there is more than one L1-L2 router. But L1-L2 routers may not do ECMP. Thus Option C is incorrect.

When MPLS PE is inside L1 domain, LDP cannot assign a label to the PE loopbacks since the remote loopbacks are not known. Internal L1 routers only learn default route as it was explained in the IS-IS chapter.

And whenever optimal routing is required, of there is available, more specific information can help for that.

Correct answer of this question is A and B.

Question 6:

How many level of hierarchy is supported by IS-IS?

A. One

B. Two

C. Three

D. As many as possible

Answer 6:

IS-IS supports two level of hierarchy. Hierarchy is common network design term, which is used to identify the logical boundaries.

IS-IS Level 1 and IS-IS Level 2 domains provide maximum two levels of hierarchy. Level 2 IS-IS domain is similar to Backbone area in OSPF, Level 1 IS-IS domain is similar to Totally NSSA area in OSPF.

Question 7:

If some prefixes are leaked from the IS-IS level 2 domain into level 1 domain, how IS-IS prevents those prefixes to be advertised back in Level 2 domain?

A. Route tag should be used

B. ATT bit prevents prefixes to be advertised back in Level 2 domain

C. U/D bit is used to prevent prefixes to be advertised back in Level 2 domain

D. They wouldn't be advertised back in Level 2 domain anyway

Answer 7:

If some reason some prefixes are leaked from Level 2 into level 1, U/D bit in IS-IS prevents those prefixes to be advertised back into IS-IS level 2 domain. This is an automatic process, doesn't require configuration. It is a loop prevention mechanism in IS-IS route leaking.

That's why the answer of this question is C.

Question 8:

Which below mechanism is used in IS-IS full mesh topologies to reduce the LSP flooding?

A. Elect a DIS and Backup DIS

B. Use IS-IS Mesh Group

C. Use DR and BDR

D. Deploy Multi Level IS-IS design

Answer 8:

Full mesh topology could be in any level, either Level 1 or Level 2 in multi level design. Thus having Multi level design won't help for LSP flooding if the topology already in any particular level.

It is similar to have BGP Confederation for scalability but still in sub AS you have to configure full mesh IBGP or for scalability you implement Route Reflector inside confederation sub AS. There is no Backup DIS in IS-IS, there is only a DIS (Designated Intermediate System), thus the Option a is incorrect. DR and BDR is an OSPF feature not the IS-IS.

That's why the correct answer of this question is Option B. Mesh Group concept was explained with a case study in IS-IS chapter.

Question 9:

If an IS-IS router is connected to three links and redistributing 100 EIGRP prefixes into the domain, and the design is flat/single level IS-IS design, how many IS-IS LSP is seen in the domain?

A. 100 IS-IS LSP

B. 3 IS-IS LSP

C. 300 IS-IS LSP

D. 1 IS-IS LSP

Answer 9:

There will be different TLVs for internal and external routes but there will be only 1 IS-IS LSP for the domain. If there would be multi level IS-IS design two LSP would be seen but since the question says that it is a flat/single level deployment, there will be only 1 IS-IS LSP, either L1 or L2.

That's why the correct answer is D.

Question 10:

Which below statements are correct for IS-IS design?

A. Topology information is not advertised between IS-IS levels

B. Starting with Flat/Single Level 2 IS-IS design makes the possible future IS-IS deployment easier

C. IS-IS level 2 route is preferred over level 1 route in IS-IS

D. IS-IS uses DIS and Backup DIS on the multi access links.

Answer 10:

There is no backup DIS in IS-IS, thus Option D is incorrect.

IS-IS level 1 routes are preferred over IS-IS level 2 routes. Similar to OSPF intra area routes preferred over Inter Area routes. Thus option C is incorrect as well.

Correct answer of this question is A and B.

IS-IS FURTHER STUDY RESOURCES

Books

White, R. (2003). *IS-IS: Deployment in IP Networks*, Addison-Wesley.

Videos

Ciscolive Session –BRKRST–2338

Podcast

http://packetpushers.net/show-89-ospf-vs-is-is-smackdown-where-you-can-watch-their-eyes-reload/

Chapter 5
EIGRP

If the requirement is to use Enterprise level, scalable, minimal configuration for the Hub and Spoke topology such as DMVPN, then the only choice is EIGRP.

EIGRP is a distance vector protocol, and unlike OSPF and IS-IS, topology information is not carried between the routers. EIGRP routers only know the networks/subnets that their neighbors advertise to them.

As a distance vector protocol, nodes in EIGRP topology don't keep the topology information of all the other nodes. Instead, they trust what their neighbors tell them.

Feasible distance is the best path. Primary path successor is the next-hop router for the route. Feasible successors are the routers which satisfy the feasibility condition. These are the backup routers.

- Feasible successors are placed in EIGRP topology table.
- Reported distance is the feasible distance of the neighboring router.

EIGRP Feasibility Condition

If node A'S next-hop router's reported distance is less than the feasible distance of node A, then A's backup router is loop free and can be used as a backup and placed in the topology table.

In order for the path to be placed in the EIGRP topology table, it has to satisfy the EIGRP feasibility condition.

ECMP

B

10 10

A D

10 10

C

From Router A's point of view, Router B and Router C are the Equal Cost routers, so both ABD and ACD path can be used. Router A installs both Router B and Router C in not only EIGRP topology table, but also in the routing table.

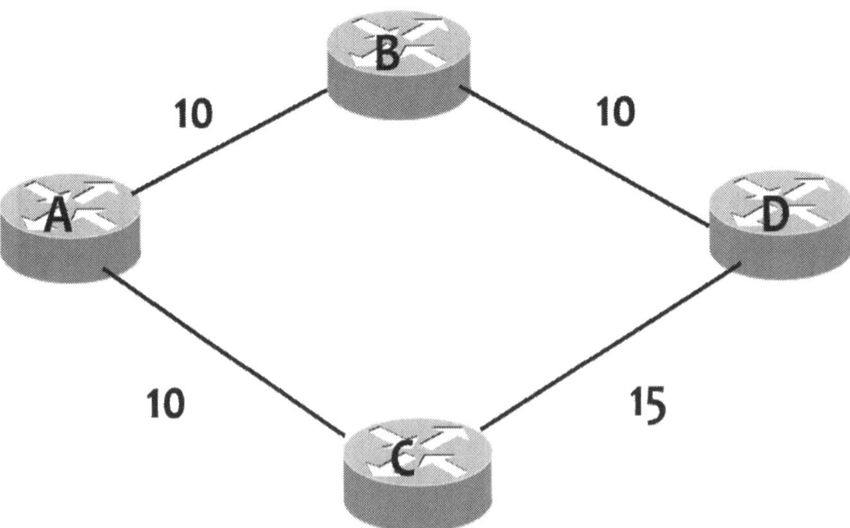

Router C to Router D link cost is 15. In order to satisfy the feasibility condition for Router A , Router C-Router D link cost should be smaller than A-B-D total cost. Since $15 < 10 + 10$, Router C can be used as a backup router by Router A to reach Router D.

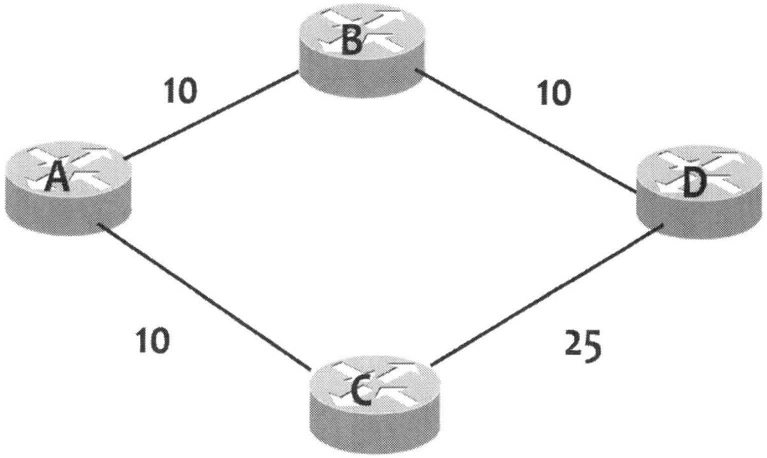

Router C to Router D link cost is 25. In order to satisfy the feasibility condition for Router A, Router C-Router D link cost should be smaller than A-B-D total cost. Since 25 > 10 (A-B) + 10(B-D), Router C cannot be used as a backup router by Router A to Reach Router D. What if C-D were 20?

EIGRP RFC 7868

EIGRP is an Informational RFC anymore.

It is not anymore Cisco's EIGRP, it is an open standard. Without a most critical feature of EIGRP, can we really say that?

Why Cisco doesn't share the most important feature, which can help in large scale EIGRP design although industry has been asking from them for a long time?

EIGRP RFC 7868 specifies EIGRP Dual Algorithm, EIGRP Packets such as Update, Query and Reply, EIGRP Operation, and EIGRP Metrics (K1, K2...K6).

And since EIGP is RFC anymore, other vendors can legally implement EIGRP. There was couple of open source EIGRP implementations already, but with the RFC status, seeing new implementations among the big vendors would not be a big deal.

In addition to EIGRP packet types and metric values, there are a couple of important things to understand about EIGRP.

Among them is how EIGRP, as a distance vector protocol, calculates a best path and advertise it to the neighbors.

Understanding what is EIGRP successor, EIGRP feasible successor, EIGRP feasibility condition, metric values and usage in real life deployments is among the most important parameters in EIGRP that should be properly understood.

EIGRP RFC is an 80-page document, which provides detailed explanations of the protocol. However, it lacks EIGRP Stub, one of the most important features if not the most important one.

Even if it is an RFC, the usability of EIGRP in large scale deployment will be limited without EIGRP Stub feature.

In large-scale network, there might be thousands of spokes routers. And waiting for each router's EIGRP reply might significantly slow down the network convergence. Not only that, Hub router would send EIGRP query to thousands of neighbors, which would be a lot of burdens on the CPU.

That's not all. Hub router has to process EIGRP reply packet from thousands of spokes nodes, most probably almost at the same time. This process would put a lot of burdens on the input queue and CPU of the Hub routers.

EIGRP Stub will be explained in more detail later in the chapter. Also case study will be provided.

EIGRP Theory Diagrams

In the below diagrams, how EIGRP prefixes are learned by the routers, then how EIGRP routers advertises the prefixes are shown.

You will see that there is no topology information in EIGRP. This is biggest difference of EIGRP from OSPF and IS-IS.

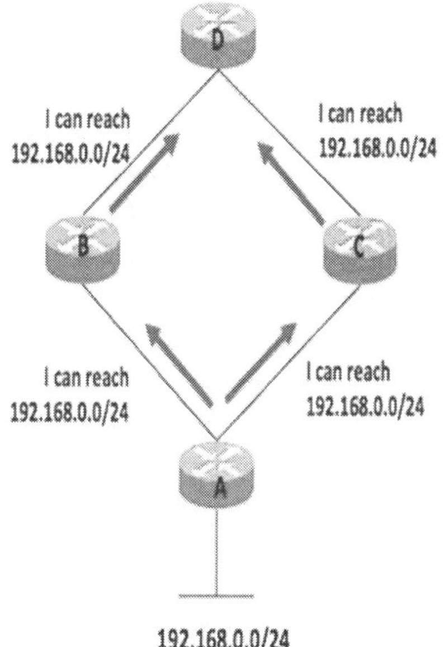

In Distance vector protocols topology information Is hidden beyond the next hop.

EIGRP only knows prefix and next hop information.

In this topology A advertises that it has 192.168.0.0/24 network.

Router B and C only advertise to Router D that they can reach 192.168.0.0/24, not that they are connected to Router A which is then connected to Router A.

Router D learn to reach to 192.168.0.0/24 , it can use Router B or Router C, but Router D doesn't know which routers or Connections exist beyond Router B and Router B.

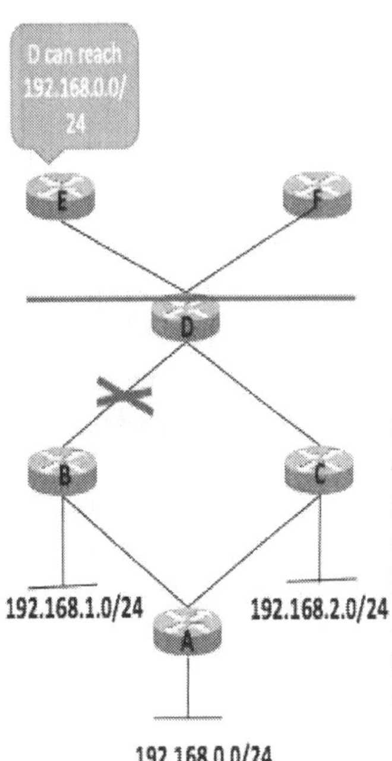
D can reach 192.168.0.0/24
E
F
D
B
C
A
192.168.1.0/24
192.168.2.0/24
192.168.0.0/24

For E and F Topology information is hidden here.
They only know that
192.168.0.0/24 can be reached via Router D

In this network, if all three subnets are summarized at the Router D and send to Router E and F, when link B-D fails (or any link between the routers in this topology) since Router D still can reach to all subnets via alternate links Router E and F doesn't need to know all the specific subnets. Because only the exit point for Router E and Router F is Router D. Summarization may create suboptimal routing if there is more than one exit point though. (This is general rule for all the IGPs)

192.168.0.0/24

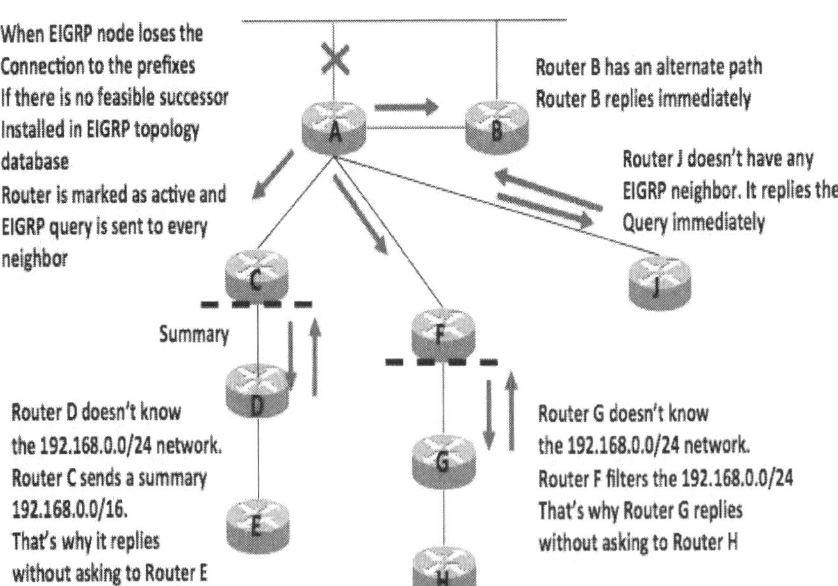
When EIGRP node loses the Connection to the prefixes If there is no feasible successor Installed in EIGRP topology database
Router is marked as active and EIGRP query is sent to every neighbor
Router B has an alternate path
Router B replies immediately
Router J doesn't have any EIGRP neighbor. It replies the Query immediately
A
B
C
J
F
Summary
D
G
E
H
Router D doesn't know the 192.168.0.0/24 network.
Router C sends a summary 192.168.0.0/16.
That's why it replies without asking to Router E
Router G doesn't know the 192.168.0.0/24 network.
Router F filters the 192.168.0.0/24
That's why Router G replies without asking to Router H

EIGRP Design over Different Network Topologies

EIGRP is best in Hub and Spoke and Mesh topologies, but is not good at Rings. See the below examples.

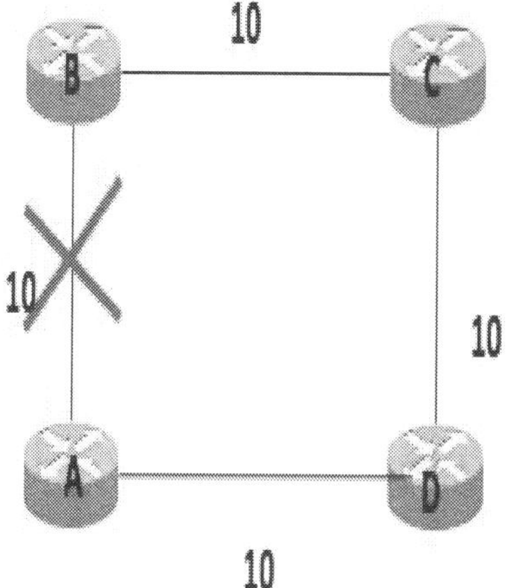

In this network If A-B link fails, Router A sends a query to Router D , Router D sends a query to Router C.

Since Router C is not using Router D to reach Router B, Query stops at Router C and Router C replies that it has an Alternate path.

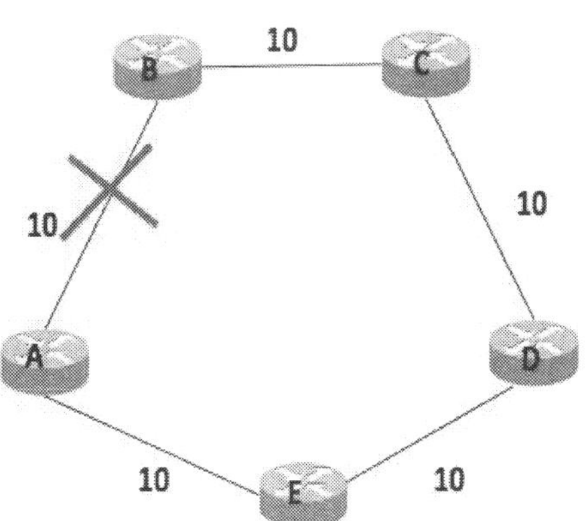

In this network if A-B link fails , Router A sends a query
to Router E , Router E sends a query to Router D and
Router D sends a query to Router C.

Query range in this network is three hops.

Ring topology is very challenging for all IGP protocols
including EIGRP.

If this topology would be triangle instead of ring EIGRP could find a feasible successor and convergence would be very fast.

In hub-and-spoke topologies, spoke nodes should be configured as EIGRP stub. This is similar to the behavior of BGP transit AS. In order to prevent Transit AS from being a customer, customer only sends its AS path to the upstream and filters all the other AS.

EIGRP STUB

EIGRP Stub allows the router to not be queried, so the router does not advertise routes to peer if the route is learned from another peer.

EIGRP Stub is the most important feature in large-scale EIGRP design.

Query

EIGRP STUB

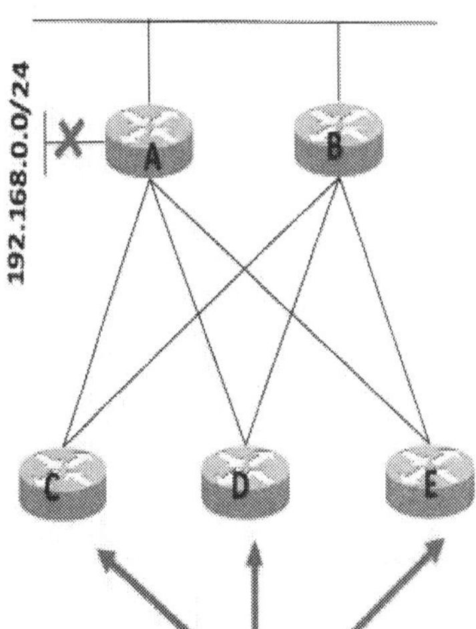

When EIGRP Stub feature is enabled spoke sites are not used as transit site.

Also Hub site doesn't even send an EIGRP query if 192.168.0.0/24 network fails as in the picture Router A sends a query only to Router B. This helps for the convergence, provide faster convergence.

If EIGRP Stub wouldn't be enabled but filtering or summarization is enabled at the Hub sites, spokes sites still would receive a query and they would process.

This might create a resource problem on the Hub for large scale Hub and Spoke deployment.

Always use EIGRP stub in Hub and Spoke topology
Spoke sites shouldn't be used transit site

EIGRP Stub Operation on Hub and Spoke Network

Access network should always be configured as EIGRP stub.

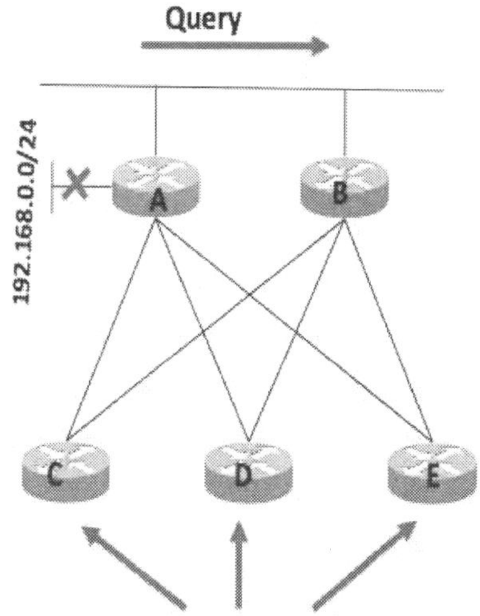

Query

192.168.0.0/24

A B C D E

EIGRP is the most scalable IGP protocol inn HUB and Spoke Topologies.

Spoke sites have two connections for redundancy not to be used as transit between Hub sites.

Having a direct link between the HUB sites is important.

Otherwise Spoke sites might be used as transit nodes.

Always use EIGRP stub in Hub and Spoke topology
Spoke sites shouldn't be used transit site

EIGRP Summary and Filters

The summarization metric is received from the route, which has the lowest metric. If that route goes down, metric changes so summarization effect to upstream will be lost.

You can create a loopback interface within the summary address range with a lower metric than any other route in the summary, but the problem with this approach is if all the routes fail in that summary range but loopback stays, then a blackhole occurs.

When this problem occurs within the EIGRP named mode you can use summary-metric so that you can statically state the metric you want to use.

EIGRP over DMVPN Case Study

Enterprise Company wants to use MPLS L3 VPN (right one in the below topology) as its primary path between its remote office and the datacenter.

Customer uses EIGRP and EIGRP AS 100 for the Local Area Network inside the office. They want to use their DMVPN network as a backup path. Customer runs EIGRP AS 200 over DMVPN

Service Provider doesn't support EIGRP as a PE-CE protocol, only static routing and BGP. Customer selected to use BGP instead of static routing since cost community attribute might be used to carry EIGRP metric over the MP-BGP session of service provider. Redistribution is needed on the R2 between EIGRP and BGP (two ways).Since customer uses different EIGRP AS numbers for the LAN and DMVPN networks, redistribution is needed on R1 too.

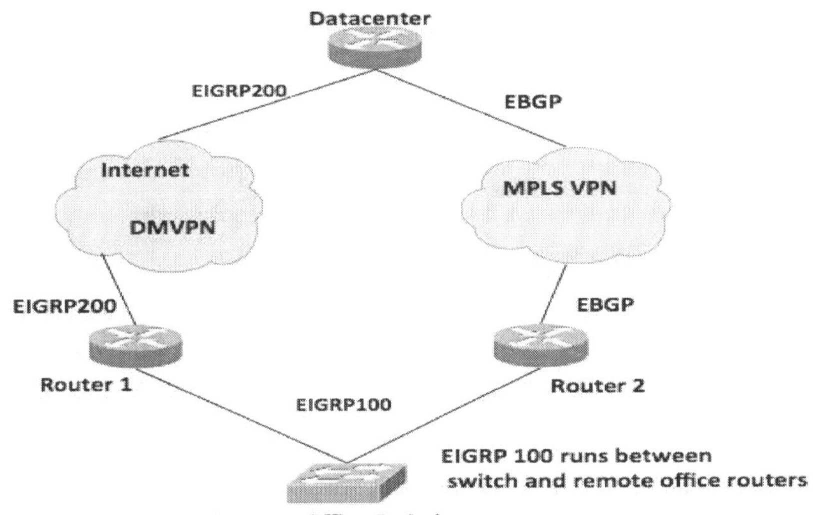

Question 1:

Should the customer use same EIGRP AS on the DMVPN network and its office LAN? What is the problem with that design?

Answer 1:

No they should not.

Since the customer's requirement is to use MPLS VPN as primary path, if the customer runs same EIGRP AS on LAN and over DMVPN,

EIGRP routes will be seen as internal by DMVPN, but external by MPLS VPN. Internal EIGRP is preferred over external because of Admin Distance so customer should use different AS numbers.

DMVPN could be used as a primary path for some delay, jitter, or loss of insensitive traffic, but the customer didn't specify that.

Question 2:

When the company changed the EIGRP AS on DMVPN and started to use a different EIGRP AS on the DMVPN and the LAN, which path will be used between the remote offices and the datacenter?

Answer 2:

Since redistribution is done on R1 and R2, remote switch and datacenter devices see the routes both from DMVPN and BGP as EIGRP external. Then the metric is compared. If the metric (bandwidth and delay in EIGRP) is the same, both paths can be used (Equal Cost Multipath- ECMP).

Question 3:

Does the result fit the customer's traffic requirement?

Answer 3:

Remember what the customer's expectation was for the links; they to use MPLS VPN for all their applications as a primary path.

So the answer is yes, it satisfies the customer's requirements. If the customer uses different EIGRP AS on LAN and DMVPN, with metric adjustment MPLS VPN path can be used as primary with the metric arrangement.

Question 4:

What happens if the primary MPLS VPN link goes down?

Answer 4:

Traffic from remote office to the datacenter goes through Switch-R1-DMVPN path. Since those will not be known through MPLS VPN when it fails, only DMVPN link is used from the datacenter. DMVPN link is used as primary if a failure happens.

Question 5:

What happens when the failed MPLS VPN link comes back?

Answer 5:

R2 receives the datacenter prefixes over MPLS VPN path via EBGP and from R1 via EIGRP. Once the link comes back, datacenter prefixes will still be received via DMVPN and MPLS VPN and appear on the office switch as an EIGRP external.

Since metric was arranged previously to make MPLS VPN path primary, no further action is required.

This is the tricky part: if using Cisco switches or those from another vendor that takes BGP weight attribute into consideration for best path selection, then redistributed prefixes weight would be higher than the prefixes which are received through MPLS VPN, so R2 uses Switch-R1 DMVPN path which violates the customer's expectations.

EIGRP vs. OSPF Design Comparison

Below table summarizes the similarities and the differences of these two Interior Gateway Dynamic Routing Protocols in great detail. Network designers should know the pros and cons of the technologies, protocol alternatives and their capabilities from the design point of view. esign requirements are given such as Scalability, Convergence, standard protocols and many others and these design parameters should be used during any design preparation. Also know that this table will be helpful in any networking exam.

Design Requirement	OSPF	EIGRP
Scalablability	2 tier hierarchy , less scalable	Support many tiers and scalable
Working on Full Mesh	Works well with mesh group	Works very poorly, and there is no mesh group
Working on a Ring Topology	Its okay	Not good if ring is big due to query domain
Working on Hub and Spoke	Works poorly, require a lot of tuning	Works very well. It requires minimum tuning
Fast Reroute Support	Yes - IP FRR	Yes - IP FRR and Feasible Successor
Suitable on WAN	Yes	Yes
Suitable on Datacenter	DCs are full mesh. So, No	DCs are full mesh so no
Suitable on Internet Edge	No it is designed as an IGP	No, it is designed as an IGP
Standard Protocol	Yes IETF Standard	No, there is a draft but lack of Stub feature
Stuff Experince	Very well known	Well known
Overlay Tunnel Support	Yes	Yes
MPLS Traffic Engineering Support	Yes with CSPF	No
Security	Less secure	Less secure
Suitable as Enterprise IGP	Yes	Yes
Suitable as Service Provider IGP	Yes	No, it doesn't support Traffic Engineering
Complexity	Easy	Easy
Policy Support	Good	Not so Good
Resource Requirement	SPF requires more processing power	DUAL doesn't need much power
Extendibility	Not good	Good, thanks to TLV support
IPv6 Support	Yes	Yes
Default Convergece	Slow	Fast with Feasible Successor
Training Cost	Cheap	Cheap

Design Requirement	OSPF	EIGRP
Troubleshooting	Easy	Easy
Routing Loop	Good protection	Open to race condition

EIGRP vs. OSPF Design Comparison

EIGRP Hub and Spoke Design and Stub Feature Case Study

Haleo is a fictitious Enterprise company that uses DMVPN Wide Area Network technology over the Internet.

They have only one datacenter and the WAN routers that connect remote branches to the datacenter and campus network are terminating many remote branches.

For redundancy and capacity purposes, Haleo is using two DMVPN hub routers.

They know that EIGRP is the best IGP for large-scale DMVPN design, but recently they had some issues with their WAN network.

Question 1:

What additional information do you need from Haleo to address their issue?

- Datacenter network topology?
- Which routing protocol Haleo is using?
- Encryption method of Haleo?
- Routing configuration?
- WAN Network Topology?

Answer 1:

Let's look at the options.

Datacenter Network topology: We don't need this information since in the background information, we are told that the problem is on the WAN network.

Which routing protocol Haleo is using: We don't need this because well in the background information we are told that it is EIGRP.

Encryption method: Nothing is said about encryption; we can't assume that they are using encryption over DMVPN network since DMVPN doesn't require encryption.

Routing configuration: We know that Haleo is using EIGRP, but we don't know if they have EIGRP Stub on the edges or whether split horizon is disabled on the hub, so we need to know their EIGRP features.

WAN network topology: We need WAN network topology since we don't know how many routers are in the branches, how they are connected. The background information only mentions that Haleo is using two hub routers.

Email:

Dear Designer,

We are using EIGRP. EIGRP Stub has been enabled on all remote branches per your suggestion.

Some critical branch offices have two routers and there is a 1 Gbps Ethernet handoff from each router to only one hub router in the datacenter. I am sending our DMVPN network diagram at the attachment. For simplicity, I have shared only a couple of sites, but the rest of the sites are connected in the same way, i.e., either one 1 router 2 links or 2 routers 2 links to the datacenter.

Hub and Spoke Case Study Customer Topology

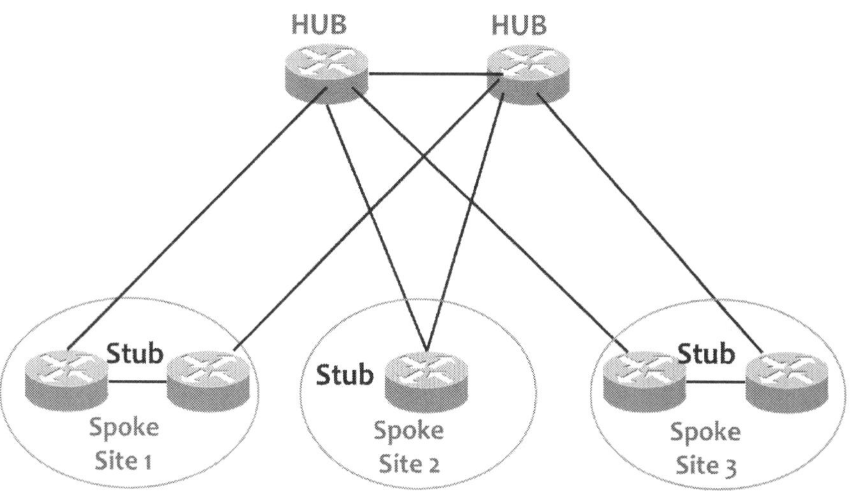

Question 2:

Based on the information provided, what might be the problem? How it can be solved?

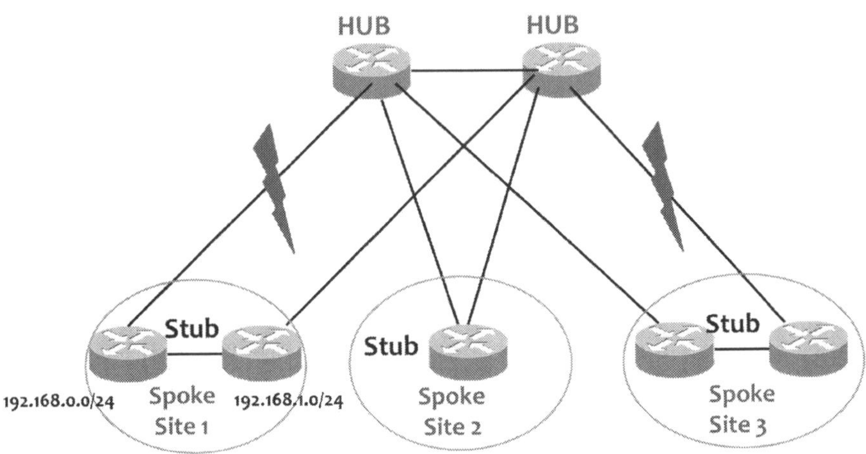

Since the spoke routers are running as EIGRP Stub, they don't send the prefixes which are learned from each other to the hubs. If the link between hub and the spoke sites which have two routers fails the router is isolated from the rest of the network

Spokes in the spoke site 1 send their network to each other. So 192.168.0.0/24 and 192.168.1.0/24 is learned by both spokes, but since they are EIGRP Stub, they don't send the learned routes to the hub. If the Hub and Spoke link failed in Spoke Site 1, 192.168.0.0/24 network will not be reachable anymore.

Same thing for Spoke Site 3, since that site also has two routers and EIGRP Stub is enabled. The solution is to enable EIGRP Stub leaking. In DMVPN it is good to send summary or default route to the spokes by the hubs. Spokes should send the routes which they learn from each other to the hub and also should send the routes which they learn from the hub to each other. In this way, sites, which have more than one router, which has EIGRP Stub configuration, do not have an issue in case of any failure.

EIGRP in MPLS Layer 3 VPN Case Study

Enterprise Company is using EIGRP on its network. They have MPLS VPN and also DMVPN network for its WAN network.

MPLS service is Layer 3 VPN, managed by the service provider. Company has 30ms end-to-end latency SLA for their MPLS VPN network and all their applications fit to this service level agreement. MPLS VPN is the desired primary path and in case of failure, DMVPN should be used as backup.

Recently, they had an outage and after researching, they realized that the convergence of their EIGRP was higher than expected. They are asking for your help to address the issue and provide a solution.

Their topology is attached.

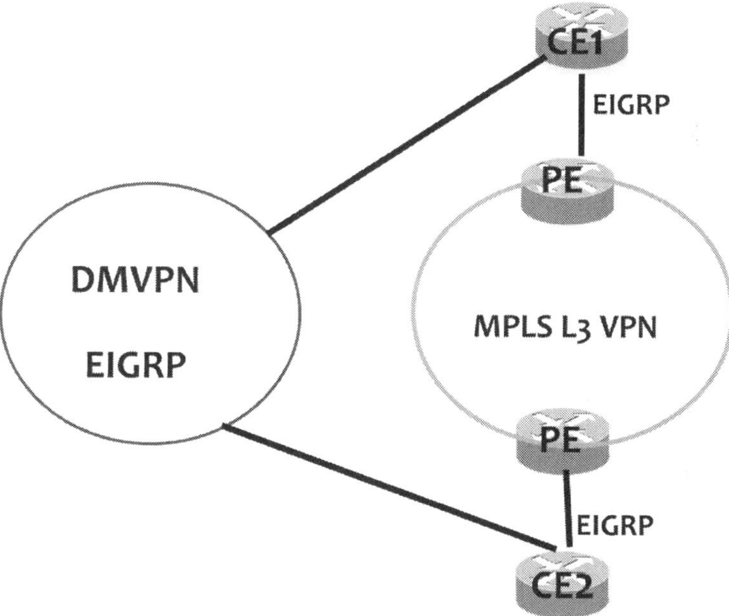

Because EIGRP is a distance vector protocol it suffers from two problems. In case of failure, either suboptimal routing or a blackhole situation will occur, both due to the EIGRP race condition.

In the topology below, if the loopback interface of CE1 fails, depending on the timing of EIGRP and MP-BGP update, you might have a routing loop.

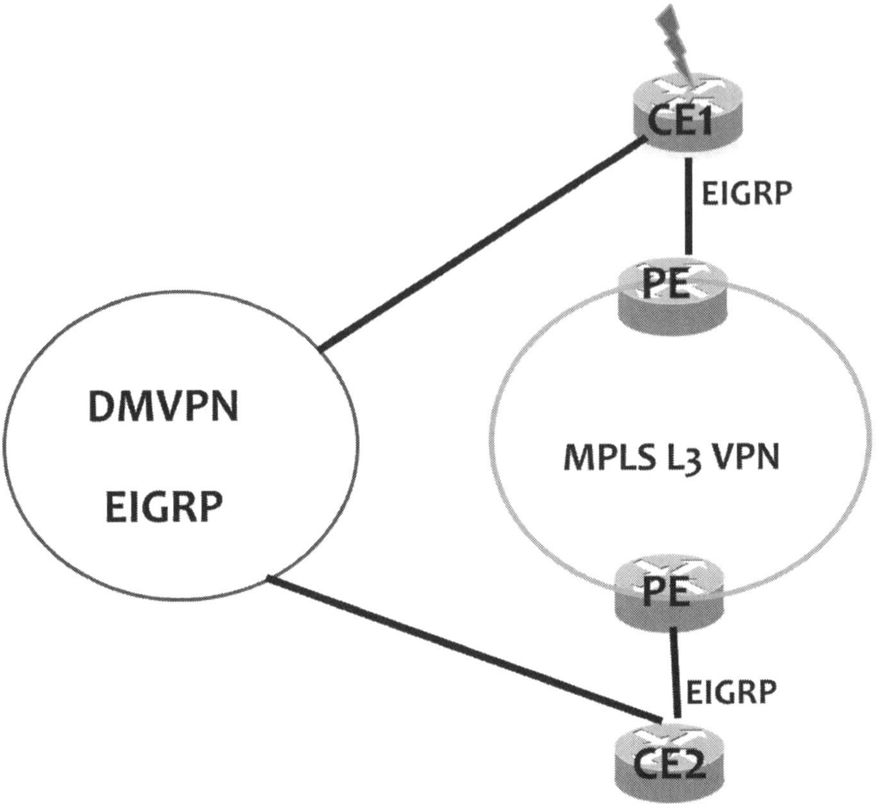

CE1 sends EIGRP queries to PE1 and CE2 asking its loopback prefix; network is using MPLS VPN as primary path.

PE1 prefers the prefix via CE1; since it learns the prefix from the CE1 it assumes that there is no alternate path. PE1 doesn't send queries further and replies with prefix unreachable to CE1.When PE1 stops learning CE'1 loopbacks from EIGRP, it removes it from its BGP table as well (EIGRP to MP-BGP redistribution).

When PE1 removes the prefix from its BGP routing table it sends a BGP withdrawal to the PE2. PE1 previously sent an EIGRP query to the CE2, and CE2 propagated it.

Here the EIGRP race condition can be a big issue.

Depending on the arrival of EIGRP query and the BGP withdrawal message to the BGP, persistent routing loop can occur. If BGP withdrawal over the MPLS VPN backbone via MP-BGP comes faster than EIGRP query through CE1–CE2 and eventually to the PE2, everything is fine. Because PE2 removes the prefix from BGP table and stops redistributing into the EIGRP (MP-BGP to EIGRP redistribution). But if EIGRP query from the CE2 comes faster than BGP it withdraws to PE2.

Since PE2 has a path to the CE1 over the MPLS VPN, it replies to the CE2 that it has an alternate path. This reply goes up to the originator (CE1) and CE1 sends it to PE1. In return PE1 sends it to PE2.

CE1 now thinks that CE2 has an alternate path for its own loopback.

Meanwhile, PE2 receives the BGP withdrawal which was previously sent by PE1.

PE2 sends an EIGRP query to CE2 so CE2 again thinks that it is not reachable, so it sends a EIGRP query to CE1.

EIGRP REVIEW QUESTIONS

Question 1:

Which below technology provides similar functionality with EIGRP Feasible Successor?

A. ISPF

B. Partial SPF

C. Loop Free Alternate Fast reroute

D. OSPF Stub Areas

E. IS-IS Level 1 domain

Answer 1:

Although EIGRP convergence was not explained in the EIGRP chapter, it is important to mention here. EIGRP Feasible successor is the backup path, which satisfies the feasibility condition.

Which means it should satisfy the EIGRP's loop free backup path condition.

There is no ISPF, Partial SPF, PRC or SPF in EIGRP. These algorithms are used in link state protocols.

Answer of this question is LFA FRR, which is one of the IP Fast Reroute mechanisms. IP FRR mechanisms will be explained in the MPLS traffic engineering section later in the book.

Question 2:

How many levels of hierarchy is supported in EIGRP?

A. One

B. Two

C. Three

D. Unlimited

Answer 2:

Unlike OSPF and IS-IS, there is no limit in EIGRP. OSPF and IS-IS support two levels of hierarchy as it was explained earlier.

There is no topology information in EIGRP and summarization can be done anywhere in EIGRP. Unlimited level of hierarchy is possible with EIGRP, that's why answer of this question is D.

Question 3:

In the below topology R3 is configured as EIGRP Stub. If the link between R1 and R2 fails, which below statements are true for the below topology? (Choose Two)

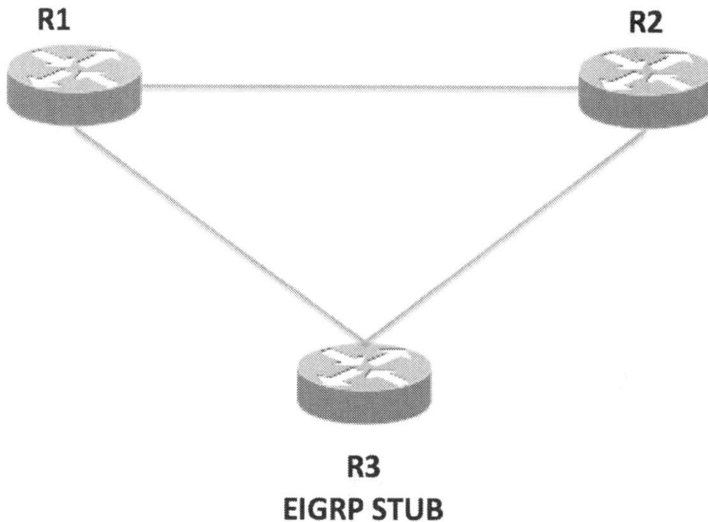

A. Since R3 is configured as EIGRP Stub, R3 is not used as transit for the traffic between R1 and R2
B. R1 can reach the networks behind R2 through R3
C. R3 has all the R1 and R2 prefixes in its routing table
D. R3 doesn't have R1 and R2 prefixes
E. R2 can reach the networks behind R1 through R3

Answer 3:

As it was explained in the EIGRP Stub section in this chapter, when node is configured as EIGRP stub, it is not used as transit node anymore.

Question is asking when the R1 and R2 link fails, whether R3 will be transit node. No, it will not be transit node.

Which mean, R1 cannot reach R2 through R3 and R2 cannot reach R1 through R3. That's why B and E are incorrect.

R3 has all the prefixes of R1 and R2 even if it is configured as EIGRP Stub.

That's why the correct answer of this question is A and C.

Question 4:

Which below option is considered as loop free path in EIGRP?

A. If reported distance is less than feasible distance
B. If reported distance is same as the feasible distance
C. If reported distance is higher than feasible distance
D. If administrative distance is higher than feasible distance

Answer 4:

In order a path to be chosen as loop free alternate which means satisfy the EIGRP feasibility condition as it was explain in the EIGRP chapter of the book, reported distance has to be less than feasible distance. That's why the answer of the question is A.

Question 5:

What happens if the backup path satisfies the feasibility condition? (Choose Two)

A. It is placed in link state database
B. It is advertised to the neighbors
C. It is placed in the topology table
D. It can be used as unequal cost path
E. It is placed in the routing table

Answer 5:

EIGRP database is called Topology database. Link state database is used in link state protocols.

If backup path satisfies feasibility condition, it is placed in topology table, not in routing table. If it would be best path (successor) or equal cost path, it would be placed in routing table. But since question says, backup path, it is only placed in EIGRP topology database.

Since it is not the best path, it is not advertised to the neighbors.

With ' variance' command, it can be used as unequal cost path and can be placed in the routing table.

That's why answer of this question is C and D.

Question 6:

Which below statements are true for EIGRP Summarization? (Choose Two)

A. EIGRP Auto-summarization is on by default for all the Internal and External routes

B. EIGRP Route summarization can reduce the query domain which helps for convergence

C. EIGRP Route Summarization can reduce the query domain which can prevent Stuck in Active problem

D. Summarization cannot be done at each hop in EIGRP

Answer 6:

Summarization can be done at each hop in EIGRP. This is different than OSPF and IS-IS. Auto-Summarization is not enabled for all the routes by default in EIGRP. Summarization helps to reduce query domain boundary, which in turn help for convergence, SIA problem, troubleshooting and so on.

That's why the answer of this question is B and C.

Question 7:

Which below statement is true for EIGRP queries? (Choose Two)

A. EIGRP queries always send

B. Limiting EIGRP query domain helps for scalability

C. If summarization is configured, EIGRP query is not sent

D. If filtering is configured, EIGRP query is not sent

E. If EIGRP Stub is configured, EIGRP query is not sent

Answer 7:

If EIGRP Stub is configured, as it was explained before, EIGRP query is not sent. With summarization and filtering still EIGRP query is sent. EIGRP query domain size affects scalability. If the query domain size is reduced, scalability increases.

That's why answer if this question is B and E.

Question 8:

Why passive interface should be enabled on the access/customer ports?

A. To prevent injecting the customer prefixes to the network

B. To reduce the size of the routing table

C. For the fast convergence

D. For higher availability

Answer 8:

Passive interface should be used on all hosts, access and customer ports. Otherwise security attack can happen and prefixes can be injected into the routing domain. It doesn't provide faster convergence. And the reason to disable routing protocols on the customer/access ports is not to reduce routing table size.

That's why the answer of this question is A.

Question 9:

If the path in the network will be changed by changing the EIGRP attribute, which below statement would you recommend as a network designer?

A. Bandwidth should be changed

B. Delay should be changed

C. Reliability should be changed

D. PBR should be configured

Answer 9:

PBR is not an EIGRP attribute. Reliability is not used for EIGRP path selection. Bandwidth and Delay attributes are used for EIGRP path selection and metric is calculated based on these two parameters.

But, since bandwidth can be used by many applications such as QoS, RSVP-TE and so on it should be changed, otherwise other things in the network can change too.

Also since the minimum bandwidth is used for path calculation, changing bandwidth can affect entire network design. Not only the path, which we want.

On the other hand, delay is additive and changing it can only affect the path, which we want.

That's why the answer of this question is B.

Question 10:

When EIGRP is used as MPLS VPN PE-CE routing protocol, which below mechanism helps for loop prevention even if there is a backdoor link?

A. Up/Down bit

B. Sham link

C. Site of Origin

D. Split Horizon

Answer 10:

EIGRP Site of Origin is used to prevent loop even if there is a backdoor link. Backdoor link causes race condition in MPLS VPN topologies and it can create sub optimal routing and routing loop.

It will be explained in the MPLS VPN section in the MPLS chapter in detail.

That's why answer of this question is C.

EIGRP FURTHER STUDY RESOURCES

Books

Pepelnjak, I. (2000). *EIGRP Network Design Solutions*, Cisco Press Core.

Videos

Ciscolive Session–BRKRST -2336

Podcast

http://packetpushers.net/show-144-open-eigrp-with-russ-white-ciscos-donnie-savage/

Articles

http://www.cisco.com/c/en/us/td/docs/ios/12_0s/feature/guide/eigrp-stb.html

http://www.cisco.com/c/en/us/td/docs/ios/xml/ios/iproute/_eigrp/configuration/xe-3s/ire/xe/3s-book/ire-ipfrr.html

Chapter 6
VPN DESIGN

In this chapter below technologies will be covered. Most of these technologies are used in the Wide Area Network but can be applied in the Campus or Datacenter as well.

For example there are use cases of LISP and GETVPN in the Datacenter, GRE in the Campus and the Datacenter. Throughout this chapter, use cases of all these technologies will be explained in detail. Comparison charts are very important to understand the pros and cons of each of these technologies. They will help in CCDE exam and they will definitely help network designers for their design projects.

- GRE
- mGRE
- IPSEC
- DMVPN
- GETVPN
- LISP

VPN THEORY

Virtual Private Network is the logical entity, which is created over a physical infrastructure. It can be setup over another private network such as MPLS or public network such as Internet

All VPN technologies add extra byte to the packet or frame, which increases the overall MTU so the network links should be accommodated to handle bigger MTU values.

VPN technologies work based on encapsulation and decapsulation.

For example GRE, mGRE and DMVPN encapsulate IP packets into another IP packet, VPLS and EVPN encapsulates Layer 2 frame into an MPLS packets.

You can run routing protocols over some VPN technologies but not all VPN technologies allow you to run routing protocols.

In order to support routing over tunnel, tunnel endpoints should be aware from each other.

For example MPLS Traffic Engineer tunnels don't support routing protocols to run over, since the LSPs are unidirectional which mean Head-end and Tail-end routers are not associated. This will be explained in detail in MPLS chapter.

All VPN technologies except IPSEC and LISP, in our list, supports routing protocols to run over.

GRE

GRE tunnels are by far most common tunneling technology. Very easy to setup, troubleshoot and operate. But in large scale deployment, configuring GRE tunnels become cumbersome.

Below are the some characteristics of GRE tunnels.

- GRE tunnels are manual point to point tunnels. Tunnel end points are not automatically derived. Network operator needs to configure the tunnel end points manually.
- Supports routing protocols to run over. You can run any routing protocols on top of GRE tunnels.
- IPv4 and IPv6 can be transported over GRE. Some VPN technologies may not support IPv6 or IPv6 routing protocols.
- Non-IP protocols such as IPX, SNA etc. can be carried over GRE tunnel as well. Most of the tunneling technologies cannot carry Non-IP traffic. We will see them throughout the chapter.
- If there are too many sites that need to communicate with each other, GRE is not scalable. But in Hub and Spoke topologies it can be used since whenever new spoke site is added, only new site and hub should be revisited. Not all the spokes need configuration.
- Even though in Hub and Spoke topologies, the configuration can be too long on the Hub site. mGRE will reduce configuration on the Hub site greatly.

- GRE add 24 bytes to the IP Packet. 4 byte GRE header and 20 bytes new IP header is added; this increases MTU size of the IP packet. Careful planning on the interface MTU is necessary.
- GRE doesn't come by default with encryption so in order to encrypt the packet; IPSEC should be enabled over GRE tunnel.

GRE Uses Cases:

- Classical use cases of GRE tunnel is over Internet with IPSEC, VRF-lite to carry different VPN information separately in the Campus, WAN or datacenter and IPv6 tunneling over IPv4 transport.
- GRE is used mostly together with IPSEC to support the traffic that is not supported by IPSEC by default. For example IPSEC tunnels don't support Multicast by default but together with GRE, GRE over IPSEC supports multicast traffic.

mGRE – Multipoint GRE

- mGRE tunnels, allow multiple destinations such as multiple spoke sites to be grouped into a single multipoint interface.
- mGRE is a multipoint bidirectional GRE tunnel
- Uses only 1 IP subnet so routing table of the routers are reduced which is good for the convergence, troubleshooting and device performance.
- Remote endpoint address is not configured that's why it requires additional mechanisms for tunnel end point discovery. These additional mechanisms can be BGP or NHRP. When it is used with NHRP, solution is called DMVPN which we will see later in detail
- Supports IPSEC and routing protocols to run on top.
- Supports IPv6 and non-IP protocols.
- Don't require a manually configured GRE tunnel that's why configuration complexity is reduced greatly.
- Suitable for full mesh topology such as spoke to spoke tunnels.

mGRE Use Cases:

- MPLS VPN over mGRE: in this case single mGRE interface is enough to carry multiple VPN information.
- Another use case is VRF Lite over mGRE that requires 1:1 VRF to mGRE interface. So each VRF requires separate mGRE interface. DMVPN uses this concept.
- mGRE adds 28 bytes of overhead because of the additional 4-byte Key field which is not typically included in the GRE header when using a point to point GRE tunnel

IPSEC

IPSEC provides secure transmission of packets at the IP layer (Not Layer2). For Layer 2 encryption MACSEC is used. With IPSEC packets are authenticated and encrypted.

Some of the characteristics of the IPSEC tunnels:

- Provides site to site and remote access VPN topologies.
- IPSEC has two modes:Transport mode and the tunnel mode. The difference between the two is that in transport mode; only the IP payload is encrypted, in tunnel mode ; the entire IP datagram(including header) is encrypted.
- IPSEC is point to point tunneling mechanism, thus in large scale implementation it can not scale.
- IP Multicast is not supported over IPSEC VPNs. Since most of the routing protocols run over multicast, this is the reason why Routing Protocols cannot run over pure IPSEC VPNs.
- QoS is supported through TOS byte preservation.
- Routing protocols don't run over IPSEC VPNs, it requires additional GRE encapsulation (GRE over IPSEC)
- IPSEC VPN is a standard protocol that supported by every vendor. Designers should know which technologies are vendor proprietary and which ones are standard based.

IPSEC VPN Use Cases:

- It is mainly used to provide encryption for the data over the Public Internet. This data shouldn't be real-time, packet loss, jitter and delay sensitive since there is no QoS SLA over the Public Internet. Internet is best effort.

DMVPN

DMVN is Point to Multipoint and Multipoint to Multipoint tunneling technology. It reduces the configuration in full mesh topologies greatly. Cisco proprietary technology but the multi point to multipoint automatic tunneling concept is supported by many vendors.

Some of the characteristics of DMVPN:

- DMVPN Works based on two standard technologies; NHRP and mGRE (Multipoint GRE).
- NHRP is used to map NBMA/Underlay address to the Tunnel/Overlay address.
- mGRE tunnel interface doesn't require manual tunnel destination configuration.
- Local address/LAN subnets are advertised over the overlay tunnels (DMVPN tunnels) through the routing protocols.

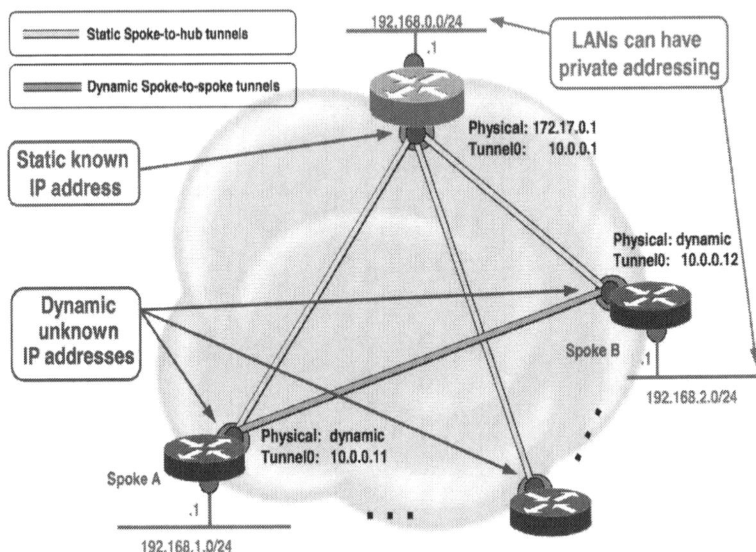

- Spoke to Hub tunnels are always up. They are permanent tunnels as it can be seen from the above picture.
- Spoke to Spoke tunnels are on demand tunnels and if there is no traffic between the spokes, they are teared down.
- Hub site IP address has to be Static and should be known by every spoke.
- Spoke IP addresses can be dynamic and they are registered to the HUB by NHRP protocol. In real life deployment, spoke sites can receive Public IP address from the dynamic pool of the Internet Service Provider.
- Multicast is not natively supported in DMVPN, Multicast is supported via ingress replication and done at the HUB, thus Multicast support of DMVPN can create scalability problem in Large scale design, especially at the Hub site.
- Per tunnel QoS is supported in DMVPN, this prevent hub to over utilized the spoke bandwidth.

- All routing protocols, except IS-IS, can run over DMVPN. IS-IS cannot run since; DMVPN only support IP protocols and IS-IS works based on Layer 2.
- DMVPN invented by Cisco but other vendors provide the capability with different name, Cisco's implementation is not compatible with the other vendors.
- IPSEC is optional in DMVPN and can be implemented as native point to point IPSEC or with GETVPN (Group key)
- DMVPN can carry IPv4 and IPv6 unicast and multicast packets over the overlay tunnels.
- DMVPN also can work over IPv4 and IPv6 private and public infrastructure transport such as Internet or MPLS VPN.
- There are three phases of DMVPN, Phase 1, Phase 2 and Phase 3.
- In all the DMVPN Phases, overlay routing protocol control packets pass through the HUB. There is no spoke to spoke control plane traffic. So routing protocol traffic always go through the HUB.

DMVPN Phase 1

- Spokes use Point to Point GRE but Hub uses a multipoint GRE tunnel.
- mGRE tunnel interface simplifies configuration greatly on the Hub.
- Spokes have to specify the tunnel destination manually as Hub since they run P2P GRE tunnel not mGRE tunnel in DMVPN Phase 1.
- Summarization is allowed from the Hub down to the spokes. The Hub can only send default route as well since Hub does not preserve the remote spokes next hop in Phase 1.
- Hub changes the IGP next hop to itself hence spoke to spoke traffic always passes through the Hub. There is no spoke to spoke tunnel in DMVPN Phase 1.
- Spoke to spoke tunnel cannot be created, that's why DMVPN phase 1 doesn't provide full mesh connectivity.

- Due to lack of spoke to spoke tunnel in DMVPN Phase 1, Cisco came up with DMVPN Phase 2.

DMVPN Phase 2

- Spoke to spoke dynamic on demand tunnels are first introduced in DMVPN Phase 2.
- In contrast to Phase 1, mGRE (Multipoint GRE, not Multicast) interface is used in Phase 2 on the Spokes.
- Thus, spokes don't require tunnel destination configuration under the tunnel interface and tunnel mode is configured as " Multipoint Gre".
- Spoke to spoke traffic doesn't have to go through the HUB. Spokes can trigger on demand tunnel between them.
- The biggest disadvantage of Phase 2 is, each spoke has to have all the Remote – LAN subnets of each other since the Hub, preserves the next hop addresses of the spokes.
- Thus, spokes have to have reachability to the tunnel addresses of each other.
- This disallows the summarization or default routing from Hub down to the spokes.
- This is a serious design limitation for the large scale DMVPN networks.
- For the distance vector protocols, Split horizon needs to be disabled and "no next-hop self" should be enabled on the HUB.

There was too many routing protocol tuning requirement in DMVPN Phase 2. Also lack of summarization was a scaling concern in large scale DMVPN deployment.

DMVPN Phase 3

- Spoke to spoke dynamic tunnels are allowed in DMVPN Phase 3 as well.
- Spokes don't have to have the next hop of each other's private addresses.
- An NHRP redirect message is sent to the spokes to trigger spoke to

spoke tunnels. Hub provides the Public/NBMA addresses (Real IP address on the Internet) of the spokes to each other.

- Since the next hop in the routing table of the spokes is HUB's tunnel address, spokes don't have to have the specific next hop IP address of each other.This allows summarization and default routing in Phase 3.
- Hub can send a summary or just a default route down to the spokes. Hence, Phase 3 is extremely scalable

GETVPN

- GETVPN is Any to Any tunnelless VPN technology, there is no tunnel configuration in GETVPN.
- Some of the characteristics of GETVPN are:
- Uses an IPSEC Tunnel mode.
- GETVPN is Cisco proprietary protocol but the concept of any to any IPSEC is supported by the other vendors with the different names as well.
- Can run over private network only, can not run over Public Internet due to IP header preservation.

In the below picture, GETVPN header is shown. You can see that it is very similar to IPSEC tunnel mode but the outside IP header is preserved. This is different from regular IPSEC tunnel mode, which uses different IP header after ESP header.

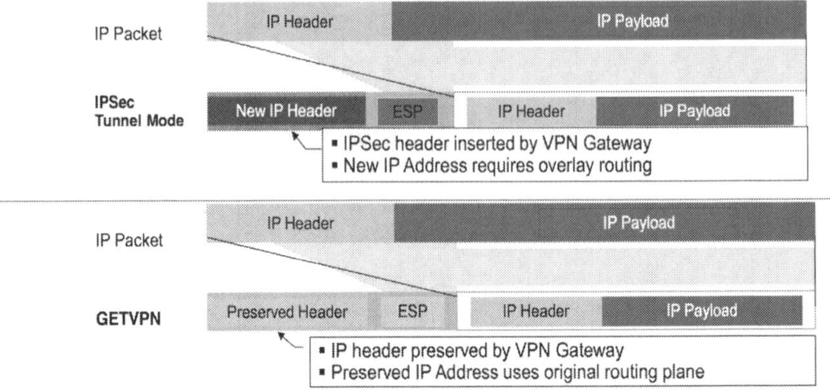

- GETVPN can run on top of any routing protocol.
- It doesn't support overlay routing protocol since there is no tunnel to run routing protocol over. GETVPN is tunnelless VPN technology.
- GETVPN provides excellent Multicast support compare to DMVPN since there is no ingress replication at the HUB but it uses native IP multicast.
- GETVPN doesn't support Non-IP Protocols.
- Uses Group Key mechanism instead of Point to Point IPSEC Keys which are used in DMVPN by default, thus from the security scalability point of view, GETVPN is much scalable technology compare to the DMVPN.

How GETVPN works:

- Group Members (GMs) "register" via GDOI with the Key Server (KS).
- KS authenticates & authorizes the GMs.
- KS returns a set of IPSEC SAs for the GMs to use.
- GMs exchange encrypted traffic using the group keys.
- Traffic uses IPSec Tunnel Mode with IP address preservation.

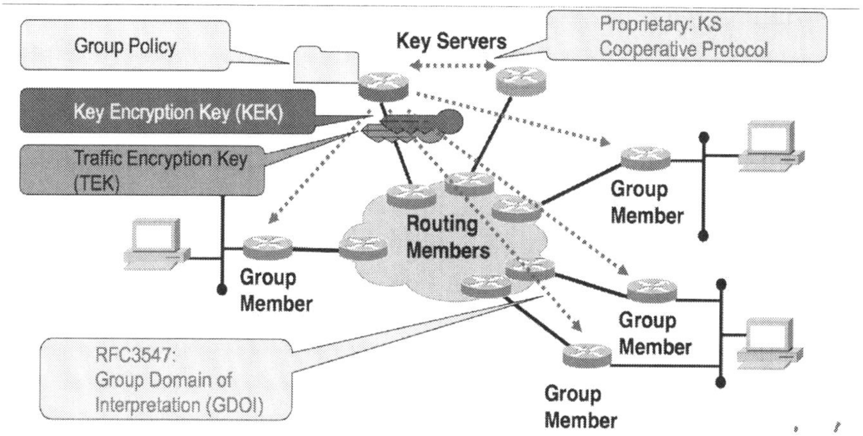

One of the common questions from the customers in real life as well as in the design exam is GETVPN to DMVPN comparison. From menu design criteria, you should know the pros and cons of each technology.

DMVPN vs. GETVPN Comparison

Below comparison chart provides the detail overview of these two overlay VPN technologies from the design point of view.

Network designers should know the pros and cons of the technologies, protocol alternatives and their capabilities from the design point of view.

Design Requirement	DMVPN	GETVPN
Scalability	Scalable	Much more scalable than DMVPN
Working on Full Mesh topology	Permanent hub and spoke tunnels and on demand spoke to spoke tunnels, it works but limited scalability	It works perfectly if the underlying routing architecture is full mesh topology, GET VPN needs underlay routing
Working on Hub and Spoke	Works very well	Works very well
Suitable on private WAN	Yes	Yes
Suitable over Public Internet	Yes	No. GETVPN cannot run over Public Internet because of IP header preservation
End point discovery	To setup the Mgre tunnels uses underlay routing, for the private address discovery uses NHRP (Next hop Resolution Protocol)	It uses underlay routing to create VPN, there is no overlay tunnels

Design Requirement	DMVPN	GETVPN
Tunnel Requirement	Yes, it uses Mgre(Multi Point GRE) tunnels to create overlays	It is tunnelles VPN, uses underlaying routing to encrypt the data between endpoints
Standard Protocol	No,Cisco proprietary	No,Cisco proprietary but Juniper also supports the same idea with Group VPN feature
Stuff Experince	Not well known	Not well known
Overlay Routing Protocol Support	Except IS-IS other routing protocols are supported, IS-IS runs on top of Layer 2 but only IP protocols can run over DMVPN	It is tunnelles VPN so routing protocols cannot run on top of GETVPN but it requires underlaying routing protocols to setup the communication
Required Protocols	NHRP and Mgre	GDOI and ESP
QoS Support	Good, can support per tunnel QoS which uses shaping on the DMVPN Hub to protect capacity and SLA	Good, it uses underlaying network's QoS architecture,in addtion to queuing,shaping at the GET VPN Group Members to protect SLA is enabled
Multicast Support	Multicast over the tunnel is handled at the DMVPN Hub. Hub replicates multicast traffic which is not efficiend	Native multicast support. Multicast replication is done in the network, doesn't need Hub device to replicate. Multicast MDTs (Source , Shared) are used in the traditional way, so multicast handling of GETVPN is much better than DMVPN
Security	Point to Point IPSEC SA	Multipoint to Multipoint IPSEC SA
Resource Requirement	More	Less
IPv6 Support	Yes,it can be setup over IPv6 transport or it can carry IPv6 payload. So IPv6 over DMVPN and DMVPN over IPv6 both are possible	Yes
Default Convergence	Slow	Fast
Can run over other VPN ?	DMVPN is already tunneled VPN technology so only routing is enough, it doesn't make sense to run tunnel over tunnel	GETVPN can run over DMVPN since GETVPN is tunnelless technology, use case of GETVPN over DMVPN is to carry private addressing over Internet. Most common use case of GETVPN is over MPLS VPN or VPLS since both VPN technologies are full mesh by default and GET VPN provides very good scalability for encryption

DMVPN vs. GETVPN

CHAPTER 6

LISP-Locator Identity Separation Protocol

LISP is an IP mobility mechanism. It is a tunnelless VPN technology. (GETVPN is the other tunnelless VPN technology). Rather than having tunnel, LISP provides network connectivity with encap/decap approach. IP packet is encapsulated at the Ingress node inside another IP packet and decapsulated at the egress node.

What is really LISP and what are the design characteristics as a VPN technology?

- Tunnel end points are known by the centralized database (Map Server/Map Resolver in LISP terminology) and the routers pull the information from the database when it is needed.
- LISP is an IP in IP encapsulation mechanism. EID space is encapsulated in RLOC space. This provides IP mobility.
- There is also attempt to provide MAC in IP encapsulation in LISP, it is still an IETF draft. This can be the LISP use case in the Datacenter. OTV uses MAC in IP encapsulation and commonly used Cisco VPN technology for the Datacenter Interconnect use case.
- There is an Experimental RFC (RFC 6830) on LISP but it has been invented by Cisco.
- Similar to DNS infrastructure. Mapping Database keeps the host to gateway mapping information.
- Host space is called EID (Endpoint Identifier) and its gateway is called RLOC (Routing Locator). RLOC IP addresses are learned through underlaying routing infrastructure. But routing protocols don't advertise EID space. EID spaces are learned from the Mapping Database whenever they are needed.
- EID space is similar to Local IP subnet and RLOC space is similar to NBMA address in DMVPN. You can remember them probably easier in this comparison.
- There are many LISP use cases. Most interesting LISP use cases are VM Mobility in the Datacenter, BGP Traffic Engineering at the Internet Edge and IPv6 transition (IPv6 over IPv4 or IPv4 over IPv6 infrastructure).

- From the security point of view MR/MS is a target point.

LISP Device Roles and Terminology

ITR – Ingress Tunnel Router

- Receives packets from site-facing interfaces
- Encapsulates to remote LISP sites, or natively forward to non-LISP sites

ETR – Egress Tunnel Router

- Receives packets from core-facing interfaces decapsulates and deliver packets to local EIDs at the site

EID to RLOC Mapping Database

- Contains RLOC to EID mappings

GRE vs. mGRE vs. IPSEC vs. DMVPN and GETVPN Design Comparison

Below table summarizes the similarities and the differences of all the VPN technologies, which have been discussed in this chapter in great detail.

Network designers should know the pros and cons of the technologies, protocol alternatives and their capabilities from the design point of view.

Many design requirements are given in the below table and the explanation is shared for each of the technology.

Design Requirement	GRE	mGRE	IPSEC	DMVPN	GETVPN
Scalability	Not scalable. Point to point technology	Scalable,one tunnel interface for multiple tunnel endpoint	Not scalable,point to point technology	Scalable for routing but not scalable for IPSEC. DMVPN is used with IPSEC in general	Very scalable technology
Working on Full Mesh topology	It works but not scalable if there are too many devices to connect	It works very well on full mesh topology	It works but not scalable if there are too many devices to connect	Permanent hub and spoke tunnels and on demand spoke to spoke tunnels, it works but limited scalability	It works perfectly if the underlying routing architecture is full mesh topology, GET VPN needs underlay routing protocol
Working on Hub and Spoke	Yes, it is suitable on Hub and Spoke	Yes works well	It works but require too much processing power on the Hub site	It woks but require too much processing power on the Hub site from the IPSEC point of view, for the routing works very well	Works very well
Suitable on private WAN	Yes	Yes	Yes	Yes	Yes
Suitable over Public Internet	Yes	Yes	Yes	Yes	No. GETVPN cannot run over Public Internet because of IP header preservation
End point discovery	Tunnel Source and Destination needs to be manually defined	Tunnel destination is not specified manually,it is automatic	Manual configuration	To setup the Mgre tunnels uses underlay routing, for the private address discovery uses NHRP (Next hop Resolution Protocol)	It uses underlay routing to create VPN, there is no overlay tunnels
Tunnel Requirement	Yes,Point to Point tunnel is required	Yes tunnel is required	Yes tunnel is required	Yes, it uses Mgre(Multi Point GRE) tunnels to create overlays	It is tunnelles VPN, uses underlaying routing to encrypt the data between endpoints

Design Requirement	GRE	mGRE	IPSEC	DMVPN	GETVPN
Standard Protocol	Yes	Yes	Yes	No,Cisco proprietary	No,Cisco proprietary but Juniper also supports the same idea with Group VPN feature
Stuff Experince	Very well known	Well known	Very well known	Not well known	Not well known
Overlay Routing Protocol Support	Can run over all routing protocols	Can run over all routing protocols	Can run over all routing protocols	Except IS-IS other routing protocols are supported, IS-IS runs on top of Layer 2 but only IP protocols can run over DMVPN	It is tunnelles VPN so routing protocols cannot run on top of GETVPN but it requires underlaying routing protocols to setup the communication
Required Protocols	GRE tunnel and IP reachability between end points	Multipoint GRE tunnel and IP reachability between end points	IP reachability between end points,IKE and ESP	NHRP and Mgre	GDOI and ESP
QoS Support	Very well.Flexible QoS	Well	Supports with TOS byte preservation	Good, can support per tunnel QoS which uses shaping on the DMVPN Hub to protect capacity and SLA	Good, it uses underlaying network's QoS architecture,in addtion to queuing,shaping at the GET VPN Group Members to protect SLA is enabled
Multicast Support	Yes	Yes	No	Multicast over the tunnel is handled at the DMVPN Hub. Hub replicates multicast traffic which is not efficiend	Native multicast support. Multicast replication is done in the network, doesn't need Hub device to replicate. Multicast MDTs (Source , Shared) are used in the traditional way, so multicast handling of GETVPN is much better than DMVPN

Design Requirement	GRE	mGRE	IPSEC	DMVPN	GETVPN
Security	No	No	Yes,point to point IPSEC Sas	Point to Point IPSEC SA	Multipoint to Multipoint IPSEC SA
Resource Requirement	More	Less	More	More	Less

VPN DESIGN REVIEW QUESTIONS

Question 1:

Which below statements are true for DMVPN? (Choose Two)

A. DMVPN can work over IPv6

B. IPv6 can work over DMVPN

C. OSPF and IS-IS as link state protocols can run over DMVPN

D. DMVPN cannot run over Internet since there may not be static Public IP address at every spoke sites

Answer 1:

As it was mentioned in this chapter, DMVPN can work over IPv4 and IPv6 and both IPv4 and IPv6 can run over on top of DMVPN.

IS-IS cannot work over DMVPN, that's why Option C is incorrect.

DMVPN can run over Internet, spoke sites don't have to have static Public IP addresses.

That's why; answer of this question is A and B.

Question 2:

Which below statements are true for GRE tunnels? (Choose Three)

A. Any routing protocols can run on top of GRE tunnels

B. Multicast can run on top of GRE tunnels

C. GRE tunnels are multi point to multi point tunnels

D. Non-IP protocols are supported over GRE tunnels

E. From the processing point of view, for the devices, GRE encapsulation and decapsulation is harder than IPSEC encryption/decryption

Answer 2:

Any routing protocols can run on top of GRE tunnels including IS-IS. Multicast can run as well.

GRE tunnels are point-to-point tunnels and Non-IP protocols are supported over GRE tunnels.

From the processing point of view, most CPU intensive task is encryption not the GRE encapsulation.

That's why the answer of this question is A, B, D.

Question 3:

Which below option is true for GETVPN over DMVPN for Internet deployment?

A. GETVPN and DMVPN cannot interoperate

B. GETVPN cannot work over Internet due to IP Header preservation

C. GETVPN key server would be an attack vector this is a security risk

D. GETVPN doesn't bring extra scalability since DMVPN already provides it

Answer 3:

GETVPN and DMVPN can work together. Thus Option A is incorrect. GETVPN cannot work over Internet, that's true but question is asking specific deployment, which is GETVPN over DMVPN that can work over Internet. That's why Option B is incorrect.

GETVPN brings scalability for the IPSEC part when it is used together with DMVPN.

Only correct option is C since GETVPN key servers would be placed on a public place which is a security risk.

Question 4:

Which below statement is true for IPSEC VPN? (Choose Two)

A. IPSEC VPN is point to point VPN

B. It can run over GRE tunnels

C. It can run over LISP tunnels

D. Routing Protocols can run over IPSEC tunnels

E. Multicast can run over IPSEC tunnels

Answer 4:

Multicast and Routing protocols cannot run over IPSEC tunnels.

IPSEC tunnels are point-to-point tunnels.

There is no LISP tunnels thus IPSEC cannot run over LISP tunnels but wording could be IPSEC can run with LISP and there is real world deployment with LISP and GETVPN (Multi Point IPSEC).

That's why the correct answer of this question is A and B.

Question 5

Which below option is important in GRE tunnel deployment? (Choose Two)

A. GRE Tunnel endpoints shouldn't be learned over the tunnel

B. GRE tunnel endpoints are manually configured

C. IPSEC is enable by default on GRE tunnels

D. Tunnel destination address is learned through an Authoritative server

Answer 5:

Tunnel destination address is not learned through an Authoritative server in GRE tunnels. This is done in LISP for example. IPSEC is not enabled by default with GRE tunnels.

One of the most important design considerations in GRE tunnels; tunnel end point address/destination address shouldn't be learned over the tunnel. Otherwise tunnel comes up and goes down. It flaps.

Another correct answer is B, because GRE tunnels are manual tunnels, which require manual tunnel destination configuration.

Thus the correct answer of this question is A and B.

Question 6:

Which below option is true for DMVPN deployments? (Choose Three)

A. DMVPN can interoperate with the other vendors

B. DMVPN supports non-IP protocols

C. DMVPN supports multicast replication at the Hub

D. DMVPN can run over IPv6 transport

E. DMVPN supports full mesh topology

Answer 6:

DMVPN is a Cisco preparatory solution that cannot interoperate with the other vendor VPN solutions. It only supports IP tunneling as it was explained in the VPN chapter. Thus IS-IS is not supported over DMVPN.

DMVPN supports multicast but replication is done at the Hub. It is not Native Multicast as it is the case in GETVPN.

DMVPN can run over IPv6 transport and Hub and Spoke, Partial Mesh and Full mesh topologies can be created with DMVPN as explained in the VPN chapter.

That's why the correct answer of this question is C, D and E.

Question 7:

Which below options are true for DMVPN vs. GETVPN comparison? (Choose Three)

A. IPSEC scalability point of view GETVPN is much better than DMVPN

B. DMVPN provides multi point to multipoint topology but GETVPN cannot

C. DMVPN is a tunnel based technology but GETVPN is tunnelless technology

D. DMVPN is Cisco preparatory technology but GETVPN is standard based

E. DMVPN can run over Internet but GETVPN cannot.

Answer 7:

IPSEC scalability point of view GETVPN is much better compare to DMVPN since GETVPN uses Group Key.

DMVPN is tunnel-based technology and GETVPN is tunnelless. Both are Cisco preparatory.

DMVPN can run over Internet but GETVPN due to IP header preservation cannot.

Both can support multi point to multi point topology.

That's why the correct answer of this question is A, C and E.

Question 8:

Which below statements are true for the GETVPN? (Choose Three)

A. It is a tunnelless technology
B. It uses GDOI for key distribution
C. Multicast replication is done at the HUB
D. It cannot run over Public Internet due to IP Header preservation
E. OSPF can run over GETVPN

Answer 8:

GETVPN is tunnelless technology but routing protocols cannot run over GETVPN. GETVPN runs over routing protocol. So it is not an underlay VPN mechanism. It uses GDOI for the key distribution as it was explained in the VPN chapter.

Multicast is native in GETVPN so there is no HUB Multicast replication as it is the case in DMVPN.

It cannot run over Public Internet due to IP header preservation.

That's why the correct answer of this question is A, B and D.

Question 9:

Which below statements are true for LISP? (Choose Three)

A. LISP is an MAC in MAC encapsulation mechanism.
B. LISP can encapsulate IPv6 in IPv4

C. LISP can encapsulate IPv4 in IPv6
D. LISP can provide IP mobility
E. LISP comes encryption by default

Answer 9:

LISP is an IP in IP encapsulation mechanism, which allows IP mobility.

It can encapsulate IPv6 in IPv4 packets and vice versa.

It doesn't come with IPSEC encryption by default.

That's why the correct answer of this question is B, C and D.

Question 10:

Which below statements are true for DMVPN Phases? (Choose Four)

A. DMVPN Phase 1 supports spoke to spoke dynamic tunnels
B. DMVPN Phase 1 uses permanent point to point GRE tunnels on the spokes
C. DMVPN Phase 2 requires IP next hop preservation
D. DMVPN Phase 3 allows summarization
E. Only DMVPN Phase 2 and Phase 3 supports dynamic spoke to spoke tunnels thus full mesh topology can be created

Answer 10:

DMVPN Phase 1 doesn't support spoke-to-spoke dynamic tunnels. It uses point-to-point permanent GRE tunnels on the spoke. Hub still uses mGRE tunnels though.

DMVPN Phase 2 requires IP next hop reservation. Hub doesn't change the IP next hop to itself.

DMVPN Phase 3 allows summarization.

And only DMVPN Phase 2 and Phase 3 supports dynamic spoke-to-spoke tunnels, which allow full-mesh topology to be created.

That's why the answer of this question is B, C, D and E.

Chapter 7
IPV6 DESIGN

This chapter will start with basic IPv6 definition. Then below sections will be covered:

- IPv6 Business Drivers
- IPv6 Address Types
- IPv6 Routing Protocols Overview
- IPv6 Design and Deployment Methodology
- IPv6 Transition Mechanisms
- IPv6 Case Study
- IPv6 Design Review Question and Answers

WHAT IS IPV6?

Internet Protocol version 6 (IPv6) is the most recent version of the Internet Protocol (IP), the communications protocol that provides an identification and location system for computers on networks and routes traffic across the Internet.

IPv6 was developed by the Internet Engineering Task Force (IETF) to deal with the long-anticipated problem of IPv4 address exhaustion.

According to Google's statistics, on December 26, the world reached 9.98 percent IPv6 deployment, up from just under 6 percent a year earlier as you can see from the below chart.

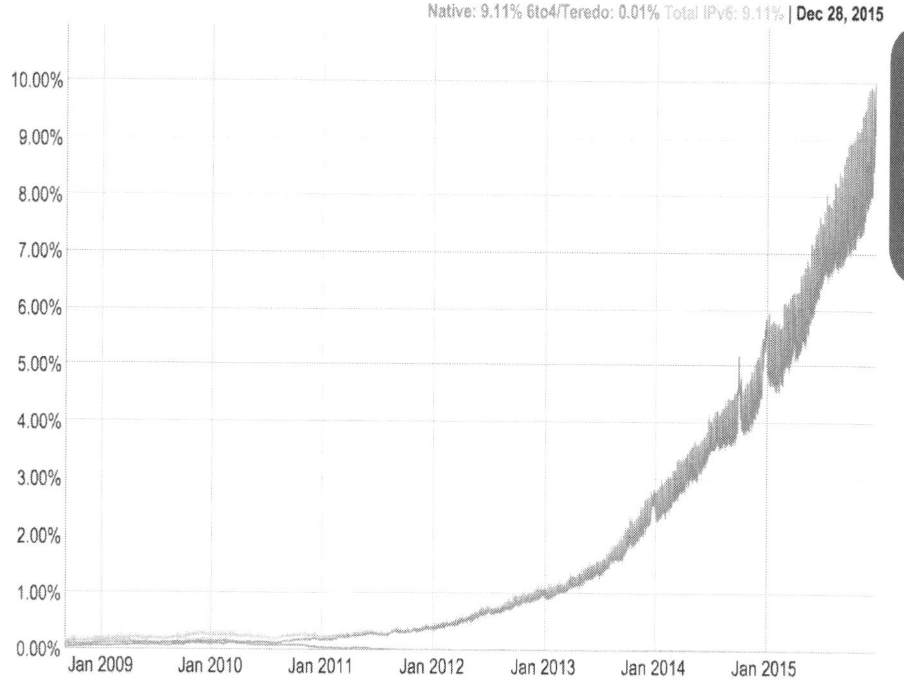

Google IPv6 Statistics 2016

Especially due to IPv4 address exhaustion, many Service Providers, Mobile Operators, and Cable MSOs have implemented Ipv6 for many years.

There are many business drivers for IPv6 in Enterprise, Internet Service Providers, Mobile Operator Networks, Cable companies today.

IPv6 Business Drivers:

IPv4 address exhaustion

Probably the biggest Business Driver for the IPv6 deployment is IPv4 address exhaustion. Almost all of the RIR (Regional Internet Registries) have allocated all IPv6 public address spaces already.

No one can receive receive an IPv4 address block from the Regional Internet Registries. There are many methods to survive without an IPv6 addresses for the Service Providers but none of them provides better ROI (Return On Investment) in the long term. These methods will be explained in the IPv6 Transition mechanisms section of this chapter.

IPv4 address exhaustion business driver is most common driver in the Service Provider/Operator domain.

Business Continuity

This business driver is applicable to any type of networks. Especially in the Enterprise networks, starting IPv6 design at the Internet Edge provides business continuity. Customers can reach to e-commerce website of the Company and business don't miss the opportunity. This approach is also called ' Thin Edge '. Thin edge IPv6 deployment method shows highest observed growth in the Enterprises.

Also there will be more IP address need in the Enterprise networks with the emerging applications such Internet Of Things (IOT).

The network today enables all enterprise business transactions. As enterprises move into emerging markets to expand their business, the network needs to grow, and more IP addresses need to be allocated.

Easier Network Mergers and Acquisitions

When one company acquires or merges with another, this often causes a conflict or "collision" in the RFC 1918 IPv4 private address space.

For example, one company might run a 192.x.x.x address space, and the company it acquires might also use this same address space.

Many companies deploy a NAT overlap pool for a period of time, where both companies communicate with each other over a non-overlapping address space such as 10.x.x.x.

This allows the hosts at both companies to communicate until one of the sites is readdressed.

IPv6 will remove the need for NAT and merger and acquisition scenarios will be much easier from the IP addressing point of view.

Government IT Strategy and Regulations

National IT strategies and government mandates across the globe have caused many enterprises and service providers to implement IPv6 to better support these government agencies (Private sector companies working with government agencies).

One example of how a government mandate influences the private sector to deploy IPv6 is when multiple U.S.-based defense contractors rapidly started their planning and deployment of IPv6 to support the U.S. federal IPv6 mandate of June 30, 2008. Many of these companies not only peer with federal agency networks but also provide IP-enabled services and products that would one day require IPv6.

Infrastructure Evolution

The underlying infrastructure for the Internet, and emerging developments in verticals such as energy management, power distribution, and other utility advancements, have matured and grown in size to the point of applying pressure to existing technologies, products, and IPv4.

The evolution of technologies in SmartGrid, broadband cable, and mobile operators now require more and more devices to connect to the Internet.

Regardless of the use case or technology, all these maturing technologies and use cases either already or soon will depend on IP as their means of communication. IPv4 cannot support these demands, and IPv6 is the way forward for each of these areas of development.

IPv6 Address Types

IPv6 Addressing rules are covered by multiples RFCs. Specifically in RFC 4291.

IPv6 Address Types are:

IPv6 Unicast: One to One (Global, Unique Local, Link local)

Anycast: One to Nearest (Allocated from Unicast)

Multicast: One to Many

Multiple IPv6 addresses of any Type (Unicast, Multicast or Anycast) may be assigned to a single Interface.

There is no Broadcast Address in IPv6. For the broadcast operation in IPv4, Ipv6 uses Multicast.

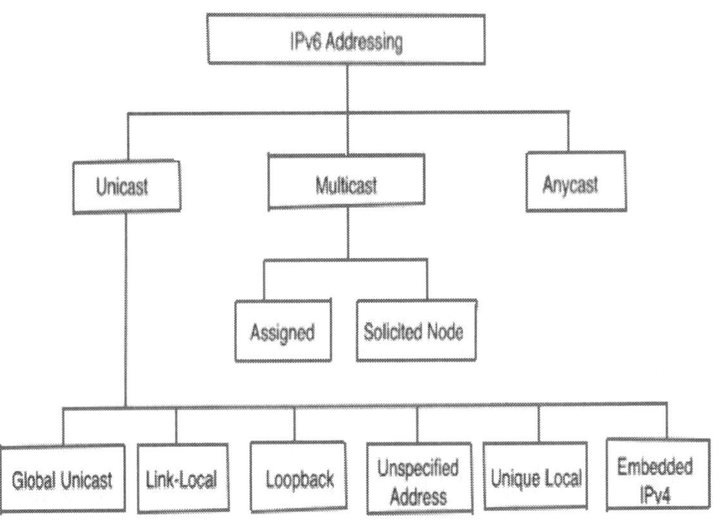

IPv6 Global Unicast Addresses: A routable address in the IPv6 Internet, similar to public IPv4 addresses.

IPv6 Link-local Addresses: Used only to communicate with devices on the same local link.

Loopback Address: An address not assigned to any physical interface and can be used for a host to send an IPv6 packet to itself.

Unspecified Address: Only used as a source address and indicates the absence of an IPv6 address.

Unique Local Addresses: Similar to private addresses in IPv4 (RFC 1918), these addresses are not intended to be routable in the IPv6 Internet.

IPv6 Routing Protocols

EIGRP and IS-IS, because of TLV (Type, Length, Value) information coding, doesn't require new protocol to support IPv6. Only the protocols extensions (New TLVs), allows these protocols to process IPv6 prefixes.

BGP doesn't require new version of protocol to support IPv6. New NLRI information for IPv6 address family is defined in BGP.

On the other hand OSPFv3 is the newer version of the OSPF that supports IPv6. OSPFv2 doesn't support IPv6 but OSPFv3, in addition to IPv6, supports IPv4 as well.

There are new LSA types in OSPFv3.

OSPFv2 vs. OSPFv3

Main advantage and the difference of OSPFv3 from the LSA structure and information processing point of view is; In OSPFv2, Router LSA contains both reachability and the topology information.

In OSPFv3, topology information is not carried in Router LSA. This brings scalability to network design because, unlike OSPFv2, if new loopback interface is added or new subnet is added to the network, routers in the network don't run Full SPF.

In OSPFv2, even creating a loopback interface would cause all the routers in the network to run full SPF, which is resource intensive task, especially for the low-end devices.

In the below OSPFv2 vs. OSPFv3 comparison table, you will see almost all similarities and the differences between the two protocols.

This table should be know by not only the network designers but also any network engineers, exam takers and those who consider to deploy IPv6 in their network.

Design Requirement	OSPFv2	OSPFv3
Scalability	Good	Better since Router and Network LSA doesn't contain prefix information but only topology information
Working on Full Mesh	Works well with mesh group	Works well with mesh group
Working on Hub and Spoke	Works poorly, require a lot of tuning	Works bad requires tuning

Design Requirement	OSPFv2	OSPFv3
Fast Reroute Support	Yes - IP FRR	Yes - IP FRR but limited platform support
Suitable on WAN	Yes	Yes
Suitable on Datacenter	DCs are full mesh. So, Not well	DCs are full mesh so Not well
Suitable on Internet Edge	No it is designed as an IGP	No it is designed as an IGP
Standard Protocol	Yes IETF Standard	Yes IETF Standard
New LSAs	None	Links LSA (Type 8) is used for adjaceny formation and link local scope only, Inter-Area-Prefix LSA (Type9) which is one of the biggest enhancement since it is used to carry prefix information only,inside an area
Transport	Multicast, 224.0.0.5 and 224.0.0.6	Same but with IPv6 addresses. Multicast. FF02::5 and FF02::6
Reachability info handeling	Inside an Area, Router and Network LSA carries the reachability information,between areas reachability info is carried in Summary(Type3) LSA	Inside an area reachability information is carried in Intra Area Prefix LSA (Type9) which is new LSA type, inter area prefixes are still carried in Type 3 LSA but name is changed as Inter-Area prefix LSA
Topology info handeling	Inside an Area Router and Network LSA carries the topology information,topology info is not carried beyond an area	Same.Inside an Area Router and Network LSA carries the topology information,topology info is not carried beyond an area
Stuff Experince	Very well known	Not well known, especially topology and reachability information handling,Multi Area Adjaceny and new LSA types should be understood better
Overlay Tunnel Support	Yes it supports	Yes it supports
MPLS Traffic Engineering Support	Yes with CSPF or external controller	Yes, with CSPF or external controller
Security	MD5 Authentication	Authentication is removed since it runs on top of IPv6, IPv6 supports IPSEC and Authentication, this simplifies the OSPF header
Suitable as Enterprise IGP	Yes	Yes
Suitable as Service Provider IGP	Yes	Definitely
Complexity	Easy	Moderate
Resource Requirement	Full SPF runs on prefix or topology change so it is worse than OSPFv3	If topology doesn't change, full SPF is not needed. Prefix information is carried in new LSA, not in Router LSA anymore
IPv6 Support	No	Yes

CHAPTER 7

Design Requirement	OSPFv2	OSPFv3
IPv4 Support	Yes	Yes
Default Convergece	Slow	Even slower if multiple address families are used
Troubleshooting	Easy	Harder,requires understanding IPv6 addressing, after that it is same packet types, LSA, LSU, DBD
Routing Loop	Inter area prefixes should be received from ABR,all non-backbone areas should be connected to the backbone area	Same as OSPFv2. Inter area prefixes should be received from ABR,all non-backbone areas should be connected to the backbone area

OSPF v2 vs. OSPFv3 Technical Comparison Table

IPv6 Design and Deployment Methodology

IPv6 deployment can be done in many ways. In this section, most common deployment methodology will be explained.

This is not a migration methodology from IPv4 to IPv6 but steps will explain how to deploy IPv6 on any type of networks.

If some feature or mechanism is only applicable for specific business type, it will be highlighted.

Prior to IPv6 deployment on the network infrastructure, some jobs need to be completed first.

First three tasks in the below should be completed before doing IPv6 related technical tasks such as Routing Protocol configuration, Transition mechanism deployment and so on.

IPv6 Deployment Steps:

1. Goal and Strategy should be identified.
2. Network Readiness Assessment
3. Network Optimization/ Garbage Collection
4. IPv6 Address Procurement
5. Developing an IPv6 Addressing Plan
6. IPv6 Strategy Deployment (Dual-Stack, Tunneling, Translation)

These are the steps we will take a look in further detail.

- **IPv6 Deployment Goal:**

Ultimate goal for the IPv6 deployment is to provide IPv6 to the end users, customers. Enterprise Company might want to provide the IPv6 for their internal users or for the customers.

Service Providers may want to provide IPv6 for their Broadband customers, wireless customers, content providers and so on.

Also IPv6 deployment strategy should be identified at the very early stage.

For the two types of networking transport, there are different strategies.

- **IP Transport**:

If the network infrasture is based on IP, then Dual-Stack, Tunneling or Translation IPv6 transition mechanisms are deployed.

MPLS Transport:

6PE and 6VPE are the best strategies for the MPLS based backbone infrastructure. These will be explained later in this chapter in detail.

1. Network Readiness Assessment:

- You should check whether your infrastructure is ready for IPv6.
- What can run IPv6 today and what needs to be upgraded?

Documentation is the key for IPv6 deployment. Good documentation helps for the IPv6 deployment a lot.

For the network infrastructure, you should first check whether the routers are IPv6 capable. Because if you cannot route the packets across the network infrastructure, your servers and the systems will not be able to serve.

Critical systems such as DNS, E-mail and others can be checked but these can be done in later stage as well.

Remote offices, POP locations, Datacenters and other places in the network should be analyzed.

Hardware capabilities of the devices such as RAM, Flash Memory,

CPU and also software versions should be documented.

You should know which technologies, protocols and the features are used in IPv4 infrastructure. Because you will look whether your software and hardware will support those in IPv6.

Does the existing software provide IPv6 features that you use for your IPv4 infrastructure?

Maybe with software upgrade you may have the capabilities that you want. Maybe upgrading software can provide the capability, which you need, but you don't have enough memory to upgrade.

In Enterprise networks, application owners should check whether their Applications are IPv6 capable.

Maybe not and need to change the hardware.

As you can see, all these information will be needed.

Many vendors provide an automation tool that you can collect all these information.

2. Network Optimization and Garbage Collection

- If you finish the second step that is Network Readiness assessment which mean the network is ready for IPv6. But before starting technical IPv6 tasks, we may want to optimize our existing network.

Network optimization mean, checking the best practices for the technologies, looking for optimal routing, removing unused features, securing the infrastructure and so on.

If you are starting RIPv2, you may want to migrate it to other protocol for example.

IPv4 might have been deployed on the network for many years and you probably haven't looked for the optimization.

IPv6 deployment is a good time to optimize the existing network so IPv6 can work on a clean infrastructure.

We should avoid the mistakes that have been done in IPv4.

3. IPv6 Address Procurement

IPv6 addresses can be received either from ISPs (Local Internet Registries) or RIR (Regional Internet Registries)

Regional Internet Registries (ARIN, APNIC, RIPE and so on) assign /32 to the Service Providers. This provides 65k /48 subnets. If company requires more, they can get as well.

If the IPv6 address space is received from the ISPs, allocation policy in general is /48. This provides 65k /64 subnets.

Multihoming issue in IPv4 is the same in IPv6.

If the Enterprise Company is looking for multihoming, address space should be received from the RIR to avoid readdressing and other issues. When the prefixes are received from the RIR, those prefixes are called **Provider Independent (PI)** prefixes. It is also known as PI space.

4. IPv6 Addressing Plan

When creating an IPv6 addressing plan, there are couple things need to be considered by every business

- Scalable plan should be created
- Assigning IPv6 addresses at the Nibble boundary
- BCP (Best Current Practices) should be known
- Address space can be distributed based on function

Let's take a look at why assigning IPv6 address at the nibble boundary is important.

Assigning an IPv6 addresses at the Nibble Boundary

IPv6 offers network engineers more flexible addressing plan.

Nibble is 4 bits of IPv6 address.

Nibble boundary means dividing IPv6 address space based on the address numbering.

Each character in IPv6 address represents 4 bits. Which mean that IPv6 addressing plan can be done on 4-bit boundaries.

Let's take a look at below example:

Consider the address block 2001:abc:0:10::/61

The range of IPv6 addresses in this block are:

2001:0abc:0000:00**10**:0000:0000:0000:0000

2001:0abc:0000:00**17**:ffff:ffff:ffff:ffff

As you can see from the above example, this subnet only runs from 0010 to 0017.

Next block is 2001:abc:0:18::/61.

In this range, the IPv6 addresses are:

2001:0abc:0000:00**18**:0000:0000:0000:0000

2001:0abc:0000:00**1f**:ffff:ffff:ffff:ffff

As you can see from the above two example, when you divide the IPv6 address by /61, you don't use the Nibble boundary.

Instead of subdividing with /61, if we divide the address range with /60,

2001:abc:0:10::/60

Then the address range would be:

2001:0abc:0000:00**10**:0000:0000:0000:0000

2001:0abc:0000:001f:ffff:ffff:ffff:ffff

Note that this subnet uses the entire nibble range, which is 0 to f.

And then this range (0 to f) can have a particular meaning within the entire IPv6 address block. For example; infrastructure addressing for a particular POP location.

There are Infrastructure addressing part and the Customer/end user part in the IPv6 addressing.

In the Service provider network, Infrastructure is Core backbone, POP locations, Datacenter and so on. Customer IPv6 addressing depends on the business. Some Service Providers can have Broadband, Cable modem, Business customers and so on.

Let's look at Service Provider IPv6 addressing plan.

Service Provider IPv6 Addressing Plan:

Service Providers receive /32 from the RIR (Regional Internet Registries)

Different Service Providers may have different allocation policy. As you will see in the below examples, one Service Provider may assign /48 for whole the infrastructure, another SP can assign one /48 per region.

It depends on the Service Providers size and geographical distribution.

1. Service provider Infrastructure Addresses:

Loopback Interfaces:

- One /64 is allocated for all loopback interfaces in the network

- /128 is assigned per loopback is assigned

Backbone Interfaces:

- One /48 is allocated for the whole backbone
- This provides 65k subnets
- Some multi national companies can assign /48 per region
- Between region summarization provides scalability

Local Area Networks:

- /64 per LAN is assigned
- Some networks in real life assign /96 as well.

Point-to-Point Links:

- Best practice is using /127 for the point to point links as per RFC 6164
- Many operators are reserving /64 but assigning /127 for the point to point links

Network Operation Center and the Shared Services:

ISP NOC is considered as the part of Infrastructure and get IPv6 address from the /48 which is allocated for the Infrastructure.

Shared services/critical systems such as ISP DNS, Email systems and so on also considered as the part of Infrastructure and get the IPv6 address from the /48 which is allocated for the Infrastructure.

2. Service Provider Customer Address Allocation Plan and Customer Point-to-Point Links Address Allocation Plan

These are the Service Provider to Customer links and should be received an IPv6 address from the different range. These links shouldn't be considered as Infrastructure links and shouldn't be carried even in the SP Infrastructure IGP.

Service Providers should keep separate their Customer and the infrastructure IPv6 addresses.

- One /48 is allocated for all the SP customer links.
- This /48 is divided per POP.
- Customer addresses shouldn't be carried in the Infrastructure IGP. For the monitoring purpose these addresses can be carried through the IBGP.

Customer Site IPv6 Address Allocation Plan

These are the IPv6 addresses assigned to the Customers by the Service Providers. These are not the point-to-point SP to customer link addresses.

Based on the size of their network, Service Providers assign different size of IPv6 address to their customers.

In general, Service Providers assign:

- /64 is for the very small network.
- /56 is for the Small to medium businesses (/56 provides 256 subnets)
- /48 is for the Enterprises (/48 provides 65k subnets)
- Similar to Customer to SP point-to-point links addresses, Customer Addresses shouldn't be carried in the SP IGP. Those prefixes should be carried in BGP. IGP is not designed to carry millions of prefixes.
- The Service Provider shouldn't assign customer IPv6 addresses per POP basis. Because Customers might be moving and allocating IPv6 address per Region basis for the Customers make more sense.

5. IPv6 Strategy Deployment

You should remember that deploying IPv6 on the existing infrastructure don't break the IPv4.

The common question is; where should we start?

Should we start from the Core to the Edge or from Edge to the Core? Or should we deploy IPv6 at the Internet Edge only?

Important to remember that IPv6 don't have to be deployed everywhere by the businesses. If the goal is to have IPv6 presence for the Enterprise e-commerce business for example, IPv6 might be deployed only at the Internet Edge.

For the Service Provider, things are different. All the backbone infrastructure, customer connections, ISP Peering links and the Transit connections are deployed IPv6.

- Core to the Edge Model IPv6 Deployment:

This model is used when you have no defined time frame for deployment, but you want to have your network prepared for eventuality of IPv6 services one day. The core of the network is chosen as you have a smaller number of devices to touch, you can deploy IPv6 without interrupting the IPv4 part of the network.

You can break the things several times, redo your addressing and still not hurt the network. Once you learn stuff like routing, addressing, QoS and other important services, you can then start dual stacking from the core towards the edge (i.e. campus, branch, POP locations etc.)

- Edge to the Core Model IPv6 Deployment:

The second model is Edge to the Core.

This is a bit more difficult deployment model as it relies nearly 100% on tunneling.

It is used by those organizations that need to connect endpoints to the Internet or their own internal Data Centers and apps that are IPv6-enabled and do it in a hurry.

This may be used by a vendor who is writing software that is IPv6-aware and they need their developers to have access to an IPv6 environment to do their job. They may not have the luxury of time or money to dual stack the whole network at once so they start small with an overlay deployment. As time goes on the network underneath the tunneling or overlay environment can be dual stack enabled and then the tunnels can go away.

This model is seen in the Enterprise businesses not in the Service Providers networks.

- Internet-Edge Only Model IPv6 Deployment:

The third IPv6 deployment model is the Internet Edge-Only model. This is quite popular these days in the E-commerce business especially

The organization can represent its services and content over both the existing IPv4 connection and the new IPv6 connection.

When the model is selected by the business, all the necessary interfaces should be configured according the IPv6 address plan, which has been done in the earlier stage.

Routing protocols are configured.

Don't forget that OSPFv2 don't support IPv6. OSPFv3 supports both IPv4 and IPv6.

Depending on the selected Model, IPv6 transition technology will be put in place.

Let's take a look at most common IPv6 transition technologies.

IPv6 Transition Mechanisms

The only available public IP addresses are IPv6 addresses. But vast majority of the content is still working on IPv4. How IPv6 users can connect to the IPv4 world and How IPv4 users can reach to the IPv6 content. This is accomplished with the IPv6 transition technologies.

Probably the IPv6 transition technologies is a misleading term. Because; IPv4 infrastructure is not removed with these technologies. Thus probably the IPv6 integration technologies is a better term.

But still throughout this section I will be using IPv6 transition technologies.

There are three types of IPv6 Transition Technology.

1. Dual Stack

- IPv6 + IPv4

The entire infrastructure is running both IPv4 and IPv6.

2. Tunnels

- IPV6 - IPv4 – IPv6
- IPv4 – IPv6 – IPv4

Two IPv6 islands communicate over IPv4 part of the network or two IPv4 islands communicate over IPv6 part of the network.

3. Translation

- IPv6 – IPv4 (NAT64)
- Private IPv4 – Public IPv4 (NAT44)

With translation, IPv6 only device can communicate with IPv4 only device. But they think that they communicate with the same version of device.

IPv6 Translation Mechanisms:

Most common IPv6 translation mechanism is NAT64 +DNS64.

It replaces older version translation mechanism NAT-PT. NAT-PT is deprecated due to DNS security issues. DNS Application Layer Gateway were integrated in NAT-PT.

With NAT64 + DNS64 mechanism, DNS entity is separated from the NAT entity.

In this mechanism, IPv6 only device can communicate with IPv4 only device over IPv6 only network.

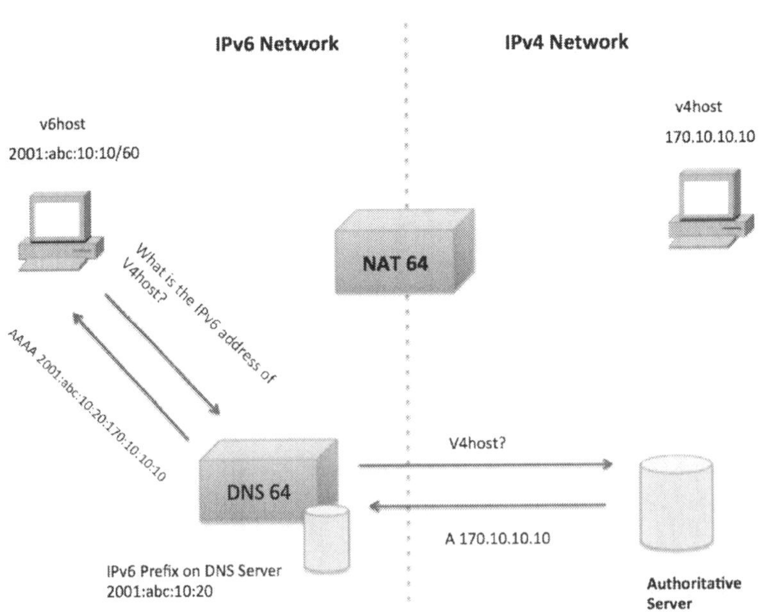

NAT64+DNS64 IPv6 Translation

In the above picture, on the left v6 host, which is in the IPv6 network, wants to communicate with v4 host, which is in the IPv4 network.

When IPv6 host wants to communicate with the ipv4 host, it sends a DNS query. This query passed through the DNS64. DNS64 then queries send this query to the authoritative DNS server, which is in the IPv4 world.

Authoritative DNS server sends an ‘ A ‘ record back.

DNS64 translate this A record into a AAAA record which is IPv4 address. It embeds IPv4 ‘ A ‘ record in to and IPv4 prefix that is assigned to DNS64. Resulting IPv6 address is called IPv6 Synthetized address.

Then packet goes to the NAT64 device; it can use the embedded IPv4 address inside the IPv6 address (AAAA from the DNS), removes the IPv6 part and create a stateful mapping table.

In this model, IPv6 host thinks that it communicates with the IPv6 device (DNS64), and v4 host thinks that it communicates with the IPv4 device (Authoritative IPv4 DNS server).

Stateful IPv6 translation mechanism problems:

There are many problems with NAT64 + DNS64 Translation. This is the common problem of Stateful address translation. Stateful Load Balancing, which is one of the techniques used in Enterprise IPv6 Internet Edge only deployment, also suffer from the same problems.

Stateful IPv6 translation problems:

- Traffic has to be symmetrical. Stateful devices drops asymmetrical traffic flows.
- Many applications will break because of NAT
- Some IPSEC modes don’t work through NAT
- There will be problems with timing in Mobile networks
- Logging will be a problem and many government forces operator to provide the logs
- There are much more problems special to the different kind of networks. These are common ones only.

IPv6 Tunneling Mechanisms:

Tunnels are used to send IPv6 traffic over IPv4 network or IPv4 traffic over IPv6 network.

There are many tunneling solutions proposed and here common ones will be shown only.

In general there are two types of Tunneling solutions.

Manual Tunnels:

For any type of tunnel, tunnel endpoints should be known and reachable. In Manual Tunnels, Tunnel endpoints are manually configured.

They are mostly used for permanent site-to-site connectivity.

IP-in-IP and GRE are the manual tunnels.

6PE and 6VPE, which are the MPLS based tunneling methods are also considered as Manual Tunneling technologies.

Automatic Tunnels:

Commonly used for transient connectivity. They could be site-to-site or host-to-host tunnels.

Within Automatic Tunnels, there must be an an automatic way to find to tunnel end points.

Every Automatic tunneling solution either encapsulates IPv4 tunnel endpoints in IPv6 Address or it consults an Authoritative server for the tunnel endpoints. (Remember LISP?).

Embedded Tunnel Endpoints Automatic IPv6 Tunneling Mechanisms:

1. 6to 4 Tunnels

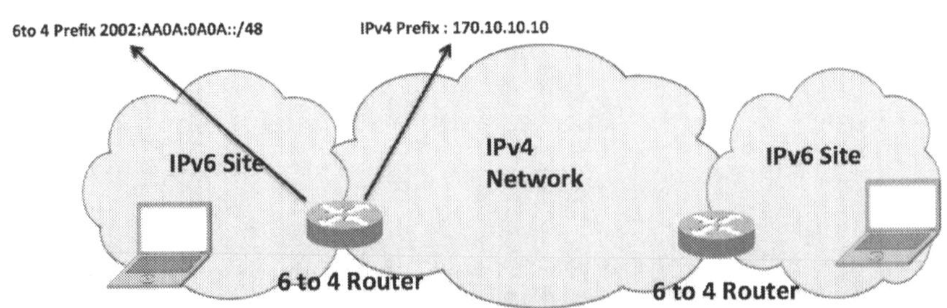

6to4 is a fairly common Automatic Tunneling mechanism in the Service Provider networks. As you can see from the above picture as well, IPv4 address is embedded in IPv6 prefix.

In the above example, there are two IPv6 sites which are connected over an IPv4 network.

There are 6to4 routers. Those routers need to understand how to tunnel IPv6 in IPv4 packets.

6to4 uses reserved 16bits prefix which is 2002, next 32 bits, after 2002 IPv6 prefix is the Hexadecimal version of the IPv4 interface address.

Although above example shows two routers connecting IPv6 islands, 6to4 tunneling mechanism could run between two hosts as well.

6to4 Automatic Tunneling Problems:

* 6to4 tunnels use IANA reserved 6to4 prefix which is 2002::/16.
* In order to reach the outside world, 6to4 relay router is needed.
* ISPs cannot use their IPv6 address pool for the Tunneling.

2. 6RD AUTOMATIC TUNNELS

6rd is a superset of 6to4 tunnels and many Service Providers deployed this tunneling mechanism in their network. First deployed by one of the France ISPs, called Free Telecom.

Operationally, very similar to 6to4 tunnels which encapsulate IPv6 packets in IPv4 packet. Thus 6rd is an IPv6 over IPv4 tunneling mechanisms.

It is commonly deployed for the Broadband customers by the Service Providers.

In order to support 6rd, broadband CPEs which are generally Modem need to support 6rd.

Basically in those deployments Broadband CPEs (Customer Premises Equipment) should have IPv6 and 6rd capable software. This can be considered, as drawback of 6rd but many of the solution requires not only IPv6 capable device but also specific tunneling mechanism capability.

There is also Host to host Automatic tunneling mechanism that uses embedded end point address concept. An ISATAP tunnel is an example for the host-to-host tunnels.

There is a Tunnel Broker concept in Automatic Tunneling mechanisms, which is also known as Semi-Automated tunnels. Uses authoritative server to find a tunnel end point.

3. Dual Stack

Dual stack is possibly the simplest IPv6 transition mechanism to implement. Every interface, applications and host runs IPv6 and IPv4 at the same time.

Dual stack operation is driven by DNS.

If destination address comes from DNS in an A record only, then communication is done via IPv4.

If destination address from DNS in a AAAA record only, then communication is done via IPv6.

If both A and AAAA record return, most of the applications prefer IPv6.

But the biggest problem in Dual Stack is, if there is no more IPv4 addresses available, how every interface can have IPv4 as well? Especially for the Service Provider networks!

Common solution for this issue by many of the companies is CGN (Carrier Grade NAT), which is also known as LSN (Large Scale NAT).

Carrier Grade NAT is doing NAT44 operation in large scale, in the Service provider network.

Service provider instead of assigning Public IPv4 address to each customer, they assign IPv4 private address.

In CGN, globally unique IPv4 address pool moves from customer edge to more centralized location in the Service Provider network.

There are three CGN architectures.

Three Carrier Grade NAT solutions:

1. NAT444
2. NAT464
3. DS-Lite

1. NAT 444

This solution uses three IPv4 layers.

Customers IPv4 private space is NATed to Service Provider assigned IPv4 private space first.

Then second NAT44 operation is done from Service Provider assigned IPv4 private address space to Service Provider IPv4 public address.

In this solution there are two layers of NAT44. One on the customer CPE another on the Service Provider network. Potential problem is many application which may work through one layer of NAT, will not work in two layers of NAT.

Second problem is Service Provider IPv4 private address space can conflict with the Customer IPv4 address space.

2. NAT464

Due to potential address conflict between customer and the Service Provider private IPv4 address spaces, another solution proposed by IETF was NAT464.

In this solution, Customer IPv4 private address space is NATed from IPv4 private to IPv6 address. On the customer CPE NAT 64 operation is needed.

Second NAT in this solution would be on the Service Provider network. Second NAT would be also NAT64.

This solution requires two times NAT64 operation and nobody implemented it.

3. Dual-Stack Lite (DS-Lite)

DS-Lite is an IPv4 in IPv6 tunneling solution from the customer site to the Service Provider.

Service Provider to customer connection is IPv6.

This solution requires DS-Lite capable CPE at the customer site. But this CPE doesn't do IPv6 to IPv4 translation. It does tunneling. It tunnels IPv4 customer packets in IPv6 packets. Then packet is sent to the CGN box in the Service Provider network.

When CGN receives IPv4 customer packets, it does the translation from IPv4 private customer address to IPv4 Public address.

Today, there is not many DS-Lite capable CPE.

Tunneling solutions should be considered as just a temporary solution. They are not IPv6 alternatives.

Some design thoughts on the Dual-Stack, Tunneling and Translation Solutions:

There are mainly three IPv6 transition methods; Dual-Stack, Tunneling and Translation.

Careful engineers can understand the difference between IPv6 migration and IPv6 transition.

All of these three technologies are used to have IPv6 protocol capabilities in addition to IPv4.

They are not migration mechanisms. Migration means removing IPv4 completely and running only IPv6 in the network, which might not be the case at least for the next decade.

There is a saying in the industry, Dual-stack where you can, tunnel when you must, translate if you have a gun in your head.

Vendor materials and many industry experts also recommend dual-stack as the best approach, but it is definitely misleading.

They shouldn't do this and you should think at least three times when you listen vendor engineer.

In order to understand why the above statement is not true (dual-stack is not the best approach for IPv6 design), we have to understand what is IPv6 dual-stack in the first place.

What does really IPv6 Dual-stack mean?

Dual-stack refers to running IPv6 and IPv4 in the network together. But not only on the routers and switches but also on all the links, host operating systems and most importantly on the applications.

In the Enterprise networks, this can be local area network, wide area network and the datacenters but in the service provider networks, it will be access nodes, pre-aggregation, aggregation, edge and core networks, also datacenters and the RAN (Radio Access Network) network, mobile handset and the applications inside handset, CPE modem and many other devices.

As you can see, it is not just about network routers that IPv6 capable but everything in the network that needs to support IPv6.

Actually the easiest part is to enable IPv6 dual-stack on the routers. Hardest two parts of the IPv6 dual-stack deployment are the applications and the CPEs.

CPE is a term used in the Service Provider networks, which define the devices in the customer location.

For example, ADSL modem is a CPE for the broadband service.

Since there might be millions of ADSL modem which need to support IPv6, imagine the size of the deployment, and time to complete these types of deployments, especially if hardware needs to be replaced.

Also since with Dual-Stack, in addition to IPv4, you will have IPv6 as well, memory and CPU requirements will be much more compare to IPv6 only network or other IPv6 transition technologies.

Thus, you change the routers with the bigger ones (Scale-UP) generally, which is good for the networking vendors (Juniper, Alcatel, Cisco etc.). It wouldn't be wrong if I say that this is one of the reasons they are advertising that dual-stack is the best approach for IPv6 design.

If you think that dual-stack is hard if not impossible for many of this network just because the scale of the deployment, you are wrong. There are other things.

IPv4 address exhaustion and common solutions:

As you know public IPv4 addresses have been exhausted. Most of the RIRs (Regional Internet Registry) already assigned their last IPv4 address blocks to the Service Providers. So if you go to the RIPE, ARIN or any other RIR today and ask IPv4 address, you might not get anything. IPv4 is done.

This doesn't mean Service Providers ran out of IPv4 addresses as well. So as an Enterprise customer, if you ask your Service Provider to assign an IPv4 address, you might still get small block, but many of my customers recently tried to get new address block (Very small, /25, /26) and their service providers asked justifications and wanted the customer to pay them a lot of money.

But how can service providers solve their IPv4 issue if they cannot receive an IPv4 address from the Regional Registries?

Very common answer is CGN (Carrier Grade NAT). Most of the Service Providers today implement Carrier Grade NAT.

CGN is also known as LSN (Large Scale NAT). And in my opinion, it should be called LSN since there is nothing for CGN to be a carrier grade. It is just a NAT.

With CGN, Service Providers do NAT44 on the CPE from private address to another private address (Well known /10 prefix which is allocated by IANA) and another NAT44 on the Service Provider network. That's why you can hear CGN, LSN, Double NAT or NAT444. All of them refer to the same thing.

But with CGN you are not enabling IPv6.

CGN is a way to solve the IPv4 depletion problem in a very problematic way. Companies are also using trade-market to purchase IPv4 public addresses. Average cost per IPv4 address is around 8-10$ currently. This might increase by the time. And it would be wise to expect to see much bigger DFZ space by the time because of de-aggregation.

With CGN, IPv4 private addresses are shared among many customers and those shared addresses are NATed at the CGN node twice.

There will be always some applications, which run IPv4 only; in this case you have to use a Translator.

I am talking about IPv6 to IPv4 translator and vice versa. So dual-stack may not be possible because fancy – free a lot of applications don't support IPv6 today. (Most common example is Skype and some VOIP applications)

Common solution for translating IPv6 to IPv4 is NAT 64 + DNS 64 which was explained earlier in this chapter.

NAT-PT was the early version of IPv6 to IPv4 translator but there were security problems such as DNSSEC thus NAT-PT is obsolete now.

NAT 64 + DNS 64 is good for translating v6 to v4 so IPv6 only host can reach IPv4 only host but wait, that's not all yet either.

How you will support an application, which doesn't rely on DNS?

Skype is very common applications, which uses hard coded IPv4 addresses and doesn't rely on DNS.

NAT 64 + DNS 64 cannot be a solution for that. Just because of these types of applications, companies that enabled dual-stack everywhere, place a translation at the host device.

For example, Mobile operators use 464XLAT on the handheld devices to support IPv4 application.

NAT46 is performed at the handset (Smart phone, tablet, etc.) by providing dummy IPv4 address to the application, and performing 4 to 6 NAT at the handset.

For example T-Mobile in U.S deployed 464XLAT to support IPv6 only devices to run over IPv6 only network.

What about IPv6 tunneling? When it might be needed?

Tunneling is necessary if the company cannot enable IPv6 on some part of the network. For example if Broadband Service Providers DSLAM doesn't support IPv6, it is hard if not impossible to replace those equipments until the hardware refresh cycle.

Most common tunneling technology by these types of companies is 6rd (6 Rapid Deployment).

Or Enterprise networks, which want to enable IPv6 in their LAB environment, need tunneling over the IPv4 network until all the links and routers support dual-stack.

IPv6 6rd can be used as a router-to-router IPv6 over IPv4 environment for this type of deployment, as well as host-to-host or host to router tunnelling technologies such as ISATAP can be used.

Conclusion:

There will always be a need to use all these transition mechanisms together in the network. Dual-Stack is the hardest to support IPv6 transition method among all the others by the large-scale companies and the IPv6 to IPv4 translation technologies breaks most of the applications.

Tunnelling is a solution to support IPv6 over IPv4 network and can be the interim solution until dual-stack is enabled on all the nodes and links.

Our end goal shouldn't be IPv6 dual-stack! Our goal is to have an IPv6 only network and remove IPv4 completely. This can be only achieved with networking vendors, Service Providers, Operating System manufacturer, application developers, website owners, CDN companies and many others.

Otherwise CGN or Trade-market (Buying IPv4 public address from the other companies) type of interim solution only buy a time and those solutions will be expensive for the companies day by day without IPv6.

There are companies, which has IPv6 only network today!

IPV6 REVIEW QUESTIONS

Question 1:

Fictitious Service Provider company has been planning IPv6 access for their residential broadband customers. Which solutions below don't require access node changes in the Service Provider domain? (Choose Three)

A. CGN

B. 6rd

C. 6to4

D. D. IPSEC

E. DS-Lite

F. Dual Stack

Answer 1:

IPSEC is not an option. Dual Stack requires IPv6 support in addition to IPv4 everywhere.

DS-Lite require IPv6 access nodes.

6rd and 6to4 are the IPv6 tunnelling mechanisms over IPv4 Service Provider infrastructure.

6rd and 6to4 don't require access node upgrade such as DSLAM, in the case of residential broadband upgrade.

But both 6to4 and 6rd still require CPE upgrade on the customer site.

CGN (LSN) doesn't require access node upgrade as well; most of the residential equipment already supports NAT44.

Thus the answer of this question is A, B and C.

Question 2:

Which below mechanisms allow asymmetric IPv6 routing design?

A. 6rd

B. 6to4

C. NAT 64 +DNS 64

D. D. DS-Lite

Answer 2:

Asymmetric routing is possible with the stateless mechanisms only.

6rd is the stateless tunnelling mechanisms.

NAT64 + DNS 64 can be stateful or stateless, thus they are not the correct answer. DS-Lite has CGN component, which is always stateful.

That's why answer of this question is A, 6rd.

Question 3:

What is the biggest cost component during IPv6 transition design?

A. CPE

B. Access Nodes

C. Core Nodes

D. Training

E. Application Development

Answer 3:

Biggest cost component is CPE (Customer Premises Equipment).

In case IPv6 is not supported on the CPE, enabling it on software requires operational expenses, changing the hardware requires both operational and capital expenses.

If Service Provider needs to change CPE for 10 Million customers and every CPE cost only 50$, 500million $ is required only for CAPEX.

That's why answer of this question is A, CPE.

Question 4:

Which below options might be a possible problems with NAT 64 + DNS 64 design? (Choose Three)

A. It may not support IPv4 only applications such as Skype

B. Duplicate DNS entries can come if company has more than one DNS

C. It doesn't support DNSSEC

D. It doesn't translate IPv4 to IPv6

E. Stateful NAT 64 + DNS 64 makes routing design harder

Answer 4:

As they have been explained in the IPv6 chapter, NAT64+DNS64 may not support IPv4 only applications such as Skype. Duplicate DNS entries can come if company has more than one DNS and Stateful NAT 64 + DNS 64 makes routing design harder.

Thus the correct answer of this question is A, B and E.

Question 5:

If IPv6 only node will reach to IPv4 only content, which below mechanism is used?

A. A. 6rd tunneling

B. B. Dual Stack

C. C. Translation

D. D. Host to Host tunnelling

Answer 5:

Translation mechanism is needed. Tunnelling cannot solve the problem.

Question 6:

Which below options are used as IPv6 transition mechanisms? (Choose Three)

A. Dual-Stack

A. B. Edge to Core Ipv6 design approach

B. C. Tunneling

C. D. Translation

D. E. IPv6 Neighbor Discovery

Answer 6:

As it is explained in detail in the IPv6 chapter, Dual-Stack, Tunneling and the Translation are the IPv6 transition mechanisms.

That's why, answer of this question is A, C and D.

Question 7:

Which subnet mask length is used in IPv6 on point-to-point links for consistency?

A. A. /56

B. B. /64

C. C. /96

D. D. /126

E. E. /127

Answer 7:

/64 is used in IPv6 on point-to-point links for consistency.

Although there was discussions around its usage and some people considered initially that it was wasting of address space, general design recommendation is using /64 or /127 for point to point links and using /64 everywhere including point to point link provides consistency.

Question 8:

Which IPv6 design method consumes more resources on the network nodes?

A. Dual-Stack

B. Tunneling mechanisms

C. Translation mechanisms

D. IPv6 only network

E. Carrier Grade NAT

Answer 8:

Dual Stack on the network nodes consumes more CPU and more memory compare to tunnelling and the translation mechanisms, which are used for IPv6 transition.

That's why; the answer of this question is A, Dual-stack.

Question 9:

What does Dual-Stack mean?

A. A. Enabling IPv6 and IPv4 on all the networking nodes

B. B. Enabling IPv6 and IPv4 on all the networking nodes and the links

C. C. Enabling IPv6 and IPv4 on all the networking nodes, links, hosts and applications

D. D. Enabling IPv6 and IPv4 on the core, aggregation and access network nodes.

Answer 9:

Dual stack is providing both IPv4 and IPv6 connectivity to all the networking nodes, links, hosts and applications. That's why; answer of this question is C.

Question 10:

Fictitious Service Provider company requires more Public IPv4 addresses but due to IPv4 exhaustion they couldn't receive from the RIRs. What is the option for them to continue providing IPv4 services without enabling IPv6 on CPE, access and core network?

A. Carrier Grade NAT

B. DS-Lite

C. NAT64 + DNS64

D. 6rd

E. 6to4

Answer 10:

IPv4 exhaustion problem requires Carrier Grade NAT solution, which share public IPv4 addresses among multiple users by using NAT 44 on the CPE and NAT 44 on the SP domain. It is also called double NAT, Large Scale NAT, Dual NAT 44 or NAT444.

That's why answer of this question is A, Carrier Grade NAT.

Question 11:

Which below terms are used interchangeably for Carrier Grade NAT (CGN)? (Choose Three)

A. LSN

B. Double NAT

C. Service Provider NAT

D. CPE NAT

E. NAT 444

Answer 11:

LSN (Large Scale NAT), Double NAT, NAT 444 are used interchangeably for CGN. Thus, the answer of this question is A, B and E.

Question 12:

Which below options are used as an IPv6 over IPv4 tunnelling mechanism? (Choose Two).

A. 6to4

B. 6rd

C. NAT 64 + DNS64

D. DS-Lite

E. MAP-E

F. 464xlat

Answer 12:

Out of given options, IPv6 tunnelling mechanisms are 6to4 and 6rd. Remaining ones is used for IPv4 tunnelling. IPv4 service is tunneled over IPv6.

That's why; answer of this question is A and B.

Question 13:

What are the problems with Carrier Grade NAT IPv6 design? (Choose four)

A. Some applications doesn't work behind CGN

B. If the users behind same LSN, stateful devices might drop traffic, thus require traffic go through CGN node even if the traffic between nodes which are behind same LSN

C. IP address overlapping if Customer uses same private address range with the Service Provider

D. It requires IPv6 on the CPE nodes, thus CPEs have to be upgraded

E. Since it is stateful, asymmetric traffic is not allowed.

F. Since it is stateless, asymmetric traffic is not allowed.

Answer 13:

Some applications doesn't work behind CGN If the users behind same LSN, stateful devices might drop traffic, thus require traffic go through CGN node even if the traffic between nodes which are behind same LSN IP address overlapping if Customer uses same private address range with the Service Provider . Since it is stateful, asymmetric traffic is not allowed.

Correct answer of this question is A, B, C and E.

Question 14:

What are the problems with dual stack IPv6 design? (Choose Three)

A. It consumes more memory and CPU on the networking nodes compare to tunnelling and translation mechanisms

B. It doesn't solve IPv4 address exhaustion problems

C. It requires IPv6 support on all the CPE and Access nodes which are the most cost associated components

D. Troubleshooting wise it is harder compare to tunnelling and translation mechanisms

E. All of the above

Answer 14:

It consumes more memory and CPU on the networking nodes compare to tunnelling and translation mechanisms. It doesn't solve IPv4 address exhaustion problems. CPEs and hosts still require IPv4 address. Host private address is NATed to the CPE public IPv4 address (NAT44) It requires IPv6 support on all the CPE and Access nodes, which are the most cost associated components.

That's why; answer of this question is A, B and C.

Question 15:

What is the best IPv6 design method for MPLS Layer 3 VPN service?

A. Dual Stack

B. NAT 64 + DNS 64

C. 6rd

D. 6VPE

E. 6PE

Answer 15:

Best IPv6 design method for MPLS Layer 3 VPN service is 6VPE.

Question 16:

Which options are the IPv6 Automated Tunneling mechanisms? (Choose Three)

A. 6rd
B. 6over4
C. 6to4
D. Tunnel Brokers
E. NAT-PT
F. GRE Tunnels

Answer 16:

6rd, 6to4 and 6over4 are the automated IPv6 tunnelling mechanisms.

6over4 requires multicast on the network thus it is deprecated.

In all three mechanisms IPv4 addresses embedded in the IPv6 address.

Tunnel broker is a semi-automated mechanism. The Authoritative server provides tunnel destination address. NAT-PT is a translation mechanism and because of security issues it is deprecated.

GRE Tunnels are manual tunnelling mechanism.

That's why the answer of this question is; A, B and C.

Question 17:

Service Provider Company wants to implement DPI (Deep Packet Inspection) node in the network. Which below method would create a problem?

A. Tunneling
B. Dual-Stack
C. Native IPv4
D. Translation
E.

Answer 17:

Most of the DPI devices cannot work with the IPv6 tunnelling mechanisms. Thus using them with the DPI element can create a problem. There is no problem with the other options. Correct answer is Option A.

Question 18:

Enterprise Company implemented QoS on their network. Which below IPv6 design option method doesn't work well with QoS?

A. Dual Stack

B. Translation

C. IPv6 only

D. Tunneling

Answer 18:

Ipv6 tunnelling mechanisms don't work well with the QoS.

Question 19:

Which below options are used for host to host IPv6 tunnelling?

A. ISATAP

B. 6to4

C. 6rd

D. Teredo

E. IPv6 DAD

Answer 19:

ISATAP and the Teredo are used for host to host or host to router tunnelling.

Question 20:

Enterprise Company wants to have an experience with the IPv6. They have 50 IT Lab facilities and want to access IPv6 application in the datacenter. They don't have currently IPv6 on their network and they want to have an access immediately from the labs to the applications

Where would they start enabling IPv6?

A. Network Core first and IT labs should enable IPv6

B. No need for IPv6 on the network, they can use translation

C. IT labs should be enabled IPv6 and tunnel to the DC

D. Placing CGN box at the central place solves is best design options for them

Answer 20:

As it is explained in the IPv6 chapter, they are looking for Edge to the Core model. IT labs should be enabled IPv6 and tunnel to the DC. Answer of this question is C.

Question 21:

Which mechanism can be used to deploy IPv6 services in an IPv4 only backbone?

A. NAT64 at the edge of the network

B. 6PE in the backbone network

C. 6RD on CPEs and 6RD BRs at the Edge of the network

D. DS-Lite at the Edge of the network

Answer 21:

Since in the requirement it is said that, IPv4 only backbone, NAT64, 6PE and DS-Lite cannot be a solution.

Because NAT64 requires IPv6 only network or Dual Stack, 6PE requires MPLS network and DS-Lite requires IPv6 only network.

Yes, NAT64 could be place at the Internet edge and the best place for NAT64 deployment is Internet edge according to RFC 7269, in this question, requirement says that IPv4 only network. That's why; answer of this question is C.

Question 22:

E-commerce company want to enable IPv6 on their network as soon as possible. Where would be the best place for them to start and which solution would you recommend?

A. All DC infrastructure, running dual stack is best option.
B. At the internet edge, NAT 64 + DNS 64 is a best solution
C. At the internet edge and dual stack is best solution
D. All over the network and dual stack is best solution

Answer 22:

In the requirement it is said that E-commerce Company and they want to enable IPv6 as fast as possible. Dual stack is very time consuming if not impossible.

Also, since the business is E-commerce, in general, IPv6 business case for the E-commerce companies is IPv6 presence.

If Happy Eye balls enabled at the customer sites, or IPv6 only users will reach to their site, it is important to have IPv6 presence for E-commerce companies. Thus Starting from the Internet Edge and enabling NAT 64 + DNS 64 is the best for the given company and the requirements.

Thus, answer of this question is B.

Question 23:

Which below options are critical as an IPv6 First Hop Security features? (Choose Three)

A. A. Suppressing excessive Multicast neighbor discovery messages
B. B. ARP Inspection
C. C. Limiting IPv6 Router advertisement
D. D. Preventing rogue DHCPv6 assignments
E. E. Broadcast control mechanism

Answer 23:

There is no ARP in IPv6. So ARP inspection is unrelated.

There is no Broadcast in IPv6 as it is explained in the IPv6 chapter, thus Option E is wrong as well. Remaining all three features are critical IPv6 First Hop Security features.

That's why; answer of this question is A, C and D.

Question 24:

Enterprise Company implemented dual stack network. It took a lot of time them to implement dual stack on all their networking nodes, links, applications, hosts and operating system. Although their network is 100 % dual stack, they only see 25 % IPv6 Internet traffic on their network.

What might be the possible problem?

A. Some of their link for the Internet may not be IPv6 enabled

B. Content which their users try to access is not enabled IPv6

C. Operating system of their users might prefer IPv4 over IPv6

D. They might have Happy Eye Balls enabled and IPv6 might have priority

Answer 24:

Because either content, which their users try to access, is not enabled IPv6 or Operating system of their users might prefer IPv4 to IPv6. Answer of this question is B and C.

Question 25:

Which below protocols are used in IPv6 Multicast?

A. MLD

B. Auto-RP

C. MSDP

D. Embedded RP

E. Anycast RP

Answer 25:

MSDP and Auto-RP is not supported in IPv6 Multicast. MLD, Embedded RP and Anycast RP are the IPv6 Multicast features.

MLD is equivalent of IGMP Snooping in IPv4 and whenever there are layer 2 switches in IPv6 Multicast design, MLD should be enabled for optimal resource usage.

Chapter 8
BORDER GATEWAY PROTOCOL

If the requirement is to use a routing protocol on the Public Internet then the only choice is Border Gateway Protocol (BGP). Scale is extremely large and robust.

BGP works over TCP that's why it is considered robust, because TCP is inherently reliable.

BGP is multi-protocol; with the new NLRI it can carry many address families. Today almost twenty different NLRI are carried over BGP. New AFI and SAFI are defined for the new address families.

EBGP and IBGP are our main focus. If the BGP connection is between two different autonomous systems, it is called EBGP (External BGP).

If BGP is used inside an autonomous system with the same AS number between the BGP nodes, then the connection is called IBGP (Internal BGP).

BGP Theory

Before starting BGP Theory, EBGP, IBGP and more advanced topics, some basic BGP definitions should be clear.

What is MP-BGP (Multi Protocol BGP)?

MP-BGP (Multiprotocol BGP) is the set of extensions to the BGP protocol. Standard BGP only supports IPv4 unicast address family, whereas MP-BGP supports more than 15 different BGP address families.

RFC4760 defines the extensions for BGP protocol and states " in order to bring extra functionality to BGP protocol, new BGP AFI (Address Family Identifier) and BGP SAFI (Sub Address Family Identifier) is introduced".

Multi protocol BGP supports IPv4 and IPv6 address families and their unicast and multicast variants.

MPBGP also supports Layer 2 VPN address families. EVPN (Ethernet VPN) is a mechanism that the mac addresses are exchanged between PE devices over BGP control plane.

All these BGP address families are exchanged between BGP neighbors over a single BGP session. BGP neighbors exchange their capability in the BGP open message.

If BGP neighborship is setup only for the IPv4 BGP address family and later on extra protocol such as L3 VPN address family is added, BGP session goes down.

That's why careful planning is an important to avoid downtime even in a maintenance window since some networks cannot even tolerate planned failure.

If MP-BGP needs to be setup between two BGP nodes (It can be between BGP Route Reflector and Route Reflector Clients in BGP Route Reflector topologies), new address family needs to be explicitly activated.

Below is an example configuration on Cisco IOS device to enable MP-BGP (Multiprotocol BGP)

- router bgp 1000
- no bgp default ipv4-unicast
- neighbor x.x.x.x remote-as 100
- address-family vpnv4 unicast
- neighbor x.x.x.x activate
- neighbor x.x.x.x send-community extended

In the above example, Router in AS 1000 creates a BGP VPNv4 neighborship with the router x.x.x.x (IP address). VPNv4 address family is activated and send-community extended configuration knob is used to send RT (Route Target) community values between the MP-BGP neighbors.

In order to enable MP-BGP, new AFI and SAFI are defined by IANA.

What does BGP free core mean?

BGP refers to an Internet protocol used between different Autonomous System on the Internet.

Let's look at the topology shown below to understand the BGP operation and IP destination-based lookup.

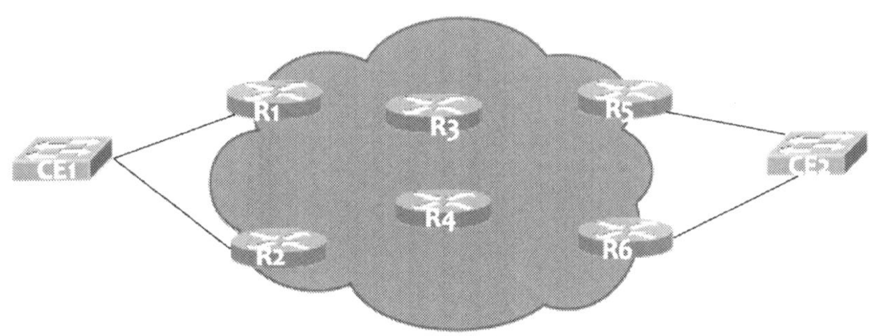

BGP Free Core

In the above topology, when CE1 wants to reach CE2 at the other side of the network, the packet reaches to either R1 or R2. If there are no tunneling mechanisms such as MPLS, GRE, or any other mechanisms, R1 or R2 makes IP destination-based lookup and sends packets to R3 or R4.

If the prefixes behind CE2 are learned by BGP, all the routers have to do an IP destination-based lookup to see if there is a route for the CE2 prefixes in the routing table from BGP.

Every router – R1, R2, R3, R4, R5, and R6 – has to run BGP.

If any Layer 3 overlay tunnelling technology runs in the network, then the routers in the middle, which are R3 and R4, do not have to keep the CE1 and CE2 prefixes.

R3 and R4 keep only the routing information of the edge nodes. As a result, R3 and R4 are used for reachability between R1, R2, R5, and R6.

Since MPLS is a tunnelling mechanism that provides Layer 2 or Layer 3 overlay, if MPLS is used in the network, intermediate devices, which are R3 and R4, do not have to run BGP.

R1, R2, R5, and R6 are called edge nodes, and R3 and R4 are known as core nodes.

That's why you can have BGP free core network if MPLS is used in the networks.

BGP Free core means, Core nodes of the network doesn't have to enable BGP.

BGP Path Selection

Unlike IGP protocols, BGP doesn't use link metrics for best path selection. Instead, it uses many attributes for the best path selection. This allows creating complex BGP policies.

BGP is a policy-based protocol which provides IP based traffic engineering inside an autonomous system. In fact, IGPs don't support traffic engineering like BGP does.BGP path vector protocol has many similarities with Distance Vector protocols such as EIGRP.

For example in EBGP and IBGP, one best path is always chosen and placed in the routing table; this path is advertised to the other BGP neighbor. This might create suboptimal routing design or slow BGP convergence. There might be vendor-specific attributes such as weight attribute. Also, there are some intermediary steps, which are not used commonly. Below is the BGP best path selection criteria list to keep in mind as a designer.

BGP Best Path Selection Steps

Below are the BGP Path selection steps in order.

Understanding them allows network designer to deploy better BGP policies. Better BGP policies lead to optimal routing, better capacity usage, easier troubleshooting and maintenance, higher network availability and scalability.

- BGP next-hop has to be reachable
- Longest match wins
- Weight (Local to the Router- Cisco attribute)
- Local Preference (Higher Local Preference wins)
- AS-Path (Shorter AS-Path length wins)
- Origin
- MED
- Prefer EBGP over IBGP

- Lowest IGP metric to the BGP next-hop (Hot Potato Routing)
- Multipath
- Prefer lowest neighbor address

Let's understand now, How BGP Local Preference attribute is used in BGP Path selection by explaining DFZ (Default Free Zone) concept.

WHAT IS DFZ (DEFAULT FREE ZONE)?

In the context of the Internet and BGP routing, DFZ – commonly known as Default Free Zone – refers to the collections of all the public IPv4 BGP prefixes without default route on the global Internet.

Most of the time, you hear full-route or full-Internet-route terms, which are the same with Default Free Zone term. Having all BGP routes, which are announced by all the available AS (Autonomous System), on the Internet.

Currently, there are more than 600,000 IPv4 BGP routes and about 30,000 IPv6 routes in the DFZ (Default Free Zone). These numbers, however, could easily be reduced to 300,000 for IPv4 and less than 20,000 for IPv6 based on the CIDR reports (IPv4 CIDR report and IPv6 CIDR report).

When you have a BGP connection with the ISP, you can receive only default route, partial route (Customer routes of your ISP), default free zone route (full BGP routing table), DFZ + default routes, DFZ + Customer routes, DFZ+ default route, and DFZ + partial route (Customer routes of your ISP). In sum, you have many options to choose from.

Actually, your preference entirely depends on your BGP policy. For instance, if the network traffic is between your users and the servers inside your ISP or if it is between your users and the servers inside the Customer datacenter of your ISP, you don't want this traffic to go through the suboptimal path.

Let's see the below topologies to understand how suboptimal routing is created with the wrong BGP policy.

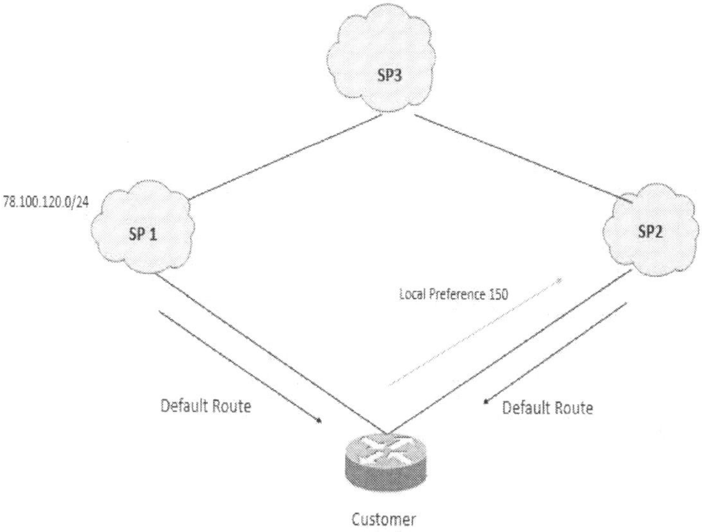

BGP Egress Path Selection with Default Route

In the above figure, the Customer is connected to the two Internet Service Providers, which are linked to the same upstream Service Provider, SP3.

The Customer is receiving only default route, thus increasing the local preference on SP2 BGP connection. The Customer wants to reach 78.100.120.0/24 network, which is the Customer of SP1.

The connection will be optimal if the Customer reaches 78.100.120.0/24 network over SP1 link directly. Nonetheless, since the Customer increases the local preference for the default route over SP2 link – for each prefix – only SP2 link is used.

And the traffic flow between the Customer and the 78.100.120.0/24 network is Customer- SP2 – SP3 – SP1. SP2 uses its upstream Service Provider that is SP3.

Let's take a look at the topology shown below.

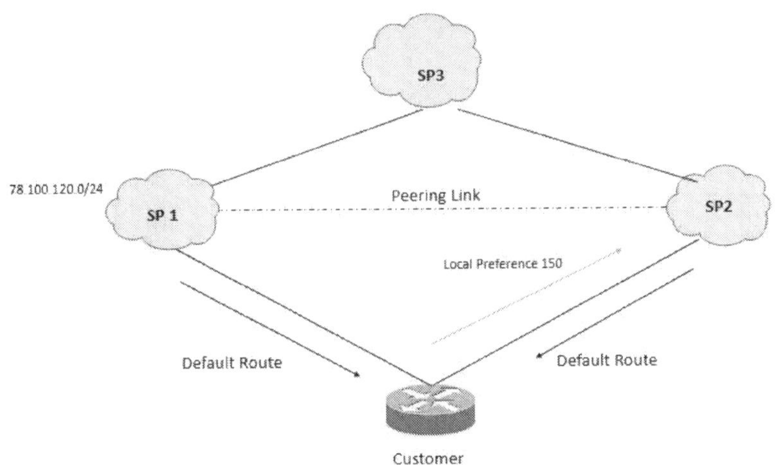

BGP Egress Path Selection with Default Route and Peering between SPs

In the above Figure, there is a peering link between the SP1 and SP2. The Customer is still receiving only default route and using BGP local preference 150 (by default 100 on SP1 connection) over SP2. What's more, the Customer wants to reach 78.100.120.0/24 network, which is the Customer of SP1.

In this traffic, the flow would be Customer-SP2-SP1.

The peering link between SP1 and SP2 prevents the packets from being sent from SP2 to SP3.

By default, SP2 prefers peering link over upstream link because of cost reduction. This is almost always the case in real life BGP design of the Service Providers and will be explain in detail in the BGP Peering section of this chapter.

But the traffic flow, from the Customer point of view, is still suboptimal because it is supposed to be directly between the Customer and SP1, not between SP2 and SP1.

Let's examine the last topology to see whether the partial routing can avoid suboptimal BGP routing.

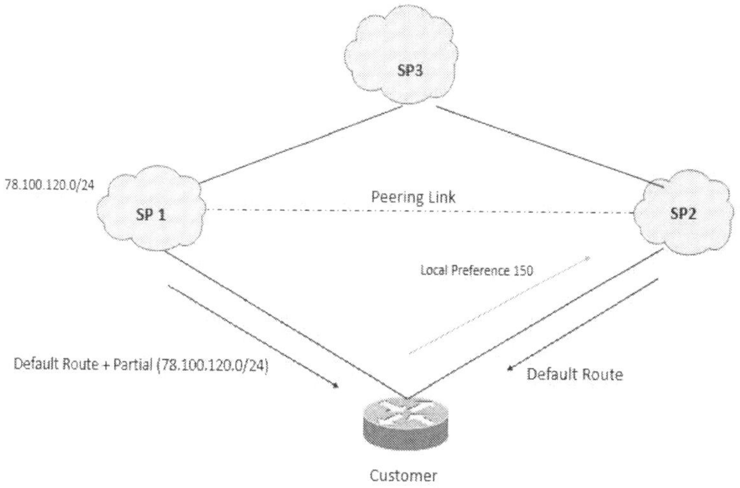

BGP Path Selection with the Default Route +Partial Route

In the above figure the partial route is received from the SP1. Everything is the same with topology; besides, only the partial route is added.

To simplify the concept, let's assume that we are receiving 78.100.120.0/24 network, including the default route, from SP1.

The Customer still uses BGP Local Preference 150 over SP2 link and BGP Local Preference 100 for the default route. The Customer doesn't change BGP local preference for the partial routes; rather, the Customer uses BGP Local Preference 100 for the 78.100.120.0/24 as well.

But since the longest match routing is evaluated and chosen over the local preference (Remember BGP Best Path Selection steps), the Customer selects SP1 as the best path for the 78.100.120.0/24 network. The remaining networks are reached through the SP2.

Receiving DFZ, which is full Internet routing table, allows network administrators to have optimal path if there are multiple ISPs or multiple links. Nonetheless, this benefit is not free.

In sum, the more the routes, the more the processing power. BGP routers, which have full internet routing table, requires much more memory and CPU compared to BGP routers which have only the default route or default + partial routes.

EBGP

EBGP is used between two different autonomous systems. Loop prevention in EBGP is done by the AS path attribute, which is why it is a mandatory BGP attribute. If BGP node sees its own AS path in the incoming BGP update message, BGP message is rejected.

BGP traffic engineering sends and receives the network traffic based on customer business and technical requirements. For example, link capacities might be different; one link might be more stable than the other or the costs of the links might be different. In all of these cases, customer may want to optimize their incoming and outgoing traffic.

For BGP outgoing traffic local preference attribute is commonly used. BGP inbound traffic engineering can be achieved in multiple ways:

* MED (BGP external metric attribute)
* AS-path prepending
* BGP community attribute

BGP weight attribute can be used for outgoing traffic optimization as well, but don't forget that it is local to the router and many implementations may not support it. MED attribute is used between two autonomous systems. If the same prefix is coming from two different AS to a third AS, although you can use always-compare MED feature, it is not good practice to enable this feature since it can cause BGP MED Oscillation problem.

Creating an inter-domain policy with the MED attribute is not a good practice.

AS path is mandatory and it is carried over entire internet, although some service providers can filter excessive prepending.

Local preference attribute is domain-wise and sent by the IBGP neighbors to each other.

BGP Next-Hop Behavior in IP and MPLS Networks

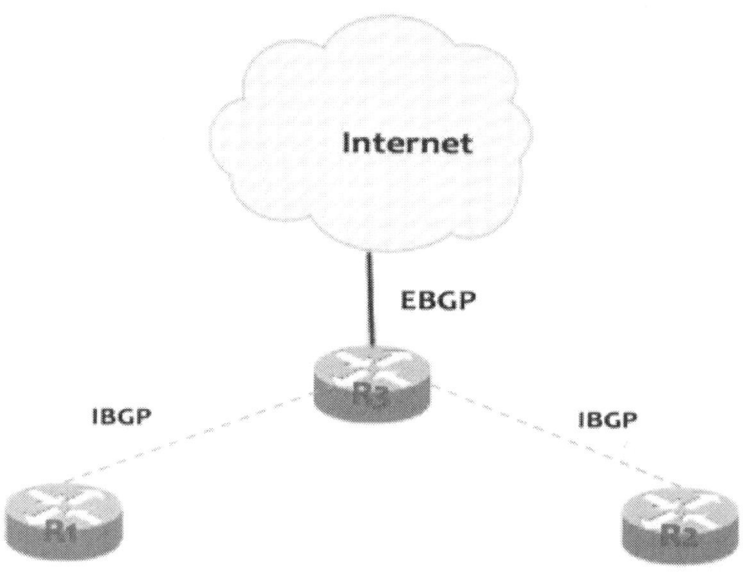

IBGP Next-hop handling in IP networks

In the above figure, there is no MPLS service in the network. What's more, R1 and R2 are running IBGP with R3.

And R3 is running EBGP with its upstream Service Provider.

When R3 sends the BGP prefix to R1 and R2, BGP next hop is unchanged.

The link between R3 and the Internet is set as BGP next hop. In other words, if you examine the BGP routing table of R1 and R2, the next hop of the BGP prefixes coming from the Internet is R3-Internet link.

Further, routers need to find IGP (OSPF, IS-IS, EIGRP) next-hop in order to send the packets to the destination. The link between R3 and Internet (External link) is not known by the IGP protocol.

That link can be redistributed to IGP or it can be set as IGP passive interface. If you don't want to see external routes in your IGP, then BGP next hop can be set to router's loopback, an internal route.

In order to set the next hop to router's loopback, you can create a route map on R3 to set the next hop as its loopback interface, or you can set BGP next hop independently and create IBGP session between Router's loopbacks. BGP sources interface in this case are R1, R2, and R3's loopback.

As you can see, if there is no MPLS VPN service, the prefixes – which are received from EBGP – are advertised to IBGP neighbor without changing the next hop. If the external link is not wanted in the network, manual operation is required on the edge router to set the next hop to it.

Important to know that, if external link is not set as next-hop, in case that link failure, traffic is black holed. (Dropped at that router) until BGP control plane is converged. BGP PIC Edge solves this problem by installing an alternate route in the forwarding table. BGP PIC concept will be explained later in this chapter.

Let's take a look at MPLS VPN network and see how BGP next-hop operation is handled.

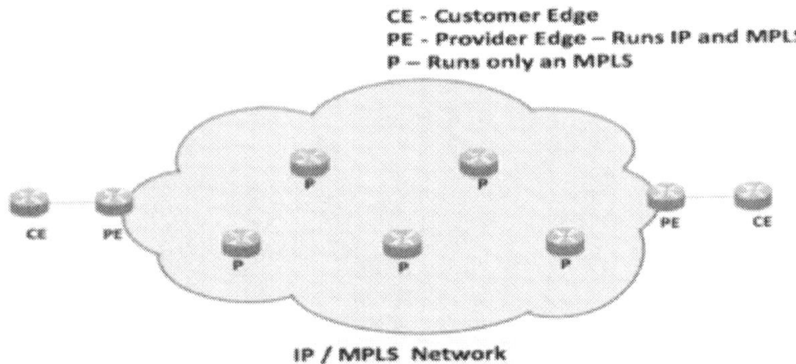

MPLS Network and the Components

In the above figure, basic MPLS network and its components are shown. MPLS Layer 3 VPN requires PE router to be the routing neighbor with the CE routers. It can be static route, RIP, EIGRP, OSPF, IS-IS, or BGP.

IP prefixes are received from the CE routers and PE appends RD (Route Distinguisher) to the IP prefixes. And a completely new VPN prefixes are created. (IPv4+RD=VPNv4)

PE routers re-originate all the customer prefixes regardless of its origin, static redistribution, and PE-CE OSPF/IS-IS/EIGRP/BGP as well advertising all MP-IBGP peers by setting the BGP next-hop to it. As for the IP network, you don't need to do the manual operation.

MP-BGP neighborship between the PE routers should be created between their loopbacks. And in that case, loopback is set as next hop without configuring BGP next-hop-self manually.

BGP Internet Edge Design and Multihoming Considerations

There are three basic flavors of BGP Internet Edge Design and Multihoming.

1. Primary/Backup
2. Load Sharing across all links
3. Best path

Also there can be forth model, which requires shifting traffic between links with any of the three options such as pushing traffic away from over utilized links.

Let's look at each option in detail.

1. Primary/Backup BGP Design Model

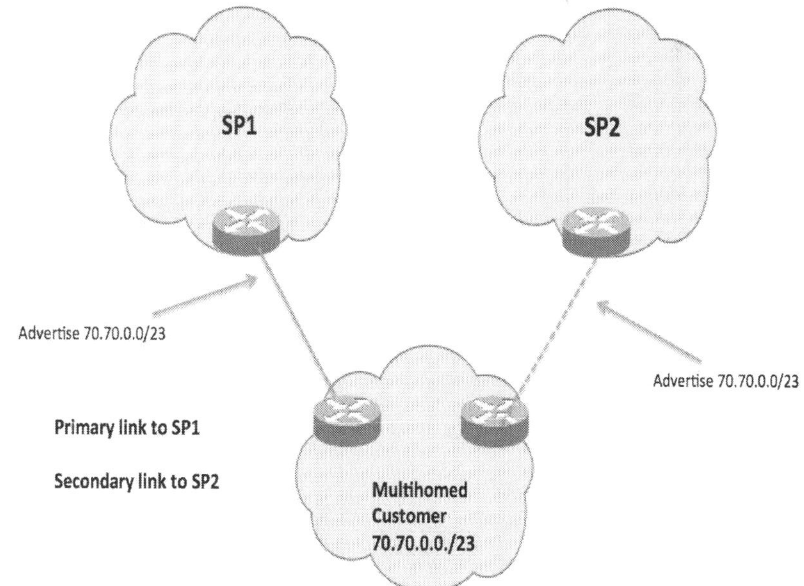

BGP Primary/Backup Design Model

In the above figure, Primary/Backup BGP Internet edge design model is shown. Common reason for design model is one link is more expensive than the other. Not only cost wise but also it can be expensive for the company from the Latency and performance point of view as well.

In this model; a link or set of links as are designated as the primary link to use for all traffic to one or more destination prefixes. The backup link should only carry traffic if the primary link goes down. BGP Traffic Engineering is done in both inbound and outbound directions. Inbound traffic means, traffic, which comes to our AS, outbound traffic, is, traffic that goes out from our AS.

If all links are connected to the same AS, inbound traffic is manipulated by setting higher MED on backup link or links. If links are terminated on different ASes, inbound traffic is manipulated by having the Provider set low local preference on backup link or links. Sending BGP community and expecting Service provider to lower the local preference on the backup link generally does this. Outbound traffic is manipulated by learning a default route and setting lower local preference on the backup link. Receiving a default route in this model is important for the router resources. Full Internet routing table requires more router resources.

2. Load Sharing BGP Design Model

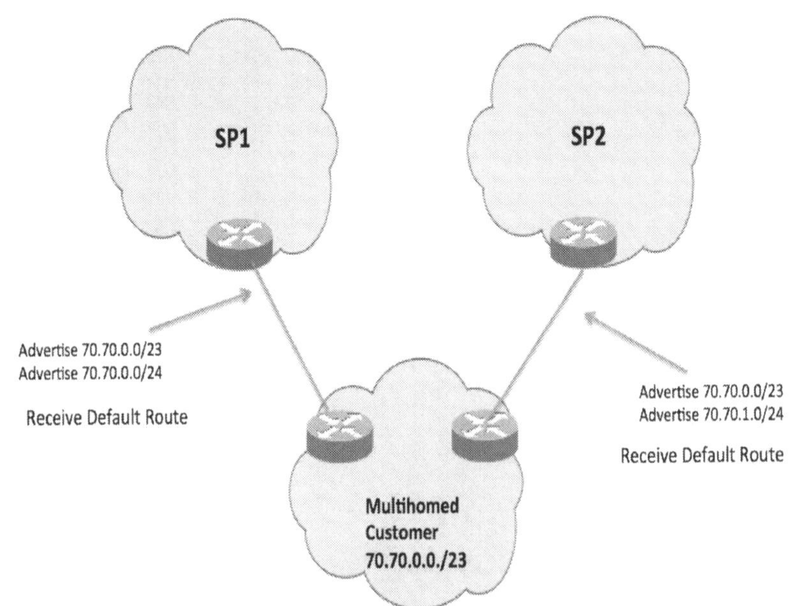

BGP Load Sharing Design Model

In the above figure, Load Sharing BGP Internet edge design model is shown. In this model, all available links are loaded. The goal is to load the links as evenly as possible without negative impact on traffic flows. Common use case of this model is to squeeze as much bandwidth out of multiple links as possible. This is often the case where larger links are cost prohibitive such as for small companies or locations where circuit cost is high.

In this model, default route is received from the upstream ISPs. Inbound traffic is manipulated by dividing IP subnets of the company and making particular more specific route announcements across different links in addition to the aggregate announcement.

In the above figure, /24 are the more specific routers and /23 is the aggregate. Aggregate announcement is sent because in case one of the links fail, remaining link can receive the traffic of the failed link.

Outbound traffic is manipulated by equal cost static default routes. If one of the links is more utilized, Hot Potato routing is done for better utilization. Hot, Cold and Mashed Potato routing will be explained later in this chapter.

3. Best Path BGP Design Model

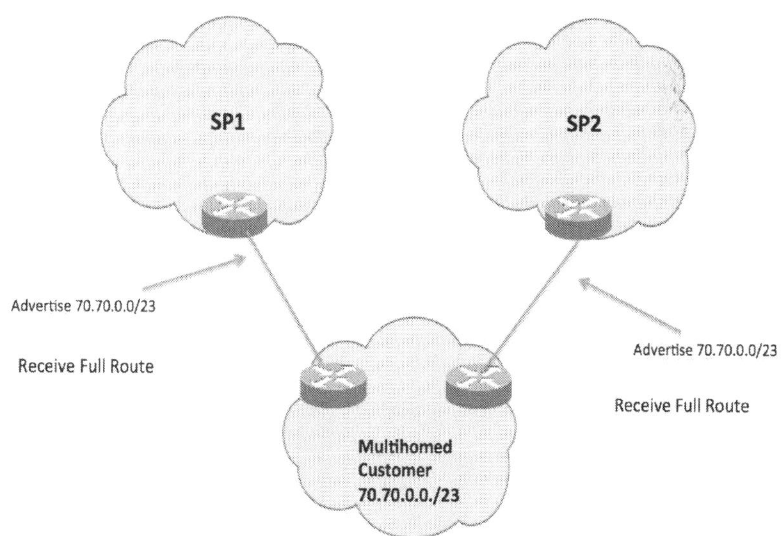

BGP Best Path Design Model

In the above figure, Load Sharing BGP Internet edge design model is shown.

In this model, rather than having default route, full Internet routing table is received from all available uplinks. Having full Internet routing table provides ability to send the traffic to the most optimal exit point or closest exit point.

In the previous design model that is Load Sharing Design Model, default route was received from the Service Providers and if necessary, more specific prefixes were created in the routine table. More configurations is necessary in that model but having smaller routing table gives an ability to use lower end devices at the Internet edge. This model requires full Internet routing table, which means more Memory and the processing power but allows utilizing the best path without doing too much configuration.

In all of the above models, when there is congestion on the link or some of the links, some amount of traffic might be shifted to less utilized ones. This might be the case even in the Primary/Backup model.

Shifting traffic from the more utilized link to the less utilized link is called Traffic Dialing. Inbound traffic is shifted to the backup link or underutilized links by advertising some, but not all, destinations as more preferred across the links to be utilized.

These destinations will be more preferred due to being more specific, having a higher local-preference, shorter AS-path, or lower MED value, etc. Out bound traffic is pushed away from the over utilized links by increasing the IGP distance to the over utilized links for some sources. (Hot Potato Routing) Outbound traffic can also be shifted away from the over utilized links by depreferencing some inbound BGP paths associated with the over utilized links.

Let's have a look at how AS-path prepending is used in BGP Best Path design model for inbound path manipulation.

BGP As-Path Prepending – Use cases, Alternatives and Challenges

BGP As-path is a mandatory BGP attribute, which has to be sent in every BGP message. BGP as-path prepending is one of the BGP traffic engineering methods

What is BGP AS-path attribute? Why BGP AS-path attribute is used?

BGP AS-Path attribute is mainly used for loop presentation in EBGP. Of course it is also used for best path selection as well. If the receiving AS finds its AS-number anywhere in the AS-path, BGP update is ignored.

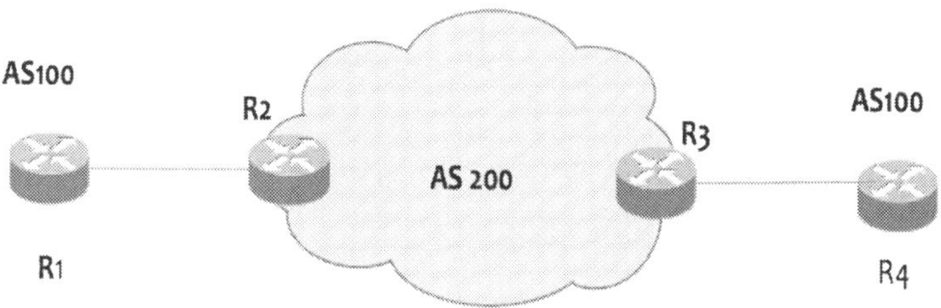

BGP Loop Prevention

In the above figure, R1 and R4 are the Internet Gateway Routers in AS 100, which is connected to AS 200.

When R2 receives prefixes from R1, it sends to R3 with BGP AS, 'AS 100'. When R3 sends a BGP update to its EBGP neighbor which is R4, it prepends AS 200 and the AS-Path is seen by the R4 as ' 200 100 '

When you examine BGP tables, at the left, always last AS is seen. At the right of the AS-Path, originator BGP AS is seen.

When R4 receives a BGP update from R3, since its own BGP AS, which is AS 100, is in the as-path (200 100), R4 doesn't accept the BGP update. In some scenarios you may need R4 to accept the prefixes though.

For example in MPLS L3 VPN.

If EBGP were used as PE-CE protocol in MPLS L3 VPN, R4 and R1 would need to accept the prefixes from each other.

There are two ways two overcome the issue. Either on the Service provider site, BGP as-override feature or at the customer site (In this example, R1 and R4) BGP allow-as features are used.

What is BGP As-path prepending?

BGP As-path prepending is used to influence inbound traffic to the company. Outbound traffic is usually done via BGP local preference attribute or BGP hot-potato routing.

BGP As-path prepending is used in BGP Best Path Design Model. It can be used in Load Sharing model as well.

What are the other alternatives for BGP as-path prepending?

BGP MED attribute is also used to influence incoming traffic to the company. BGP Med attribute is not sent between the providers.

If company has multi home connection to the two Service Providers, those service providers won't send the MED setting of the company to each other.

That's why best practice with BGP MED, don't use it if you have connection to more than one service provider to influence inbound path selection.

Another BGP as-path prepending alternative is BGP Communities.

How BGP traffic engineering is achieved with BGP as-path prepending?

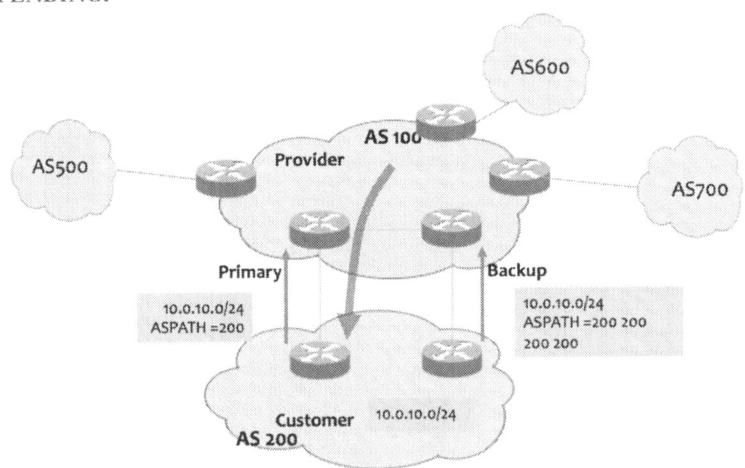

BGP as-path prepending with single ISP

In the above figure, Customer AS 200 wants to use of the links as backup. 10.0.10.0/24 prefix is sent via backup link with the 3 prepend. Thus AS path is seen through the backup link by the upstream service provider which is AS 100 as ' 200 200 200 200 '.

Every BGP neighbor of the Service Provider (AS 100) will see only AS 200 without AS path prepend, because internal BGP speaker will chose the best path and that best path will be sent to EBGP neighbor of the Service Provider.

Internal BGP speakers will receive the prefixes from primary path as BGP AS 200, from backup BGP AS 200 200 200 200 as prepended, thus they will choose the shorter AS Path and will use it. In this topology BGP MED could be used as well since Customer AS 200 is connected to only one service provider, which is AS 100.

Don't forget that BGP as-path prepending will not affect outbound traffic from the customer to the Service Provider. So if local preference is not implemented, backup link is still used to send the traffic from customer to the Internet. But from Internet to the company traffic is handled by BGP As-Path Prepending. (Inbound Traffic manipulation).

What are the challenges which BGP as-path prepending cannot handle and what are the solutions for incoming BGP path manipulation?

There are some challenges with BGP As-Path Prepending when it is used in multi-homed BGP setup.

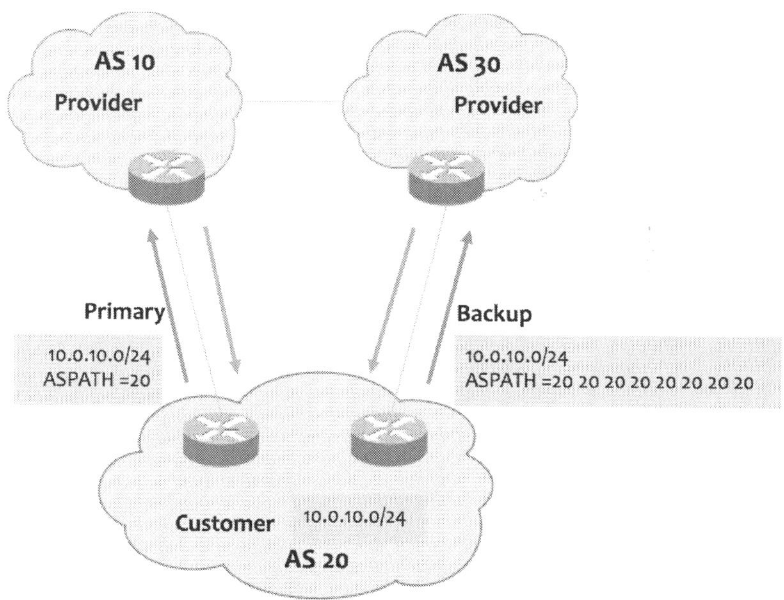

BGP As-Path Prepending with Multiple ISP

In the above figure, Customer AS 20 is connected to two Service Providers. Customer is sending 10.0.10.0/24 prefix to both ISP. They are advertising this prefix to their upstream ISPs and also each other through BGP peering.

AS 30; will be used as backup. Thus Customer is sending the 10.0.10.0/24 prefix towards AS30 with As-Path Prepends. Customer prepends its own AS path with 7 more AS.

You might think that link from; AS 30 won't be used anymore so it will be used as backup. But that is not totally true.

Traffic from their upstream ISPs will go to the AS 10 because all the other ASes over Internet will see the advertisement from AS 30 with lots of prepends. But all the customers of AS 30 will still send the traffic for 10.0.10.0/24 prefix over the link which wants to be used as backup, although AS 30 learns 10.0.10.0/24 prefix over BGP peering link with AS 10 as well, its upstream providers as well.

But important to know that, Service Providers always chooses to send the traffic for their customer prefixes over the customer link first, then peering links, lastly through upstream ISP. Because they want to utilize the customer link as much as possible to charge more money.

Service Providers implement Local Preference attribute to achieve this. Basic local preference policy could be; Local Pref 100 towards Customer, local pref 90 towards peering link and local pref 80 towards upstream ISP.

With this knowledge we can understand why customer of AS 30 would still use customer link for 10.0.10.0/24 prefix although customer wants that link to be used as backup.

Customer is sending that prefix with AS-path attribute and service provider implements local pref for that prefix. Since local preference attribute is more important in the BGP best path selection process, if the traffic comes to any of the BGP routers of AS 30, it is sent through customer link. Not through BGP peering link with AS 10 or any upstream provider of AS 30.

This problem can be solved with BGP community. If Customer sends 10.0.10.0/24 prefix with the BGP community which effects local preference value of AS 30, link between customer and AS 30 is not used anymore.

Customer could send the community as 30:70, which reduces the local pref to 70 for the customer, prefixes over the customer BGP session, AS 30 would start to use BGP peer link to reach to 10.0.10.0/24 prefix.

BGP Soft Reconfiguration and Route Refresh

BGP is a policy-based protocol and it uses inbound and outbound filters with the attributes. BGP updates are kept in many different places in the router:

* BGP RIB, which is the routing table of BGP, RIB which is a router's general routing table created by all the routing protocols, and FIB which is a forwarding table.

In addition to BGP RIB, BGP uses adjacency RIB-IN and RIB-OUT databases. All the prefixes from the remote BGP neighbor are placed in the BGP RIB-IN database first. Then, inbound filter is applied and prefixes are taken into BGP RIB database.

If we enable BGP soft reconfiguration inbound, we keep received prefixes in the BGP RIB-IN database. If it is not enabled, we ignore them. If BGP soft reconfiguration inbound is enabled, even if you filter the prefixes after receiving from the neighboring BGP device, the prefixes are still reachable. This helps to verify whether the filter is working correctly.

This is memory-intensive, since you keep those prefixes in BGP RIB-IN database in addition to BGP RIB database. By contrast, BGP route refresh works in a different way to accomplish the same task. Filter is still applied for the incoming or outgoing prefixes. However, they are not kept in a separate database. They are either taken into the BGP RIB database or ignored, making memory consumption more efficient.

Don't forget that router memories are expensive!

Community attribute is sent over the BGP session by the customer to the service provider. Upon receiving the prefixes ISP takes action for their predefined communities.

ISPs publish their supported community attribute values. For example, they can say that if a customer sends prefixes with the attached 5000:110 community then local preference 110 is applied towards that circuit.

BGP Peering

BGP Peering is an agreement between different Service Providers. It is an EBGP neighborship between different Service Providers to send BGP traffic between them without paying upstream Service Provider.

To understand BGP peering, first we must understand how networks are connected to each other on the Internet. The Internet is a collection of many individual networks, which interconnect with each other under the common goal of ensuring global reachability between any two points.

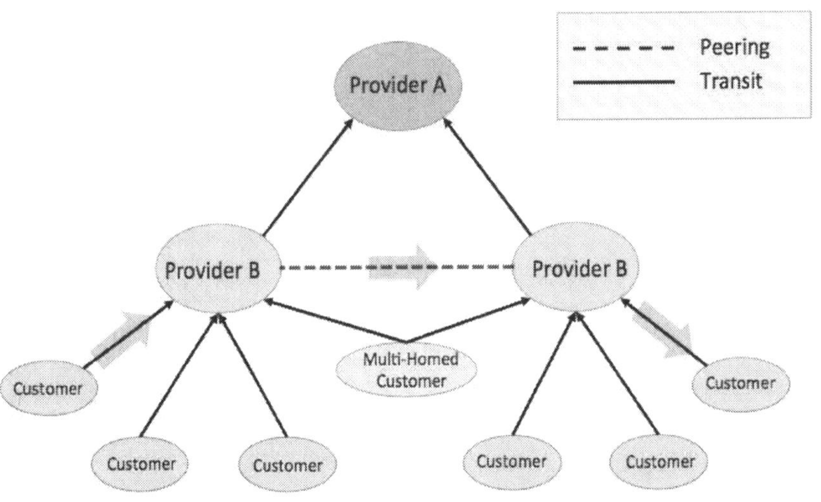

BGP Peering and Transit Links

There are three primary relationships in this interconnection:

- **Provider:** Typically someone who is paid and has the responsibility of routing packets to/from the entire Internet.
- **Customer:** Typically someone who pays a provider with the expectation that their packets will be routed to/from the entire Internet.
- **Peers:** Two networks that get together and agree to exchange traffic between each others' networks, typically for free. There are generally two types of peering: public and private. Both will be explained in this session.

Benefits of BGP Peering

Reduced operating cost: A transit provider is not being paid to deliver some portion of your traffic. Peering traffic is free!

Improved routing: By directly connecting with another network with whom you exchange traffic, you are eliminating a middle-man and potential failure point.

Distribution of traffic: By distributing traffic over interconnections with many different networks, the ability to scale is potentially improved.

BGP Peering Types

Private BGP Peering

Private Peering is a direct interconnection between two networks, using a dedicated transport service or fiber.

- May also be called a Private Network Interconnect, or PNI.
- Inside a datacenter this is usually a dark-fiber cross-connect.
- May also be a Telco-delivered circuit as well.

Done at the exchange point. Commonly referred as IX.

Some considerations in public vs. private BGP peering:

- Route servers are used in the Internet Exchange Points in the same way as route reflectors in IBGP design.
- Route servers provide scalability in the IX and don't change the BGP next-hop of the prefixes.
- An exchange point is typically the optimal choice for a network maintaining a large number of small interconnections and little traffic.
- Not every company peers publicly with all others; some have closed peering agreements or require a number of POP locations or some amount of bandwidth or other criteria to be a peer with others.

Trying to maintain private interconnections with dedicated physical links for every peer is often financially or logistically prohibitive. For example, maintaining one hundred GigE cross-connects to a peer with one hundred small peers would probably exceed the cost of an exchange point port, not to mention the overhead of provisioning and maintaining the ports. A private peer is typically the optimal choice for two networks exchanging a large volume of traffic.

For example, if two networks exchange 10 Gbps of traffic with each other, it is probably cheaper and easier to provide a dedicated 10 GE between them, rather than have them each pay for another 10 GE exchange port.

Many networks maintain a mix of public and private peers. When we talk about service provider network interconnections in real life, we mostly use a tier definition.

BGP Peering Case Study

Network A is a customer of Network Z and Network B is a peer of Network Z.

Network A becomes a transit customer of Network B.

Network A announces 4.0.0.0/16 aggregate to Network Z and more specific prefixes, 4.0.0.0/24 and 4.0.1.0/24 to Network B. Network B sends more specifics to its peer Z.

Network Z only announces the aggregate to the world. What is the impact of this design?

How can it be fixed?

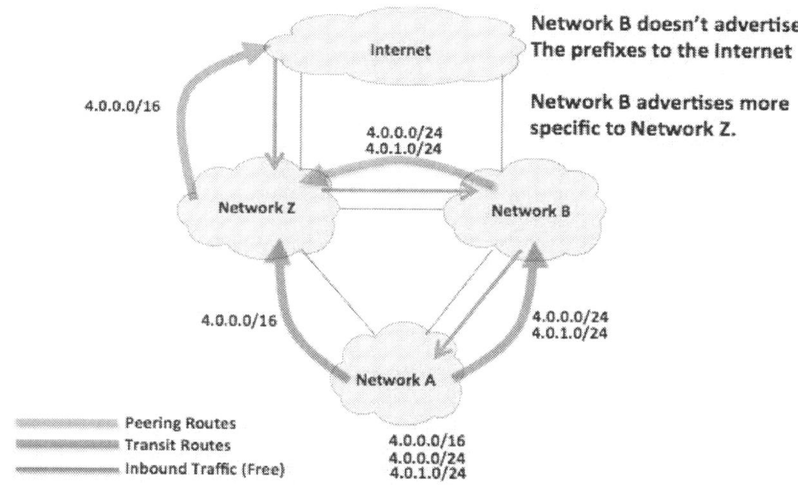

BGP Peering Case Study

As depicted in the above diagram, Network B doesn't announce the specific to the world. As a result, traffic from Internet to Network A goes through Network Z and then through Network B over peer link.

Network A doesn't have to pay its provider Network Z. This is known as the Jack Move. Here Network A and Network pull the Jack Move on Network Z. As previously seen in the peering section, most, if not all networks prefer customers over peers and this is implemented with local preference.

However, here the customer (Network A) is sending aggregates only to Network Z, but more specific routes are coming from Network B, which is a peer network.

Prefix length overrides the local preference during forwarding.

The only way to prevent this situation is Network Z should watch whether their peers advertise more specific announcements for the routes learned from its customers.

Tier 1, 2, and 3 Service Providers

Tier 1: A network, which does not purchase transit from any other network, and therefore peers with every other Tier 1 network to maintain global reachability.

Tier 2: A network with transit customers and some peering, but that still buys full transit to reach some portion of the Internet.

Tier 3: A stub network, typically without any transit customers, and without any peering relationships.

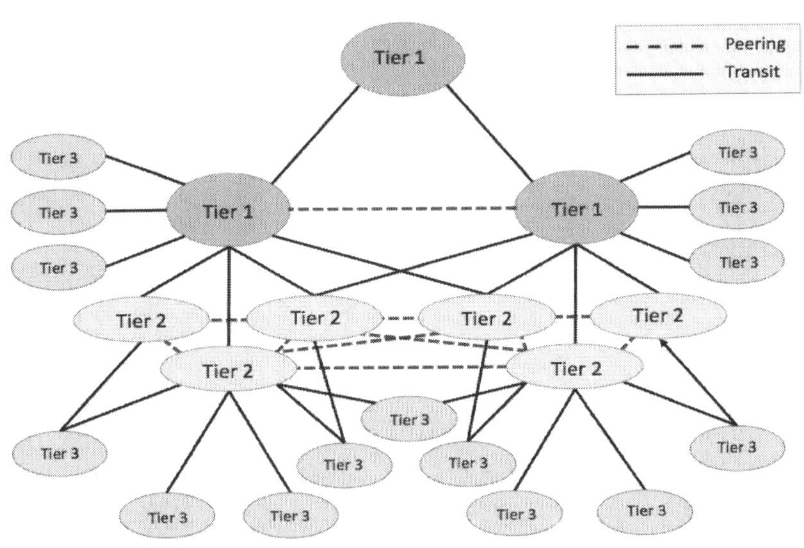

Tier 1, 2 and 3 Service Provider Interconnections

Unless the customer changes their path preference with communities, service providers almost always choose customer over peering links vs. transit links. Because they want to utilize customer links, they pay for the transit and peering brings them some cost.

For example, service providers set BGP local preference of 100 towards customer, 90 towards peer, and 80 towards transit provider. Higher local preference is preferred, thus if same route is received from all of these links, traffic is sent to the customer due to higher local preference.

IBGP

IBGP is used inside an autonomous system. In order to prevent routing loop, IBGP requires BGP nodes to have full mesh interconnections amongst them. Full-mesh IBGP sessions may create configuration complexity and resource problems due to a high number of BGP sessions in large-scale BGP deployment.

Route reflectors and confederations can be used to reduce the sessions on each router. The number of sessions and configurations can be reduced by the route reflectors and confederations, but they both have important design considerations.

- Confederations divide the autonomous system to smaller sub-autonomous systems.
- Confederations give the ability to have EBGP rules between Sub-ASs. Also, inside each Sub-AS a different IGP can be used. Merging a company's scenarios is easier with confederation than route reflectors.

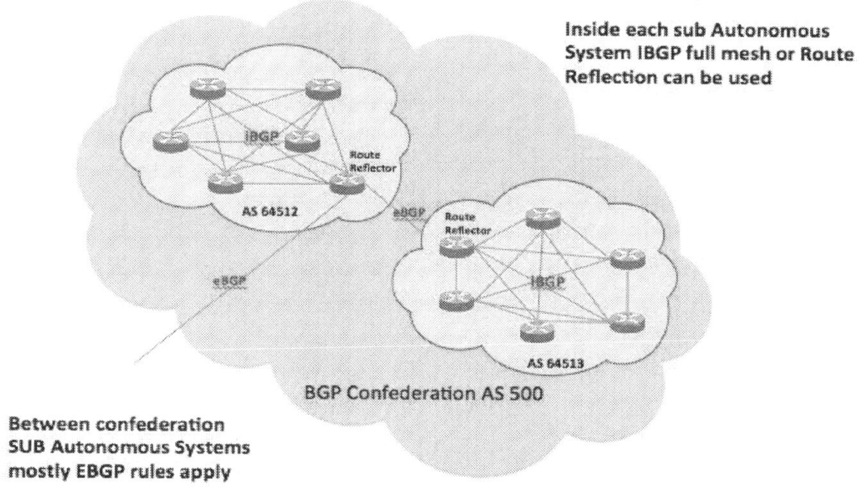

BGP Confederation

BGP Route Reflectors

Route reflectors create a hub-and-spoke topology from the control plane standpoint. RR is the hub and the clients are the spokes.

RRs and RR clients form a cluster. There should be more than one RR in a cluster for redundancy and load-sharing. For different address families a different set of route reflectors can be used. This avoids fate sharing.

For example, if IPv4 RR is attacked, VPN customers may not be impacted if different sets of RR are used. One RR can be a client of another RR. Hierarchical RR deployment is possible for very large-scale scenarios. It is like an EIGRP summarization at every tier. Don't forget that RR hides the path You need additional mechanisms to advertise all or selected paths to the route reflector clients if necessary.

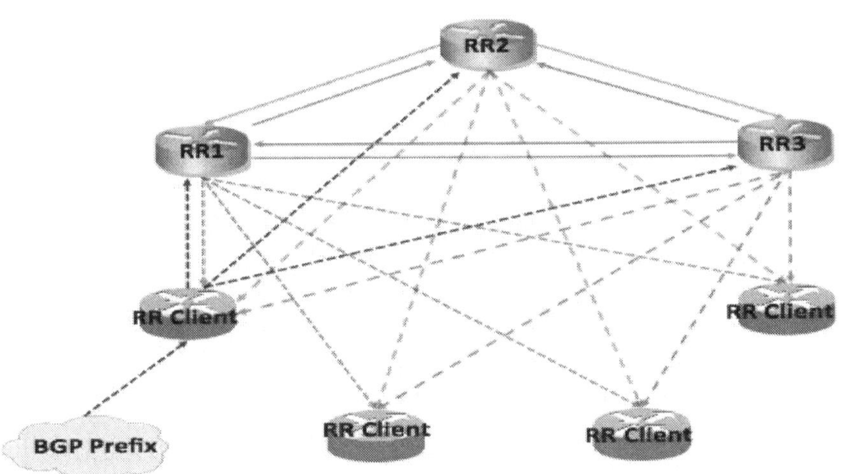

Prefix p/24 is sent from the RR client to three of the RRs. Route reflector has full mesh among them. They send the prefixes to each other. BGP route reflector cluster is the collection of BGP route reflectors and route reflector clients. The RR uses Cluster ID for loop prevention. RR clients don't know which cluster they belong to.

In the above picture, instead of P router, if we had a BGP route reflector then PE3 wouldn't receive the backup path. Because route reflectors hide the paths, select the best path and advertise only the best path to the route reflector clients.

BGP Route Reflector Clusters

BGP route reflectors, used as an alternate method to full mesh IBGP, help in scaling.

BGP route reflector clustering is used to provide redundancy in a BGP RR design. BGP Route reflectors and its clients create a cluster.

In IBGP topologies, every BGP speaker has to be in a logical full mesh. However, route reflector is an exception.

IBGP router sets up BGP neighborship with only the route reflectors.

Some Terminology first:

Route Reflector Cluster ID has four-byte BGP attribute, and, by default, it uses a BGP router ID.

If two routers share the same BGP cluster ID, they belong to the same cluster.

Before reflecting a route, route reflectors append its cluster ID to the cluster list. If the route is originated from the route reflector itself, then route reflector does not create a cluster list.

If the route is sent to EBGP peer, RR removes the cluster list information.

If the route is received from EBGP peer, RR does not create a cluster list attribute.

Cluster list is used for loop prevention by only the route reflectors. Route reflector clients do not use cluster list attribute, so they do not know to which cluster they belong.

If RR receives the routes with the same cluster ID, it is discarded.

Let's start with the basic topology.

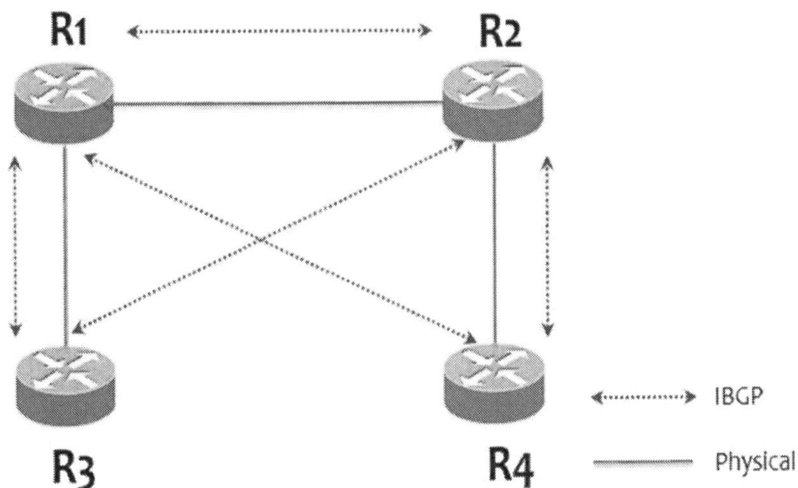

ROUTE REFLECTOR USES SAME CLUSTER ID

In the diagram shown above, R1 and R2 are the route reflectors, and R3 and R4 are the RR clients. Both route reflectors use the same cluster ID. Green lines depict physical connections. Red lines show IBGP connections.

Assume that we use both route reflectors as cluster ID 1.1.1.1 that is R1's router ID.

R1 and R2 receive routes from R4.

R1 and R2 receive routes from R3.

Both R1 and R2 as route reflectors append 1.1.1.1 as cluster ID attributes that they send to each other. However, since they use same cluster, they discard the routes of each other.

That's why; if RRs use the same cluster ID, RR clients have to connect to both RRs.

In this topology, routes behind R4 are learned only from the R1-R4 direct IBGP session by the R1 (R1 rejects from R2). Of course, IGP path goes through R1-R2-R4, since there is no physical path between R1-R4.

If the physical link between R2 and R4 goes down, both IBGP sessions between R1-R4 and R2-R4 goes down as well.

Thus, the networks behind R4 cannot be learned.

Since, the routes cannot be learned from R2 (the same cluster ID), if physical link is up and IBGP session goes down between R1 and R4, networks behind R4 will not be reachable either, but if you have BGP neighborship between loopbacks and physical topology is redundant, the chance of IBGP session going down is very hard.

Note: Having redundant physical links in a network design is a common best practice. That's why below topology is a more realistic one.

WHAT IF WE ADD A PHYSICAL LINK BETWEEN R1-R4 AND R2-R3?

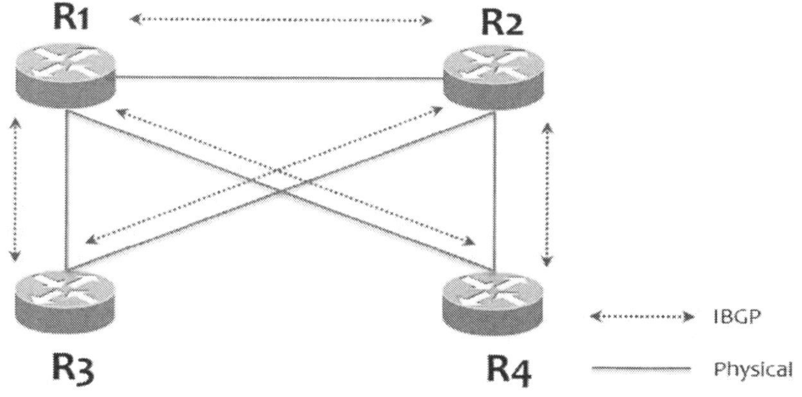

Figure-2 Route Reflector uses same cluster-ID, physical cross-connection is added between the RR and RR clients

In Figure-2 physical cross-connections are added between R1-R4 and R2-R3.

Still, we are using the same BGP cluster ID on the route reflectors. Thus, when R2 reflects R4 routes to R1, R1 will discard those routes. In addition, R1 will learn R4 routes through direct IBGP peering with R4. In this case, IGP path will change to R1-R4 rather than to R1-R2-R4.

In a situation in which R1-R4 physical link fails, IBGP session will not go down if the IGP converges to R1-R2-R4 path quicker than BGP session timeout (By default it does).

Thus, having the same cluster ID on the RRs saves a lot of memory and CPU resource on the route reflectors even though link failures do not cause IBGP session drop if there is enough redundancy in the network. If we would use different BGP cluster ID on R1 and R2, R1 would accept reflected routes from R2 in addition to routes from direct peering with R4.

I recommend using same BGP Cluster ID for the Route Reflector redundancy otherwise route reflectors would keep an extra copy for each prefix without extra benefit though some designs, depending on the physical topology might require accepting those prefixes as well.

BGP Route Reflector behavior in MPLS VPN

If BGP topology is not full mesh but there is Route Reflector then in MPLS/VPN environment unique RD is configured on the PEs to advertise different VPN prefixes to the Route Reflectors

Because RD is different the VPNv4 prefixes are different. Both PE1 and PE2's advertisements are reflected to PE3. Now on the PE3 Load sharing or Fast Reroute (BGP PIC) is possible

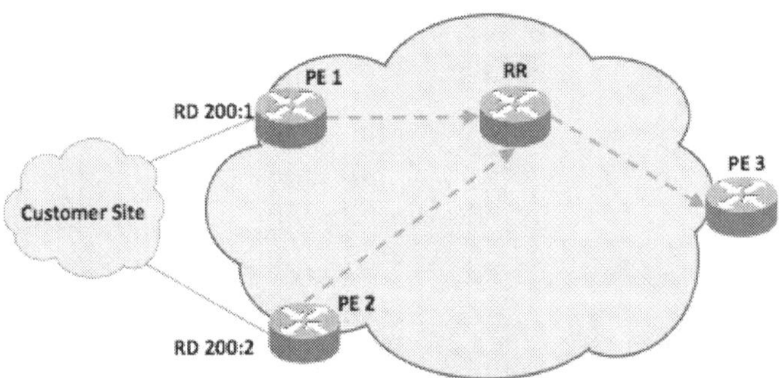

Changing BGP Route Reflector Behavior

If you want to send more than one best path by the BGP Route Reflectors for multi-pathing or fast reroute purpose, then use these approaches.

- Unique RD per VRF per PE. Unique route distinguisher is used per VRF per PE. No need, Add-Path, Shadow RRs, Diverse Paths. Only applicable in MPLS VPNs.
- BGP Add-Path
- BGP Shadow Route Reflectors
- BGP Shadow Sessions

BGP Shadow Route Reflectors to send more than one best path

Shadow Route reflectors. There are two route reflectors; one route reflector sends best path, the second one calculates the second best and sends the second best path.

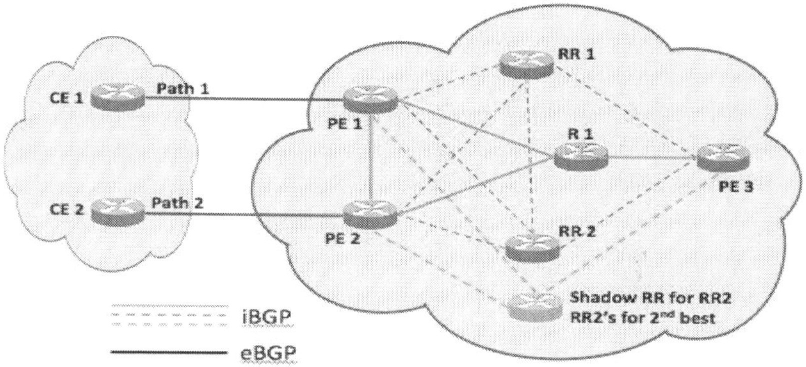

R1 and R2 is used for redundancy and they advertise the best path to the PE3 RR2' calculates and advertises only the second best path.

In the topology above, path P1 and P2 is learned by both RR1 and RR2. Customer sends lower MED on path P2 to use their links active/ standby. In order to send both paths to the RRs, BGP best external is enabled on PE1 and PE2, thus RR1 and RR2 receives both P1 and P2 paths. Since BGP MED is lower from the P2 path, RR1 and RR2 choose PE2 as best exit. Only PE2 is advertised as best path towards R3.

By deploying RR2, we can send the second best which is path from PE1 towards PE3. Shadow route reflector deployments don't require MPLS in the network.

Shadow sessions: Second IBGP session can be created between RRs and PE. PE is used here as a general term for edge BGP node. Shadow RR and shadow sessions design don't require MPLS in the network.

On the above topology, second sessions can be created between RR1, RR2, and PE3. Over the second IBGP session, second best can be sent. This session is called a shadow route reflector session.

BGP Add-Path

With shadow RR or shadow sessions, there are secondary IBGP sessions between RR and PEs. But the same behavior can be achieved with BGP Add-Path without an extra IBGP session between Route Reflector and the Route reflector clients.

BGP Add-path uses path-identifier to distinguish the different next hops over one IBGP session.

In BGP, if multiple paths are sent over the same BGP session, the last one is kept since it is seen as the latest update. When using VPN route reflectors, you can use multiple route reflectors for different prefixes if scalability is a concern. Based on route targets, we can use route reflector Group-1 to serve odd route target values and route reflector Group-2 to serve even route target values.

In this solution, PEs send all the RT values to both route reflector groups. They receive and process all the prefixes, but based on odd/even ownership they filter out the unwanted ones. However, processing the prefixes which will be filtered anyway is not efficient.

Instead, route target constraints should be deployed so route reflectors can signal to the PE devices that are route reflector clients their desired route target values.

BGP Add-Path vs. BGP Shadow RR vs. BGP Shadow Sessions vs. Unique RD per VRF per PE Approaches Design Comparison

When route reflectors are deployed in the network, they only send the best path to clients. Some applications such as Fast Reroute, Multipath and Optimal Routing as explained before, requires more than one best path to be advertised from the Route Reflectors to the Route Reflector clients. There are many approaches for that as they were explained earlier in the chapter. Below table summarizes the similarities and the differences of these design models in great detail.

In MPLS deployment, the Unique RD per VRF per PE is the best method.

Network designers should know the pros and cons of the technologies, protocol alternatives and their capabilities from the design point of view.

Design Requirement	BGP Add Path	BGP Shadow RR	BGP Shadow Sessions	MPLS Unique RD per PE per VRF
Best in MPLS	No	No	No	Yes
How many IBGP Session between RR and RR-Client	One IBGP session, Path IDs are different for different next-hop	One session per Route reflectos. If there is only one more Shadow RR which sends second best path, two IBGP sessions on the RR Client, one for each RR	One session per next-hop. Only one RR but multiple separate IBGP session is required between RR and RR Client	One IBGP session between VPN RR and RR Client, different RDs make the same IP prefixes unique
Resource Requirement	Best	Worst, requires separate RR and IBGP session per next-hop	Better than Shadow RR because doesn't requre separate Route reflector, worse than ADD path because require extra IBGP session per next-hop	Same as Add-path, doesn't require extra IBGP session or Route Reflector
Migration of existing Route Reflectors	Very hard,all Route Reflectors and clients need to be upgraded to support Add-path	Easy, only Route Reflector code needs to be upgraded	Easy,only Route Reflector code needs to be upgraded	Easiest because there is no upgrade on any device. Only unique/separate Route Distinguisher needs to be configured on the Pes per VRF
Standard Protocol	Yes IETF Standard	Yes IETF Standard	Yes IETF Standard	Yes IETF Standard
Stuff Experince	Not well known	Not well known	Not well known	Known
Troubleshooting	Hard,default behaviour of BGP which is advertising only one best path is changing. Operation stuff needs to learn new troubleshooting skill	Easy	Easy	Easy
IPv6 Support	Yes	Yes	Yes	Yes
Provisioning	Easy, only one IBGP session between Route reflector and the client	Hard, one IBGP session per next-hop	Hard, one IBGP session per next-hop	Easiest,only the consideration is to have unique RD per VRF per PE

BGP Add-Path vs. BGP Shadow RR vs BGP Shadow Sessions vs. Unique RD per VRF per PE Design Comparison

BGP Route Reflector Case Study

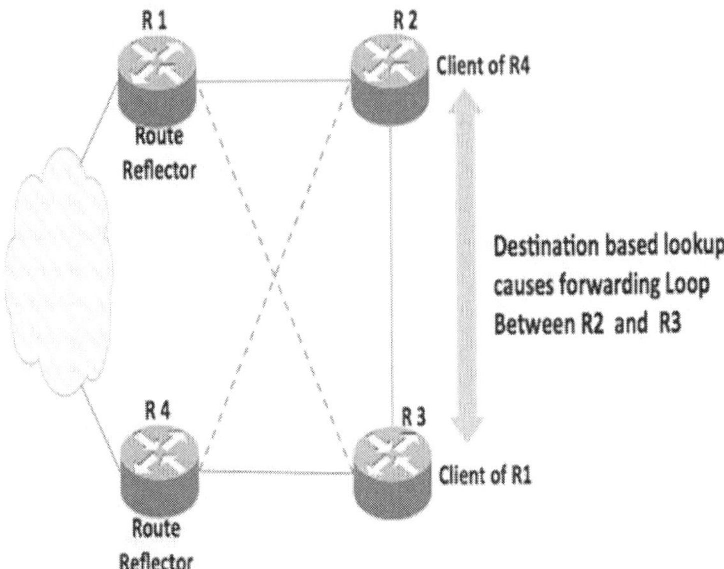
R1
R2
Client of R4
Route
Reflector
Destination based lookup
causes forwarding Loop
Between R2 and R3
R4
R3
Client of R1
Route
Reflector
R3 should be a client of R4 instead of R1 . R2 should be a client of R1 instead of R4.
Then, we wouldn't have this problem

BGP Route Reflector logical topology should follow physical topology in IP backbones

In the above topology, R2 is the route reflector client of R4 and R3 is the route reflector client of R1.

- MPLS or any tunneling mechanism is not enabled. What is the problem with this design?
- Would this be a problem if MPLS were enabled?

In this topology, permanent forwarding loop occurs. (Not micro-loop, which is, resolved automatically when the topology converged.)

- Suppose prefix A is coming from the cloud in the topology above to the Route Reflectors.
- Route Reflectors reflects to their clients by putting themselves as next-hop.

For example, when the packet comes to R2, R2 will do IP-based destination lookup for prefix A and find the next hop as R4, so it will send the packet to R3, because R3 is the only physical path towards R4.

When R3 receives the packet, it will do the destination-based lookup for prefix A, and then it will find R1 as next hop.

To reach R1, R3 will send the packet to R2.

R2 will do the lookup for prefix A and send it to R2; R3 will send it back. Packet will loop between R2 and R3.

If MPLS were enabled, we wouldn't have the same behavior, since when R2 does the destination lookup for prefix A, it will find the next hop R4, but in order to reach R4, it would push the transport label. When R3 receives the packet from R2, R3 wouldn't do the IP-based lookup, but instead MPLS label lookup, so it would swap the incoming label from R2 to outgoing label towards R4.

BGP Route Reflector Design Considerations and Hot and Cold Potato Routing

If someone tosses you a hot potato, do you want to hold it a long time? If you like pain maybe the answer is yes – but how many of us like pain? In the same way, hot potatoes are very applicable to the IBGP design. When a service provider receives a packet, if the destination is another service provider, they don't want to keep the traffic in their network long time.

Why? The answer lies in simple economics, including the different types of peering relationships between providers. Before going further into an explanation and design cases for hot, cold and mash potatoes, let's take a look what are these arrangements.

Service providers can be grouped as Tier 1, 2, or 3 depending on their topology, traffic, and the geographically separation of their networks. This concept was explained earlier in this chapter.

If a service provider receives a service and/or connection from a provider at a higher tier, this arrangement is called a transit relationship. A tier 2 SP is upstream the service provider of Tier 3 SP, and tier 2 SP gets their service and/or connection from Tier1 provider.

Tier 1 providers have their own transmission facilities, connecting geographically separated regions.

Service providers pay to transit traffic to a service provider at a different tier; tier 2 providers pay tier 1 provider for transit, and tier 3 providers pay tier 2 providers for transit, etc. Along the same tier, or among providers that exchange about an equal amount of traffic, providers create settlement free peering relationships. How does all of this relate to hot potato routing?

Service providers don't want to keep their customer traffic in their network if they can push it off onto another provider's network, especially if it's the destination is reachable through a peering connection for which they don't pay the other provider, so they will move the traffic quickly out of their network into a peering provider's network.

This is hot potato routing. Hot potato routing aims to bring traffic to the closest exit point from where it enters the network.

I will use the below figure to explain some of the concepts. In AS1, there are 2 Route reflectors, which can be in same or different clusters. Route Reflector clustering design will be explained in this chapter.

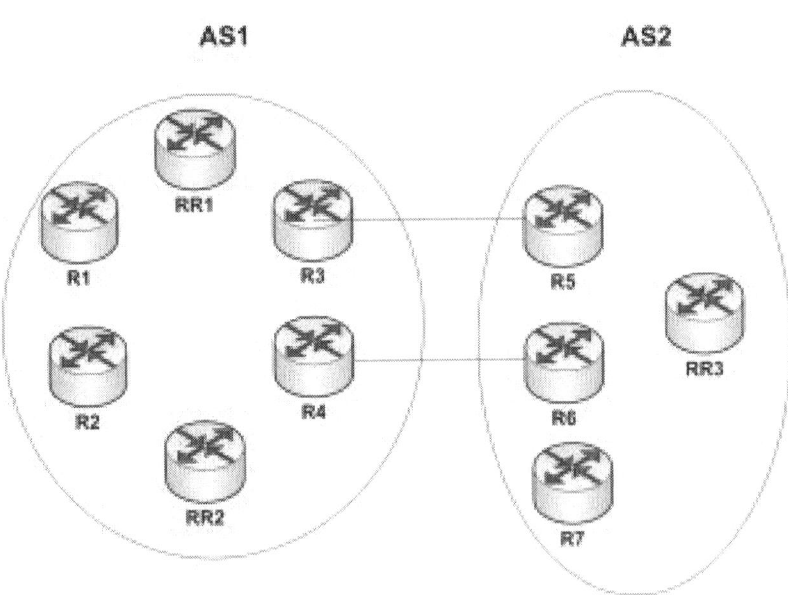

Service Providers Hot Potato Routing

Between AS1 and AS2 there are 2 links to exit from the domain. For the traffic behind AS2, AS1 wants to send the traffic the nearest BGP exit point. To accomplish this, the IGP metric to the BGP next hop is used as the tiebreaker, in other words, R1 needs to find the closest EBGP speaker, which can reach the destination in AS2.

If R5 or R6, in AS2, are sending the prefix with a MED attribute set, AS1 should remove the MED for the incoming prefixes to get hot potato routing.

Different vendor BGP implementations may vary for using the MED attribute although latest RFC defines if the MED is not set from the sender AS, then receiving AS handle as minimum possible value.

This can remove the inconsistency.

But to get hot potato routing, the network designer needs to move beyond BGP metrics, and work with the internal topology of the provider's network. Inside an AS, three type of BGP topology can exist.

BGP Full mesh, confederation or route reflector. Full mesh IBGP topologies where the MED is ignored will naturally choose the exit point closest to the entrance point. For route reflector topologies, the closer the RRs to the EBGP speakers along the edge of the network, the more accurately traffic will follow the IGP metrics, so the closer the AS will come to achieving optimal hot potato routing.

Service providers, especially when their BGP topologies get bigger, implement route reflector or confederations. Route reflectors increase scaling by hiding alternate paths from their clients, which involves a set of tradeoffs.

Instead of having every potential exit point from the AS, any given EBGP speaker will now only have the set of exit points the RR sends the optimal exit points from the RR's perspective. But this best path may not be the best path to exit from the domain from the internal IBGP device point of view; it is the best path from the route reflector point of view.

Traditional BGP works like this, there is couple paper out there about path-state vector, the idea is sending the policy information more than one hop away and overcome the BGP slow converge issue. (Here I am comparing the speed with the IGP protocol, not full mesh vs. route reflector in BGP.). But even with that idea, route reflector best path selection and advertisement behavior doesn't change.

Three different proposals have been put forward which can be used to resolve this problem: BGP add paths, diverse path, and computing the best path from the client's point of view. Add path and diverse path can be used to send more than one exit point to internal BGP speaker. But with these approaches, idea is to send more than one best path, which is seen by the RR to the internal IBGP speaker. (Add Path and Diverse Path/Shadow RR was explained earlier in this chapter.)

IBGP speaker holds these path, can be installed into the RIB if multipath is enabled, or can even be programmed into the FIB as an alternate/backup path with the BGP PIC.

The Problem with Add Path and diverse paths is simply carrying the additional paths. The RR clients don't know all possible paths to exit from the domain, they need to know closest one to achieve hot potato routing, or the most optimal exit point for cold potato routing.

Although implementations support sending `"1, 2,, n," paths, sending less than and may not give the correct result, sending all possible paths defeat the use of route reflector. Routers has to keep all the states in their at least BGP RIB-IN database.

The alternate idea is to select the best path on the RR from the internal IBGP speaker point of view and distribute the best path to internal speakers based on their topology view. Whenever a BGP route reflector would need to decide what path or paths need to be selected for advertisement to one of its clients, the route reflector would need to virtually position itself in its client IGP network location in order to choose the right set of paths based on the IGP metric to the next hops from the client's perspective. This is called BGP Optimal Route Reflector Placement and will be explained in this chapter.

Cold potato routing is used for the opposite situation – when the provider wants to carry the traffic inside its network for as long as possible, or bring the network as close to the actual recipient as possible. Cold potato generally is used for content delivery network, where the target is to manage the user experience.

To achieve cold potato routing, R1 needs to know which exit point is topologically closest to the destination. Why should we use cold potato maybe you are asking right now. One answer is content delivery networks; another is that service providers prefer to keep traffic that is destined to paying customers within their network. For peering it can vary, sending site the traffic may pay, or can be related with the traffic volume or can be totally based on mutual benefit.

In the above figure, if Service Provider B is receiving transit service from the Service Provider A, then it can choose the exit whichever Service Provider B wants.

Service Provider B could send a MED attribute or prepend one advertisement while leaving another advertisement without any prepend to influence inbound traffic.

Or it could send a community as a signal to Service Provider A to raise the Local Preference of one path over another. But all these attributes can be easily remove from the BGP update depends on the agreement between the Service Providers.

Google, Facebook, and Akamai bring their cache engines and servers to IXP (Internet exchange point) or directly into the service provider network to avoid hot potato routing to their network. This is actually good for end users, providers, and Google, while reducing the value of the services transit providers well. When their cache engine is closer to the actual users, service providers can better control the traffic and use best exit to reach to content.

Hot and cold potato routing sends the traffic either exit closest to the entry, or the exit, closest to the actual destination.

Route reflectors can be deployed to avoid operational concern, avoid keeping the routing states in each BGP devices.

Route reflectors also need to be fully meshed to allow prefix distribution inside an AS, and in some topologies, Hierarchical BGP Route reflection can be created as second level hierarchy.

Full-Mesh IBGP vs. BGP Route Reflectors vs. BGP Confederation Design Comparison

Below table summarizes the similarities and the differences of these three IBGP design models in great detail.

Network designers should know the pros and cons of the technologies, protocol alternatives and their capabilities from the design point of view.

Although BGP Route Reflectors are most widely deployed in large-scale networks, still there are some BGP confederation deployments in real life as well.

Design Requirement	Full Mesh IBGP	BGP Route Reflector	BGP Confederation
Scalability	Least, between each BGP node there is an IBGP session, number of session and configuration is highest	High since there is only one IBGP session on the RR client, if there are two RRs, two sessions per RR client	Medium since it requires Route Reflector inside each Sub AS for scalability
Logical Topology	Full Mesh	Hub and Spoke between Route Reflectors and the RR Clients	Point to point between Sub Ases, Hub and Spoke RR- RR client in Sub AS or Full mesh IBGP inside Sub AS
Resource Requirement	Highest	Lowest	Medium
Number of Next Hop	All available next-hops are sent thus highest resource consumption on the BGP routers.	Only one best path is sent by RR to RR Clients. Thuslowest resource consumption among other options	Depends on Full mesh IBGP or RR inside Sub AS, if full mesh all the available paths, if RR is used, then only one best path is sent
Loop Prevention	No loop since all the BGP routers direct IBGP peer	Cluster List and Originator ID are used for loop prevention	Between Sub Ases EBGP rules apply,if Sub AS sees it's own AS number in the AS path, packet is dropped
Migration from Full Mesh	No	Migration from Full Mesh IBGP is easy compare to Confederation	Migration from Full Mesh IBGP is hard compare to BGP Route Reflectors
Standard Protocol	Yes	Yes	Yes

Design Requirement	Full Mesh IBGP	BGP Route Reflector	BGP Confederation
Different IGP inside an AS	Technically Yes but running same IGP is the best practice inside an AS	Technically Yes but running same IGP is the best practice inside an AS	Definitely yes and there is no problem.One of the advantages of BGP Confederation,compare to BGP RR design. Inside an each Sub AS, different IGP can run, IGP topologies are not extended between SUB Ases
Commonly Used	Small scale environment most common	Large scale environment most common	Not very common
Path Visibility	All the available path are known by the IBGP routers. Highest level visibility	Route Reflectors only advertise best path to RR client, path visibility is worst	Depends.Inside Sub AS if Full Mesh IBGP, it is best, if RR is running, worst.
Provisioning	Hard since it requires too much configuration	Very easy, one IBGP session per RR	Medium. Worse than Route Reflector.
IPv6 Support	Yes	Yes	Yes
Default Convergence	Fastest since all IBGP routers connected directly,second best path is already known by the routers	Worst since RR adds extra convergence time and the RR clients know only the best path when RR is deployed	Depends.If Full Mesh IBGP then fast, if RR inside an AS, then slow.
MPLS VPN support	Yes	Yes	Yes but hard to manage since Inter-AS VPN operation is required

Full-Mesh IBGP vs. BGP Route Reflectors vs. BGP Confederation Design Models Comparison

BGP Hot and Cold Potato Routing Case Study

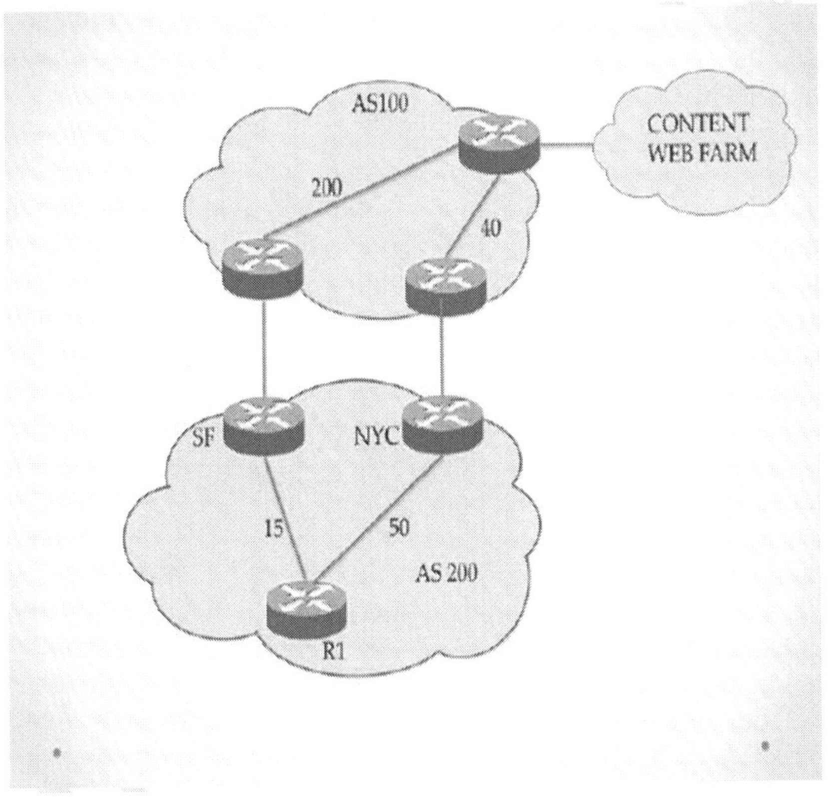

BGP Hot and Cold Potato Routing Case Study

AS 200 is a customer service provider of AS 100 transit service provider. Customers of AS 200 are trying to reach a web page located behind AS 100. AS 200 is not implementing any special BGP policy.

What would be the ingress and egress traffic for AS 200?

The illustration depicts the AS 100 and AS 200 connections. They have a BGP peer (customer-transit) relationship in two locations, San Francisco and New York.

IGP distances are shown in the diagram. Since there is not any special BGP policy, hot potato rule will apply and egress path will be chosen from AS 200 and AS 100 based on IGP distances.

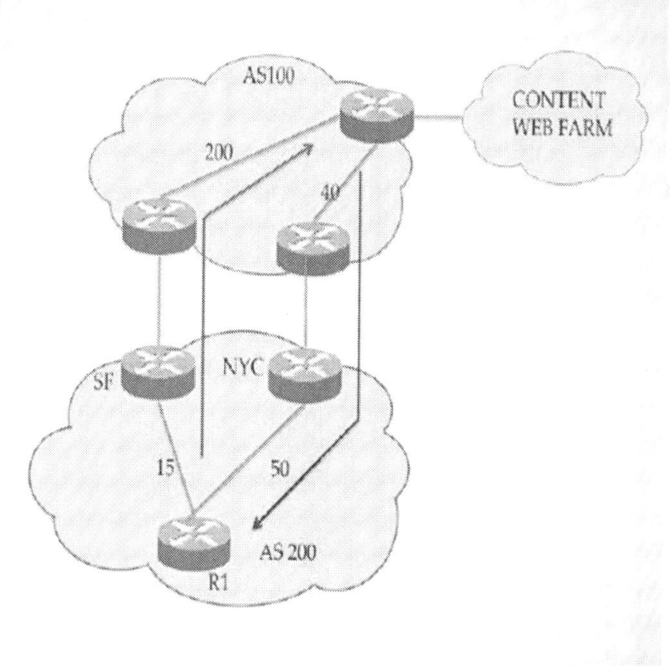

BGP Hot and Cold Potato Routing

In this diagram, egress traffic from AS 200 is the green arrow, since SF path is shorter IGP distance. Ingress traffic to AS 200 from AS 100 is the blue arrow, since NYC connection from AS 100 is shorter IGP distance (40 vs. 200).

AS 200 is complaining about the performance and they are looking for a solution to fix the problem behavior. What would you suggest to AS 200?

- Customer AS 200 should force AS100 for cold potato routing. Since they are customers, their service providers have to do cold potato routing for them.
- By forcing for cold potato routing, AS 100 has to carry the Web content traffic to the closest exit point to AS 200, which is San Francisco.

That's why AS 200 is sending its prefixes from SF with lower MED than NYC as depicted below.

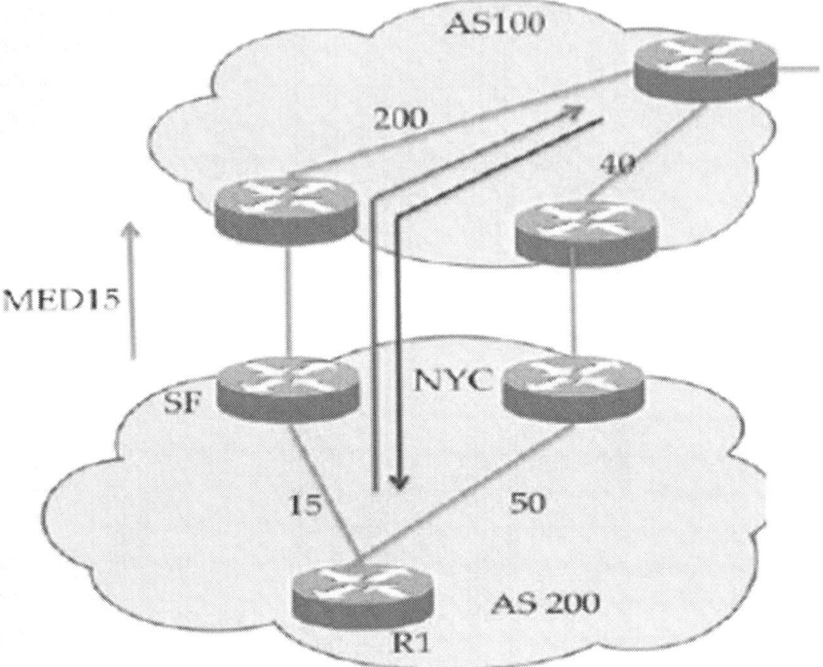

Problem with the Hot Potato Routing

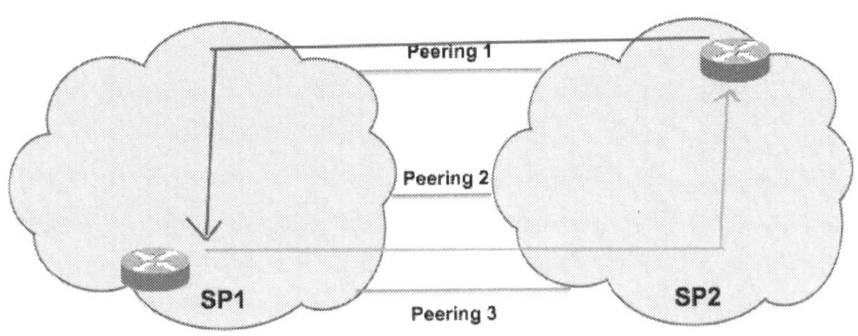

Hot Potato Routing Traffic Pattern over Peering links

In the above figure, there are two Service Providers, SP1 and SP2. They have three peering connections in different places.

There is a traffic demand between the two routers as it is depicted in the figure. Both Service Providers would do the Hot Potato routing because the links are peering links. Not the customer, provider connections.

In this case SP1 to destination traffic would be similar to the Green path. SP2 to destination traffic would be similar to the Blue Path.

But what if they would coordinate and would send the traffic towards peering link 2 for this traffic demand?

If they would coordinate and wouldn't do Hot Potato routing, traffic pattern would be as below figure. Obviously below traffic would be beneficial for both providers.

In the above figure their Internal uplinks are used more than below one. I call below option as Coordinated Routing.

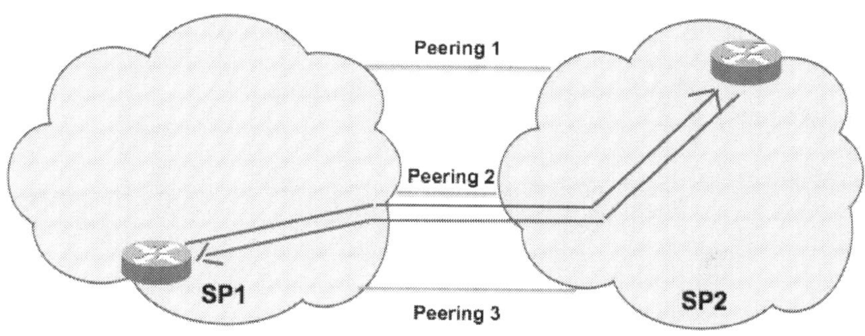

Coordinated Routing Traffic Pattern over Peering Links

BGP PIC (BGP Prefix Independent Convergence, a.k.a BGP FRR)

BGP PIC (Prefix Independent Convergence) is a BGP Fast reroute mechanism which can provides sub second convergence even for the 500K Internet prefixes by taking help of IGP convergence.

BGP PIC uses hierarchical data plane in contrast to flat FIB design, which is used by Cisco CEF and many legacy platforms.

In a hierarchical dataplane, the FIB used by the packet-processing engine reflects recursions between the routes.

There are two implementation of BGP PIC concept and it can protect from multiple failures. Link, node in the core or edge of the network can be recovered under a second and most of the case under 100ms (It mostly depends on IGP convergence, so IGP should be tuned or IGP FRR can be used).

As I mentioned above there are two implementation of BGP PIC namely, BGP PIC Edge and BGP PIC Core.

Let's start with BGP PIC Core.

BGP PIC CORE

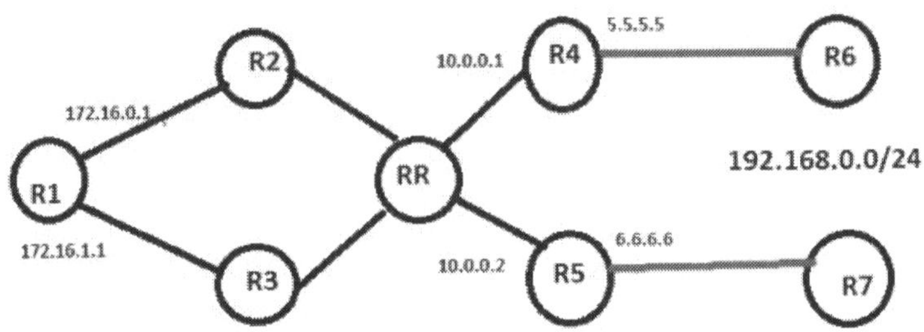

BGP PIC Core

In the above figure, R1, R2, R3, R4, R5 and RR (Route Reflector) belongs to AS 100, R6 and R7 belongs to AS 200.

There are two EBGP connections between ASBRs of the Service Providers.

Everybody told you so far that BGP converges slow because BGP is good for scalability not for the fast convergence, right?

But that is wrong too.

If BGP relies on control plane to converge of course it will be slow since the default timers are long (BGP MRAI, BGP Scanner and so on, although you don't need to rely on them as I will explain now).

Default free zone is already more than 500K prefixes. So approximately we are talking about 50 MB of data from each neighbor, it takes time to process. If you have multiple paths, amount of data that needs to be processed will be much higher.

Let's look at BGP control plane convergence closer.

BGP Control Plane Convergence:

Imagine that R1 in the above picture learns 192.168.0.0/24 prefix from R4 only. R4 is the next hop. (You have chooses maybe R4 as primary link with Local preference, MED or you don't do anything but R4 is selected by the hot potato routing because of Route Reflector position)

If R4 is the best path, R5 doesn't send 192.168.0.0/24 prefix to the IBGP domain unless BGP best external is enabled (It should be enabled if you want additional path information in Active/Standby link scenarios).

Now imagine that R4 fails. Convergence on the Route Reflector will depend on if BGP Best External is enabled on the R5.

If it is not enabled, R5 should perform best path calculation, advertise the prefixes to the Route Reflector, Route Reflector will run best path selection and advertise them to the R1, and R1 will run best path selection and place the prefixes to the RIB.

How IBGP routers learn that R4 is failed?

There are two mechanisms for that. They will either wait for the BGP Scanner time (60 seconds in most implementation) to check whether the BGP next hop for the BGP prefixes are still up, or the newer approach is BGP Next Hop tracking (Almost all vendors support it).

With BGP next hop tracking, BGP next hop prefixes are registered to the IGP route watch process, so as soon as IGP detects the BGP next hop failure, BGP process is informed.So R1 learned the R4 failure through IGP. Then R1 has to delete all the BGP prefixes, which are learned from R4. If it is full Internet routing table, it is very time consuming process as you can imagine.

In the absence of already calculated backup path, BGP will rely on control plane convergence so of course it will take time. But you don't have to rely on that. I recommend many service providers to start consider BGP PIC for their Internet and VPN services.

In the routers routing table there is always a recursion for the BGP prefixes. So for the 192.168.0.0/24 subnet the next hop would be 10.0.0.1, if the next-hop self is enabled, otherwise since IBGP doesn't change BGP next hop by default when the prefixes are received from an EBGP peer, 5.5.5.5 would be a next hop.

But in order to forward the traffic, router need to resolve immediate next hop and layer 2 encapsulation.

So for the 10.0.0.1 or 5.5.5.5, R1 selects either 172.16.0.1 or 172.16.1.1. Or R1 can do the ECMP (Equal Cost Multipath).

In the many vendors FIB implementation, BGP prefixes resolve immediate IGP next hop. Cisco's CEF implementation works in this way too. This is not necessarily a bad thing though. It provides better throughput since the router doesn't have to do double/aggregate lookup. But from the fast convergence point of view, we need a hierarchical data plane (Hierarchical FIB). With the BGP PIC, both PIC Core and PIC Edge solutions, you will have hierarchical data plane so for the 192.168.0.0/24 you will have 10.0.0.1 or 5.5.5.5 as the next hop in the FIB (Same as RIB).

For the 10.0.0.1 and 5.5.5.5 you will have another FIB entry which points to the IGP next hops, which is 172.16.0.1 and 172.16.1.1. These IGP next hops can be used as load shared or active/standby manner.

BGP PIC Core helps to hide IGP failure, from the BGP process. If the links between R1-R2 or R2-R3 fails, or as a device, R2 or R3 fails, R1 starts to use backup IGP next hop immediately.

Since the BGP next hop doesn't change and only the IGP path changes, recovery time will be based on IGP convergence. For the BGP PIC Core you don't have to have multiple IBGP next hop. BGP PIC Core can handle core IGP link and node failures.

BGP PIC Edge on the other hand, provides sub second BGP fast recovery in the case of Edge link or node failure.

BGP PIC EDGE

BGP PIC Edge provides sub second convergence time in the case of edge link or node failure. BGP PIC Edge is especially useful for MPLS VPN service and can be provided by the Service provider as a value added service thus might provide additional revenue.

Sub second convergence is not possible without PIC – Prefix Independent Convergence for BGP.

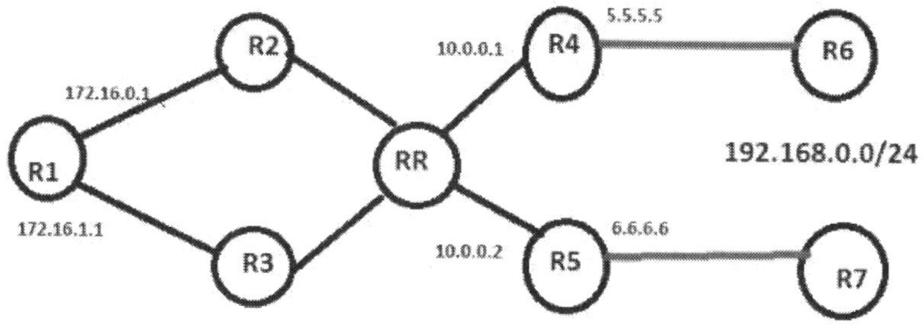

BGP PIC (Prefix Independent Convergence) Edge

In order BGP PIC Edge to work, edge IBGP devices (Ingress PEs and ASBRs) need to support BGP PIC and also they need to receive backup BGP next hop.

In the above topology, R1 is the ingress PE, R4 and R5 are the ASBR nodes. Route Reflector is shown in the data path but it is not recommended in real network design. Unfortunately backup next hop is not sent when BGP Route Reflector is introduced since RR selects and advertises only the best path for the given prefix. For example, in the above topology, R6 and R7 both sends, 192.168.0.0/24 network but R1 can learn from the RR only one exit point (BGP next-hop), either R4 or R5.

There are many ways to send more than one best path from BGP RR as we have seen earlier in this chapter. But let's assume, R1 learns the 192.168.0.0/24 prefix from R4 and R5 by using one of those ways.

How BGP PIC Edge Works?

Let's assume link between R1 learns the 192.168.0.0/24 prefix from R4 and R5 and choose the best exit point as R4. In this case R5 is marked as backup/alternate next hop and programmed into the FIB (Forwarding Information Base) of R1. Let's examine some failure and see how BGP PIC takes an action. BGP PIC edge in case of edge link fails but ASBR doesn't set next-hop self

In case R4-46 link fails and R4 doesn't set next-hop to itself (No next-hop self). In that case, link between R4 and r6 is advertised to the IGP. When R4-R6 link fails, R1 learns the failure from the IGP. BGP Next-hop tracking feature helps here. IGP protocols register to the BGP Next-hop tracking process.

When R1 learns the link failure between R4-R6, it immediately changes the BGP next hop for the 192.168.0.0/24 prefix to the R5. This switchover is done in less than a second regardless of the number of prefixes. Which mean even though you have million of BGP prefixes which need to be updated, still sub second convergence. (In this example for the simplicity only 192.168.0.0/24 prefix)

BGP PIC edge in case of edge link fails and ASBR set's next-hop self

When R4 sets BGP next hop to it self (It is done by setting the loopback as next-hop), since the loopback interface won't go down, even though R1 learns the link failure (if the R4-R6 link is redistributed into IGP) from IGP, it doesn't trigger BGP next-hop tracking to fails the BGP next hop, because BGP next hop for the 192.168.0.0/24 prefix is not the R4-R6 link address but the R4 loopback.

In this case R1 continue to send the traffic for the 192.168.0.0/24 prefix to the R4. But since the link between R4-R6 fails, when R4 receives the traffic destined to 192.168.0.0/24, it should send towards R5 immediately. (That's why; not only Ingress nodes, but also ASBRs should learn the alternate next-hop)

When do you set next-hop self on the edge BGP node?

In MPLS VPN environment it is the best practice and almost mandatory to set the BGP next hop to the PE loopback. With that, transport LSP can be created to that PE loopback.

So far in the examples, BGP PIC edge protected the link failures.

BGP PIC edge in case of edge node failure

What if R4 fails? How R1 would reach to that failure?

In case R4 fails, IGP will trigger the BGP Next-hop tracking and R1 can change the next-hop as R5 for all the BGP prefixes. Convergence is again sub-second regardless of a number of BGP prefixes.

BGP PIC Conclusion:

- BGP PIC – Prefix Independent Convergence is a BGP data plane convergence mechanism, not a control plane. Thus convergence time is only related with IGP convergence and it is prefix independent. If you have 500K full Internet routing table, all of them will be installed in the FIB before the failure as a backup route and when the failure happens, next BGP next hop is used immediately.

- BGP PIC is also known as BGP Fast Reroute.
- BGP PIC is very suitable for MPLS VPN service, especially when the customers pays and ask tight convergence time in any failure scenario.
- When BGP PIC is enabled, adding backup path for the million pf prefixes require additional memory and CPU, that's why resources should be monitored carefully
- BGP PIC is not a Cisco proprietary protocol; most of the vendors implement BGP PIC today. Juniper Networks is implementing BGP PIC as well.

Hierarchical Service Provider Networks and BGP Best External

BGP Best External is used in Active Standby BGP Topologies generally but not limited with that.

BGP Best External feature helps BGP to converge much faster by sending external BGP prefixes, which wouldn't normally be sent if they are not overall BGP best path.

There are BGP best internal, BGP best external and BGP Overall best path.

BGP Best external in active-standby scenarios can be used in MPLS VPN, Internet Business Customers, EBGP Peering Scenarios, Hierarchical large scale Service Provider backbone and many others.

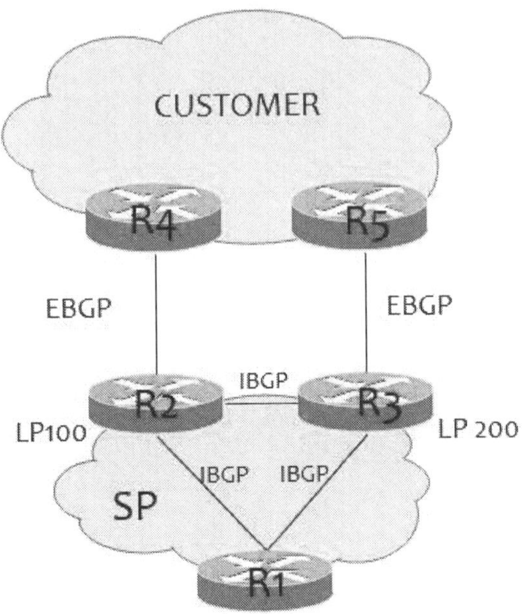

BGP Active-Standby Path Selection

In the above figure, IBGP is running in the Service Provider network. Between R1, R2 and R3 there is an IBGP full mesh sessions.

R2 and R3 are connected to customer network and EBGP is running between them. Since BGP Local Preference attribute is set on R3 as 200, R3 is used as egress point. In this case, best path in the Service Provider domain for this customer is R3 and it is advertised to R1 and R2.

Although R2 has a connection to customer network, since overall best path is IBGP path, R2 doesn't even send its connection to R3 and R1. This is against to BGP RFC but almost all vendors implemented their BGP in this way.

Before starting to explain BGP best external impact let's remember how BGP would converge in case primary link fails.

In case R3 to Customer link fails, R2 can learn the failure through IGP or BGP. If BGP next hop is the R3 loopback (It is always the case with MPLS Layer 3 VPN), when the external link fails, R2 cannot understand the failure from IGP update. R2 in that case waits BGP withdrawal and update messages from R3. When BGP update is completed, R2 install prefixes with its external path into the RIB and FIB.

Now let's enable BGP best external on R2.

When BGP best external is enabled on R2, although overall best path in BGP comes from IBGP neighbor, which is R3, R2 would send its best external path. Since R2 has only 1 external path, R2 would send its path to both R3 and R1.

Here is the trick. Implementations don't install best external path into the RIB and FIB of the routers unless BGP PIC is enabled. (Some vendors enable BGP PIC by default when BGP best external is enabled, Ex: Cisco)

Is BGP Best External helpful without BGP PIC?

Yes it is. Since in that case, R3 wouldn't wait BGP update from R2, it would only install prefixes into the RIB and FIB, because prefixes would be received from R2 and installed in BGP RIB when best external is enabled.

If BGP PIC and also BGP best external is enabled on R3, then in case R3 external link fails, R3 would start to send the traffic towards R2 because prefixes would be installed in RIB and FIB with the backup flag.

You can think that this solves the issue. You think that in the case of primary link fails; secondary link immediately is used without packet loss. Actually No.

If its pure IP network then microloop occurs. Because when R3 starts sending the traffic towards R2 (BGP PIC is enabled), R2 doesn't know yet that external link of R3 failed. R2 sends the traffic back to R3 and R3 sends it back to R2 because both does the IP lookup for the BGP prefix.

In MPLS VPN it is solved if the VPN label allocation is done per prefix or per CE since R2 and R3 in that case wouldn't do the IP lookup but based on inner (VPN) label, they would start to send the traffic towards customer. If VPN allocation is done per VRF, then in that case if two CEs are connected to R2, R2 has to do the IP lookup to distinguish the correct CE and because of IP lookup, R2 would send the traffic back to R3 and microloop would occur again.

So BGP best external and PIC in IP network will suffer from microloop but instead of loosing seconds or minutes for waiting BGP to convergence, when IGP is tuned, microloop can be resolved in less than a second, because R2 would be notified about the R3's external link failure as fast as possible.

Now let's look at the other example to see how BGP best external works and how it will help for the convergence. Also this example shows that you may not need BGP Add-path, BGP Shadow RRs/Shadow Sessions to send more than one path from Route Reflector in the specific topologies.

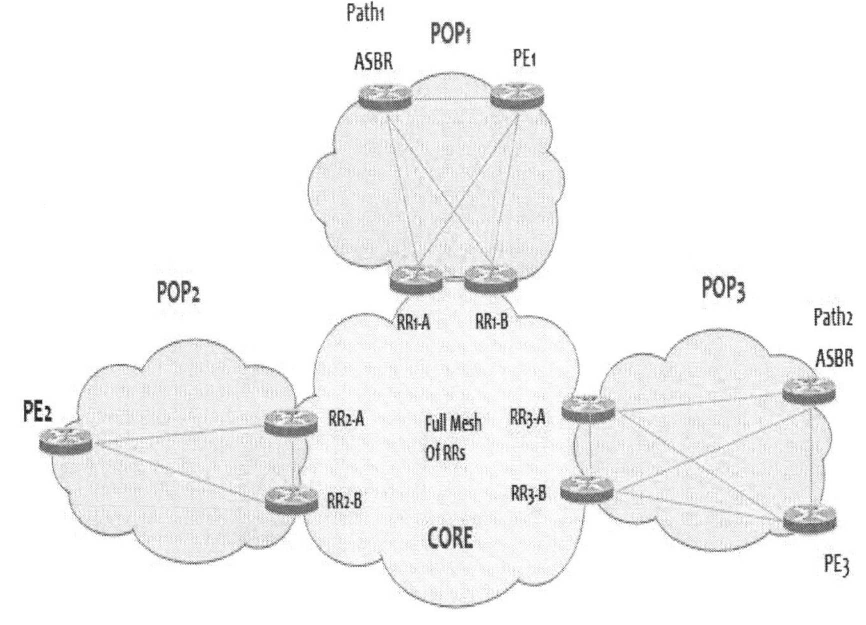

BGP Hierarchical Service Provider Backbone

Above topology was common in the past and still is used in some Service Provider networks. Pop and Core architecture is shown, without MPLS in the core. POP has Route Reflectors in the data path. For redundancy there are more than one Route Reflector. And the routes are summarized at the Core to POP boundary.

In the above figure, for the simplicity there are only 3 POPs, which are connected to the Core network is shown. Each pop has two RRs, which have full mesh IBGP sessions between them. In the core, there is PE, which is connected to the customer and ASBR, which is connected to upstream provider and receive BGP prefix. In the POP there is full mesh IBGP session as well.

Note that, there would be second level Hierarchy in the Core as well, because when the number of POP locations grow, required full mesh IBGP sessions between RRs would be too much.

For a given prefix, in this picture, we have two paths. Path1 from POP1 and Path 2 from POP3.

BGP best external in this topology can be enabled on two places. It can be enabled on the ASBRs and also Route Reflectors.

Let's assume Local preference is set to 200 on ASBR in Pop1 and 100 on ASBR in Pop3. This makes ASBR in Pop1 is the overall BGP best path for the prefix. If BGP best external is enabled only on the ASBRs but not on the Router Reflectors, then Route Reflectors in POP 1 and POP2 doesn't receive the best external path, which is Path 2 from POP3.

But POP3 RR3-A and RR3-B does receive overall best path which is Path 1 and best external path which is Path 2 because simply the ASBR in POP3 sends best external path to its RR which is RR3-A and RR3-B.

In this topology, BGP Add-path could be used to send best external path from RR3-A and RR3-B to the POP 1 and POP2 Route Reflectors. But the problem with BGP Add-path, it requires every PE, ASBRs and Route Reflector software and hardware upgrade.

Instead, BGP Best External is enabled on Route Reflector as well. This allows RR3-A and RR3-B to send best external path, which is Path 2 to POP1 and POP2 RRs. When we have overall best path and the BGP Best External path on the RRs, in case overall best path goes down, network convergence is greatly increased, especially when BGP PIC is used together with BGP best external on ASBRs and RRs.

For example, if traffic comes from POP2 that doesn't have ASBR and needs to go to the prefix, RR2-A and RR2-B will have two paths in this case. One is overall best path which is Path1 and another is best external path which is Path2.

Both paths would be installed in RRs RIB and FIB (BGP PIC is enabled in addition to BGP best external). In case Path 1 fails, since best external path is already in the RIB and FIB, BGP PIC would just changed the pointer to the best external BGP path and you wouldn't even lose packet.

Hierarchical SP Networks and Best External Conclusions:

- BGP best external helps BGP convergence both in IP and MPLS network.

- BGP best external is especially useful with BGP PIC and some vendors enable BGP PIC by default when the BGP best external is enabled.
- If you will use BGP best external in the network, test before deployment because your vendor implementation might be slightly different.
- BGP best external can be enabled at the Edge of network such as at the ASBR but as well as on the RRs.
- Depends on the topology, BGP best external and BGP PIC would be just enough to send more than one path without BGP Add-path or other mechanisms
- With BGP best external and BGP PIC, for certain topologies, you can have sub second convergence
- BGP best external was already specified in the original BGP RFC but never implemented by the vendors but now it is popular again.
- Drawback of BGP best external is resource consumption. Since routers start to keep additional path, this requires extra memory and CPU.

EIGRP vs. OSPF vs. IS-IS vs. BGP Design Comparison

Below table summarizes the similarities and the differences of the dynamic routing protocols in detail from the design point of view.

This table is shared here because, all the protocols are so far covered and the all design requirement is explained throughout the book.

Network designers should know the pros and cons of the technologies, protocol alternatives and their capabilities from the design point of view.

Design Requirement	OSPF	IS-IS	EIGRP	BGP
Scalablability	2 tier hierarchy , less scalable	2 tiers hierarchy , less scalable	Support many tiers and scalable	Most scalable routing protocol
Working on Full Mesh	Works well with mesh group	Works well with mesh group	Works very poorly, and there is no mesh group	Works very poorly, but RR removes the requirement
Working on a Ring Topology	Its okay	Its okay	Not good if ring is big due to query domain	Good with Route Reflector
Working on Hub and Spoke	Works poorly, require a lot of tuning	Works bad requires tuning	Works very well. It requires minimum tuning	IBGP works very well with Route Reflector
Fast Reroute Support	Yes - IP FRR	Yes - IP FRR	Yes - IP FRR and Feasible Successor	Requires BGP PIC + NHT + Best external + Add-Path
Suitable on WAN	Yes	Yes	Yes	Yes, but in very large scale or when policy is needed
Suitable on Datacenter	DCs are full mesh. So, No	DCs are full mesh so No	DCs are full mesh so no	Yes, in large scale DC and it is not uncommon
Suitable on Internet Edge	No it is designed as an IGP	No it is designed as an IGP	No, it is designed as an IGP	Yes, it is designed to be an Inter domain protocol
Standard Protocol	Yes IETF Standard	Yes IETF Standard	No, there is a draft but lack of Stub feature	Yes, IETF Standar
Stuff Experince	Very well known	Not well known	Well known	Not well known
Overlay Tunnel Support	Yes	Doesn't support IP tunnels	Yes	Yes
MPLS Traffic Engineering Support	Yes with CSPF	Yes, with CSPF	No	No
Security	Less secure	More secure since it is on layer2	Less secure	Secure since it runs on TCP
Suitable as Enterprise IGP	Yes	No, it lacks Ipsec	Yes	Not exactly, very large scale networks only
Suitable as Service Provider IGP	Yes	Definitely	No, it doesn't support Traffic Engineering	Maybe in the datacenter but not as an IGP
Complexity	Easy	Easy	Easy	Complex

Design Requirement	OSPF	IS-IS	EIGRP	BGP
Policy Support	Good	Good	Not so Good	Very good
Resource Requirement	SPF requires more processing power	SPF requires more processing power	DUAL doesn't need much power	Requires a lot of RAM and decent CPU
Extendibility	Not good	Good, thanks to TLV support	Good, thanks to TLV support	Very good, it supports 20 + address families
IPv6 Support	Yes	Yes	Yes	Yes
Default Convergece	Slow	Slow	Fast with Feasible Successor	Very slow
Training Cost	Cheap	Cheap	Cheap	Moderate
Troubleshooting	Easy	Very easy	Easy	Moderate
Routing Loop	Good protection	Good protection	Open to race condition	Good protection

EIGRP vs. OSPF vs. IS-IS vs. BGP Design Comparison

BGP Case Study – Inter AS BGP Policies create Sub Optimal Routing

The customer is running a BGP session with one service provider; they are considering receiving a transit service from the second service provider as well. The customer is using their own AS number, which is AS20 There are two connections to their service provider and it seems fro the topology that the left path will be used as primary for their incoming traffic.

Question 1:

How can you achieve this?

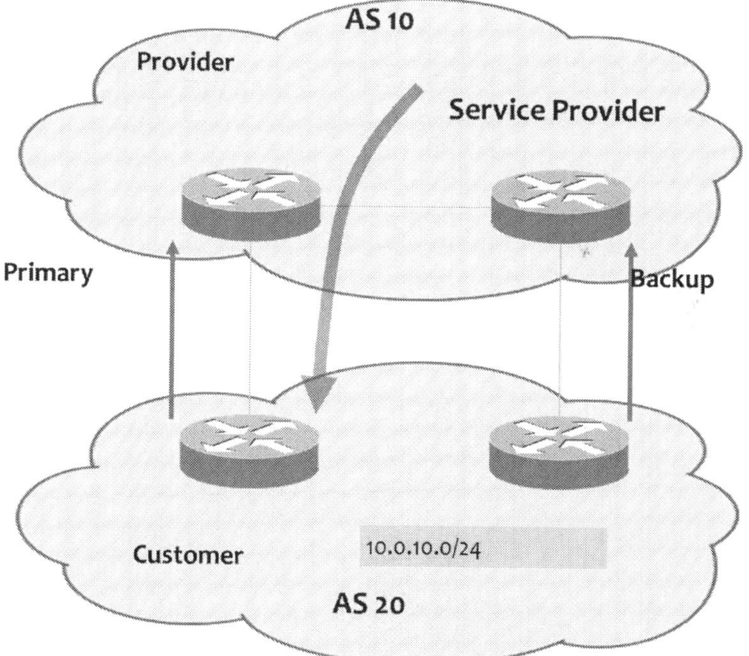

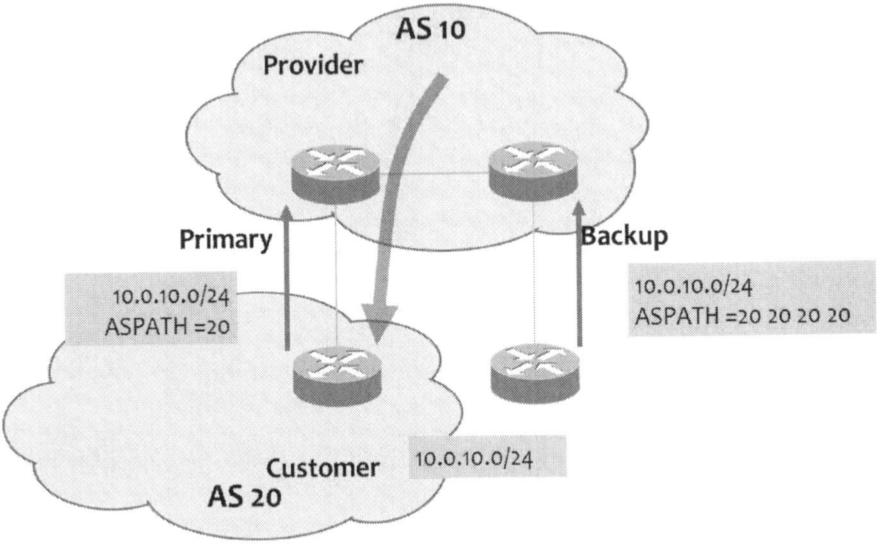

Prepending will (usually) force inbound traffic from AS 10 to take primary link.

The customer purchased a new link from the second service provider which uses AS number 30 and decommissioned one of its links from the old service provider. The customer wants to use the second service provider link as a backup link. They learned the AS-path prepending trick from early experience.

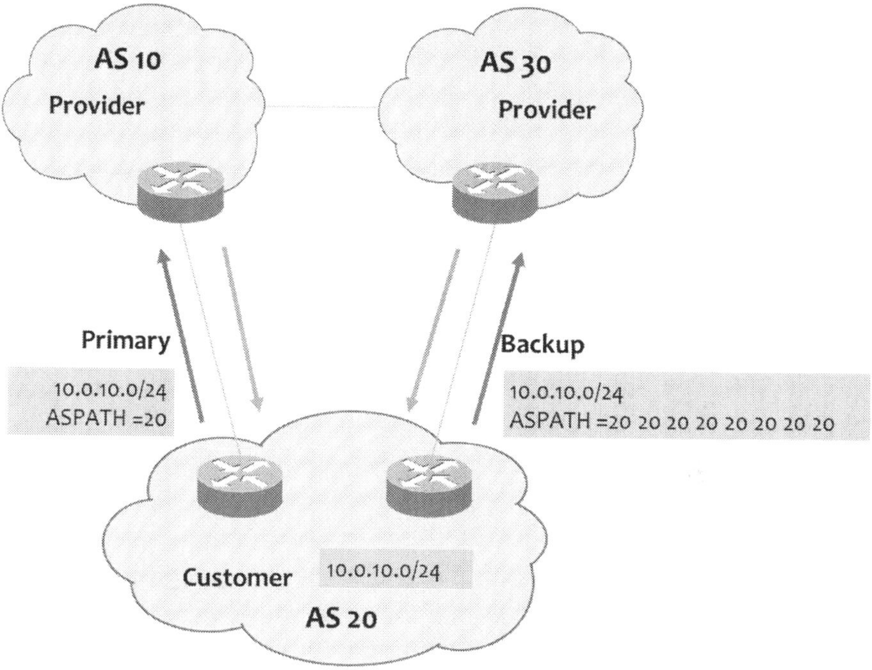

AS 10
Provider

AS 30
Provider

Primary
10.0.10.0/24
ASPATH =20

Backup
10.0.10.0/24
ASPATH =20 20 20 20 20 20 20 20

Customer
10.0.10.0/24
AS 20

Question 2:

Is there a problem with this design?

Question 3:

If there is a problem, how can it be solved?

Answer

There is a problem with the design since the customer wants to use the second service provider as a backup. AS-path prepending in this way is often used as a form of load balancing

However, AS 30 will send traffic to backup link, because it prefers customer routes due to higher local preference that service providers use the customer link rather than the peer link. Local preference is considered before AS-path length, so AS-path prepending is not affected in this design.

The solution is to use communities.

COMMUNITY 30:80 is okay to send the traffic through peer

AS 10
Provider
AS 30
Provider
AS 30: Normal customer local pref is 100, peer local pref is 90
Backup
10.0.10.0/24
ASPATH =20 20 20 2020 20 20
Primary
10.0.10.0/24
ASPATH =20
Customer
10.0.10.0/24
AS 20
Customer import policy at AS 30:
If 30:90 in COMMUNITY then
set local preference to 90
If 30:80 in COMMUNITY then
set local preference to 80
If 30:70 in COMMUNITY then
set local preference to 70

Question 4:

What if the customer uses second service provider link as primary and the old provider as secondary with the second provider peering connection as depicted in the below topology?

Does community help?

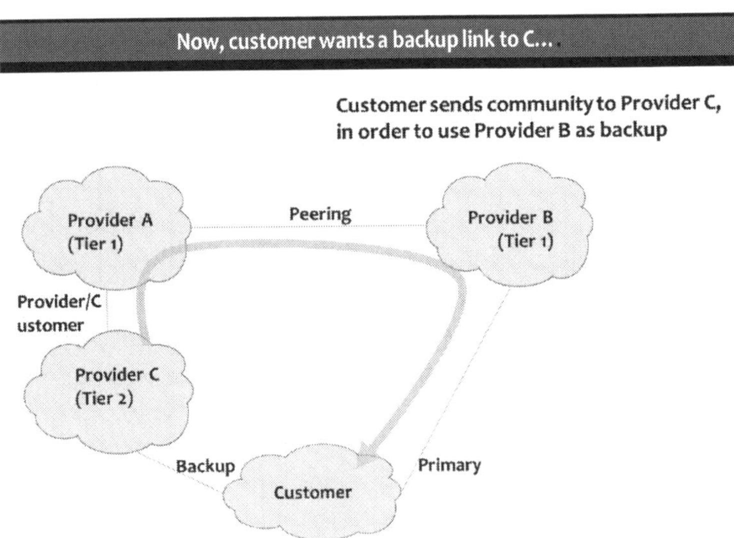

Yes, community helps, now Provider B can be used as primary.

Question 5:

What happens if primary link fails?

Provider A
(Tier 1)
Peering
Provider B
(Tier 1)
Provider/C
ustomer
Provider C
(Tier 2)
Backup
Customer
Primary

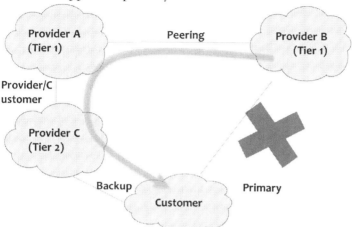

Backup link is installed and can be used by the customer.

Question 6:

What happens when the primary link comes back?

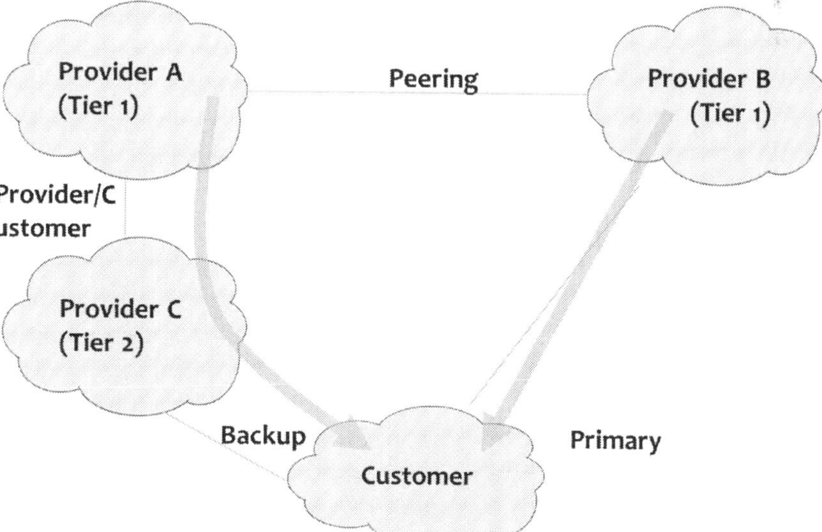

When the primary link comes back, both paths are used for incoming traffic, because Provider A continues to choose to send to Provider C since the community attribute is sent by Customer to Provider C, not to Provider A.

Solution:

Either Provider C will send a Provider A for its customer a community attribute, or Backup BGP link will be reset the when primary link comes back.

BGP Case Study – Connecting Internet Gateways between Datacenters without Stateful Devices

Enterprise Company has two datacenters. They have 200 remote offices and all the locations access the Internet from the datacenters. They recently had an outage on the Internet circuit and all the Internet sessions from the remote offices that use that link were dropped.

What are the solutions to prevent session failure in case of a link failure on the Internet gateways of this company?

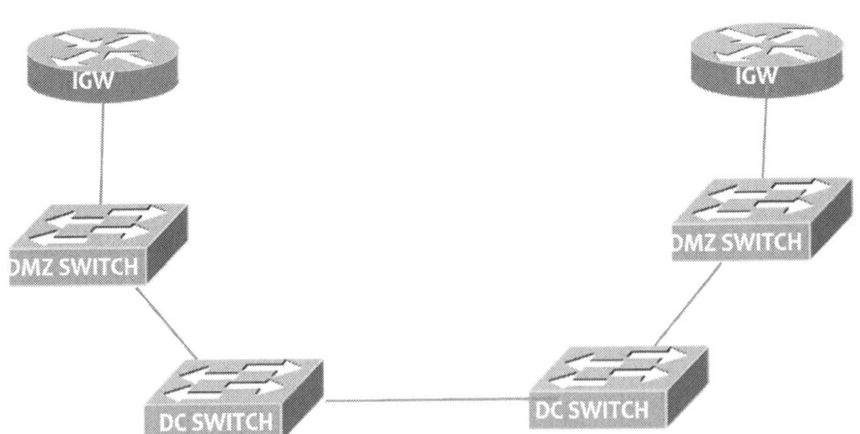

Note: In any solution, stateful devices such as Firewalls, Load Balancers, IDS/IPS are not considered in design. In real life design scenarios you will most likely have them in the Enterprise environment.

Solution 1:

IBGP over direct physical link. Best option, but can be costly. Budget might be concern, also deployment might take longer compared to other solutions.

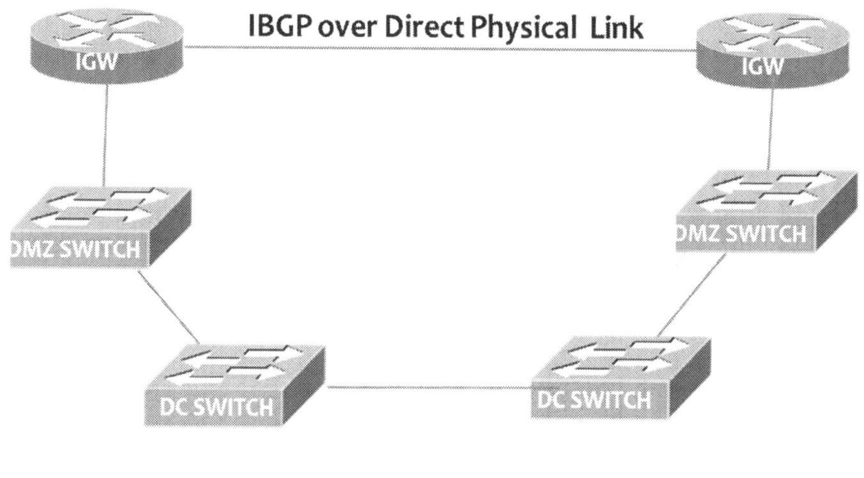

IBGP over direct physical link

Solution 2:

IBGP over GRE tunnels between the datacenters. Fastest option and does not require service provider interaction.

It should be used as a short-term solution.

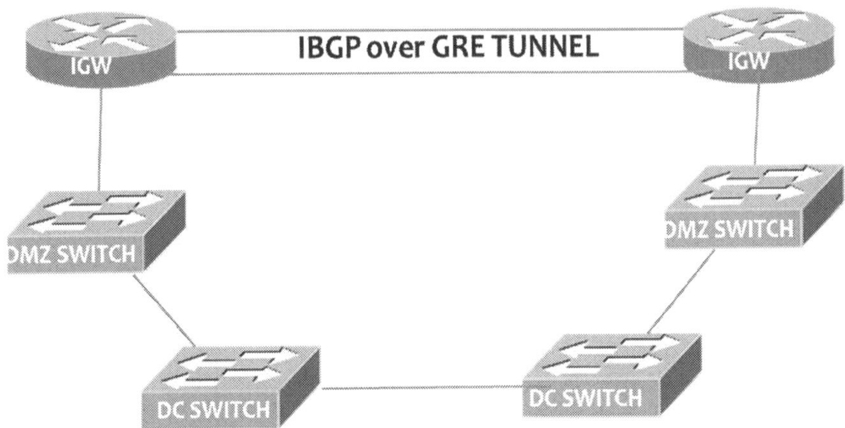

IBGP over GRE tunnels

Solution 3:

Another solution could be IBGP over MPLS VPN. In this solution, assumption is Company has already an MPLS VPN and with configuration at the Service Provider site, new logical circuit can be provisioned.

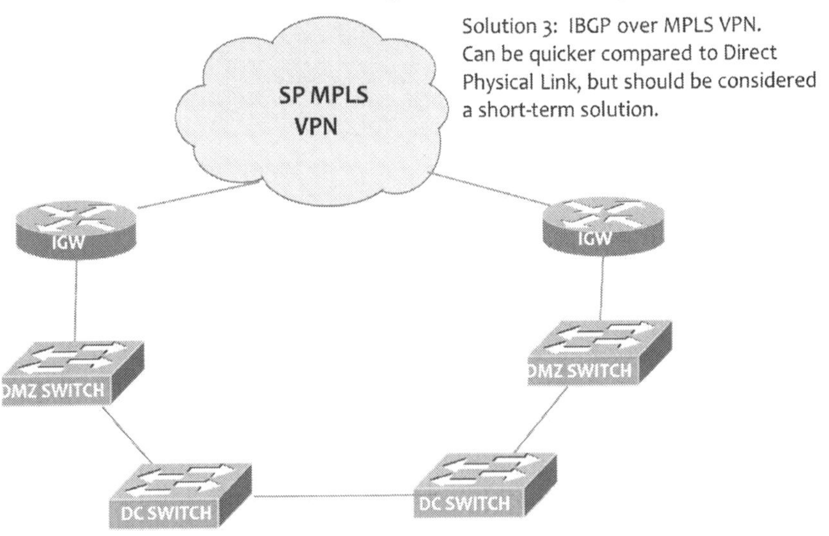

IBGP over MPLS VPN service

BGP Case Study – Internet Edge Design Considerations in the Enterprise

A U.S.-based Enterprise e-commerce company is designing a new network. They have two datacenters and both datacenters will host many servers.

Design Requirements:

- There are 1000km between the two datacenters.
- Their networking team knows that for the best user performance traffic should be symmetrical between servers and the users/clients.
- In addition to datacenter interconnect link they also have a direct physical connection.
- Based on the below topology, what might be the issue?

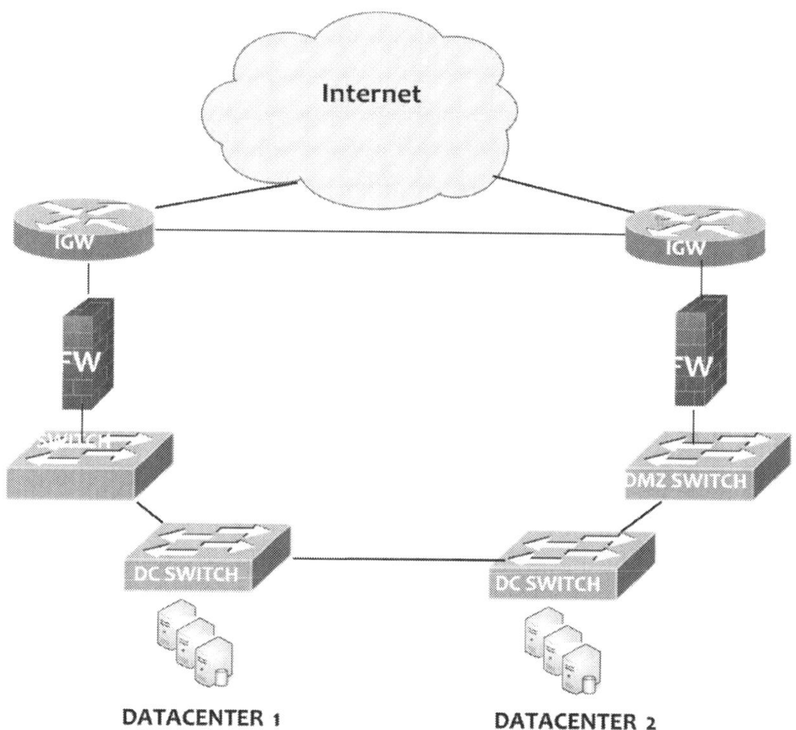

Internet Edge connections in the Enterprise between the Datacenters

The requirements say that traffic from DC1 should come back to DC1 directly. Firewalls drop all asymmetric traffic.

If the users are accessing DC1 servers it should go back from the DC1. Typically, servers use DC switch as default gateway. DC switches receive default route redistributed to their IGP from BGP by the IGW. IGP cost is used to reach to the closest IGW by the DC switches.

Incoming traffic always a problem when there is a stateful device in the path.

In the above topology if traffic comes to DC1 it has to go back from DC1 and vice versa, it is not only for asymmetric flow on the firewalls, load balancers, etc., but also to avoid a bottleneck. If traffic destined for DC1 comes to DC2, it has to go through direct physical internet link to DC1, this adds additional latency and consumes unnecessary bandwidth.

Question 2:

How can the company achieve symmetrical traffic flow so they don't have traffic drops or performance issues?

- They can split their public IP space by half and advertise specifics from each datacenter and summary from both datacenters as a backup in case first DC IGW link or node fails.
- Imagine they have /23 address space, they can dive 2x/24 and advertise each /24 from local datacenters only and /23 from both datacenters (Load Balancing Model which was explained in this chapter). Since their upstream SP will prefer longest match routing over any other BGP attribute, traffic returns to the location where it is originated.

BGP REVIEW QUESTIONS

Question 1:

Which of the below option is the reason to run IBGP? (Choose Two)

A. It is used for the reachability between PE devices in MPLS network

B. It is used to carry EBGP prefixes inside an Autonomous System

C. It is used with Route Reflectors for the scalability reason in large scale networks

D. It is used to prevent failures outside your network from impacting your internal network operation

Answer 1:

One of the correct answers of this question is to carry EBGP prefixes inside an Autonomous system.

IGP is used for the reachability between PE devices in an MPLS network.

Option C is valid but not the correct answer, because; question is asking the reasons, not the best practices.

Option D is one of the correct answers as well because with IBGP, internal network is protected from the outside failures by separating the local failure domains.

That's why; answers of this question are B and D.

Question 2:

Which of the below options are true for the BGP Route Reflectors? (Choose Three)

A. Route Reflectors provide scalability in large scale network design

B. Route Reflectors hide the available paths

C. Route Reflectors selects and advertise only the best path to

Route Reflector clients

D. Route Reflectors can be placed anywhere in the IP backbone as an IPv4 RR.

Answer 2:

Route reflectors as explained in the BGP chapter, are used to improve scalability of the BGP design in large-scale deployments.

Route reflectors hide the available path information by selecting and advertising only the best path to the clients.

Thus the correct answer of this question is A, B and C.

Option D is wrong because, Route Reflectors should follow the physical topology in an IP backbone, it cannot be placed everywhere, careful planning is required. Otherwise forwarding loop occurs as it was explained in one of the case studies in the BGP chapter.

Question 3:

Which below attributes are commonly used for BGP path manipulation? (Choose Three)

A. Local Preference

B. Origin

C. As-Path

D. Community

E. Weight

Answer 3:

Origin is not used commonly for the BGP path manipulation. Weight is Cisco preparatory and it is only local to the routers. It shouldn't be used for path manipulation.

BGP path manipulation was explained in detail in BGP chapter.

Answer of this question is A, C and D.

Question 4:

Which of the below options is used in the Public Internet Exchange Points to reduce configuration overhead on the BGP devices?

A. BGP Route Reflectors
B. BGP Prefix Lists
C. BGP Route Servers
D. BGP Map Servers

Answer 4:

There is nothing called BGP Map Servers. In the Public Internet Exchange points BGP Route Servers are used to reduce configuration overhead. They improve scalability. Very similar to Route Reflectors but Route Reflectors are used in IBGP, not in the Public Exchange Points. That's why answer of this question is C.

Question 5:

Which below options are true for the BGP Confederation? (Choose Three)

A. It is done by creating Sub-Autonomous system
B. It is easier to migrate from full-mesh IBGP, compare to BGP Route Reflectors
C. Between Sub Autonomous Systems mostly EBGP rules apply
D. Compare to BGP Route Reflector design, it is less commonly deployed in the networks.

Answer 5:

From the migration point of view, Full mesh IBGP to BGP Confederation is harder, compare to BGP Route Reflectors. Thus Option B is invalid.

All the other options are correct thus the answer of this question is A, C and D.

Question 6:

Which below option is used for inbound BGP path manipulation?

A. Local Preference

B. MED
C. As-Path prepending
D. Community
E. Hot Potato Routing

Answer 6:

Hot Potato Routing and Local Preference are used for Outbound BGP Path manipulation as explained in the BGP chapter in detail.

MED should be used if there is only one upstream ISP but still it is used for inbound path manipulation. AS-Path prepending and the communities are used for the multihoming connections as well.

That's why; answer of this question is B, C and D.

Question 7:

Fictitious Service Provider is considering providing an availability SLA for their MPLS VPN customers. They want to provide sub second convergence in case link or node failure scenarios.

What would you suggest to this company to achieve their goal? (Choose Two)

A. Implementing BFD
B. Implementing BGP PIC Core and Edge
C. Implementing BGP Route Reflectors
D. Implementing IGP FRR

Answer 7:

They should implement BGP PIC features to protect BGP from the link or node failure. Especially Edge node failures, even if MPLS Traffic Engineering or IP FRR deployed, couldn't be recovered in sub second.

Since BGP PIC convergence is mostly depends on IGP convergence as well, deploying IGP FRR (Fat Reroute) provides a necessary infrastructure for the BGP PIC. They should be deployed together. BFD is just a failure detection mechanism. IGP Convergence is depends on many other parameters tuning as it was explained in the IGP chapters of the book.

That's why; answer of this question is B and D.

Question 8:

What does MP-BGP (Multi Protocol BGP) mean?

A. BGP implementation which can converge less than a second

B. BGP implementation which is used in Service Provider networks

C. BGP implementation which can carry multiple BGP Address Families

D. BGP implementation which is used in Enterprise Networks

Answer 8:

MP-BGP (Multi Protocol BGP) as explained in the BGP chapter, is the BGP implementation, which can carry multiple Address Families. BGP in 2016, can carry more than 20 different Address Families such as IPv4 Unicast, IPv6 Unicast, IPv4 Multicast, L2 VPN, L3VPN, Flowspec and so on.

That's; why; answer of this question is C.

Question 9:

What does Hot Potato Routing mean?

A. Sending the traffic to the most optimum exit for the neighboring AS

B. Sending the traffic to the closest exit to the neighboring AS

C. By coordinating with the neighboring AS, sending traffic to the closest exit point

D. It is the other name of BGP Multipath

Answer 9:

Hot Potato Routing means, sending the traffic to the closest exist point from the Local Autonomous system to the neighboring Autonomous System by taking the IGP metric into consideration. It was explained in the BGP chapter in great detail.

There is no coordination between the Autonomous System in Hot Potato Routing definition. But Coordination with the Hot Potato Routing case study was provided in the BGP chapter.

That's why; answer of this question is B.

Question 10:

With which below options, internal BGP speaker can receive more than one best path even if BGP Route Reflectors are deployed? (Choose Three)

A. BGP Shadow RR

B. BGP Shadow Sessions

C. BGP Add-path

D. BGP Confederation

E. BGP Multipath

Answer 10:

As it was explained in the BGP Route Reflectors section of the BGP chapter, Shadow Sessions, Shadow RR and BGP Add-path design provides more than best path to the internal BGP speaker even if BGP Route Reflectors are deployed.

BGP Multipath requires more than one best path and all the path attributes to be the same. Thus it requires one of the above mechanisms. BGP Confederation doesn't provide this functionality.

That's why; answer of this question is A, B and C.

Question 11:

Which below option is recommended to send more than one best path to the VPN PEs in the MPLS VPN deployment if VPN Route Reflectors are deployed?

A. BGP Add-path

B. BGP Shadow RR

C. BGP Full Mesh

D. Unique RD per VRF per PE

Answer 11:

BGP Add-path, BGP Shadow RR and Sessions deployments are suitable for the IP backbones.

If there is an MPLS backbone, configuring unique RD per VRF per PE is best and recommended design option since there is no software or hardware upgrade, no additional BGP sessions and so on.

That's why the answer of this question is D.

Question 12:

What are the reasons to send more than one BGP best path in IP and MPLS deployment? (Choose Four)

A. BGP Multipath

B. BGP Fast Reroute

C. BGP Multihop

D. Preventing Routing Oscillation

E. Optimal BGP routing

Answer 12:

As it is explained in the BGP chapter, there are many reasons to send more than one BGP best path in both IP and MPLS deployments.

These are; avoiding routing oscillations, BGP Multipathing, Fast convergence/Fast Reroute and Optimal Routing.

Sometimes for the optimal routing, just sending more than one BGP best path is not enough but may require all available paths though.

That's why, answer of this question is A, B, D and E.

Question 13:

What is the drawback of sending more than one BGP best path in BGP?

A. More resource usage
B. Sub Optimal Routing
C. Slower Convergence
D. Security Risk

Answer 13:

Sending more than one BGP best path requires more memory, CPU, network bandwidth, thus more resource usage in the network.

As a rule of thumb, whenever more information is sent, it consumes more resource, may provide optimal routing, better high availability, better convergence.

All other options are wrong, except Option A.

Question 14:

What below options are the advantages of Full Mesh IBGP design compare to BGP Route Reflector design? (Choose Four)

A. It can provide more optimal routing compare to Route Reflector design
B. It can provide faster routing convergence compare to Route Reflector design
C. It provides better resource usage compare to Route Reflector design
D. It can provide better protection against route churn
E. Multipath information is difficult to propagate in a route reflector topologies

Answer 14:

Although there are advantages of using BGP Route Reflectors, there are many drawbacks as well. Probably it is more harmful than deploying Full Mesh IBGP if the requirement is optimal routing, faster convergence and avoiding route churns.

Sending multiple paths is difficult since it requires Shadow Sessions, RR or Add-path deployments in Route Reflector topologies.

Full Mesh IBGP design consumes more device and network resources and requires more configurations on the devices compare to Route Reflector design.

That's why the answer of this question is A, B, D and E.

Question 15:

In the below topology IP backbone is shown. R2 is the RR client of R4 and R3 is the RR client of R1.

What is the next hop of R2 and R3 for the 70.70.0.0/24 prefix?

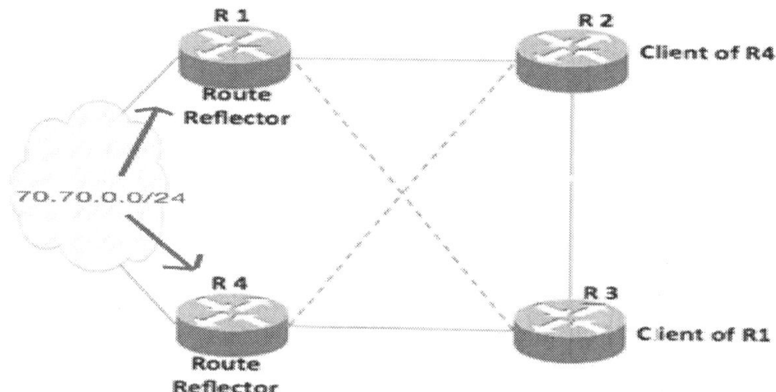

A. R1 is the next hop of R2, R4 is the next hop of R3

B. R1 is the next hop of R3, R4 is the next hop of R2

C. R2 is the next hop of R3, R3 is the next hop of R2

D. R4 is the next hop of both R2 and R3

Answer 15:

Since it is given as IP backbone, IP destination based lookup is done for the BGP prefixes.

Sine BGP prefixes require recursion and IGP next hop needs to be found for the BGP prefixes, R2's and R3's IGP next hops for the BGP prefixes should be found.

On R2, For the BGP next hop of 70.70.0.0/24 BGP prefix is R4. R2 can only reach R4 through R3.

Thus, R2's IGP next hop is R3. It applies for the R3.

R2's IGP next hop is R3 and R3's IGP next hop is R2. That's why the answer of this question is C.

Please note that in this topology BGP Route Reflectors don't follow the physical topology, which is against to BGP Route Reflector design requirement in IP networks.

That's why, in this design between R2 and R3, routing loop occurs.

Correct design is R2 should be the Route Reflector client of R1 and R3 should be the Route Reflector client of R4.

Question 16:

What can be the problem with BGP design in the Enterprise if there are more than one datacenter?

A. Convergence is very slow

B. Asymmetric routing issues if there are stateful devices

C. Route Reflector deployment is harder compare to SP deployment

D. Traffic flow cannot be optimized

Answer 16:

All the options are wrong except Option B.

Asymmetric can be a problem in Enterprise design, which has stateful devices as it was explained in the BGP chapter. Because stateful devices require symmetric routing for the flow information and firewalls, load balancers, IDS/IPS are common elements at the Internet edge or within the datacenters in Enterprise design.

In the Service Providers, CGN (LSN) is deployed to overcome IPv4 exhaustion problem as it was explained in IPv6 chapter. These nodes also require symmetric routing.

Answer of this question is B.

Question 17:

Which below option is true for the VPN Route Reflectors in MPLS deployments? (Choose Two)

A. It can be deployed in centralize place

B. It doesn't have to follow physical topology, can have more flexible placement compare to IP Route Reflectors

C. It is best practice to use VPN Route Reflectors for the IP Route Reflectors as well

D. It always provides most optimal path to the Route Reflector clients

Answer 17:

VPN Route reflector can be deployed in the centralized placed and they have more flexible placement advantage compare to the IP Route Reflector.

The reason is there is no IP destination based lookup in the MPLS networks. Thus there is no layer 3 routing loop problem as in the case of IP Route Reflector which was explained in the Answer 15.

It is not best practice to deploy IP and VPN services on the same node. Reason will be explained in Answer 18.

VPN RR, similar to IP RR, cannot always provide most optimal path to their clients. Because they selects the BGP best path from their point view, not from their clients point of view.

That's why the answer of this question is A and B.

Question 18:

What can be the problem with using IP and VPN Route Reflector on the same device? (Choose Two)

A. Attack for the Internet service can affect VPN Customers

B. Attack for the VPN service can affect Internet Customers

C. Scalability of the Route Reflectors are reduced

D. They have to participate in the IGP process

Answer 18:

When a Route Reflector is used for more than one service, it is called Multi Service Route Reflector. The problem of using Internet and VPN services on the same BGP Route Reflector is Fate Sharing.

Internet based attacks can affect VPN customers and any problem on the VPN service users affect Internet customers. Also in case of failure, all the customers fail.

Thus using a separate BGP Route Reflector per service is a best practice.

Using Multi Service RRs don't reduce the scalability. And when using multi service RRs, they still don't have to participate in IGP process.

They can be designed as inline RR that participates IGP process in specific design such as Seamless MPLS. Seamless MPLS and its five different variations will be explained in MPLS chapter.

Answer of this question is A and B.

Question 19:

In the below topology there are two datacenters of the Service Provider. If the requirement were to provide closest exit for the Route Reflector clients, in which datacenter would you deploy the Route Reflectors?

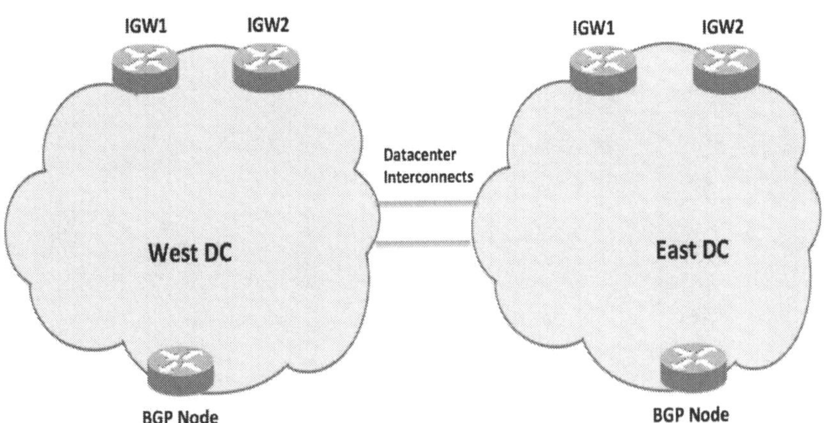

A. In West DC

B. In East DC

C. Doesn't matter the placement

D. Both in East and West DC

Answer 19:

Route Reflectors should be placed in both East and West DC. Otherwise Route Reflector would choose the best path from their point of view and would send the best path to the Route Reflector Clients from their best path.

If RR would be placed in West DC, all BGP RR Clients in East DC would choose the West DC IGW (Internet Gateways) as exit point and vice versa.

Thus the correct answer of this question is D.

Question 20:

Which below options are true for the BGP PIC deployment? (Choose Two)

A. BGP PIC can provide sub second convergence even if there are millions of prefixes in the routing table

B. BGP edge devices don't have to receive more than one best path for BGP PIC Edge to work

C. BGP PIC Edge can protect both from Edge link and Node failure

D. BGP PIC has to work with BGP Add-Path

Answer 20:

BGP edge nodes have to receive more than one best path for BGP PIC Edge operation. This was explained in the BGP chapter in detail. BGP Add-Path is one of the mechanisms, which is used to send multiple paths even RR is deployed in the network.

But BGP Add-Path is not mandatory for BGP PIC.

BGP PIC Edge can protect from both Edge link and node failures and can provide sub second convergence even if there are millions of prefixes.

That's why the correct answer of this question is A and C.

BGP FURTHER STUDY RESOURCES

Books

Zhang, R. (2003). BGP Design and Implementation, Cisco Press.

Videos

https://www.nanog.org/meetings/nanog38/presentations/dragnet.mp4
https://www.youtube.com/watch?v=txiNFyvWjQ

Articles

https://www.nanog.org/meetings/nanog51/presentations/Sunday/NANOG51.Talk3.peering-nanog51.pdf
http://ripe61.ripe.net/presentations/150-ripe-bgp-diverse-paths.pdf
https://www.nanog.org/meetings/nanog48/presentations/Tuesday/Raszuk_To_AddPaths_N48.pdf

Chapter 9
MULTICAST

If the requirement is to send flow in real time to multiple receivers, then the most efficient way to do this is multicast. Multicast is a thirty-year-old protocol, yet many people still struggle to understand it. Probably the biggest difficulty in understanding multicast is source based routing. IP unicast routing works based on destination based routing; IP multicast routing works based on source based routing.

Tree in IP unicast routing is created from the source towards destination, in IP Multicast routing from destination (receiver) towards source (sender).

Unicast vs. Multicast Flows

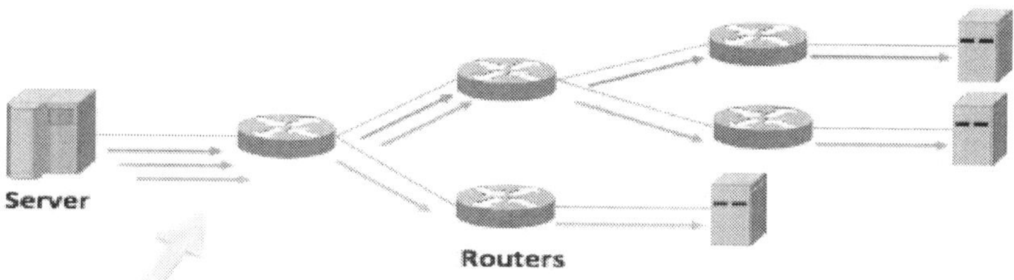

Number of Streams

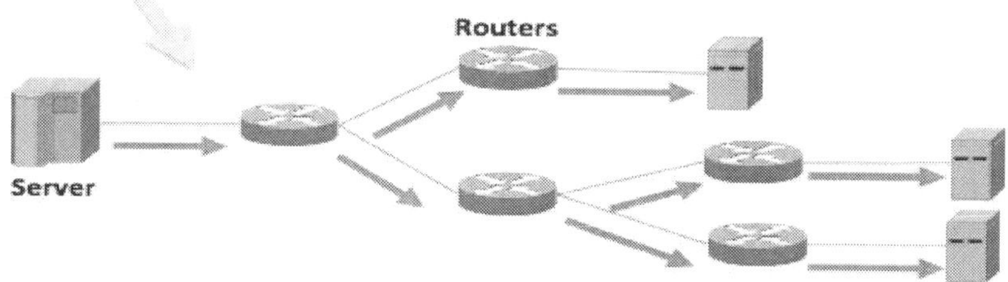

The server has to send three copies of stream for three receivers in unicast. Server sends one copy and network replicates the traffic to its intended receivers in multicast.

Multicast works on UDP, not TCP. That's why there is no error control or congestion avoidance, it is purely best effort. Receiver can receive duplicate multicast traffic in some situations. SPT switchover is an example of where duplicate traffic delivery occurs. During an SPT switchover, multicast traffic is received both from shared tree and shortest path tree.

This is one of inefficiency of multicast.

Unicast and Multicast Addressing

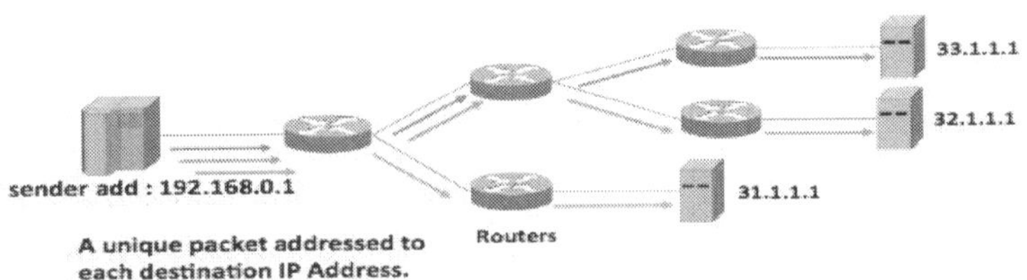

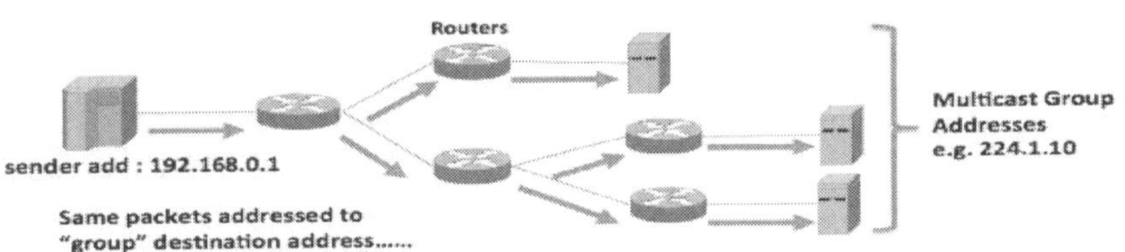

Source addresses in multicast always unicast address. Multicast address is a class D address range. 224/4. You should never see multicast Class D address as a source multicast address.

Source address can never be class D multicast group addresses. Separate multicast routing table is maintained for multicast trees. Sources do not need to join a group, they simply send the traffic. Multicast routing protocols (DVMRP, PIM) are used to build the trees. Tree is built hop by hop from the receivers to the source. DVMRP was the first multicast routing protocol, but it is depreciated and not used anymore.

Source (sender) is the root of the tree in shortest path tree.

Rendezvous point is the root of the shared tree (rendezvous point is used in ASM and bidir-PIM)

Unicast and Multicast Addressing

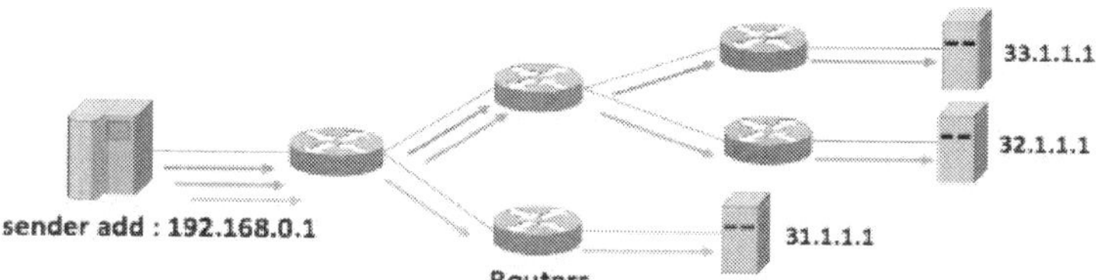

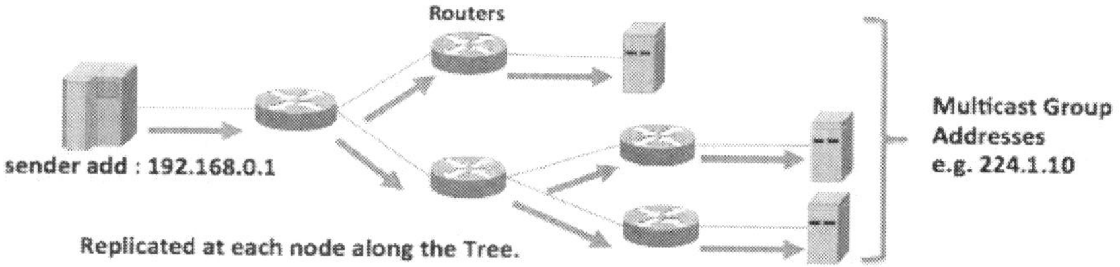

Link local addresses 224.0.0.0-224.0.0.255.

TTL of link local address multicast is 1. They are used in the local link. OSPF, EIGRP, etc. uses addresses from this range.

IANA reserved address scope ; 224.0.1.0-224.0.1.255

This address range is used for the networking applications such as NTP, 224.0.1.1 TTL is greater than 1. Administratively scoped multicast addresses; 239.0.0.0 – 239.255.255.255. This address range is reserved for use in the domain. Equivalent to RFC 1918 private address space. There is 32/1 Overlapping between IP Multicast IP and Mac Addresses.

- 224.1.1.1
- 224.129.1.1
- 225.1.1.1
- 238.1.1.1
- 238.129.1.1
- 239.1.1.1
- 239.129.1.1

All above address uses same multicast MAC address, which is 0100.5e01.0101

We will talk about below Multicast Protocols

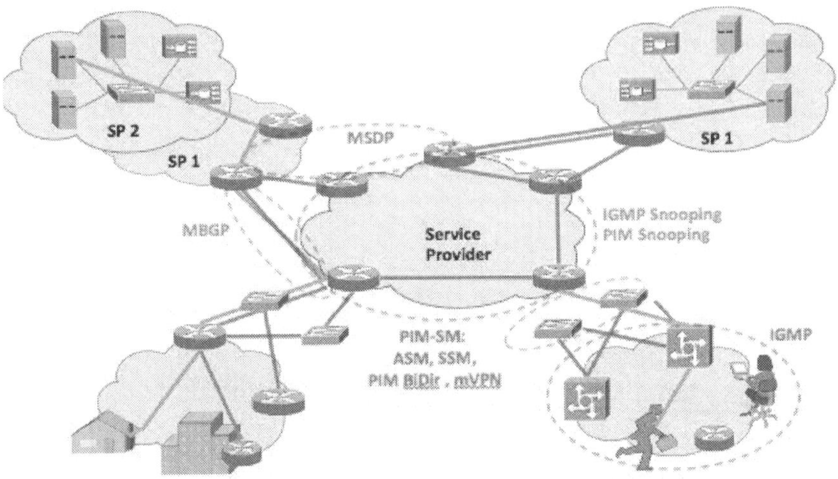

Receiver uses IGMP to communicate with the router. IGMP v2 is used in PIM ASM (any source multicast) and only IGMPv3 can be used with PIM-SSM (source specific multicast). IGMP is a host-to-router protocol. After first-hop router you don't see IGMP messages. IGMP membership report, which is also known as IGMP join is sent by the host application to the first-hop router, then first-hop router creates a PIM join towards the root of the tree

Receiver sends an IGMP membership report to the first-hop router which in return sends PIM join to the root of the tree.

By default, switch sends multicast traffic to every port, so that even uninterested hosts receive the multicast packets; this is not efficient. This is why IGMP snooping is used to help with multicast scaling.

When IGMP snooping is enabled, switch tracks the multicast traffic. When the traffic comes from the upstream router, switch sends the traffic to the interested receivers. Switches with IGMPv2 have to track every multicast packet to catch the control plane traffic. Every multicast data packet is inspected with IGMPv2, since there is no IGMPv2 router multicast group address. This is why in IGMPv2, IGMP snooping should be enabled on the hardware, otherwise performance impacts can be seen.

This problem is solved in IGMPv3. IGMPv3 uses special 224.0.0.22 multicast group address. Switch only tracks these multicast control plane packets. In this way, IGMPv3 provides scalability. Even in the software platform, IGMP snooping can be used if IGMPv3 is enabled.

Multicast Distribution Trees

Shortest-path tree or source tree is created between the source and the receiver in PIM-SSM. Shortest-path tree is created between the source and the rendezvous point in PIM ASM before the SPT (shortest-path tree) switchover.

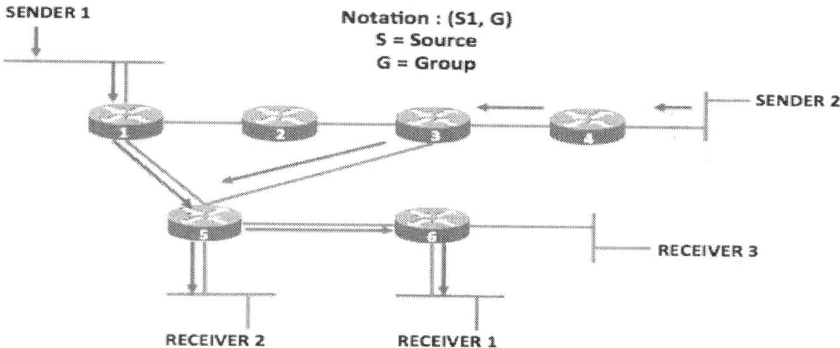

Shared tree is created between the rendezvous point and the receiver only in PIM ASM; still there is shortest-path tree between the source and rendezvous point in PIM ASM.

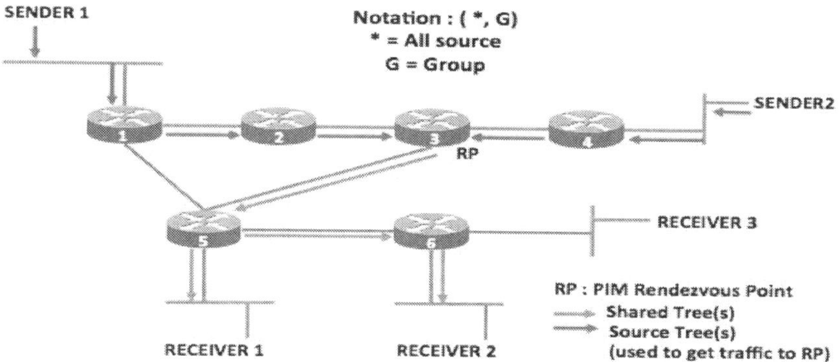

Shortest-path tree uses more memory but provides optimal path from the source to all receivers, therefore minimizing delay.

Shared tree uses less memory because there are not separate multicast states for each source for the given multicast group address. However, it may create suboptimal routing for some receivers. That's why shared tree may introduce extra delay.

PIM: Protocol Independent Multicast

PIM is a multicast routing protocol. There are two PIM modes, PIM sparse and PIM dense mode.

PIM Dense Mode (PIM-DM):

PIM dense mode is a flood and prune based (pushing) protocol. It consumes extra resources (bandwidth, CPU, and memory). Even though there are no intended receivers, multicast traffic is sent everywhere. Then if there are no receivers, routers prune the traffic. Flood and prune mechanism is repeated routinely.

PIM Sparse Mode (PIM-SM):

The most commonly used PIM mode is PIM sparse mode. PIM-SM is based on a pull mechanism, unlike PIM-DM, which is a push-based mechanism.

Receivers in PIM-SM request to join a specific multicast group. Tree is created from the receivers up to the root. Root is a sender if the tree is shortest/source based, it is a rendezvous point if the tree is shared tree.

PIM-SM (Sparse Mode) can be implemented in three ways:

- PIM ASM (any source multicast)
- PIM-SSM (source specific multicast)
- Bidir-PIM (bidirectional multicast)

PIM ASM (Any Source Multicast)

If the source is known then there is no need for PIM ASM.

If source is not known, there is a common element, which is called Rendezvous Point in PIM ASM for source registration. All the sources are registered to the PIM Rendezvous Point. Receiver join information is sent to the rendezvous point as well.

Rendezvous point redundancy in PIM ASM is supported through Anycast RP concept. Anycast RP supports both redundancy and the load balancing. This is different in PIM-Bidir Phantom RP concept, which provides only redundancy not load-balancing.

If there is no backup RP and RP fails new Multicast sources cannot be discovered since the RP is used for source discovery. This applies both PIM ASM and PIM Bidir since both deployment methods use Rendezvous Point. PIM ASM can be thought of as a dating service: it arranges meetings between the receivers and senders (source). Since PIM ASM requires rendezvous point and RP engineering, it is considered the hardest multicast routing protocol mode.

The default behavior of PIM ASM is that routers with directly connected members will join the shortest-path tree as soon as they detect a new multicast source.

Rendezvous point information can be configured as static on the every router; it can be learned through Auto-RP which is a Cisco-specific protocol or BSR which is IETF-standard. There is no Auto-RP anymore in IPv6 multicast.

PIM-SSM (Source Specific Multicast)

PIM-SSM is a source specific multicast. It does not require a rendezvous point, because sources are known by the receivers. Receivers create a shortest-path tree towards the source root of the tree is the sender. If SSM is enabled, only (S,G) entries are seen in the multicast routing table.

IANA reserves 232/8 Class D multicast address range for PIM-SSM but it's not enough to use this address range though.

Requires IGMPv3 at the source or IGMPv2 to v3 mapping on the first-hop routers. Source specific multicast is most suitable for one-to-many applications. IPTV is an example of a one-to-many application.

Bidir-PIM (Bidirectional PIM)

Bidir-PIM is suitable for many many multicast applications such as trading-floor applications where all senders are simultaneously receivers. Only uses shared tree, thus only (*,G) entries are seen in the multicast routing table.

Traffic is brought up from the sources to the rendezvous point and then down to the receivers. Since there is only shared tree, Bidir-PIM uses less state than the other PIM modes. Only (*,G) state is used. In bidir-PIM all trees are rooted at the RP. In PIM ASM, RFC check is used to prevent a routing loop; in bidir-PIM in order to prevent a loop, a designated forwarder is elected on every limb. The router with best path to the rendezvous point is selected as designated forwarder (DF).

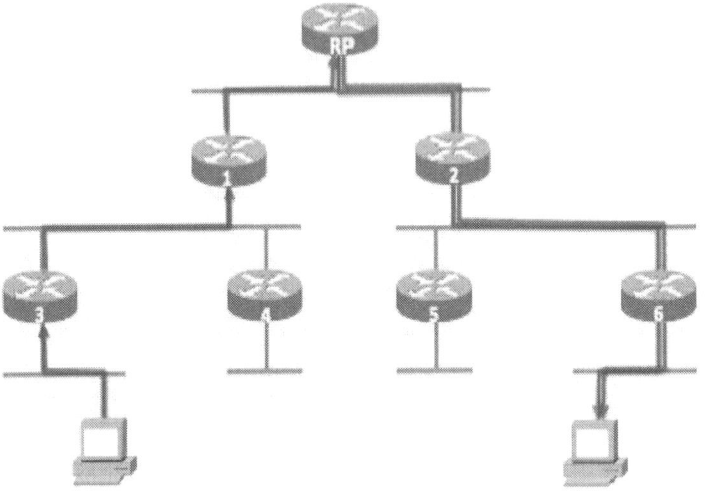

Arriving causes router and RP to create (G) state.

PIM ASM vs. PIM SSM vs. PIM Bidir Multicast Deployment Models Comparison

Below table summarizes the similarities and the differences of the multicast deployment models in great detail.

PIM Any Source Multicast, PIM Source Specific Multicast and PIM Bidir (Bidirectional PIM) are shared in this comparison table.

Design requirements and the comparison parameters work similarly for both IPv4 and IPv6 deployments.

Network designers should know the pros and cons of the technologies, protocol alternatives and their capabilities from the design point of view.

Design Requirement	PIM - ASM/Any Source Multicast	PIM - SSM/Source Specific Multicast	PIM - Bidir/ Bidirectional PIM
Scalablability	Moderate since the routers keep (S,G) state after SPT transition. Even before Shortest Path Tree transition, always Shortest Parth Tree is created between Sources and RPs	Worst. Routers have to keep every source-multicast group pair state in the multicast routing table. Thus SSM consumes a lot of router resources and sitatution get worse if there are more source and multople groups	Very scalable since the flows always on shared tree which means routers only keep (*,G) multicast entry in their multicast routing table. That's why it is used in many to many application design.
Suitable for One to Many Applications	It is suitable but Randevous Points Engineering is a disadvantage. IPTV is one of the one to many applications which PIM ASM can be used	Best.It is designed for One to Many applications. Source address information should be known by the receivers though	Not so suitable, PIM Bidir is designed for many to many multicast application traffic. Sender and Receiver both can send and receive multicast traffic at the same time. It is best for many to many application traffic pattern
Optimal Traffic Flow	Moderate.Before the SPT transition,receivers and senders communicate through Randevous Point. When receiver discovers the sources, they join the shortest path tree and they don't use Randevous Point anymore but until SPT transition traffic may flow suboptimaly	Its optimal flow since source is known and IGP best path is used to reach to the sources	Not good since all the traffic always have to pass through Randevous Point
Duplicate Multicast Traffic	Yes during SPT transition, receivers gets multiple coipes of same Multicast traffic	No, there is no duplicate	No,there is no duplicate
Fast Reroute Support	Yes - IP FRR and Multicast only FRR	Yes - IP FRR and Multicast only FRR	Yes - IP FRR and Multicast only FRR
Stuff Experince	Well known	Well known	Less known, especially Phantom RP operation for the load balancing
Loop Avoidance	Its done via RPF Check	Its done via RPF Check	Designated Forwarder is elected per subnet
Security	Less secure since all the sources can send to any multicast group	More secure because receivers specifically states which source and group pair thet are interested in	Less secure, same reason as the PIM ASM

Design Requirement	PIM - ASM/Any Source Multicast	PIM - SSM/Source Specific Multicast	PIM - Bidir/ Bidirectional PIM
Complexity	Complex since it requires randevous point, Anycast RP for the Randevous point redundancy, Randevous point engineering for the optimal multicast routing	Easy, it requires source information only. There is no Randevous Point in Source Specific Multicast, no RP Engineering , no Anycast RP	Complex since it requires Randevous point, Phantom RP for the redundancy, RP Engineering for the optimal multicast routing
Resource Requirement	Moderate among other options since routers have to keep (*,G) state between the hosts and the RP and (S,G) state between source and the RP. (*,G) state can be thought as a summarization in the IP routing. After the SPT transition, still (S,G) state though	Worst.In PIM SSM all the routers every source-group address state. Thus it requires more memory and cpu on the devices, there is no (*,G) state in PIM SSM, only (S,G)	Best since PIM Bidir enabled routers only keep (*,G) states. Only shared tree is used in Bidirectional PIM.
Troubleshooting	Easy	Very easy	Easy

PIM ASM vs. PIM SSM vs. PIM Bidir Multicast Deployment Models Comparison

Multicast Case Study – Automatic Tunneling Protocol (AMT)

Terrano is a European-based manufacturing company.

Users of Terrano want to watch the stream from the content-provider which has peering with Terrano's service provider. However, Terrano doesn't have multicast in the network.

What solution could Terrano users use without enabling IP multicast on their network?

Solution:

Solution can be provided with Automatic Multicast Tunneling (AMT) RFC 7450.

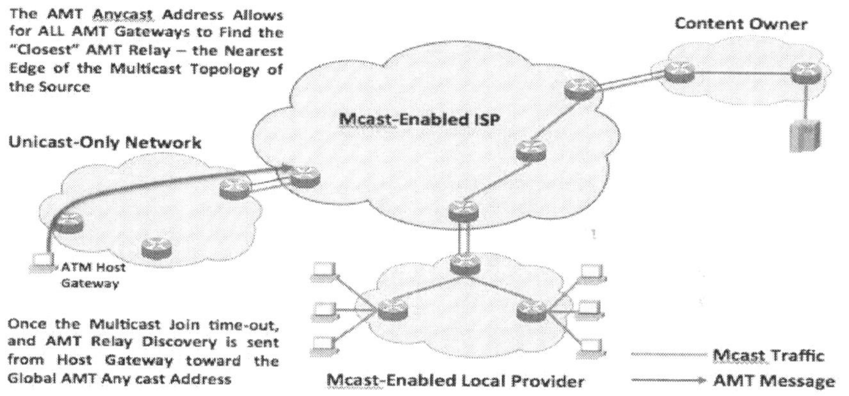

AMT (Automatic Multicast Tunneling) protocol is an IETF attempt to encapsulate multicast traffic in unicast packets and deliver multicast traffic from the source to the intended receivers.

Receivers network may not provide Multicast but this tunneling protocol allows Multicast traffic to be received over Unicast only network.

AMT discovery messages are sent to the Anycast address. In our case study, a service provider of Terrano supports multicast, so they can send the PIM messages.

(S,G) join to the content provider. Service provider needs to have AMT Relay software on their router.

AMT messages are unicast messages. Multicast traffic is encapsulated in unicast packets. Terrano can receive multicast content at this point, because end-to-end tree is built.

AMT host gateway feature can be implemented on the receiver PC.

Ideally, the first-hop routers of Terrano should provide AMT host gateway feature.

AMT is considered for some people for CDN (Content Delivery Network) replacement. I shared this case study to get your attention to this technology.

As a network designer you should always look for better alternatives for any technology.

MULTICAST REVIEW QUESTIONS

Question 1:

Which below technology is used between Multicast host and the first hop default gateway of the host?

A. PIM Snooping

B. PIM Any source Multicast

C. IGMP

D. Rendezvous Point

Answer 1:

IGMP is used between the multicast host and its default gateway. Answer is C.

Question 2:

Which below statement is true for PIM Sparse mode? (Choose Three)

A. Multicast traffic always has to go through RP

B. If there is no backup RP and RP fails new Multicast sources cannot be discovered

C. RP is used for Source Discovery

D. Anycast RP is one of the redundancy mechanisms in PIM Sparse Mode

E. There is no RP in Any Source Multicast

Answer 2:

As it was mentioned in the multicast chapter, RP is used for source discovery. If there is no backup RP and RP fails, new multicast sources cannot be discovered.

Multicast Traffic only in PIM Bidir always has to go through RP, in PIM ASM it doesn't have to.

Anycast RP is one of the redundancy mechanisms in PIM Sparse

Mode. Another one is Phantom RP, which is used in PIM Bidir.

There is RP in Any Source Multicast, that's why Option E is incorrect.

Correct answer of this question is B, C and D.

Question 3:

Which below statements are true for IP Multicast design? (Choose Three)

A. There is overlap between Multicast IP and MAC addresses

B. Most optimal multicast routing is achieved with PIM SSM

C. Least resource intensive Multicast deployment model is PIM Bidir

D. Phantom RP is the load balancing mechanism in PIM Bidir

E. Any Source Multicast RP doesn't require Rendezvous Point

Answer 3:

Phantom RP is used in PIM Bidir but it doesn't support load balancing. Most Optimal routing is achieved with PIM SSM because the three uses always the shortest IGP path. There is no need to send the traffic towards RP. Least resource intensive Multicast deployment model is PIM Bidir because there is only (*,G) multicast entries are kept in Multicast routing table. In ASM, after SPT switchover traffic continues over the shortest path. And as it was explained before there is overlap between the Multicast IP addresses and the MAC addresses. Any Source Multicast requires Rendezvous Point thus Option E is incorrect. That's why the correct answer of this question is A, B and C.

Question 4:

If the requirement is not to use Rendezvous point, which of the below options provide most efficient IP Multicast deployment?

A. Deploy PIM SSM and implement IGMPv2

B. Deploy PIM SSM and implement IGMPv3

C. Deploy Anycast RP

D. Deploy Bidirectional PIM

E. Deploy PIM Any Source Multicast

Answer 4:

In Anycast RP, Bidirectional PIM and Any Source Multicast, there is always an RP.

Only valid solutions could be A and B but since in the Option A it says that IGMPv2, and Source Specific multicast although doesn't have an RP, requires IGMPv3

That's why the correct answer of this question is Option B.

Question 5:

Which of the below solutions provide RP redundancy in case of failure in IPv4 Multicast?

A. Embedded RP
B. MSDP Anycast RP
C. Auto RP
D. BSR
E. PIM SSM

Answer 5:

There is no RP in PIM SSM.

Embedded RP is not in IPv4 Multicast. Auto RP and BSR is used to teach RP to the Multicast routers.

That's why the correct answer of this question is MSDP Anycast RP, which is used in PIM ASM only.

Question 6:

Which below Multicast PIM Sparse Mode deployment model provide one to many multicast traffic and can work with IGMPv2?

A. PIM ASM
B. PIM SSM
C. PIM Dense

D. PIM Bidir

E. IGMPv3

Answer 6:

PIM SSM and PIM ASM can provide one to many application traffic pattern but PIM SSM requires IGMP v3. That's why the correct answer is PIM ASM, Option A.

Question 7:

Which below Multicast technology provide any to any connectivity?

A. IGMP

B. PIM SSM

C. PIM Bidir

D. Anycast RP

Answer 7:

Any to any connectivity for the applications is provided by the PIM Bidir (Bidirectional PIM) as it was explained in the Multicast chapter in detail.

That's why the correct answer of this question is C.

Question 8:

How redundancy is achieved in PIM Bidir?

A. MSDP is configured between two RPs

B. Phantom RP is used and the two RP IP address is advertised with different subnet masks

C. Static multicast routing table entries are configured on the RPs

D. Phantom RP is used and the two RP IP address is advertised with the same subnet masks

Answer 8:

As it was explained in the Multicast chapter, Phantom RP concept is used in PIM Bidir for the redundancy. It doesn't provide load balancing but only the redundancy can be achieved.

Two Rendezvous Points (RP) are configured and different subnet mask is advertised for the RP IP address.

That's why the correct answer of this question is B.

Question 9:

Which below technologies are used in IPv6 multicast?

A. IGMP Snooping

B. MLD

C. Embedded RP

D. PIM Auto RP

E. DVMRP

Answer 9:

PIM Auto RP is Cisco preparatory and not supported in IPv6.

DVMRP was one of the layer 3 multicast routing protocols that was not implemented in IPv4 and not supported in IPv6.

Instead of IGMP, there is MLD in IPv6 between multicast host and the first hop multicast gateway.

Embedded RP is used for embedding RP IPv6 address as part of the multicast group address.

That's why the answer of this question is B and C.

Question 10:

If both IPv4 and IPv6 Multicast will be enabled on the campus network. Which multicast protocols should be enabled on the access switches? (Choose Two)

A. PIM Bidir

B. IGMP Snooping

C. MLD

D. Any Source Multicast

E. PIM Rendezvous Points

Answer 10:

On access switches, layer 3 multicast protocols are not enabled. On the first hop multicast routers, IGMP to PIM conversion are made. But IGMP Snooping in IPv4 and MLD (Multicast Listener Discovery) in IPv6 is critical for efficiency in IP multicast deployments.

That's' why answer of this question is B and C.

MULTICAST FURTHER STUDY RESOURCES

Books

Williamson, B. (1999). *Developing IP Multicast Networks, Volume I*, Cisco Press.

Videos

Ciscolive Session-BRKIPM-1261: Speaker Beau Williamson

Podcasts

http://www.cisco.com/c/en/us/products/collateral/ios-nx-os-software/multicast-enterprise/whitepaper_c11-474791.html

http://packetpushers.net/community-show-multicast-design-deployment-considerations-beau-williamson-orhan-ergun

Articles

https://tools.ietf.org/html/rfc7450

http://www.cisco.com/c/en/us/products/collateral/ios-nx-os-software/ip-multicast/whitepaper_c11508498.html

https://www.juniper.net/techpubs/en_US/release-independent/nce/information-products/topic-collections/nce/bidirectional-pim-configuring-bidirectional-pim.pdf

http://www.juniper.net/documentation/en_US_junos13.3/topics/concept/multicast-anycast-rp-mapping.html

http://d2zmdbbm9ferqf.cloudfront.net/2015/usa/pdf/BRKIPM-1261.pdf

CHAPTER 10
QUALITY OF SERVICE (QOS)

Quality of service (QoS) is the overall performance of a telephony or computer network, particularly the performance seen by the users of the network.

Two QoS approaches have been defined by standard organizations.

These are:

- Intserv (Integrated Services) and
- Diffserv (Differentiated Services).

Intserv demands that every flow requests a bandwidth from the network and that the network would reserve the required bandwidth for the user during a conversation.

Think of this as on-demand circuit switching, each flow of each user would be remembered by the network. This clearly would create a resource problem (CPU, memory , bandwidth) on the network, and thus it was never widely adopted.

The second QoS Approach is Diffserv (Differentiated Services).

Diffserv doesn't require reservation; instead flows are aggregated and placed into classes. Each and every node can be controlled by the network operator to treat differently for the aggregated flows.

Diffserv is a more scalable approach compared to Intserv.

If traffic exceeds the CIR or PIR and if it will be marked down, follow standard-based marking values. For example, if the application class for conforming traffic is AF31, exceeding traffic should be marked down with AF32 and violating traffic should be marked down with AF33.

QoS Application Marking Recommendation

Application	Layer 3 Classification			Layer 2 CoS MPLS EXP
	IPP	PHB	DSCP	
IP Routing	6	CS6	48	6
Voice	5	EF	46	5
Interactive Video	4	AF41	34	4
Streaming Video	4	CS4	32	4
Locally Defined Mission Critical Data	3	Cs3	24	3
Call Signals	3	AF31/CS3	26/24	3
Transactional Data	2	AF21	18	2
Network Management	2	CS2	16	2
Bulk Data	1	AF11	10	1
Scavenger	1	CS1	8	1
Best Effort	0	0	0	0

Recommended Application to PHB Marking Deployment

Voice QoS Requirements

Voice traffic should be marked to DSCP EF per the QoS Baseline and RFC 3246.

Loss should be no more than 1%. One-way Latency (mouth-to-ear) should be no more than 150 ms. Average one-way jitter should be targeted less than 30 ms.

21–320 kbps of guaranteed priority bandwidth is required per call (depending on the sampling rate, VoIP codec and Layer 2 media overhead).

Voice quality is directly affected by all three QoS quality factors: loss, latency and jitter.

Packet loss, latency and the jitter is most critical performance indicators for Voice and most of the video applications.

Video QoS Requirements

In general we are interested in two types of video traffic: interactive video and streaming video.

Interactive Video:

- When provisioning for interactive video (IP Videoconferencing) traffic, the following guidelines are recommended:
- Interactive video traffic should be marked to DSCP AF41; excess interactive video traffic can be marked down by a policer to AF42 or AF43.
- Loss should be no more than 1%.
- One-way latency should be no more than 150 ms.
- Jitter should be no more than 30 ms.
- Overprovision interactive video queues by 20% to accommodate bursts

Video Best Practices:

- Streaming video, whether unicast or multicast, should be marked to DSCP CS4 as designated by the QoS baseline.
- Loss should be no more than 5%.
- Latency should be no more than 4–5 seconds (depending on video application buffering capabilities).
- There are no significant jitter requirements.
- Guaranteed bandwidth (CBWFQ) requirements depend on the encoding format and rate of the video stream.
- Streaming video is typically unidirectional and, therefore, branch

routers may not require provisioning for streaming video traffic on their WAN/VPN edges (in the direction of branch-to-campus).

Data Applications QoS Requirements

- Best-effort data
- Bulk data
- Transactional/interactive data

Best-Effort Data

The best-effort class is the default class for all data traffic. An application will be removed from the default class only if it has been selected for preferential or deferential treatment.

Best-effort traffic should be marked to DSCP 0. Adequate bandwidth should be assigned to the best-effort class as a whole, because the majority of applications will default to this class; reserve at least 25% of bandwidth for best-effort traffic.

Bulk Data

The bulk data class is intended for applications that are relatively non-interactive and drop-insensitive and that typically span their operations over a long period of time as background occurrences.

Such applications include the following:

- FTP
- E-mail
- Backup operations
- Database synchronizing or replicating operations
- Content distribution
- Any other type of background operation

Bulk data traffic should be marked to DSCP AF11; excess bulk data traffic can be marked down by a policer to AF12; violating bulk data traffic may be marked down further to AF13 (or dropped).

Bulk data traffic should have a moderate bandwidth guarantee, but should be constrained from dominating a link.

Transactional/Interactive Data

The transactional/interactive data class, also referred to simply as transactional data, is a combination of two similar types of applications: transactional data client-server applications and interactive messaging applications.

Transaction is a foreground operation; the user waits for the operation to complete before proceeding.

E-mail is not considered a transactional data client-server application, as most e-mail operations occur in the background and users do not usually notice even several hundred millisecond delays in mail spool operations.

Transactional data traffic should be marked to DSCP AF21; excess transactional data traffic can be marked down by a policer to AF22; violating transactional data traffic can be marked down further to AF23 (or dropped).

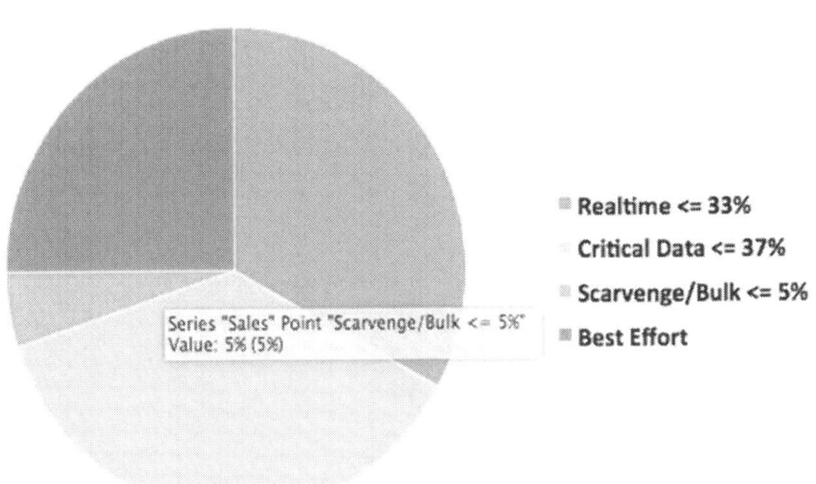

Real time, Best Effort, Critical Data, and Scavenger Queuing Rule: Four Classes of QoS Deployment

Congestion Management and Congestion Avoidance

Queuing, or congestion management, is used to manage the frames or packets before they exit a device.

In routers this is known as output queuing because IP forwarding decisions are made prior to the queuing.

Congestion avoidance is a term for managing traffic to decide when packets will be dropped during congestion periods.

The most common congestion avoidance tools are RED (Random Early Detection) and Weighted Random Early Detection (WRED).

If RED or WRED is not configured, by default all packets get same drop treatment. It is called Tail drop.

Queuing tools can also be used along side traffic shaping, which basically delays packets to ensure that the traffic rate for a class doesn't exceed the defined rate.

Congestion management deals with the front of the queues and the Congestion avoidance mechanisms handles the end of the queues.

MPLS QoS

MPLS QoS is done based on MPLS EXP bits. EXP bits are 3 bits. QoS tools; classification, marking, policing, shaping, and queening works similar to IP QoS. When the packet receives from the IP domain, packet is tunneled throughout the MPLS network.

DSCP bits are mapped to the EXP bits on the Ingress PE in the MPLS network and tunneled up to the Egress PE.

There are three MPLS QoS Tunnelling mechanisms.

- Uniform Mode
- Short Pipe
- Pipe (Also known as Long-Pipe)

As a network designer Understanding the different MPLS tunneling modes and their affects on Customer QoS policy is very important.

Uniform Mode

Uniform mode is generally used when the customer and SP share the same Diffserv domain, which would be the case if customer creates its MPLS network. The first three bits of the DSCP field are mapped to the MPLS EXP bits on the ingress PE

If a policer or other mechanism remarks the MPLS EXP value, new value is copied to lower level EXP bits. At the egress PE, MPLS EXP value is used to remark the customer DSCP value.

Short Pipe Mode

It is used when customer and SP are in different Diffserv domains. This mode is useful when the SP wants to enforce its own Diffserv policy but the customer wants its Diffserv information to be preserved across the MPLS domain. The Ingress PE sets the MPLS EXP value based on the SP Quality of Service policy.

If remarking is necessary, it is done on the MPLS EXP bits of the labels but not on the DSCP bits of the customers IP packet.

On the Egress PE, the queuing is done based on the DSCP marking of the customer's packet.

Customer doesn't need to remark their packet at the remote site.

Pipe Mode

Pipe mode is also known as Long-Pipe mode and Service Provider controls the QoS policy end to end. Pipe mode is same as short pipe mode except for that the queuing is based on MPLS EXP bits at the Egress PE and not on the customers DSCP marking.

Customer may need to remark their packet if they want consistent end-to-end QoS deployment.

Uniform vs. Short-Pipe vs. Pipe MPLS QoS Tunneling Models Comparison

Below table summarizes the similarities and the differences of these three MPLS QoS tunneling models in great detail.

Network designers should know the pros and cons of the technologies, protocol alternatives and their capabilities from the design point of view.

Design Requirement	Uniform Mode	Short Pipe	Pipe
Suitable for Customer Managed MPLS VPN	Yes,the changes in the core of the network is reflected to the IP DSCP or Presedence	No,Customer won't have control of EXP to DSCP mapping,DSCP doesn't change end to end	No,Customer won't have control of EXP to DSCP mapping,DSCP doesn't change end to end
Resource Requirement	Normal	Too much on the Eggress PE since Service Provider has to know all the Customers QoS architecture and configure the Egress PE accordingly	Normal
End to End Customer QoS setting	No,If EXP changes in the core it is copied to the DSCP at the Egress PE	Yes,Customer DSCP is preserved	Yes Customer DSCP is preserved
Special MPLS Label Requirement	No	No	Yes,Explict Null label (Label 0 for IPv4, Label 2 for IPv6) is sent by the Egress PE to the Penultimate Router
Requires QoS Remarking on the remote CE	Yes,since the DSCP information can change in the SP core,egress PE copies EXP bit to the DSCP at the Egress PE.Receiving CE needs to remark the DSCP	No,Customer QoS marking is preserved. If it comes to Ingress PE as DSCP EF, it is sent by the Egress PE as EF as well	No,Customer QoS marking is preserved. If it comes to Ingress PE as DSCP EF, it is sent by the Egress PE as EF as well
Alternative name	Unified MPLS QoS Tunneling	Short Pipe MPLS QoS Tunneling	Long Pipe MPLS QoS Tunneling
Standard Implementation	Yes IETF Standard	Yes IETF Standard	Yes IETF Standard
Customer-Service Provider Interaction	For the initial DSCP to EXP mapping only	For the initial DSCP to EXP mapping and also SP has to know each and every customer's QoS requirement to arrange egress scheduling and dropping strategy on the Egress Pe	For the initial DSCP to EXP mapping only
E-LSP and L-LSP support	Yes	Yes	Yes

Uniform vs. Short-Pipe vs. Pipe MPLS QoS Tunneling Modes Comparison

QOS BEST PRACTICES

- Always classify and mark applications as close to their sources as possible.
- Classification and marking usually done on both ingress and egress direction but queuing and shaping usually are done on Egress.
- Ingress Queening can be done to prevent Head Of Line blocking.
- Less granular fields such as CoS and MPLS EXP should be mapped to DSCP as close to the traffic source as possible.
- Follow standards based Diffserv PHB markings if possible to ensure interoperability with SP networks, enterprise networks or merging networks together.
- If there is real time, delay sensitive traffic, LLQ should be enabled.
- Enable queuing at every node, which has potential for congestion.
- Limit LLQ to 33% of link bandwidth capacity.
- Enable Admission Control on LLQ.
- Policing should be done as close to the source as possible.
- Do not enable WRED on LLQ.
- Allocate 25% of the capacity for the Best Effort class if there is large number of application in the default class.
- For a link carrying a mix of voice, video and data traffic, limit the priority queue to 33% of the link bandwidth.
- Use WRED for congestion avoidance on TCP traffic.
- Use DSCP based WRED wherever possible.
- Always enable QoS in hardware as opposed to software if possible.
- Because 802.1p bit gets lost when the packet enters the IP or MPLS domain, mapping is needed. Always implement QoS at the hardware, if possible, to avoid performance impact.
- Switches support QoS in the hardware, so, for example, in the campus,

classify and mark the traffic at the switches.

- QoS design should support a minimum of three classes:
  EF (Expedited Forwarding)
  DF (Default Forwarding/Best Effort)
  AF (Assured Forwarding)
- If company policy allows YouTube, gaming, and other non-business applications, scavenger class is created and CS1 PHB is implemented. CS1 is defined as less than best effort service in the standard RFC.
- On AF queues, DSCP-based WRED should be enabled. Otherwise, TCP synchronization occurs. WRED allows the packet to be dropped randomly and DSCP functionality allows packet to be dropped based on priority.

DO YOU REALLY NEED QUALITY OF SERVICE?

Some thoughts on End-to-End QoS Design:

Quality of service (QoS) is the overall performance of a telephony or computer network, particularly the performance seen by the users of the network.

Performance metrics can be bandwidth, delay, jitter, pocket loss and so on.

Two Quality Of Service approaches have been defined by the standard organizations. Namely Intserv (Integrated Services) and Diffserv (Differentiated Services).

As it was mentioned briefly earlier in this chapter; Intserv was demanding each and every flow to request a bandwidth from the network and network would reserve the required bandwidth for the user during a conversation.

Think this is an on demand circuit switching, each flows of each user would be remembered by the network. This clearly would create a resource problem (CPU, Memory, Bandwidth) on the network thus never widely adopted.

Although with RSVP-TE (RSVP Traffic Engineering) particular LSP can ask a bandwidth from the network nodes, and in turn nodes reserve a bandwidth, number of LSP between the Edge nodes of the network is order of magnitude less than individual flows of the users.

The second Quality of Service Approach is Diffserv (Differentiated Services) doesn't require reservation but instead flows are aggregated and place into the classes.

Network operator can treat differently for the aggregated flows by controlling each and every node.

Obviously Diffserv QoS approach is more scalable compare to the Intserv Quality of Service model.

When you practice Quality of Service, you learn Classification, Marking, Queuing, Policing, Shaping tools.

And you are also told that in order to have best Quality Of Service for the user, you need to deploy it end to end.

But where are those ends?

The name of the nodes might differ based on business. In Enterprise campus, your access switch is one end and the branch router, datacenter virtual or physical access switches; Internet gateways might be the other end.

Or in the Service Provider business, Provider Edge router is one end, other provider edge router, datacenter virtual or physical access, Internet gateways, service access devices such as DSLAM, CMTS devices might be other end.

So end to end principle will fail since the end to end domain might be too broad and too much devices to manage.

But definitely some tools make sense in some place in some networks.

For example " Policing " in the Service Provider Networks. It can be used for the billing purpose. Provider can drop the excess usage or charge for the premium service.

Policing is deployed together with classification/marking but you don't need to deploy QoS tools on the other nodes so those classification and marking will be locally make sense. This tool is also used for the Call Admission Control purpose.

Imagine you have 200Mb links and each Telepresence flow requires 45mb traffic. You can place 4 calls onto the link. If 5th call is setup, all other 4 calls suffer as well since packets has to be dropped. (45 * 5 - 200 - buffer size)

Another Quality of Service tools is queuing; and in particular it is used whenever there is an oversubscription. Oversubscription can be between the nodes (On the links) or within the nodes.

If the congestion is within the node, queuing in the ingress direction is applied to protect some traffic (maybe real time) from the Head of Line Blocking in the switching fabric of the node. Or in the egress direction, between the nodes to protect selective traffic.

The problem is if there is enough traffic, buffers (queue) will get full and eventually all the traffic will be dropped no matter what queuing method (LLQ, WFQ, CBWFW) is used.

So if you try to design end-to-end Quality of Service by enable queuing to cover all possible oversubscription in the network you fail.

When the congestion happens, some flows will just die couple milliseconds after another.

The design tradeoff here is to add more bandwidth vs. engineering all possible congestion points. I am not talking only the initial QoS design phase but the complexity brought by the QoS in the design as well.

Network Operator need to manage understand, troubleshoot QoS during steady state and in the case of failure as well.

Bandwidth is getting cheaper and cheaper everyday but the complexity of Quality of Service will stay there forever. So do you still think that you need an end-to-end QoS deployment?

QOS REVIEW QUESTIONS

Question 1:

Which below statements are true for QoS design?

A. Classification and marking should be done at every hop

B. Classification and marking should be done as close to the sources as possible

C. Instead of DSCP based marking COS based marking is recommended for end to end QoS design

D. Quality of Service increases availability bandwidth capacity

Answer 1:

QoS doesn't increase available capacity. It is used to manage fairness between the applications for current capacity.

Classification and marking should be deployed as close to the sources as possible, not at every hop.

And Instead of COS, DSCP based marking should be deployed to prevent mapping throughout the network.

That's why the answer of this question is B.

Question 2:

Which below option is true for the Congestion Avoidance mechanisms?

A. When it is enabled, router marks the packets based on some criteria

B. When it is enabled, router classify the packets

C. When it is enabled, router handles the possible congestion by using RED or WRED

D. When it is enabled, router can place the important traffic into the LLQ

Answer 2:

As it was explained in the QoS chapter, congestion avoidance mechanisms are different than congestion management mechanisms.

Congestion avoidance mechanism coordinates the front of the queues and a congestion avoidance mechanism handles the tail of the queues.

RED and WRED are the congestion avoidance mechanisms. And when it is enabled, router handles the possible congestion by using one of these mechanisms. Other options are related with classification, marking and queuing.

Only the correct answer of this question is Option C.

Question 3:

What should be the one-way latency for the Voice traffic in QoS design?

A. Less than 1 second

B. Less than 500 milliseconds

C. Less than 150 milliseconds

D. Less than 300 milliseconds

Answer 3:

As a general design rule of thumb, one way latency which is also known as mouth to ear latency for the Voice traffic should be less than 150ms.

That's why the answer of this question is C.

Question 4:

Which are the options are important in Voice over IP design? (Choose Three)

A. Delay

B. Echo

C. Packet Loss

D. Variance in delay

E. CDR records

Answer 4:

For the Voice traffic, as it was explained in the QoS chapter of the book, Packet loss, latency and the jitter is most critical performance indicators.

Latency is also known as delay and Variance in delay is known as Jitter.

CDR (Call detail record) is log information, which is not critical in Voice design as the others.

That's why the correct answer of this question is A, C and D.

Question 5:

Which below QoS mechanism is commonly deployed on the Service Provider ingress PE device for their customer traffic?

A. Policing

B. Shaping

C. WRED

D. MPLS Traffic Engineering

Answer 5:

On the customer site shaping is deployed and the Service Provider commonly deploy Policing. Exceeding traffic can be either dropped, pass normally but it is charged extra or markdown and threated worse.

Question 6:

Which of the below statements are true for the Voice Traffic in QoS design? (Choose Two)

A. Voice traffic should be marked with EF, DSCP 46

B. Voice traffic sensitive to packet loss, jitter and delay

C. Voice traffic should be placed in Best Effort Queue

D. For the voice traffic queue, WRED should be enabled

E. Voice requires one way latency less than 2 seconds

Answer 6:

Voice traffic should be marked with EF, DSCP 46. It is sensitive to packet loss, jitter and delay.

It should be placed in LLQ (Low Latency Queue) not the best effort. WRED should be enabled for the TCP based application, not for the voice traffic.

It requires one-way latency to be less than 150ms, not 2 seconds.

The correct answers of this questions are A and B.

Question 7:

Enterprise Company receives Gigabit Ethernet physical link from the local Service Provider. But the Committed Information Rate is 250Mbps. Which QoS mechanism Enterprise Company should deploy to ensure low packet loss toward the Service Provider?

A. Priority Queening

B. WRED

C. Marking

D. Policing

E. Shaping

Answer 7:

When the customer receives a service from the actual physical link speed, they can send more traffic than the committed information rate (Actual service bandwidth).

In this case common action on the Service Provider networks is to police the traffic.

The Service Provider might drop customer critical traffic unless Customer doesn't do the Shaping at their site. Correct answer of this question is shaping which is Option E.

Question 8:

Which below options are true for the QoS design? (Choose Two)

A. MPLS QoS is done based on EXP bits

B. IP DSCP uses 6 bits

C. Marking should be done at the every hop for better QoS

D. Queening is enabled when the interface utilization reaches 80%

E. Queening shouldn't be enabled in the Local Area Network since there is too much available bandwidth already

Answer 8:

MPLS QoS is done based on 3 bits EXP field. IP DSCP uses 6 bits of IP TOS byte (8 bits)

Marking and Classification should be done as close to the sources as possible. If mapping is necessary for example between PE-CE in MPLS deployments, then at the WAN edge is also remarking can be done. But not at every hop.

Queening is enabled only when the interface utilization reaches 100%. Not 80! Queening should be enabled even in the LAN to protect the applications from the micro burst. For the best QoS design, LAN shouldn't be missed and QoS should be deployed on the LAN as well.

That's why the correct answer of this question is A and B.

Question 9:

Which below statements are true for the MPLS QoS tunneling models? (Choose Three)

A. There are two types of tunneling models; uniform mode and non-uniform modes

B. There are three types of tunneling models; uniform mode, short-pipe and pipe modes

C. Pipe model is known as Long-pipe modes as well

D. With uniform modes customer may need to remark their traffic at the remote site

E. Short-pipe modes requires MPLS between the customer and the Service Provider

Answer 9:

There are three types of tunneling models; uniform mode, short-pipe and pipe modes. Pipe mode is also known as long pipe mode.

With uniform mode customer QoS policy may require remarking at the remote site.

None of the three modes require MPLS between customer and the Service Provider.

That's why the answer of this question is B, C and D.

Question 10:

Which below options are true for the MPLS QoS deployment? (Choose Two)

A. Classification and marking is done on the P devices.

B. It requires MPLS between PE and CE

C. With Short-Pipe MPLS QoS tunneling mode, queening is done based on the customer policy

D. Shaping should be done to drop the exceeding customer traffic on the Ingress PE

E. Policing should be done to drop the exceeding customer traffic on the Ingress PE

Answer 10:

Classification and marking is done on the PE devices.

It doesn't require MPLS between PE and ce

With Short-Pipe MPLS QoS Tunneling mode, queening is done at the Egress PE based on the customer QoS policy.

Policing is done on the Ingress PE to drop or remark exceeding customer traffic.

That's why the correct answer of this question is C and E.

QOS STUDY RESOURCES

Books

Szigeti, T. (2013). *End-to-End QoS Network Design: Quality of Service for Rich-Media & Cloud Networks (Second Edition)*, Cisco Press.

Videos

Ciscolive Session-BRKCRS-2501
https://www.youtube.com/watch?v=6UJZBeK_JCs

Articles

http://www.cisco.com/c/en/us/td/docs/solutions/Enterprise/WAN_and_MAN/QoS_SRND/QoS-SRND-Book/QoSIntro.html
http://ww.cisco.com/c/en/us/td/docs/solutions/Enterprise/Video/qos-mrn.pdf
http://orhanergun.net/2015/06/do-you-really-need-quality-of-service/
http://d2zmdbbm9feqrf.cloudfront.net/2013/usa/pdf/BRKCRS-2501.pdf
https://ripe65.ripe.net/presentations/67-2012-09-25-qos.pdf

CHAPTER 11
MPLS

If the requirement is to have a scalable VPN solution that can provide fast reroute traffic protection, then the only choice is MPLS.

MPLS is a protocol-independent transport mechanism. It can carry Layer 2 and Layer 3 payloads. Packet forwarding decision is made solely on the label without the need to examine the packet itself.

MPLS interacts as an overlay with IGP and BGP in many ways. For example, in multi-level IS-IS design, Level 1 domain breaks end-to-end LSP.

- In this chapter:
- MPLS Theory will be explained very briefly, basic concepts in MPLS which will be applicable to all of its applications will be mentioned.
- MPLS Applications such as Layer 2 and Layer 3 VPNs, Inter-AS MPLS VPN Deployment Options, Carrier Supporting Carrier Architecture, Seamless MPLS, MPLS Transport Profile and MPLS Traffic Engineering will be explained in detail. Comparison tables will be provided whenever is applicable from the design point of view.
- Many Case Studies will be provided to better understand the concepts in a holistic manner.
- So many MPLS design questions will be provided and answers will be shared at the end of the chapter. These questions will be complementary to the topics in the chapter and will be useful in real life MPLS design as well as CCDE Written and Practical exams.

MPLS Theory

- MPLS is a transport mechanism.
- It supports label-stacking which allows many applications to run over MPLS.
- All applications need additional labels. MPLS Layer 2 VPN, Layer 3 VPN and MPLS Traffic Engineering as a common MPLS applications require minimum two labels.
- In MPLS Layer 3 VPN, Transport, and BGP labels are used to create VPN.
- In Layer 2 VPN, Transport and VC labels are used.
- Label can be assigned by four protocols currently. LDP, RSVP, BGP, and Segment Routing

MPLS APPLICATIONS

Important MPLS applications/services for the network designers are listed below.

All that will be explained in this chapter.

- Layer 2 MPLS VPN
- Layer 3 MPLS VPN
- Inter-AS MPLS VPNs
- Carrier Supporting Carrier
- MPLS Traffic Engineering
- Seamless MPLS
- MPLS Transport Profile (MPLS-TP)

MPLS infrastructure can have all of the above MPLS application/ services at the same time.

You can provide protection for Layer 2 and Layer 3 VPN customers by having MPLS traffic engineering LSPs for SLA or FFR purposes.

MPLS Layer 2 MPLS VPN

In MPLS Layer 2 VPN, Layer 2 frame is carried over the MPLS transport.

If you are extending MPLS towards the access domain of the backbone then you can have end-to-end MPLS backbone without the need for protocol translation. Two different Layer 2 VPN architectures provide similar services defined in MEF (Metro Ethernet Forum).

Label Switched path which provides end-to-end MPLS label reachability, between the PE devices of the network is called Transport LSP. It is also known as Tunnel LSP.

MPLS Layer 2 VPN can be point-to-point, which is called virtual private wire service (VPWS), or multi-point-to-point, which is called virtual private LAN service (VPLS).

Benefits of MPLS, Why MPLS is used and MPLS Advantages

As an Encapsulation and VPN mechanism, MPLS brings many benefits to the IP networks.

Below list shows the benefits of MPLS. MPLS as a very mature VPN technology has many benefits. Below are the some of the important use case of MPLS technology and will explained in great detail throughout this chapter.

- Faster packet processing with MPLS compare to IP

Initially MPLS invented to provide faster packet processing compare to IP based lookup. With MPLS instead of doing IP destination based lookup, label-switching operation is done. Smaller MPLS header compare to IP header is processed and provides performance benefit. Although today nobody enables MPLS for this reason, this was the initial reason for MPLS as I stated above.

- BGP Free Core with MPLS

Without MPLS, if BGP is running on the network, it needs to run on every device on the path. MPLS removed this need, less protocol means, simpler network and easier maintenance.

- Hiding service specific information (customer prefixes, etc.) from the core of the network

When MPLS is used on the network, only the edge devices has to keep the customer specific information such as MAC address, Vlan number, IP address and so on. Core of the network only provides reachability between the edges.

- More scalable network

Not having service specific information on the core of the network provides better scalability. CPU and Memory point of view as well as dealing with the routing protocol updates, link state changes and many other problems abstract from the core of the network by using MPLS.

- MPLS VPNs -MPLS Layer 2 and Layer 3 VPNs

Probably the most important reason and main benefit of MPLS is MPLS VPNs. MPLS as you might know allows to create Point-to-point, point-to-multipoint and multipoint-to-multipoint type of MPLS layer 2 VPN and MPLS layer 3 VPNs.

By using BGP, LDP and/or RSVP protocols, VPNs can be created. There are tens of articles on MPLS VPNs on the website.

- Traffic Engineering

MPLS with the RSVP-TE provides traffic engineering capability which allows better capacity usage and guaranteed SLA for the desired service. MPLS Traffic Engineering are explained with the many articles on the website in detail.

- Fast Reroute

With RSVP-TE, MPLS provides MPLS Traffic Engineering Fast Reroute Link and Node Protection. RSVP-TE is one option but with LDP, LFA and Remote LFA can be setup if RSVP-TE is not used in the network. MPLS Traffic Engineering Fast Reroute can protected the important service in any kind of topology and provides generally less than a 50msec protection.

On the other hand, IP FRR mechanisms require highly meshed topology to provide full coverage in the case of failures.

When LDP is used without RSVP-TE, solution is also called as IP Fast Reroute. There was CR-LDP (Constrained based) draft but since it is deprecated I don't mention here.

MPLS doesn't bring security by default. If security is needed then IPSEC should run on top of that. Best IPSEC solution for the MPLS

VPNs is GETVPN since it provides excellent scalability.

MPLS is used mainly for the Wide Area Network but there are implementation for Datacenter Interconnect, Datacenter Multi segmentation as well.

Today with PCE (Path Computation Element), MPLS is considered to be used in SDN (Software Defined Networking) for network programmability, WAN bandwidth optimization, new emerging services such as bandwidth calendaring, multi area and multi domain traffic engineering and automation purposes as well.

MPLS Layer 2 VPN Deployment Options:

Both VPWS and VPLS can be accomplished in two ways.

These are Kompella and Martini methods.

In both methods, Transport LSP is created between the PE devices via LDP protocol.

In Kompella method, pseudo-wire is signaled via BGP.

In Martini method, pseudo-wire is signaled via LDP (Label Distribution Protocol).

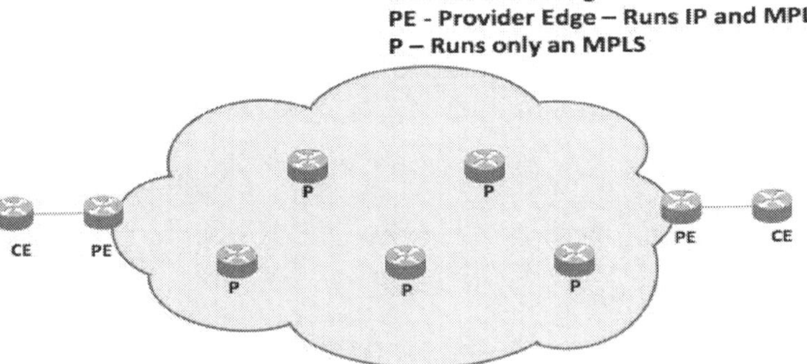

CE is customer equipment, which can be managed by Service Provider or Customer depending on SLA.

PE is the Provider Edge device, which has a connection to Customer, and the Service Provider internal devices.

In MPLS networks, all the intelligence is at the edge. Core is kept as simple as possible. KISS principle in network design comes from the “intelligent edge, dummy core” idea.

P is the Provider device and only has a connection to P or PE devices. P device doesn't have a connection to the Customer network.

PE device looks at the incoming frame or packet and identifies which egress PE device is used for the transport.

Second lookup is made to determine the egress interface on the egress device.

Packet gets two labels in both MPLS Layer 2 and MPLS Layer 3 VPN. The outer label, which is also called topmost or transport label, is used to reach the egress device.

The inner label is called pseudo-wire or VC label in MPLS Layer 2 VPN and is used to identify the individual pseudo-wire on the egress PE.

In Martini method, both transport and VC (virtual circuit) label is sent (signaled) via LDP (label distribution protocol).

Targeted LDP session is created between the PEs.

In Kompella method, transport label is signaled via LDP, VC label is signaled via MP-BGP (multiprotocol BGP). New address family is enabled if there is already BGP for other services.

MPLS Layer 2 VPN Service Types:

There are mainly two services in MPLS Layer 2 VPN. These are VPWS and VPLS.

VPWS is also known as EoMPLS (Ethernet Over MPLS). In Cisco books, you can see it as ATOM (Any Transport over MPLS) as well.

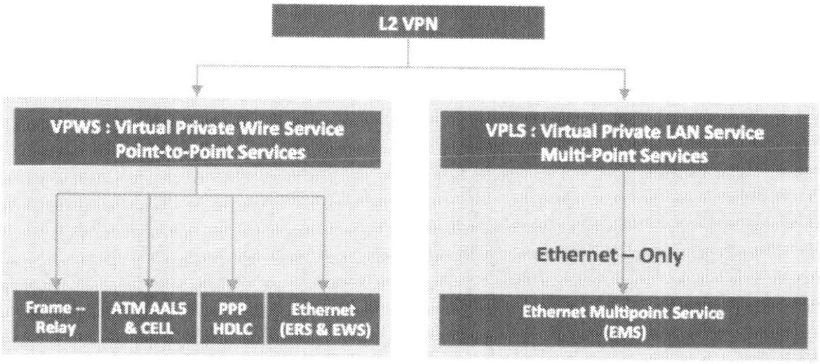

VPWS can carry almost all Layer 2 payloads as can be seen from the above diagram.

VPLS can carry Ethernet frames only. There is an attempt in the IETF for the other Layer 2 payloads over VPLS though.

In VPWS, PE devices learn only VLAN information if the VC type is VLAN. If the VC type is Ethernet, then the PE device doesn't keep any state. VLAN is not learned as well.

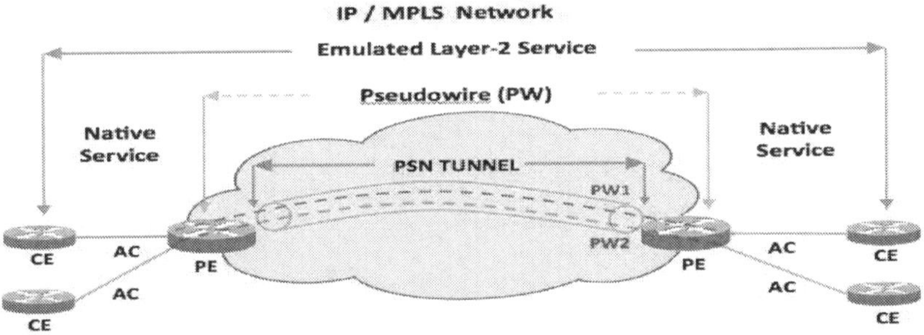

There is only one egress point for the VPWS service at the other end of the pseudo-wire, thus PE device doesn't have to keep MAC Address to PW binding.

PE device doesn't have to learn MAC address of the customer in VPWS (EoMPLS) MPLS Layer 2 VPN service. This provides scalability.

But in VPLS, since service provider provides an emulated bridge service to the customer, MAC to PW binding is necessary. Destination might be any PE since the service is multipoint.

PE devices keep MAC addresses of the customer. Although there is PBB-VPLS, which provides more scalability by eliminating learning of customer MAC addresses, it is not widely implemented.

That's why from the PE device scalability point of view, VPWS is better compare to VPLS in MPLS Layer 2 VPN.

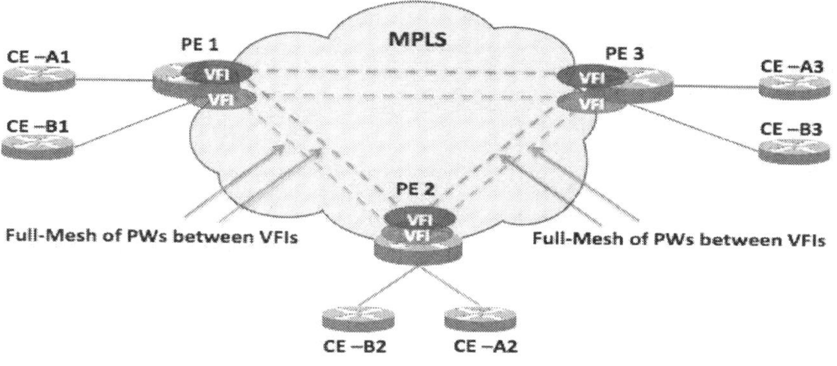

VPLS Topology

Above is the VPLS topology. In VPLS, VFI (a.k.a VSI) is a virtual forwarding/switching instance is an equivalent of VRF in MPLS Layer3 VPN.

It is used to identify the VPLS domain of the Customer.

As depicted in the above topology, point-to -point pseudo-wire is created between the PE devices for the VPWS (EoMPLS, point-to-point service). In order to have VPLS service full-mesh of point-to-point pseudo-wire is created between all the PEs, which has a membership in the same VPN.

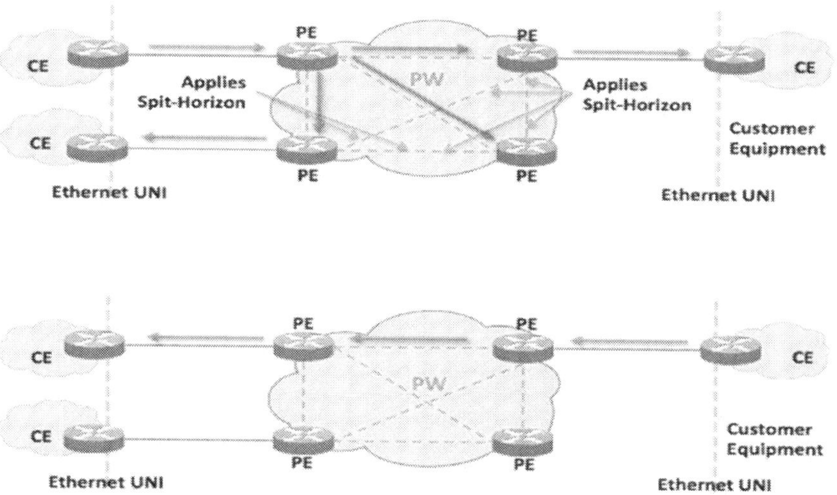

Loop Prevention in VPLS

In the above figure, loop prevention is shown in the VPLS.

There is no STP in the service provider core network for loop avoidance in VPLS.

Instead, there is a split horizon rule in the core and it is enabled by default. No need for configuration.

According the VPLS split horizon, if the customer frame is received from pseudo-wire, it is not sent back to another pseudo-wire. Since there is full-mesh pseudo-wire connectivity between the all VPLS PEs in a given customer VPN, full reachability between the sites is achieved. The number of PE nodes that need to join the VPLS instance (also known as VSI, or virtual switch instance) might be too high.

In this case, ' auto-discovery ' to learn the other PEs in the same VPN is highly important from the scalability point of view. Otherwise all the PEs in a given VPLS instance have to be manually configured.

Auto-discovery can be achieved in multiple ways. Radius server is one way, but a more common one is BGP. Kompella method uses BGP for both Auto-discovery and the pseudowire signaling.

Multi-protocol BGP can carry VPLS membership information in Kompella method.

EVPN

EVPN is a next-generation VPLS. In VPLS customer MAC addresses are learned through data plane. Source MAC addresses are recorded based on source address from both AC (attachment circuit) and pseudo-wire. In VPLS, active-active flow-based load balancing is not possible.

Customer can be dual-homed to the same or different PEs of service provider, but either those links can be used as active/standby for all VLANs or VLAN-based load-balancing can be achieved. EVPN can support active active flow-based load-balancing so same VLAN can be used on both PE devices actively. This provides faster convergence in customer link, PE link, or node failure scenarios.

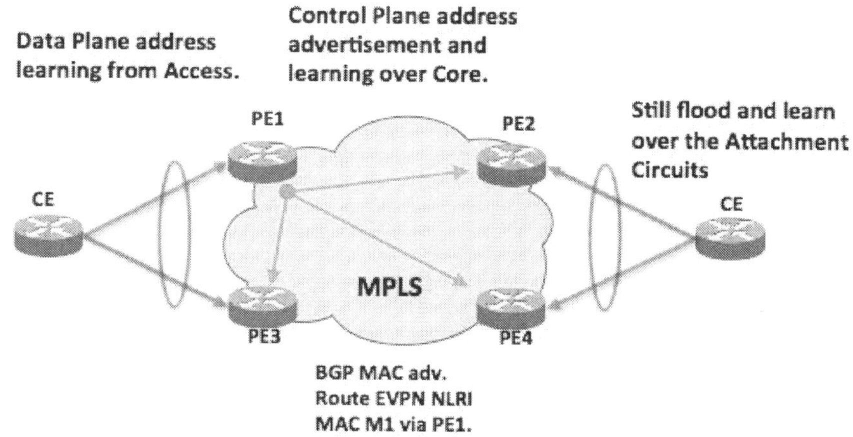

Customer MAC addresses are advertised over the MPBGP (multiprotocol BGP) control plane. There is no data plane MAC learning over the core network in EVPN. But Customer MAC addresses from the attachment circuit are still learned through the data plane.

Layer 3 MPLS VPN

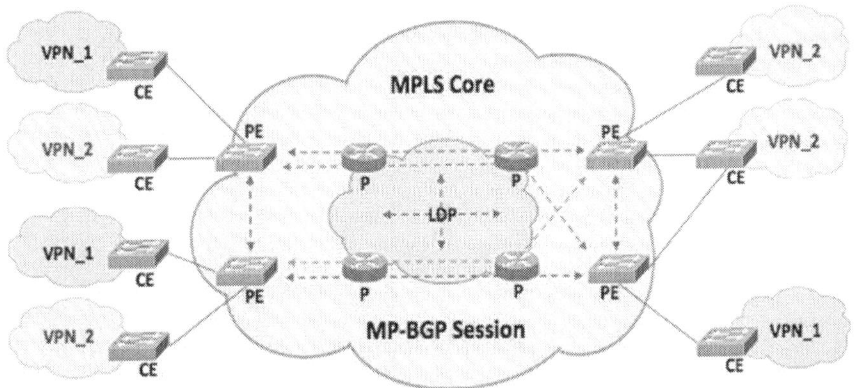

Customer runs a routing protocol with the service provider to carry the IP information between the sites. As stated earlier, static routing is a routing protocol. CE devices can be managed by the customer or service provider depending on the SLA.

Service provider might provide additional services such as IPv6, QoS, and multicast. By default, IPv4 unicast service is provided by the service provider in MPLS Layer 3 VPN architecture. Transport tunnels can be created by LDP or RSVP. RSVP is extended to provide MPLS traffic engineering service in MPLS networks.

The inner label, also known as the BGP label, provides VPN label information with the help of MPBGP (multiprotocol BGP). This label allows data plane separation. Customer traffic is kept separated over common MPLS network with the VPN label. MPBGP session is created between PE devices only. P devices do not run BGP in an MPLS environment. This is known as BGP Free Core design.

Route Distinguisher is a 64-bit value that is used to make the customer prefix unique throughout the service provider network. With RD (route distinguisher), different customers can use the same address space over the service provider backbone. Route target is an extended community attribute and is used to import and export VPN prefixes to and from VRF. Export route target is used to advertise prefixes from VRF to MP-BGP, import route target is used to receive the VPN prefixes from MP-

BGP into customer VRF. MPLS Layer 3 VPN by default provides any-to-any connectivity (multipoint-to-multipoint) between the VPN customer sites. If the customer wants to have hub-and-spoke topology, route target community can provide flexibility.

EoMPLS vs. VPLS vs. MPLS Layer 3 VPN Comparison

Below table summarizes the similarities and the differences of the three common MPLS VPN technologies in great detail.

MPLS Layer 2 VPN models; EoMPLS (Ethernet over MPLS, a.k.a ATOM) and VPLS will be compared with MPLS Layer 3 VPN.

Network designers should know the pros and cons of the technologies, protocol alternatives and their capabilities from the design point of view.

Design Requirement	EoMPLS	VPLS	MPLS L3 VPN
Scalability for the Customer	Not scalable compare to VPLS and MPLS L3 VPN	Very Scalable architecture for the layer 2 service	Very scalable architecture for the layer 3 service
Scalability for the Service Provider	Not good	Same as EoMPLS if BGP Auto Discovery is not used, if BGP AD is used,better than EoMPLS	
Service Type	Carries Layer 2 frames	Carries Layer 2 Frames	Carries Layer 3 IP packets
Working on Full Mesh	Scalability is very bad for full mesh topology	It works very well for the full mesh topology	Vey good with the MPBGP VPN Route Reflectors but RT Constraints should be used to hide unnecessary information from the unintended PE devices
Working on Hub and Spoke	Works quite well but if the number os sites too much, scalability for both customer and service provider becomes an issue	Better than EoMPLS for both the Service Provider and Customer from the scalability point of view	Requires extra configuration on the Service Provider side but it is doable and commonly used
Suitable as WAN technology	Yes but not scalable	Yes it is very scalable	Yes it is very scalable

Design Requirement	EoMPLS	VPLS	MPLS L3 VPN
Suitable as DCI technology	It is suitable but if there are so many sites to interconnect, it's scalability is not good	It is originally designed as Datacenter Interconnect Technology,it is most suitable one among all these three options	It can be used as Layer 3 datacenter interconnect technology but cannot provide layer 2 extension thus not good as DCI
Who controls the Backbone Routing	Customer	Customer	Service Provider
Standard Protocol	Yes IETF Standard	Yes IETF Standard	Yes IETF Standard
Service Provider Stuff Experince	Not well known	Limited knowledge	Well known
Routing Protocol Support	All routing protocols can be enabled over Ethernet over MPLS Service	VPLS provides LAN emulation so allows layer 2 to be streched over the customer locations.Any routing protocol can run over VPLS service	In theory any routing protocol can run as PE-CE but most Service Provider only provides BGP and Static Routing
MPLS Traffic Engineering Support	Yes	Yes	Yes
Security	Same as Frame Relay, doesn't provide IPSEC by default	Same as Frame Relay,doesn't provide IPSEC by default	Same as Frame Relay,doesn't provide IPSEC by default

Design Requirement	EoMPLS	VPLS	MPLS L3 VPN
Multicast Support	Yes	Yes	Service Provider should offer, otherwise Customer has to create overlays to carry Multicast traffic, that's why Multicast support may nor be good
Best technology for IPSEC	GETVPN,it provides excellent scalability	GETVPN,it provides excellent scalability	GETVPN,it provides excellent scalability
Resource Requirement for the Service Provider	Best since the PE devices don't have to keep the customer MAC addresses	Worst since the PE devices have to keep all the MAC addresses of the customer and MAC addresses are not aggregatable	Bad since the PE devices have to keep the routing tables of the customer but since the IP addresses can be aggregated, some sites may not need entire routing table of the customer
Resource Requirement for the Customer	Basic,it requires only layer 2 switch	Basic,It requires only layer 2 switch	More, it requires either Layer 3 switch or Router at the customer site
IPv6 Support	Yes, Service Provider is transparent for the IPv4 and IPv6 packets	Yes,Service Provider is transparent for the IPv4 and IPv6 packets	Yes with 6vPE technology it provides IPv6 supports for the VPN customers

Design Requirement	EoMPLS	VPLS	MPLS L3 VPN
Hierarchy	None	With H-VPLS full mesh PW requirement is avoided	Route Reflector for the MPBGP sessions between PE devices
Loop Prevention	It is only point to point, there is no chance to loop	In the core split horizon prevents loop. If traffic comes from PW it is not sent back to another PW	OSPF Down Bit,IS-IS Up/Down Bit, EIGRP Site of Origin prevents loop when CE is multihomed to the MPLS L3 VPN PE

EoMPLS vs. VPLS vs. MPLS L3 VPN Design Comparison

MPLS Layer 3 VPN Case Study – Protocols and Technology Placement

Enterprise Company is using MPLS Layer 3 VPN for their WAN connections. Their IGP protocol is EIGRP.

Service provider of the company is using IS-IS as an internal infrastructure IGP in their backbone and LDP for the label distribution.

Can you select all the required protocols from the checkbox near the routers?

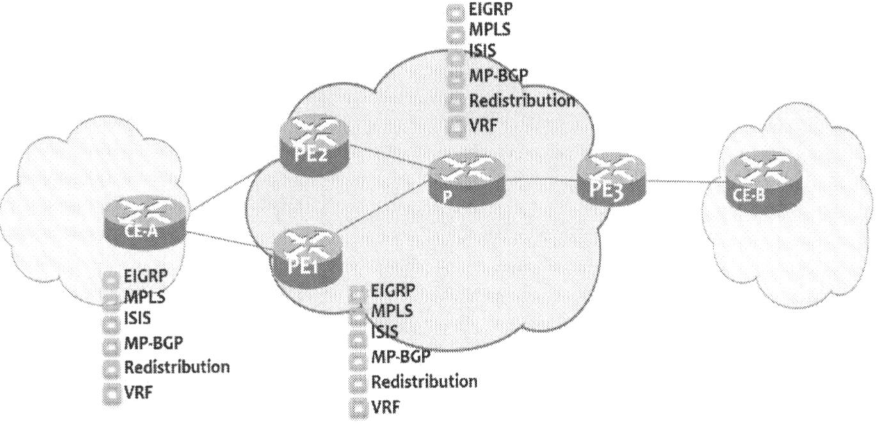

Answer should be as below.

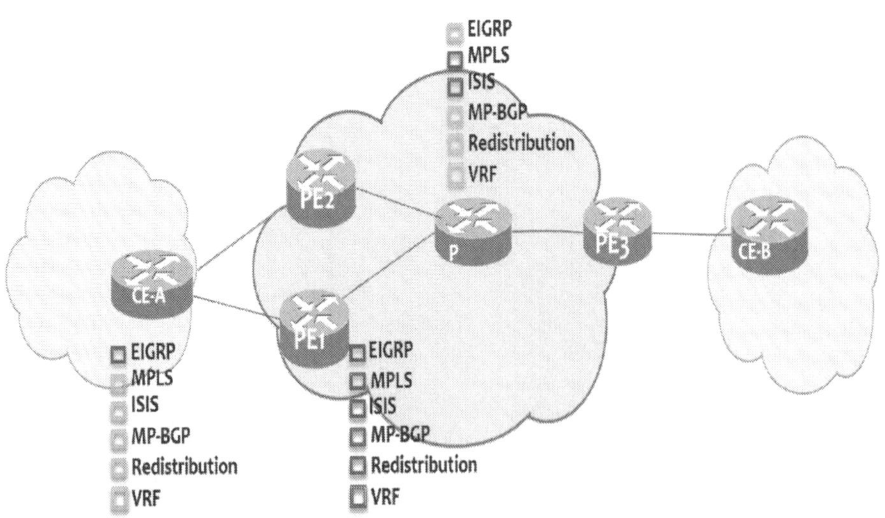

HUB-AND-SPOKE MPLS VPNs

Hub and Spoke MPLS Layer 3 VPN or any other topology in MPLS Layer 3 VPN is done by playing with the route Target attribute.

If Route Target Import and Export values are set on all the PEs in a given VPN, Full mesh topology is created. In the below figure, Hub and Spoke topology is shared. It is created by configuring the different RT values on the Hub and Spokes. Hub imports all the Spokes RT values; spokes import the HUB RT value but not the other Spokes RT values. On the Spokes, different RT values are configured.

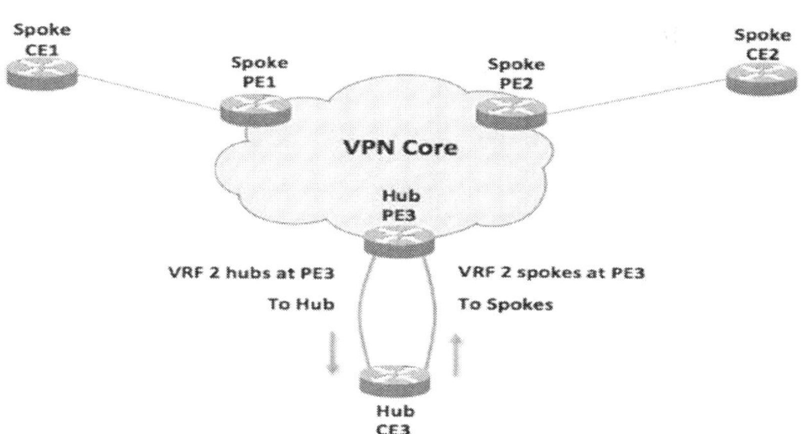

MPLS VPN RESILIENCY

Customers needing to have increased resiliency may want to have two MPLS connections from two different service providers. Primary and secondary VPNs are same type of VPN in general, so if the primary is Layer 2 VPN, since this is the operational model that the customer wants to use, secondary link from the other provider also is chosen as Layer 2 VPN.If Layer 3 VPN is received from one service provider, second link from the second provider is also received as Layer 3 VPN. Of course, neither MPLS Layer2 VPN nor Layer 3 VPN have to have MPLS VPN as a backup, but the Internet or any other transport can be a backup for the Customer.

The table below shows the selection criteria for choosing single vs. dual providers.

Single vs. Dual Carrier MPLS VPN Design Comparison

Below table summarizes the similarities and the differences of these two design models in detail.

Network designers should know the pros and cons of the technologies, protocol alternatives and their capabilities from the design point of view.

Design Requirement	Single Carrier	Dual Carrier
Complexity	Less Complex	More complex, due to more protocols technically, also two different business to deal with
Cost	Disadvantage compared to same level of availability with dual carrier	Two providers give an ability to discuss the costs with them
Availability	Less available	More available
Quality of Service	Easy	Difficult to manage
IPv6	Easy	Difficult to deploy
Multicast	Easy	Difficult. Service provider offering or overlay for multicast is difficult to manage
Convergence	Easy to manage	Difficult to manage
Service	Less service offering	More service offerings (One service provider may not provide VPLS etc.)
Merger /Acquisition	Easy Migration	Difficult to manage the migration process
Network Design	Easy	Difficult, since there are lots of considerations such as , transit sites, bandwidth, TE, and so on
Traffic Engineering	Easy	Difficult
Routing Protocols	Easy to manage	Difficult to manage

Single vs. Dual MPLS VPN Carrier Design Models Comparison

MPLS Layer 3 VPN OSPF as a PE-CE Protocol Case Study

Orefe is a supermarket company, based in Turkey. Most of their stores are in Istanbul, but they have forty-six stores operating in cities close to Istanbul.

They recently decided to upgrade their WAN. They have been using Frame Relay between the stores, HQ, and their datacenters, and, due to limited traffic rate of frame relay, they want to continue with a cost-effective alternative. The new solution also should allow Orefe to have higher capacity when needed. After discussing with their network designer, they decide to continue with the MPLS layer 3 VPN.

The main reasons for Orefe choosing MPLS Layer 3 VPN is to hand over the core network responsibility to the service provider. If they chose Layer 2 service, their OSPF internal IGP would be extended over WAN as well, and their networking team's operational load would increase. Thus, Orefe has chosen MPLS Layer 3 VPN.

Since they are using OSPF as their internal IGP in two headquarters, three datacenters, and 174 branch offices across the country, Orefe wants to have OSPF routing protocol with their service provider.

Kelcomm is the service provider that provides an MPLS VPN service to Orefe. Unlike other service providers, that only provide BGP and static routing to their MPLS Layer 3 VPN customers, Kelcomm agreed to run OSPF with Orefe.

Orefe has a VPN link between its two headquarters. They will keep that link as an alternate to MPLS VPN. In case the MPLS link fails, best effort VPN link over the Internet will be used as a backup.

- Explain the traffic flow between Orefe's two headquarters.
- What might be the possible problems? How could those problems possibly be avoided?

Both headquarters are in OSPF Area 1, as is the backdoor VPN link. The topology is seen below. If OSPF is used as a PE-CE protocol in MPLS Layer 3 VPN environment routes are received as Type 3 LSAs over the MPLS backbone if the domain ID is the same. If they are different then the routers are received as OSPF Type 5 LSAs. If domain ID is not set exclusively, then process ID is used as domain ID by default.

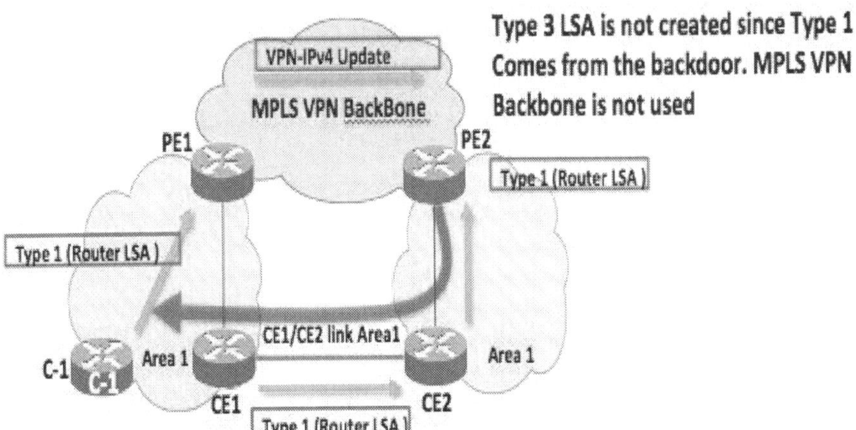

As it can be seen from the above picture, the backdoor VPN link (best-effort no-service guarantee) is used as primary. Customer does not want that because they pay for guaranteed SLA so they want to use MPLS backbone as primary path. OSPF sends prefixes over the backdoor link as Type 1 LSA.

When PE2 at the remote site receives the prefixes via Type 1 OSPF LSA, it doesn't generate Type 3 LSA to send down a CE2.

Two approaches can help to fix this problem. One option is shown as below. OSPF Sham-link.

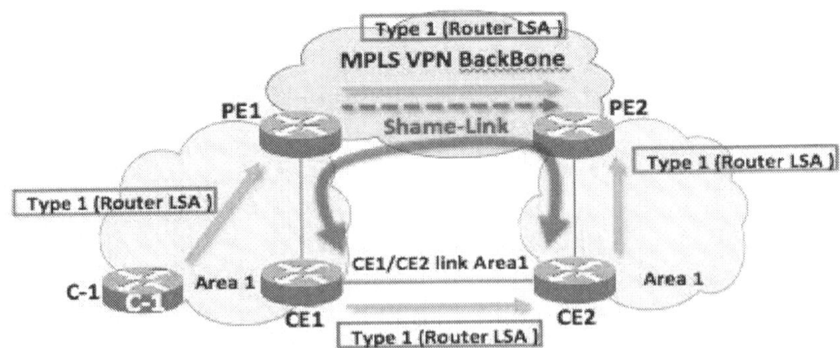

With only Metric manipulation now, MPLS Backbone can be made preferable

With the OSPF Sham-link, PE2 will send OSPF Type 1 LSA towards CE2. With only metric manipulation, MPLS backbone can be made preferable.

Another approach would place the PE-CE link into Area 0. For the headquarters, Orefe would have already put those links in Area 0. If multi-area design is required, then Orefe should place the branch offices in a non-backbone area.

Once PE-CE links are placed in Area 0, then the backdoor link should be placed in different area. This makes CE1 and CE2 an ABR. Prefixes are received over backdoor link as Type 3.

Without Sham-link they are also received as Type 3 (assuming domain ID, process ID match between PEs), and then with metric manipulation, MPLS backbone can be made preferable.

MPLS Layer 3 VPN BGP as a PE-CE Protocol Case Study

Orko is an Enterprise company that has stores in seven countries throughout Middle East. Orko's headquarters and main datacenter are in Dubai. Sixty-five of Orko's stores are connected to the datacenter in Dubai via primary MPLS L3 VPN link.

Orko's availability is important, so secondary connections to the datacenter are provided via DMVPN over the Internet.

Orko is working with a single service provider. MPLS and Internet circuit terminate on the same router.

In order to have better policy control and for scalability reasons; Orko decided to run BGP with its service provider over the MPLS circuit.

Orko doesn't have public ASN and its service provider provides its private AS 500.

Orko uses unique AS number 500 on every locations, including its datacenter. In the datacenter, Orko has two MPLS circuit for redundancy and they are terminated on different routers.

- Would this solution work with BGP as a PE-CE routing protocol? What can be done to make the solution work?
- What are the possible risks and how they can be mitigated?

Since Orko is running BGP everywhere and it uses unique AS numbers, BGP loop prevention mechanism doesn't allow the BGP prefixes with the same AS in the AS-path.

The solution wouldn't work unless service provider implements AS-

Override or Orko implements the every router allow-AS command. Even though both solutions would allow the BGP prefixes of Orko in the BGP table of the routers, due to multi-homing in the datacenter, the solution also creates the problem of BGP routing loop.

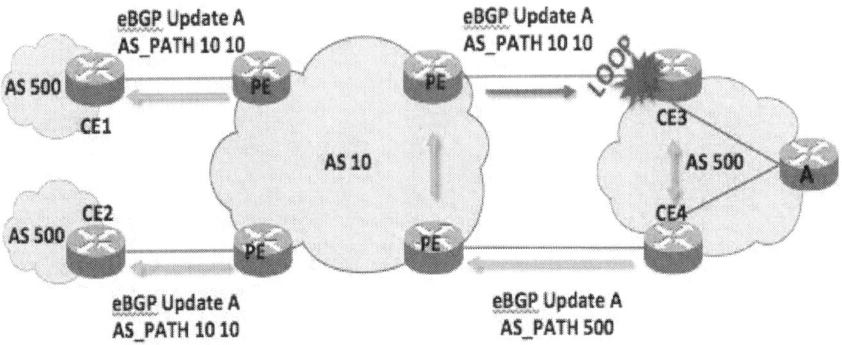

As can be seen in the above topology, Site 3, which is Orko's datacenter, originates BGP prefixes that are advertised to service provider PE device, PE3.

PE3 advertises these prefixes to PE4. Service provider configures BGP AS Override on its PE toward Orko's PE-CE link. This creates a problem on the PE4 to CE3. Since prefixes come as "AS 10, 10" , CE 3 would allow locally originated prefixes from the MPLS backbone, thus creating a BGP routing loop

If BGP AS override or allow-AS is configured it creates a routing loop at the multi-homed site. One solution to this problem can be with BGP site-of-origin (SoO).

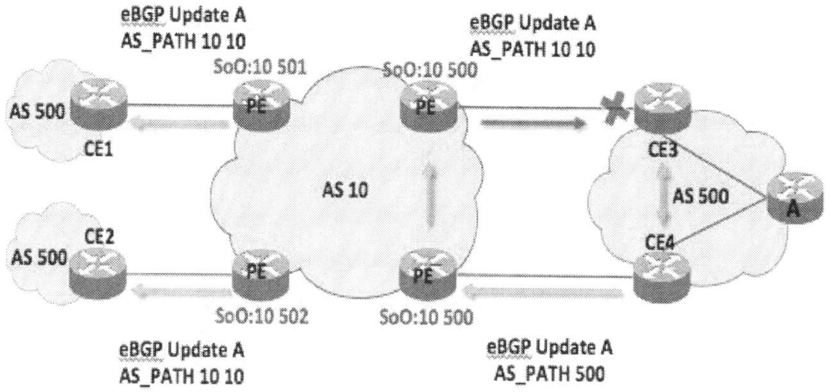

SoO 10:500 is set on the PE3-CE3 and PE3-CE4 links. When the PE4 receive the prefixes from PE3, it doesn't advertise the prefixes to CE3. SoO 10:500 is set on the PE1-CE1 and SoO 10:500 is set on the PE2-CE2 links.

SEAMLESS MPLS

Seamless MPLS provides the architectural baseline for creating a scalable, resilient, and manageable network infrastructure.

Seamless MPLS architecture can be used to create large-scale MPLS networks.

It reduces the operational touch points for service creation.

Seamless MPLS architecture is best suited to the very large scale Service Provider or Mobile Operator networks that have 1000s or 10s of thousands access nodes and very large aggregation networks.

IP traffic increases rapidly due to video, cloud, mobile Internet, multimedia services and so on. To cope with the growth rate of IP Traffic, capacity should be increased but at the same time operational simplicity should be maintained.

Since there might be 1000s to 10s of thousands of devices in the Access, Aggregation and Core network of large Service Providers or Mobile Operators; extending MPLS into the Access networks comes with the main problems:

- Large flat routing designs adversely affect the stability and convergence time of the IGP.

- Resource problems on the low-end devices or some access nodes in the large-scale networks.

In Seamless MPLS Access, Aggregation and Core networks are portioned in different IP/MPLS domains.

Segmentation between the Aggregation and the Core networks can be based on Single AS Multi Area design or Inter-AS.

Partitioning Access, Aggregation and Core network layers into an isolated IGP domains helps reduce the size of routing and forwarding tables on individual routers in these domains.

This provides better stability and faster convergence.

In Seamless MPLS, LDP is used for label distribution to build MPLS LSPs within each independent IGP domain.

This enables a device inside an access, aggregation, or core domain to have reachability via intra-domain LDP LSPs to any other device in the same domain. Reachability across domains is achieved using RFC 3107 (BGP+Label). BGP is used as an Inter domain label distribution protocol. Hierarchical LSP is created with BGP.

This allows the link state database of the IGP in each isolated domain to remain as small as possible while all external reachability information is carried via BGP that is designed to carry millions of routes.

In Single AS multi-area Seamless MPLS design, IBGP labeled unicast is used to build inter-domain LSPs.

In Inter-AS Seamless MPLS design, IBGP labeled unicast is used to build inter domain (Aggregation, Core domains) LSPs inside the AS.

EBGP labeled unicast is used to extend the end-to-end LSP across the AS boundary.

There are at least five different Seamless MPLS models based on access type and network size. Network designers can use any of the below models based on the requirements.

1. Flat LDP Aggregation and Core
2. Labeled BGP access with flat LDP Aggregation and Core
3. Labeled BGP Aggregation and Core
4. Labeled BGP Access, Aggregation and Core
5. Labeled BGP Aggregation and Core with IGP Redistribution into Access network

Let's describe these models briefly.

Seamless MPLS Deployment Models:

Flat LDP Aggregation and Core

This Seamless MPLS model applies to small networks.

In this model access network can be; a non-MPLS IP/Ethernet or TDM based and network is small in size. There is no MPLS in the access network. There is no Hierarchical BGP LSP as well.

Also, small-scale aggregation network is assumed to be composed of core and aggregation nodes that are integrated in a single IGP/LDP domain consisting of less than 500 to 1000 nodes.

Since there is no segmentation between the network layers, a flat LDP LSP provides end-to-end reachability across the network.

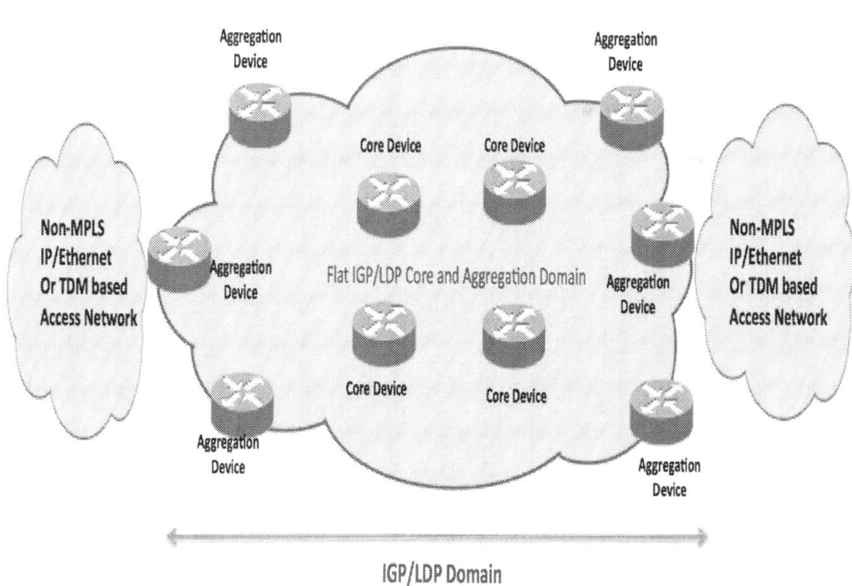

Flat LDP Aggregation and Core Seamless MPLS model

Labeled BGP access with flat LDP Aggregation and Core

This model applies to small networks as well.

This type of architecture assumes an MPLS enabled access network and small scale Aggregation and Core network.

Small-scale aggregation network is assumed to be composed of core and aggregation nodes that are integrated in a single IGP/LDP domain consisting of less than 500 to 1000 nodes.

Very similar to Flat Aggregation and Core with Non-MPLS access model but in this model; access network nodes also run IP/MPLS.

Access network runs separate IGP domain from the Aggregation and Core. The separation can be enabled either by making the access network part of a different IGP area from the Aggregation and Core nodes, or by running a different IGP process on the Aggregation nodes.

Access, Aggregation and Core networks are integrated with labeled BGP LSPs, with the aggregation nodes acting as ABRs performing BGP next-hop-self (NHS) function to extend the IBGP hierarchical LSP across the network.

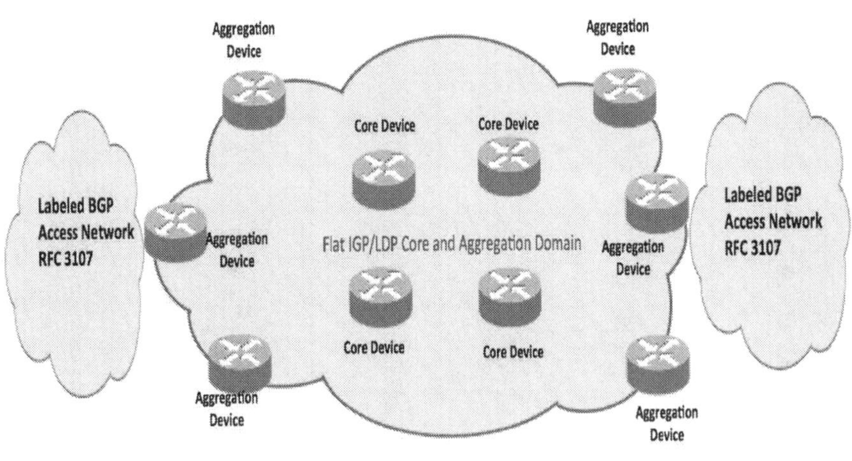

Labeled BGP Access with Flat Aggregation and Core Seamless MPLS model

Labeled BGP Aggregation and Core

This model applies to medium to large scale networks.

This model assumes a Non MPLS access network and the fairly large Aggregation and Core networks.

In this model, network is organized by segmenting the Aggregation and Core networks into independent IGP domains.

The segmentation between the core and aggregation domains could be based on a Single-AS multi-area design or an Inter-AS.

In the Single-AS multi-area option, the separation can be enabled by making the Aggregation network part of a different IGP area from the Core network, or by running a different IGP process on the Core ABR nodes. Access network can be based on an IP, Ethernet, TDM or Microwave links. LDP is used to build intra-area LSP within each domain.

The Aggregation and Core domains are integrated with labeled BGP LSPs. In the single-AS multi-area option, the Core Devices as an ABR perform BGP NHS function to extend the IBGP hierarchical LSP across the aggregation and core domains.

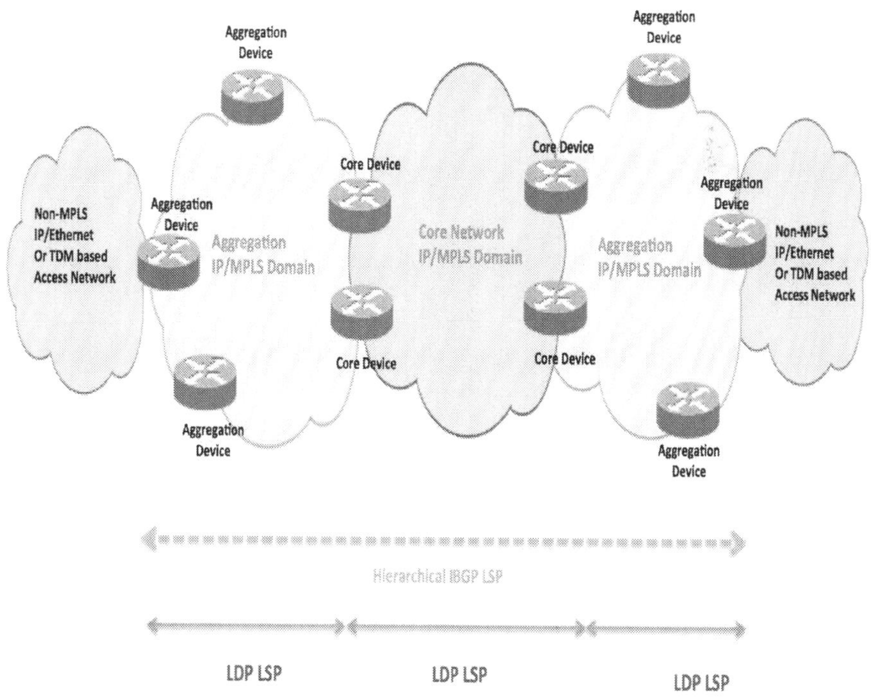

Labeled BGP Aggregation and Core Seamless MPLS model

Labeled BGP Access, Aggregation and Core

This model can be used in very large-scale networks.

This model assumes an MPLS enabled access network with large Aggregation and Core networks.

The network infrastructure is organized by segmenting the Access, Aggregation and Core into independent IGP domains.

The segmentation between the Access, Aggregation and Core networks domains could be based on a Single-AS multi area design or an Inter-AS based.

The difference of this model from the ' Labeled BGP Aggregation and Core' model is, Access network nodes run MPLS as well and RFC 3107, BGP LU (Labeled BGP) is extended up to the Access network nodes.

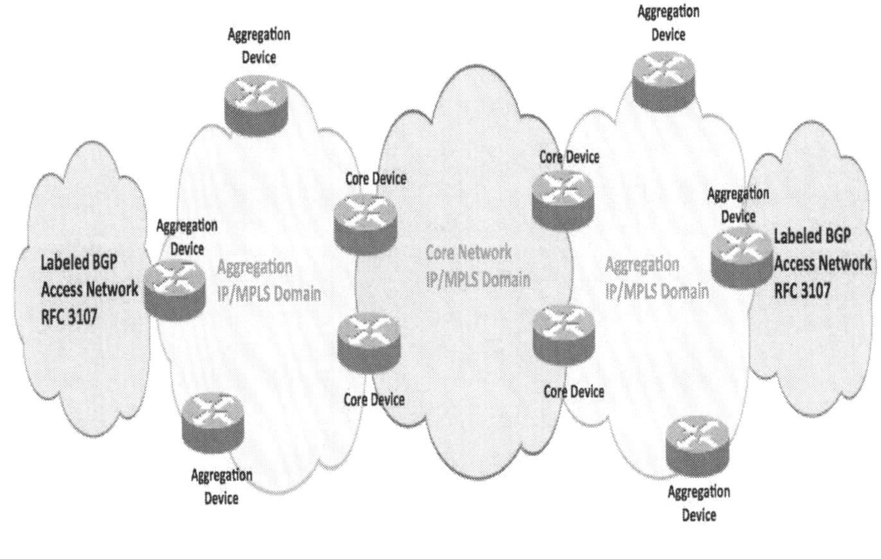

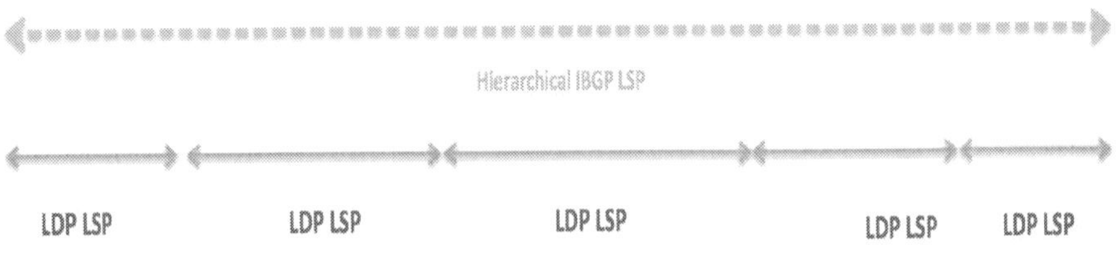

Labeled BGP Access, Aggregation and Core Seamless MPLS model

Labeled BGP Aggregation and Core with IGP redistribution into access network

In this model, Access network runs MPLS but not with labeled BGP. LDP LSPs are created in the Access network.

This model applies to very large networks.

The network infrastructure organization in this architecture is similar to 'Labeled BGP Access, Aggregation and Core '. Redistribution is performed on the Aggregation nodes. Access network loopback addresses are redistributed into the network.

There is no Hierarchical end-to-end BGP LSP in this model.

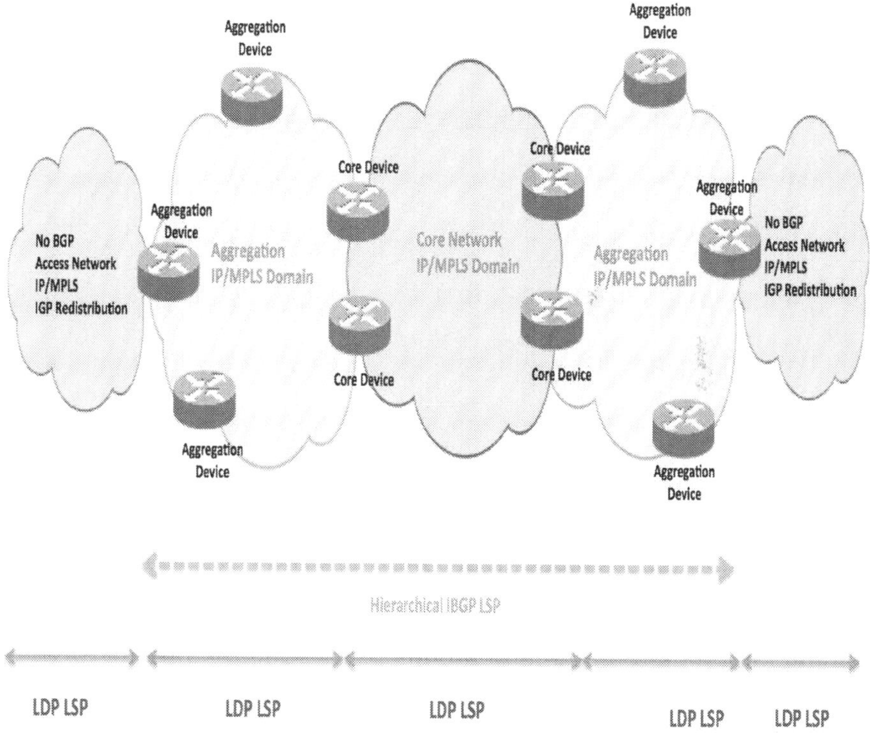

Labeled BGP Aggregation and Core with IGP Redistribution into Access Network

Inter-AS MPLS VPNs

In the simplified topology shown below, customer A has two locations: location A1 and location A2.

Location A1 is the dual home connected to service provider A.

Location A2 is the dual home connected to service provider B.

It is not compulsory that locations should be dual-homed.

However, there is a restriction: service provider A does not have a POP to connect to the location of customer A2.

For Customer A to has reachability between A1 and A2 locations via MPLS VPN service, service providers must create Inter AS MPLS VPN connection between the two locations.

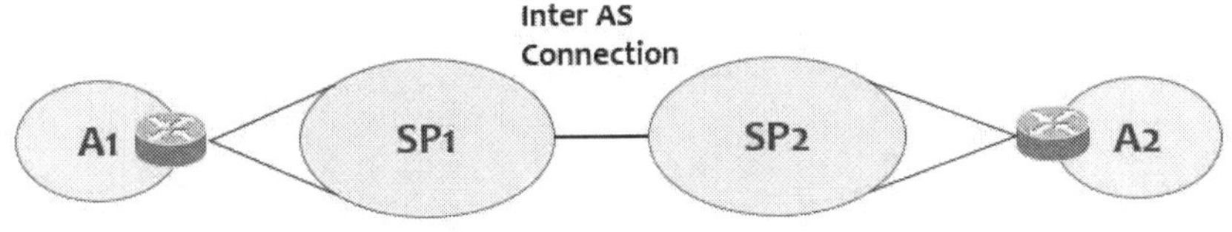

Basic Inter-AS MPLS VPN Connection

Three models defined in RFC 2547 for Inter-AS MPLS VPNs. Inter-AS Option A is the first. It is also known as 10A.There is also fourth Inter-AS MPLS VPN deployment option which has been invented by Cisco. It is known as Option AB (A.K.A Option D). Option AB will be explained in this chapter as well.

Inter-AS MPLS VPN Option A

Inter AS Option A is the easiest, most flexible, most secure Inter autonomous system MPLS VPN technology.

Inter-AS Option A is known as back-to-back VRF approach as well. Service providers treat each other as customers.

Between the service providers, there is no MPLS; only IP routes are advertised. For each customer VPN, one logical or physical link is set up. Over the link, any routing protocol can run.

But in order to carry end-to-end customer routing attribute, it is ideal to run the same IGP at the customer edge and between ASBRs.

How Inter-AS MPLS VPN Option A Works

In the below topology VPN Customers A and B are connected to two different service providers via MPLS Layer 3 VPN.

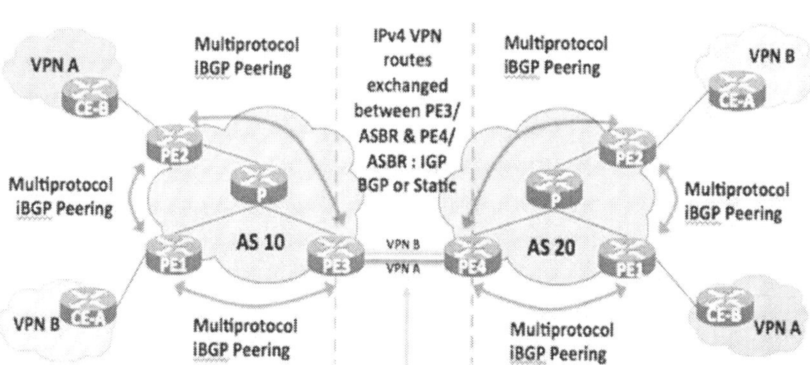

Inter-AS MPLS VPN Option A

The above topology would be used to explain Inter AS Option A operation.

In the above diagram, we have two service providers and the two customers that require Inter-AS MPLS VPN service.

The PE routers that connect the two providers are also known as ASBR (Autonomous System Boundary Router). (PE3 in AS10 and PE4 in AS20). In Inter AS Option A; ASBR router in one Autonomous System attaches directly to an ASBR router in another Autonomous System.

The two ASBR routers connected through multiple sub-interface or physical interfaces. They connect two Autonomous Systems to each other.

In addition, those sub interfaces associate with the VRF table. For each customer, service providers could use separate physical connection, instead of sub interface.

However, doing that would not produce optimal result for resource utilization.

PE routers connected to the CE devices (Customer device) run MP-IBGP, either through full mesh or through RR (Route Reflector).

In Inter AS Option A, ASBR routers have to keep all the VRFs of Inter-as MPLS service customers. This can create memory and CPU problem on the ASBRs. In other Inter-AS MPLS VPN deployment options, ASBR don't keep VRF routing table of the Inter-AS MPLS VPN customers.

SP-A and SP-B ASBR routers maintain VPN forwarding table in LFIB. Furthermore, they keep routing information in RIB and FIB.

Compared to other AS options, ASBRs have high memory usage in Inter AS Option A.

ASBR to ASBR routing protocol can be either IGP per customer or EBGP for all customers.

For example if the requirement for customer A, is to keep routing information, such as metric, end to end, SP-A and SP-B runs same routing protocol on the ASBRs and the PE devices where the Customer CE device is attached to.

So in our example, VPN A customer can run OSPF with the local PE, but ASBR to ASBR routing protocol for VPN A customer can be OSPF, EBGP or any other IGP.

There is no IGP routing protocol in Inter-AS Option B and C.

If ASBR to ASBR routing protocol for the customer is IGP, SP-A and SP-B in Inter AS Option A will have to manage redistribution at the ASBRs because the routes appear to the ASBR as BGP route from remote PEs.

ASBRs associate each such sub-interface with a VRF.

Inter AS Option A does not require MPLS at the ASBRs unlike the other Inter AS options.

Since we need to have a separate VRF and sub interface for each customer VPN, separate routing protocol configuration and dealing with redistribution for each customer VPN is operationally cumbersome, thus Inter-AS Option a is hard to scale if there too much Inter-AS MPLS VPN customers.

Among all other Inter AS options since there is only IP routing between the AS and there is no information sharing between the Autonomous Systems, Option A is considered as most secure Inter-AS MPLS VPN deployment option.

In addition, it is the easiest option to implement between the Autonomous Systems because Option A does not require control plane mechanism, except routing protocol, between the service provider ASBRs; such as LDP, BGP+Label (BGP LU) or BGP-VPNv4. Those protocols will be required in other Inter-AS MPLS VPN deployment options.

Since only IP traffic passes (Not MPLS) between the service providers and there is separate physical or sub-interface per VPN, most granular QoS implementation is achieved with Option A. (Per sub-interface and IP DSCP vs. MPLS EXP)

For all Inter AS Options, it is very common that customers have to trust to the service provider for data integrity, confidentiality, and availability.

MPLS does not encrypt the packets but if the design requirement is to have an encryption, they should deploy an IPSEC.

Last but not least, since there is no internal routing information shared between the service providers, Inter-AS Option A is seen as the most secure amongst all the Inter-AS VPNs.

INTER-AS MPLS VPN OPTION B

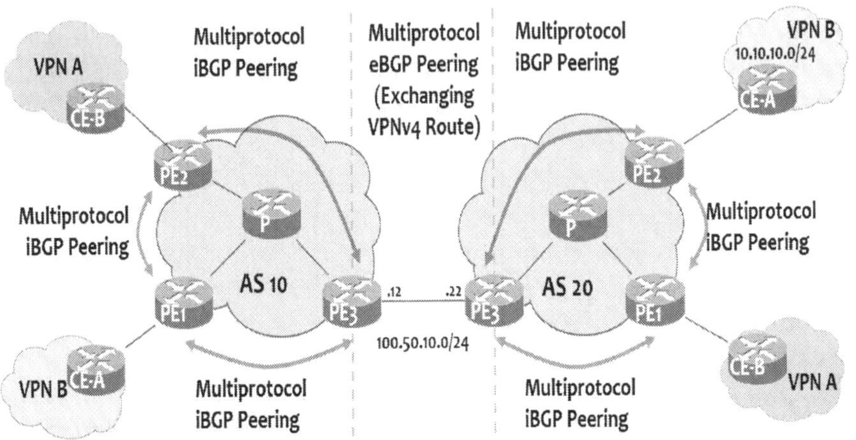

Inter AS MPLS VPN Option B

In the topology shown above, AS10 and AS20 are the service providers.

There are two Inter-AS MPLS VPN customers, VPNA and VPN B.

NOTE: All the customers of the service providers could run different routing protocol at different sites. For example, while customer VPN A who connected to the AS10, can run OSPF as PE-CE routing protocol, same customer (VPN A) can run EIGRP as PE-CE routing protocol with the AS20.

In the service provider network, PE routers are connected to the customer locations. This is regular MPLS Layer 3 VPN operation.

Only the technologies and the protocols are different at the ASBR in Inter-AS MPLS VPN deployment options. Inside the Autonomous Systems regular MPLS VPN rules apply.

PE routers run MP-BGP with route reflector to advertise VPNv4 prefixes. (It could be full mesh BGP VPN deployment as well).

PE router that connects the two providers at the edge is known as ASBR (Autonomous System Boundary Router).(Similar to other Inter-AS MPLS VPN options). ASBR learns all the VPN routes from Inter AS customers. But the main advantage from the scalability point of view in Inter-AS Option B, ASBR doesn't have to keep the customer prefixes in the VRF. It was the case in Inter-AS MPLS VPN Option A.

Inter AS Option B does not require separate sub interfaces and different IGP protocols per sub-interface between the ASBRs. (Another scalability advantage, this time scalability advantage comes from the configuration complexity point of view).

Between the ASBRs, VPNv4 address family is enabled on the ASBR routers in Inter-AS Option B.

ASBRs (Autonomous System Boundary Routers) advertise the customer prefixes that are learned from local BGP route reflector, to another Service Provider through MP-BGP VPNv4 session.

Route-target extended community is placed on the VPNv4 update. Route Target help to place the VPN prefixes to appropriate VRF. (This is also regular MPLS VPN behavior).

When PE receives the customer IP prefixes, it changes next hop as themselves (This is done by default in MPLS VPN, you don't have to enable next-hop-self)

Customer IP prefixes are sent as VPN prefixes, by adding Route Distinguisher to the IP prefixes and VPN prefixes are sent to the VPNv4 route reflector. Route reflector does not change the next hop; rather, it only reflects the route to the ASBR.

ASBR does not place MP-BGP prefixes (Customer prefixes) into VRF, since it does not have to keep VRF table but customer prefixes are maintained in the VPNv4 BGP table in Inter AS Option B.

By changing the next hop, ASBR from SP-A sends VPNv4 prefixes through MP-BGP session to SP-B ASBR.

SP-B ASBR sends the customer prefixes to its local route reflector.

Route reflector in the SP-B domain reflects the prefixes as is, send to the PE that is connected to Customer A2 location. SP-B PE sets the next hop again and sends the prefixes to the customer A2 router.

As shown in the service provider domains, there are three LSP. Because whenever BGP next hop changes, LSP is terminated at the point where the next hop is changed, and new VPN label is assigned on that router for all the VPN prefixes.

Inter AS Option B does not require LDP or IGP protocols between the Autonomous Systems; thus service providers do not need to know the internal addressing structure of each other.

Similar to Inter AS Option A, you do not need to redistribute VPN prefixes at the ASBR.

Route reflectors store all the VPN routing information for each customer, and they advertise those prefixes to ASBR.

Operators need to manage MP-BGP on the ASBRs as well as on the route reflectors.

Caveats in Inter-AS MPLS VPN Option B:

- By default ASBR would not accept the VPN prefixes if there is no corresponding Route Target for that VPN.
- Since ASBRs do not have a VRF and the Route Target for the VPN customers in Inter-AS MPLS VPN Option B, ASBR would reject the VPN prefixes."no bgp route-target filter" configuration knob allows a router to accept the VPN prefixes even if it doesn't have the corresponding Route Target for that VPN.
- Route Target Rewrite may be necessary on the ASBR routers. Because Route Target attributes has to be the same end to end for a particular VPN. If one AS uses different RT for a given VPN, another AS need to Rewrite and use the same RT value on the ASBR.

INTER-AS MPLS VPN OPTION C

As for Inter AS Option B, ASBR routers – the provider-edge devices between the service providers – maintain only the VPN prefixes of the customers in the BGP table.

In fact, I have shown that VPNv4 BGP session has been set up between the ASBRs.

The high-level operational differences between Inter AS Option C and Inter AS Option B are in two folds: one is that ASBRs do not have VRF table; the other is that unlike Inter AS Option B, Inter AS Option C do not keep VPN prefixes for the customer on the ASBR.

ASBR is the edge routers that are used to connect the Service Provider each other. As depicted in the below figure, as for Inter AS Option C, the VPNv4 BGP session is set up between route reflectors of the service providers.

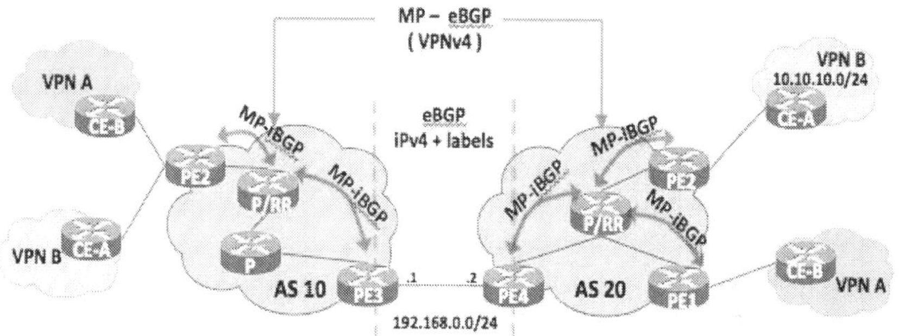

In the above figure, there are two service providers: service provider A and service provider B.

Service Provider A:

Service provider A has two customers: customer A and B

For scaling purposes, all the provider-edge routers run VPNv4 BGP session with VPNv4 route reflector.

Service provider B:

Service provider B has two customers: customer A and B.

A and B are the companies which require Inter AS MPLS VPN service.

Service provider B runs IS-IS internally (It could run other IGP protocols as well for sure). PE-CE routing protocols are enabled on the VRF; thus service provider A has two separate VRF table.

For scaling purposes, all the provider-edge routers run VPNv4 BGP session with VPNv4 route reflector.

Inter AS Option C runs VPNv4 BGP session between the Route Reflectors of the Service Providers.

ASBR PEs know the loopback address of Route reflector through OSPF in the Service Provider A network, through IS-IS in the Service Provider B network.

Since the VPNv4 EBGP neighborship is set up between VPNv4 RR of the service providers in Inter-AS Option C, the next hop for the VPN route is the route reflector.

Traffic trombones on the RR unless " no bgp next-hop unchanged " configured on the Route Reflectors. This is one of the important caveats in Inter AS MPLS VPN Option C.

Once this feature is enabled, Route Reflector does not change the next hop to itself even though the peering is EBGP VPNv4, between the RRs. (Whenever there is an EBGP session between two BGP speaker, next hop is changed since they are not client of each other but regular EBGP neighbors). As internal PEs continue to be a next hop for the customer prefixes, internal PE loopback is advertised through IPv4 BGP session between ASBRs.

As for the VPN next hop, transport label should be assigned to MPLS VPN to work efficiently, and MPLS label is assigned to the IPv4 unicast routes, which are the loopback of RRs and Internal PEs of ASBR.

Inter-As Option C Design Objectives:

- Inter AS Option C is unique, since it requires internal addressing advertisement between the Service Providers. Those addresses are leaked into the global routing table of the providers, a process that providers dislike.
- Inter-AS Option C can be used in large scale design if the company has multiple autonomous system. (Not between the Service Providers).
- Inter AS Option C is very difficult to implement because it requires meticulous redistribution at the edge of the networks, VPNv4 neighborship between the route reflectors, IPv4 BGP neighborship between the ASBRs, label advertisement, Route Target agreement between the Service Providers (Same in the Inter-AS Option B), and so on.
- Considered as insecure because the internal addresses of the Autonomous Systems are leaked in Inter-AS Option C.

Inter-As MPLS VPN Option AB (A.K.A Option D)

Inter-AS Option AB is also known as Option D or Hybrid Inter AS Option. It is called Hybrid because Inter-AS Option B uses the best capabilities of Inter-AS Option A and Inter-AS Option B. These capabilities will be explained throughout this post.

Inter-AS Option AB first deployed by Cisco but today many vendors including Juniper provides Inter-AS Option AB feature.

But what are the best capabilities of the Inter-AS Option A and Inter-AS Option B?

Inter-AS Option A is most secure, least scalable Inter-AS MPLS VPN solution. Since separate sub-interface is setup for each VPN and traffic between the ASBRs is IP traffic, QoS can be provided in much granular level compare to the other Inter-AS MPLS VPN Options (Option B and Option C). Also having separate sub-interface per VRF provides data plane isolation that brings security to the solution. Thus Inter-AS Option A is seen as most secure Inter-AS Option.

In contrast, Inter-AS Option B doesn't require separate sub-interface per VRF. In fact, ASBRs don't even have VRF per customer. Only the VPN prefixes are kept by the ASBRs. Single interface and single MP-BGP VPNv4 neighborship is enough to signal the customer prefixes between the Service Providers.

How we can have very good QoS, good scalability, good security without advertising the Infrastructure prefixes (Internal prefixes) of the Service Providers to each other in Inter-AS MPLS VPNs?

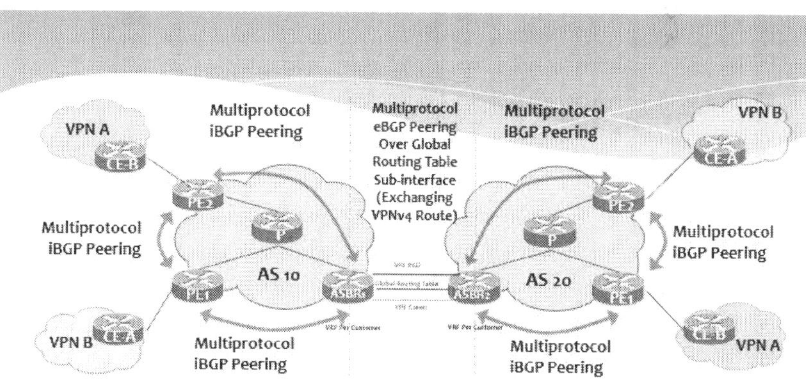

Inter AS MPLS VPN Option AB (a.k.a Option D)

Inter-AS Option AB (a.k.a Option D)

Answer is the Inter-AS Option AB. As you can see from the above figure, on the ASBRs, separate sub-interface is created per VRF.

This provides data plane isolation. QoS configuration can be applied per customer. As customers traffic are isolated via VRFs, better security is achieved as well compare to the single interface.

The difference between Inter-AS Option AB and the Inter-AS Option A is, customer prefixes is advertised through the single EBGP session between the ASBRs in Option AB.

There is no separate EBGP session per VRF between the ASBRs as in the case of Inter-AS Option A.

Control plane traffic that is the routing advertisement and other routing protocol packets are sent through the single EBGP connection over the Global routing table.

Customer data plane traffic is sent as IP traffic without MPLS encapsulation.

Uses Case of Inter-AS MPLS VPN Option AB:

- When the customer requires an MPLS VPN service from the two service providers with strict QoS SLA and the number of Inter-AS MPLS VPN customer is too much between the two service providers, it can be used.
- At least, initially it is created for these reasons but in my opinion real applicability would be the migration from Inter-AS Option A to Inter-AS Option B. During the migration from Option A to Option B, Inter-AS Option AB can be used as transition solution.

INTER-AS MPLS VPNs Case Study

In order to support their customers in different regions, two service providers decided to create VPN neighborships between them.

However, there will be a significant amount of VPN customers and the companies' security teams believe that the companies should not be sharing internal routing information with each other.

Question 1:

Which VPN solution would be best to address this problem so that the agreement can go forward?

Answer 1:

Among the available Inter-AS MPLS VPN options, Option B and Option C are the most suitable ones because of the number of expected VPN customers. However, Option C requires internal routing information such as PE and VPN RR addresses to be leaked between the service providers.

So the best solution based on these requirements is Inter- AS MPLS Option B

Question 2:

Based on the provided simplified network topologies of the two service providers, please select the protocols, which need to be used on the devices that have a check box next to them.

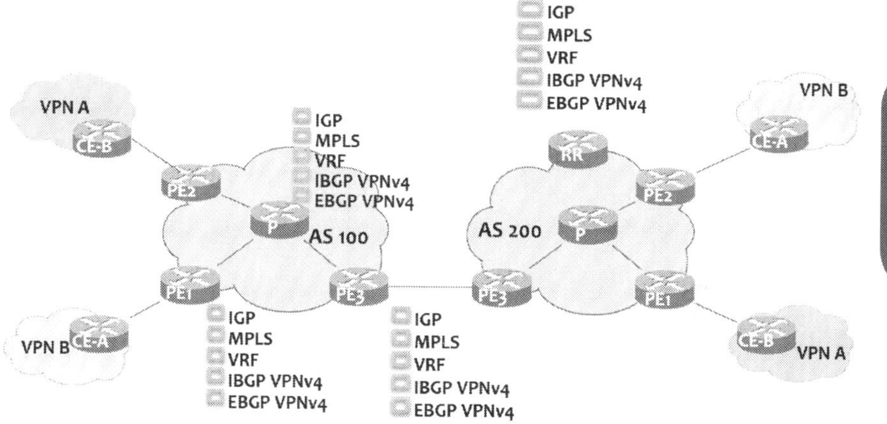

Inter AS MPLS VPN Option B

Answer 2:

Below is the answer of the second question.

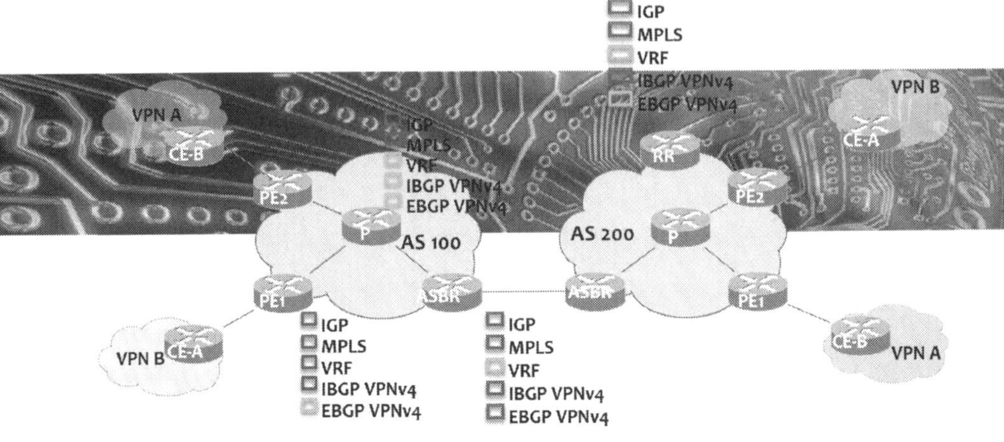

Inter AS MPLS VPN Option B

INTER-AS MPLS VPN OPTIONS COMPARISON

Knowing and understanding the different options of the technologies is very important. Network designers should know the alternatives of the technologies so they can select the best tool for the requirements.

Below table summarizes most important benefits and drawbacks of the Inter-AS MPLS VPN deployment options.

Inter-AS Option AB is not placed in the table since it is not commonly deployed option.

	Option A	Option B	Option C
Scalablability	Less scalable, due to VRF and sub interface configuration requirement for each customer VPN	Scalable since VRF doesn't have to be provisioned on the ASBR and no need to have separe VRF per customer	Very scalable since doesn't have to have VRF and VPN information on the ASBRs, VPN information is kept on the Router Reflectors
Secure	Most secure since routing information is not shared between the domains	Secure since only interlink between ASBR is leaked between domains if next-hop self is not implemented on the local ASBR	Worst.All the PE loopback subnets and the Route Reflector subnets need to be leaked between two Autonomous Systems.Thus, Option C is preferred between the two AS of the same company , not between two different companies.
Quality of Service support	Most flexible but hard to manage	Only MPLS EXP bits and one link for every customer	Same as Option B, 3 EXP bit for every customer but easy to manage compare to Option A
Stuff Experince	Easy to understand, reduces training cost	Moderate,MPLS VPN operation needs to be understood	It requires MPLS VPN, route reflector knowledge so training cost would be high and hard to find already experienced engineers
MPLS between Carriers	No	Yes	Yes
Complexity	Easy	Hard to implement and understand	Most complex
Resource Requirement on the ASBR	VRF,VPN and BGP info on the ASBR thats why require too much resource on the ASBR	Moderate,ASBR doesn't keep VRF information of all the customers but still VPN routing table is kept for the all customers on the ASBR	Best. ASBRs doesn't have to keep VRF or VPN information for all the customers. If ASBR also a PE, then it only keeps VRFrouting table and the VPN route information for the directly connected customers.
Default Convergece in case of a ASBR failure	Slow, VRF, RIB, FIB , LFIB needs to convergce	Fast, only LFIB needs to convergece	Very fasy due to only LDP adjacency between ASBRs
Troubleshooting	Easy	Moderate	Hard, requires MPLS VPN, Route reflector and good routing knowledge

	Option A	Option B	Option C
Redistribution	Yes for each customer VRF	Only interlink between two domains are redistributed if the next-hop self is not implemented on the local ASBR	Yes Pprovider Edge router loopbacks and Route Reflector subnets
Merger&Acqusition	Not suitable if there is time constraint for the operation each and every customer VRF needs to be provisiones thus it requires very long time for the migration	Requires MPLS between ASBRs and VPN configuration on the ASBRs but there is no configuration for each and every customer thus operation can be much faster compare to Option A migration	Same as Option B additionaly, since it is required to leak internal routing information between two AS, Option C is suitable for the same conpany's different administrative domain.Thats why it is very suitable for the company merger design

Inter-AS MPLS VPN Options Comparison

MPLS Carrier Supporting Carrier Case Study

Smallnet is an ISP that provides broadband and business Internet to its customer. Biggercom is a transit service provider of Smallnet, which provides Layer 3 IP connectivity between Smallnet sites. Smallnet wants to carry all its customers' prefixes through BGP over Biggercom infrastructure. Biggercom doesn't want to carry more than 1000 prefixes of Smallnet in the Smallnet VRF.

Smallnet has around 3200 customer prefixes.

Provide a scalable solution for Biggercom and explain the drawbacks of this design, given that Biggercom provides IP connectivity for Smallnet and does not want to carry more than 1000 of Smallnet's prefixes through Carrier supporting Carrier (CsC) architecture.

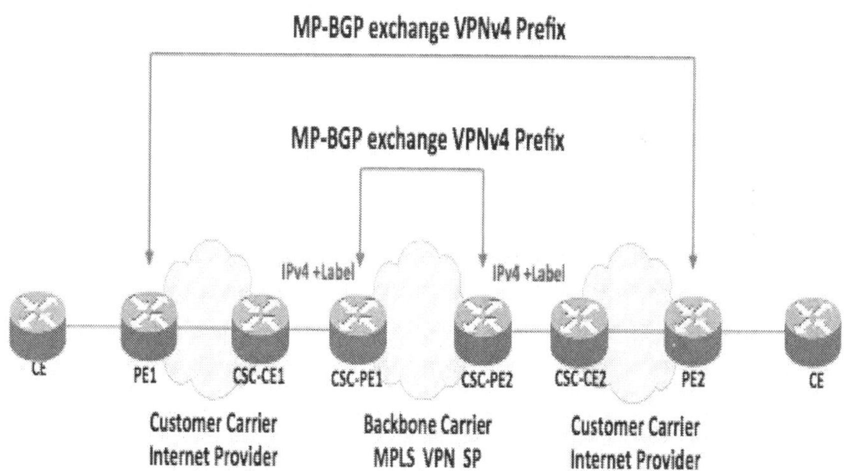

In the above picture, CsC architecture is shown. In CsC terminology, there is a customer and a backbone carrier. In our case study, Smallnet is a customer carrier and Biggercom is a backbone carrier.

There is no customer VRF at the Smallnet network. Biggercom has different VRFs for its individual customers and Smallnet is one of those customers. Smallnet has many Internet customer routes that have to be carried through backbone carrier networks. BGP is used to carry large amounts of customer prefixes. If customer demands full Internet routing table (at the time of this writing it is over 520K prefixes) then BGP already is the only way.

A BGP session is created between Smallnet and Biggercom.

Smallnet is NOT advertised over the BGP session's prefixes. Instead, loopback interfaces of Smallnet route reflectors or PEs are advertised. IBGP session is created between the Smallnet route reflectors and customer prefixes of Smallnet are advertised and received over this BGP session. One big design caveat for CsC architecture is that between the customer carrier and backbone carrier MPLS has to be enabled. So between Smallnet and Biggercom network, MPLS and BGP are enabled. The purpose of MPLS is to hide the customer prefixes of Smallnet from Biggercom.

If MPLS were not enabled on the link between Smallnet and Biggercom, Biggercom would have to do IP destination lookup on the incoming IP packet containing the customer prefixes of Smallnet. Since Biggercom doesn't have a clue about the customers of Smallnet, the packet would be dropped.

MPLS Traffic Engineering

MPLS Traffic Engineering allows network engineers to optimize network resources by sending traffic across a less congested physical path, rather than the default shortest path designated by the routing protocol. This is achieved by adding a label to each packet with specific routing instructions that direct packets from router to router, rather than allowing the routers to forward them based on next-hop lookups. The new paths can be created manually or via signaling protocols, and they help to speed traffic.

How MPLS Traffic Engineering Works?

In MPLS traffic engineering, all configurations are done on a specific network node called the headend or ingress node. Here is where all tunnels and constraints are created.

Tunnel destination address is also specified at the headend.

For example, if an MPLS traffic engineering tunnel will be set up between R2 and R6 in the below figure, all the definitions are done at R2. The tunnel destinations are called tailend or egress node.

MPLS traffic engineering tunnels are unidirectional tunnels and not congruent. This means that if one tunnel is created to carry traffic between R2 and R6, the return tunnel from R6 to R2 is not created automatically.

Reverse tunnels must also be created, but this time R6 is used as the headend and R2 as the tailend. The tailend has no configuration.

If return tunnel is not created, return traffic follows the IGP shortest path, not MPLS Traffic Engineering tunnels.

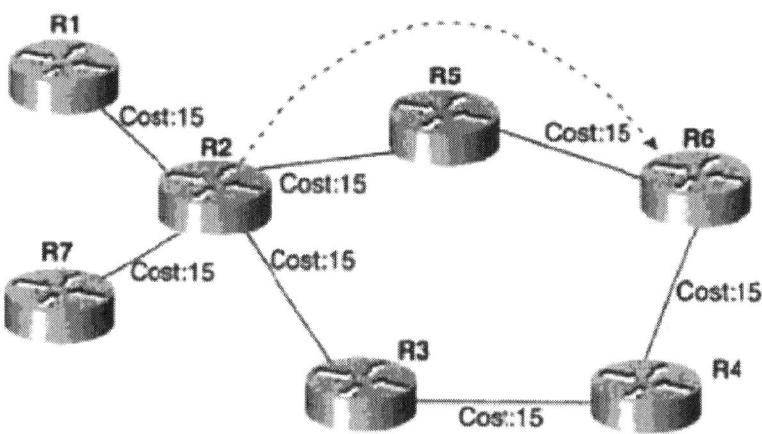

MPLS Traffic Engineering Fish Diagram

Four steps are required for MPLS traffic engineering to take place:

- Link-state protocols carry link attributes in their link-state advertisements (LSAs).
- Based on the constraints defined, the traffic path is calculated with the help of Constrained Shortest Path First (CSPF) algorithm.
- The path is signaled by Resource Reservation Protocol (RSVP).
- Traffic is then sent to the MPLS traffic engineering tunnel.

LET'S TAKE A LOOK THESE STEPS IN DETAIL:

1. By default, link-state protocols send only connected interface addresses and metric information to their neighbors. Based on this information, the Shortest Path First (SPF) algorithm creates a tree and builds the topology of the network. MPLS traffic engineering allows us to add some constraints. In the above figure, let's assume the R2-R5 link is 5 Mbit/s; R5-R6 is 10 Mbit/s; and all the interfaces between the bottom routers are 6 Mbit/s.

If we want to set up a 6-Mbit/s tunnel, SPF will not even take the R2-R5-R6 path into consideration, because the link from R2 to R5 does not satisfy the minimum requirement.

In addition, we could assign an administrative attribute, also called a "color," to the link. For example, the R2-R5-R6 interfaces could be designated blue, and the R2-R3-R4-R6 route could be assigned red. At the headend, the constraint can then specify whether to use a path that contains a red or blue color.

The color/affinity information, as well as how much bandwidth must be available, reserved, and unreserved for the tunnel are carried within the link-state packet. In order to carry this information, some extensions have been added to the link-state protocols.

Open Shortest Path First (OSPF) carries this information in the Opaque LSA (or Type 10 LSA), and Intermediate System to Intermediate System (IS-IS) uses TLV 22 and 135 for traffic engineering information.

Below table summarizes link attributes, which are carried in OSPF and IS-IS for MPLS Traffic Engineering purpose.

Link Attributes for MPLS Traffic Engineering Database	
Additional link Characteristics	• Interface Address • Neighbor Address • Physical bandvidth • Maximum reservable bandwidth • Unreserved Bandwidth (at eight priorities) • TE metric • Administrative group (attribute flags)
ISDIS or OSPF flood link information	
All TE nodes build a TE topology database	
Not required if usingoffDline path computation	

2. As we stated earlier, SPF is used to calculate the path for destinations. For traffic engineering, a slightly modified version of SPF is used, called constrained SPF (CSPF). With the extensions to link state protocols that Opaque LSAs and TLVs provide, an MPLS traffic engineering database is created that is only accessible by CSPF. CSPF can understand that the link from R2 to R5 is 5 Mbit/s and does not satisfy the 6 Mbit/s tunnel constraint. So it will not take that path into consideration in its calculation.

3. If there is an appropriate path, the path is signaled by RSVP. Previously used to provide Integrated Services QoS, RSVP incorporated new messages, including path and reservation messages, to enable MPLS traffic engineering. Label information is carried within the reservation messages.

4. Once a path is signaled, traffic is put into the tunnel. This can be accomplished via many methods including static routing, policy-based routing, class-of-service-based tunnel selection (CBTS), policy-based tunnel selection (PBTS), autoroute, and forwarding adjacency. These methods will be explained later in this chapter.

Below figure summarizes these four steps.

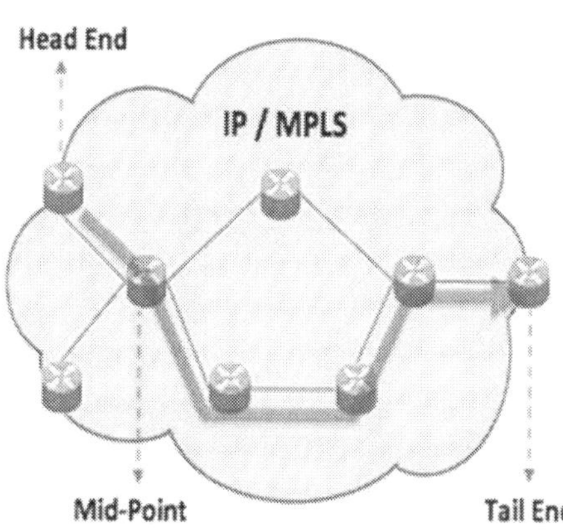

Link Information Distribution
-- ISIS –TE
-- OSPF-TE
Path Calculation (CSPF)
Path Setup (RSVP-TE)
Forwarding Traffic down Tunnel
-- Auto-route announce
-- Static route
-- CBTS
-- PBR
-- Forwarding Adjacency
-- Pseudowire Tunnel selection

Four steps of MPLS Traffic Engineering Operation

Multi-Protocol Label Switching (MPLS) traffic engineering has three main uses.

MPLS Traffic Engineering Use Cases:

1. Bandwidth Optimization:
2. Service-level agreement (SLA) support
3. MPLS Traffic Engineering fast reroute

1. Bandwidth Optimization

Let's have a look at a classic example of traffic engineering with the Fish Diagram to understand bandwidth optimization/better capacity usage use case of MPLS Traffic Engineering.

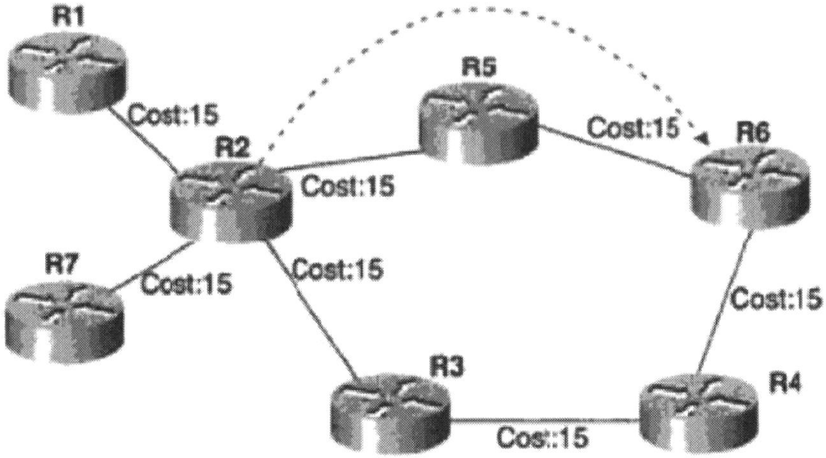

In the above figure, there are two paths you could take to get from Router 2 (R2) to Router 6 (R6):

R2-R5-R6 with the cost of 15+15=30

R2-R3-R4-R6 with the cost of 15+15+15=45

Since MPLS Traffic Engineering can only work with the link-state protocols Open Shortest Path First (OSPF) and Intermediate System to Intermediate System (IS-IS), unless otherwise specified, all our examples will be given by using link-state protocols.

Link-state protocols use the Shortest Path First (SPF) or Dijkstra algorithm to calculate the route from point A to point B.

In this example, they will choose the path R2-R5-R6, because the total cost is less than the cost for R2-R3-R4-R6.

The bottom path will not be used until the primary path fails, because link-state protocols traditionally don't support unequal cost multi-path load sharing, although enhancements had been proposed at the IETF to change this.

Source routing and policy-based routing (PBR) can be used to force traffic to the bottom path. However, these are complex from a configuration point of view, and open to administrative mistakes.

In the above example, R5 is connected only to R6. If PBR is used, only R2 needs to be configured. For a different topology, you may need to implement PBR at each router to send the traffic through the intended path.

MPLS traffic engineering helps to send selected traffic to alternate paths, which may not be the best paths from the IGP point of view.

To accomplish this, a traffic engineering tunnel is configured at the headend to create a point-to-point traffic engineering Label Switch Path (LSP).

There are two approaches to creating an LSP: tactical and strategic, also called proactive and reactive. Strategic is the systematic approach, in which a traffic matrix is identified between each ingress and egress node and a traffic engineering tunnel reservation is made based on the requirements. This is the long-term solution for an MPLS traffic engineering LSP.

Alternatively, the tactical approach can be used as a short-term solution to fix a sudden peak traffic load. The LSP can be created through the lower utilized path for a short time until the primary path traffic issue is resolved. As an example, the link might be utilized after a major news announcement causes a large surge in media traffic

2. **Service-level agreement (SLA) support**

Traffic engineering can be used to meet an SLA. Not all traffic is the same, and not all customers can get the same service. This is business, and there is no free lunch, of course.

Traditionally, voice and video traffic were carried over circuit-based TDM links. These applications are very delay and loss sensitive, so we need to design our packet-switching networks to ensure that they are adequately supported.

MPLS traffic engineering and quality of service (QoS) can both be used -- either alone or together -- to accomplish this goal. These technologies are sometimes confused, but they are independent subjects and not exclusive.

Reservation for the traffic engineering tunnels, however, is made on the control planes of devices.

As an example, you can have a 100 Mbit/s link between point A and point B. Assume you reserve bandwidth for two Label Switch Paths with 60 Mbit/s and 40 Mbit/s link requirements.

From the Point A, 80 Mbit/s of traffic can be sent over the 60 Mbit/s signaled LSP.

Since, by default, MPLS traffic engineering tunnels are not aware of the data plane actions, 20 Mbit/s of traffic exceeding the limit will be dropped.

Some of that dropped traffic might be very important, so it's in our best interest to protect it.

To make traffic engineering tunnels aware of the data plane traffic, the " **auto bandwidth " feature** of MPLS traffic engineering might be used.

When auto bandwidth is enabled, the tunnel checks its traffic periodically and signals the new LSP.

If a new LSP is signaled in this way, only the 80 Mbit/s LSP can survive over the 100 Mbit/s link. There is not enough bandwidth for the 40 Mbit/s LSP.

If there is an alternative link, 40 Mbit/s of traffic can be shifted to that link.

Otherwise, circuit capacity must be increased or a new circuit must be purchased.

If there is no alternate link and no time to bring in a new circuit, QoS could potentially be configured to protect critical traffic.

Diffserv QoS with MPLS traffic engineering is mature and commonly used by service providers in these cases.

How can one MPLS traffic engineering LSP beat another LSP?

This is accomplished with the priority feature of the tunnels. Using priority, some LSPs can be made more important than others. To achieve this, the setup priority value of one LSP should be smaller than the hold priority value of the other LSP.

Once the path is computed and signaled, it doesn't mean that traffic by default follows the traffic engineering path.

Actually, it still follows the underlying interior gateway protocol path. Since traffic engineering can work only with the link-state protocols Open Shortest Path First (OSPF) and Intermediate System to Intermediate System (IS-IS), traffic follows the shortest path from the cost point of view.

There are many methods for sending traffic into the MPLS traffic engineering LSP. These are static routing, policy-based routing, class-of-service-based tunnel selection (CBTS), policy-based tunnel selection (PBTS), Autoroute, and forwarding adjacency.

Static routing, policy-based routing and CBTS are static methods and can be cumbersome to manage.

But to send specific, important traffic into tunnels, classed-based tunnel selection can be a good option.

Based on the EXP bit in the label stack, traffic can be classified and sent to an LSP that is QoS-enabled for protection.

Autoroute and forwarding adjacency, on the other hand, are dynamic methods to send traffic into traffic engineering LSPs.

MPLS Traffic Engineering Autoroute

By default, the shortest path is used for the destination prefix, and next-hop resolution is done for the next direct connection. When the autoroute feature is implemented, the next hop automatically becomes the destination address of the tunnel tailend (Tunnel destination).

The drawback of this approach is there is no traffic classification or separation, so all the traffic -- regardless of importance -- is sent through the LSP. Once MPLS traffic engineering is enabled and Autoroute is used, traffic can be inserted only from the ingress node (label-switched router). Any LSR other than the ingress point is unable to insert traffic into the traffic engineering LSP. Thus autoroute can only affect the path selection of the ingress LSR.

MPLS Traffic Engineering Forwarding adjacency

Once we enable this feature, any MPLS traffic engineering tunnel is seen as a "point-to-point link" from the interior gateway protocol point of view. Even though traffic engineering tunnels are unidirectional, the protocol running over an LSP in one direction should operate in the same way on the return path in a point-to-point configuration.

3. **MPLS Traffic Engineering Fast Reroute**

Before explaining how fast reroute is used in the context of MPLS traffic engineering, you'll need to understand the basics of fast reroute.

In the below figure, there are two paths between Router 2 (R2) and Router 6 (R6).

If we assume that Open Shortest Path First (OSPF) is used in this topology, then based on end-to-end total link cost, the R2-R5-R6 path would be chosen.

The information for the R2-R3-R4-R6 link is also kept in the OSPF link-state database table.

If the R2-R5-R6 path fails, the SPF algorithm runs on every router in the same area, and R2 selects R3 as the next hop. It puts this information into the routing table, and if the router supports separated control and data planes, the routing information is distributed into a forwarding information base as well.

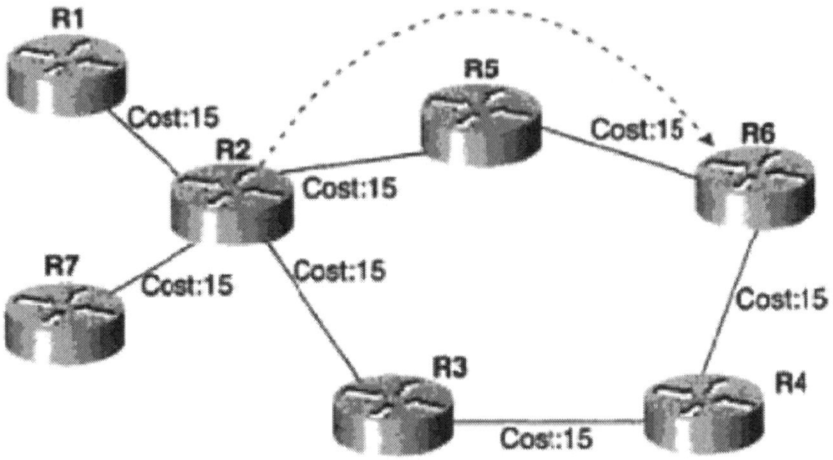

The detection of link failure, the propagation of information to every device in the flooding domain, and calculating and installing the new paths into the routing and forwarding tables of the devices will require some time. Interior gateway protocol parameters for propagation and detection can be changed, and convergence time might be reduced to even less than one second.

But for some applications like voice, this may not be enough.

We may need latency to be less than 100 or 200 ms in order to reroute traffic without experiencing adverse effects. MPLS traffic engineering can often provide a backup path within 50 ms, because the alternate path is calculated and installed into the routing and forwarding information bases before failure happens.

Below figure summarizes the benefits of MPLS Traffic Engineering Fast Reroute and also shows Primary and Backup TE LSPs.

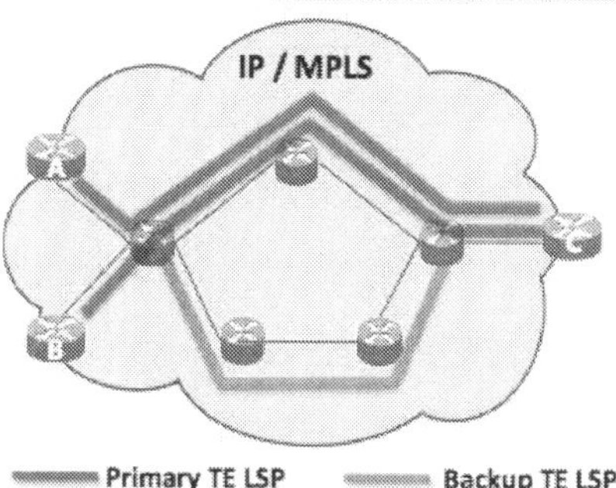

Benefits of MPLS Traffic Engineering Fast Reroute

MPLS traffic engineering is a local protection mechanism. There are two modes of local protection: link and node protection. MPLS Traffic Engineering Fast Reroute Link and Node Protection:

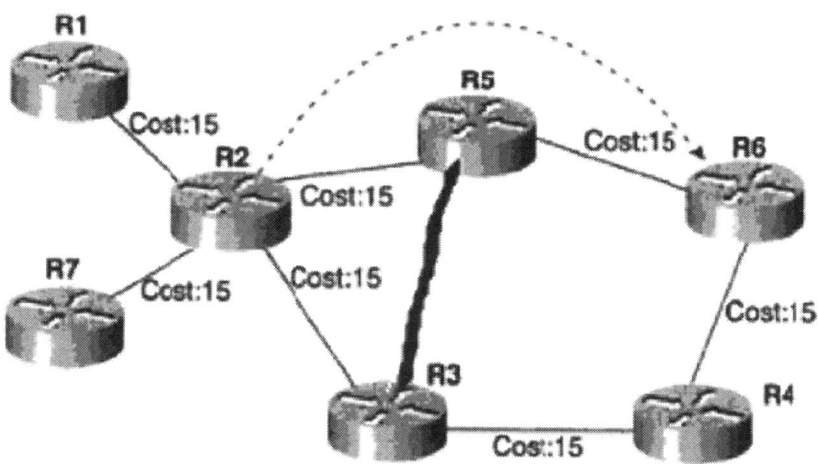

If the R2-R5 link fails and we need to protect that link, we call that link protection. Backup and pre-signaled paths can be created between R2-R3 and R5, so that if the R2-R5 link fails, traffic is automatically redirected to the backup path. Because the failure is local to R2, it is called local protection.

It's also possible for R5 to fail. In this case, the R2-R3-R5 path will not work, so we need to bypass R5 completely. An R2-R3-R4-R6 pre-signaled path could be created for node protection purposes, because in this case, we want to protect the node, rather than the link.

Below figure summarizes MPLS Traffic Engineering Fast Reroute Link Protection operation.

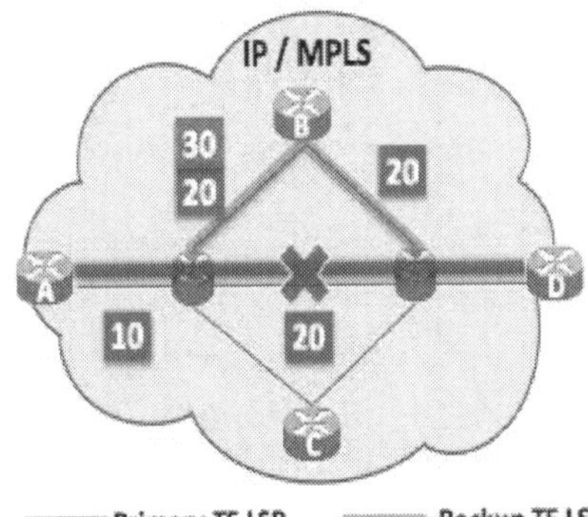
MPLS Link Protection Operation
IP / MPLS
30
20
20
A
B
C
D
10
20
Primary TE LSP
Backup TE LSP
Requires pre-signaled next-hop (NHOP) backup tunnel
Point of local Repair (PLR) swaps the topmost label and pushes backup label
Backup terminates on Merge Point (MP) where traffic rejoin primary LSP
Restoration time expected under ~ 50 ms because failure is local

MPLS Traffic Engineering Fast Reroute (FRR) Link Protection

Below figure summarizes MPLS Traffic Engineering Fast Reroute Node Protection operation.

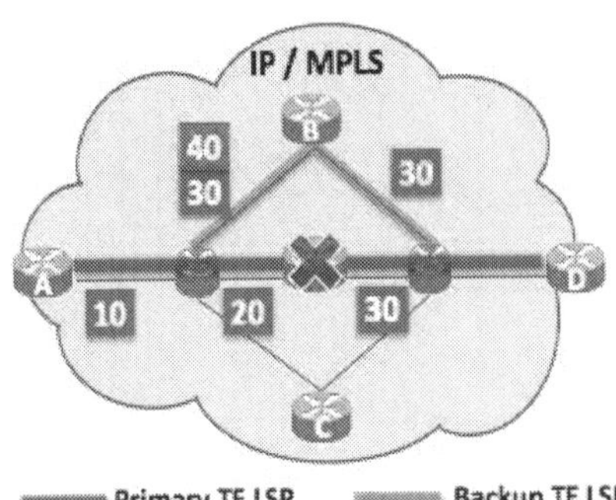
MPLS Node Protection
IP / MPLS
40
30
30
A
B
C
D
10
20
30
Primary TE LSP
Backup TE LSP
Requires pre-signaled next-next- hop (NNHOP) backup tunnel
Point of local Repair (PLR) swaps the next-next hop label and pushes backup label
Backup terminates on Merge Point (MP) where traffic rejoin primary LSP
Restoration time depends on failure detection time

MPLS Traffic Engineering Fast Reroute (FRR) Node Protection

Most failures are a link failure in the networks. Node failure is less common compares to link failure. Thus, many networks only enable link protection. MPLS Traffic Engineering Fast Reroute can cover all the failure scenarios. An IP Fast reroute technology such as LFA (Loop Free Alternate) requires high-mesh topologies to find an alternate path, which will be programmed in the data plane.

If the topology is a ring, then LFA cannot work. It requires a tunnel to the PQ node. Remote LFA is another IP fast reroute technology, which allows to be created a tunnel from the PLR to the PQ node.

There are more Fast Reroute Protection mechanisms beside MPLS Traffic Engineering. In the below section these mechanisms are briefly introduced.

MPLS Traffic Engineering Case Study

Maynet is a fictitious service provider. They have MPLS on their core network. They provide MPLS Layer 2 and Layer 3 VPN services to their business customers. Maynet in access and aggregation network does not run MPLS, but they are also considering enabling MPLS towards aggregation first and then to the access networks.

Recently, they reconsidered the core network availability and they decided to enable MPLS Fast Reroute between all edge devices in their core network.

Due to the limited size of edge devices, full-mesh RSVP-TE LSP is not a problem for Maynet, but a protection mechanism suggested by their transport team has serious concern.

They would like your opinion about the issue and ask the following questions.

- What is MPLS Traffic Engineering Path Protection?
- What are the pros and cons of having MPLS Path Protection?
- Why is the transport department suggesting MPLS TE FRR Path protection instead of local protection technologies?

Please compare the two architectures and highlight the similarities and differences for Maynet to decide the final architecture.

MPLS Traffic Engineering Fast Reroute is a local protection mechanism where the nodes local to the failure react to the failure. Control plane convergence follows the data plane fast reroute protection and if a more optimal path is found, new LSP is signaled in a MBB (make before break) manner.

Fast reroute backup LSP can protect multiple primary LSP, thus in the MPLS Traffic Engineering chapter, it is showed as 1:N protection. By contrast, path protection is a 1:1 protection schema where the one backup LSP only protects one primary LSP.

There are two drawbacks of path protection:

- Backup LSP waits idle and can only carry traffic if the primary LSP fails. This conflicts with MPLS Traffic Engineering, since the idea behind MPLS Traffic Engineering is to optimize traffic usage and cost saving.

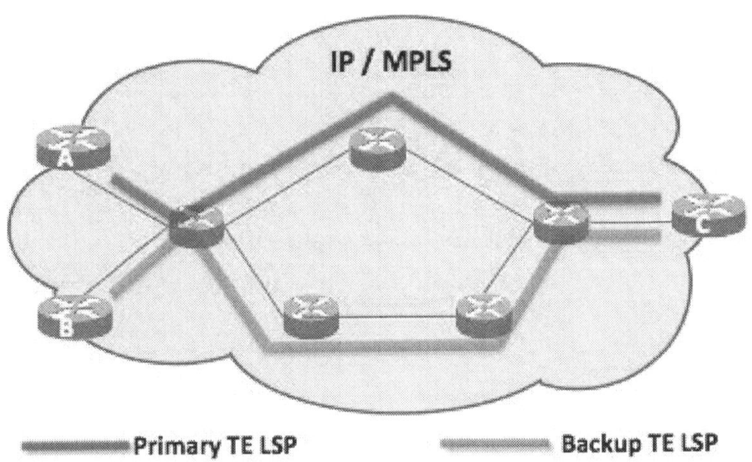

As depicted in the above picture, the green path is a backup path and it cannot pass through any devices or links that primary LSP passes.

- The second biggest drawback of having MPLS Traffic Engineering path protection as opposed to local protection with the link or node protection is the number of LSPs.

Since one backup LSP is created for each primary LSP, the number of RSVP-TE LSPs will be almost double compared to 1:N local protection mechanisms. In the transport networks SONET/SDH, OTN, MPLS-TP all have linear protection schema which are very similar to MPLS Traffic Engineering Path Protection.

If the decision is made with the transport team, it is suggested to continue with their operational model, but at the end core the network will have scalability and manageability problems.

Finally, switching to alternate path-in-path protection might be slower than local protection mechanisms since the point of local repair (node which should reach failure) may not be directly connected to a failure point. Thus, failure has to be signaled to the head end, which might be many hops away from the failure point.

In the above topology, even if the router in the middle of a topology fails, failure has to be signaled to the R2 and R2 switchover to the backup (green) LSP.

FAST REROUTE MECHANISMS IN DETAIL

Network reliability is an important measure for deployability of sensitive applications.

When a link, node or SRLG failure occurs in a routed network, there is inevitably a period of disruption to the delivery of traffic until the network reconverges on the new topology. Fast reaction is essential for the failed element. There are two approaches for the fast reaction: Fast convergence and fast reroute. When a local failure occur four steps are necessary for the convergence.

1. Failure detection
2. Failure propagation
3. New information process
4. Update new route into RIB/FIB
5. For fast convergence, these steps may need to be tuned.

Tuning of these steps and the recommendation was provided in the OSPF chapter of the book.

Although the RIB/FIB update is hardware dependent, the network operator can configure all other steps. One thing always needs to be kept in mind; Fast convergence and fast reroute can affect network stability. Unlike fast convergence, for the fast reroute, routes are precomputed and preprogrammed into the router RIB/FIB. Additional, an alternate is found, if possible, and pre-installed into the RIB/FIB. As soon as the local failure is detected, the PLR (Point of Local Repair) switches the routes to use the alternate path. This preserves the traffic while the normal convergence process of failure propagation and SPF recomputation occurs.

There are many drafts and RFCs in the IETF for the fast reroute mechanisms

- Loop Free Alternates (RFC5286, deployable today)
- Remote Loop Free Alternates (draft in RTGWG, implemented by some vendors)
- MRT-FRR (draft in RTGWG, proto-types in progress)
- MPLS RSVP-TE FRR (RFC 4090, deployable today)
- U-turns Alternates (historical interest)
- Not-via Address (RFC6981, academic interest)

We will use the below figure to demonstrate the mechanisms.

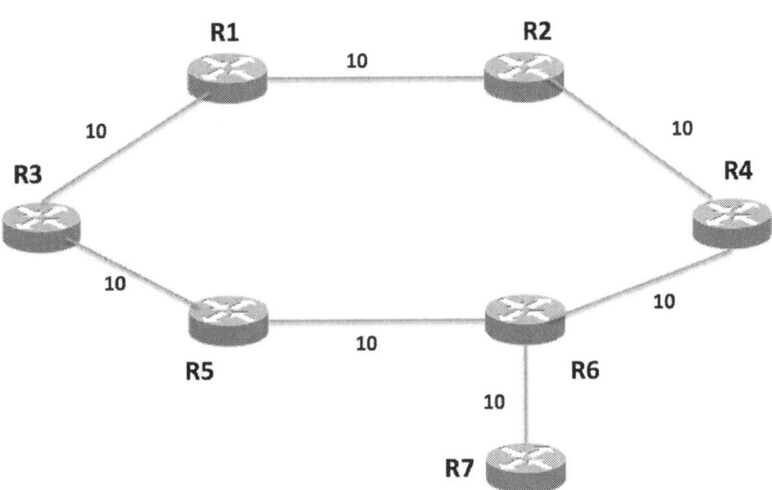

Fast Reroute Mechanisms

Assume all the link cost is the same and link-state protocol is used, in the above figure, if R1-R2 link fails, to reach the destination networks which are behind R2; R1 needs to find a way to send a packet.

When R1-R2 link fails, for the IP and MPLS networks, if R1 sends a packet to R3, since all the link cost is the same, R3's next-hop for the R2 is

R1. This is called micro-loop. Until R3 learns of the failure and computes its new primary next-hop R5, packets are looped in between R1 and R3. This is can cause a congestion on the link.

Loop free alternate mechanism looks for the alternate path for the R1 to send a packet to R2 when R1-R2 link fails. In order mechanism to work, R1 runs additional SPFs from its neighbor point of view by using **CSPF**. It is obvious that R1 cannot use R3 as its alternate next-hop. All other five mechanisms can solve this issue with the different ways. This is the drawback of LFA – there may not be either node or link protection because it is very topology dependent. Some small topologies (RFC6571) can work very well.

If somehow R3 would know that packet is coming from its primary next-hop and it should send the packet to its alternate next-hop then packet could reach to R2 through R1-R3-R5-R6-R4-R2. This is called U-turn alternate since packet is sent back to R3 from R1 without causing a micro-loop.

Mechanism to work, R3 either explicitly marked or implicitly learns that packet is coming from its primary next hop. Also R3 needs to have loop-free node-protecting alternate path. Loop-free alternate traffic is sent to a neighbor who will not send it back. In U-turn alternate, traffic is sent to a neighbor who will send it to a neighbor's alternate instead of back.

The other three mechanisms rely on tunnels. Before going further explanation, it is important to understand some general concepts.

First, there is Remote LFA. The basic concept is to find a node that the PLR can reach without going through the failure point *and* where that node can also reach the destination (or a proxy for the destination) without going through the failure point. Then the PLR can tunnel traffic to this node and it will reach the destination without going across the failure point.

To find this node, there are two steps. First, the PLR determines all nodes that it can reach without going through the primary next-hop. This set of nodes is called the extended P-space. Either the PLR's shortest path to these nodes avoids the primary next-hop *or* the PLR has a neighbor whose shortest path to these nodes avoids the primary next-hop.

- For example, the set of routers that can be reached from R1 without traversing R1-R2 is called the extended P-space of R1 with respect to the link R1-R2.

Second, the set of routers from which the node R2 can be reached, by normal forwarding, without traversing the link R1-R2 is termed the Q-space of R2 with respect to the link R1-R2.

Any nodes that are both in extended P space and Q space are candidate PQ nodes that can be the end of the repair tunnel.

In the above example, R6 is a PQ node. R3 and R5 are not in Q space because when either decapsulate a packet destined to R2, the packet would be sent back to R1 and thus cause a loop.

R4 is not in extended P space because neither R1 nor R3 can reach R4 without potentially going via R1-R2. While any tunnel technology, such as IP in IP, GRE or L2TPv3 could be used; current implementations depend upon using MPLS tunnels signaled via LDP (and targeted LDP sessions to protect LDP traffic).

When R6 is chosen as the tunnel end point, once packet is decapsulated, packet is sent towards the R2 without looping back. Different implementations may implement different policy to select among PQ nodes.

Remote LFA works based on this principle. Currently only MPLS tunnels are supported. R6 is chosen in this topology for MPLS tunnel endpoint. For an IP packet, R1 stores an alternate next-hop to R3 with the MPLS label that R3 provided to reach R6.

If the packet has an LDP-distributed label, R1 must learn the MPLS label that R6 uses for the FEC for R2; this can be done via a targeted LDP session.

Then, the label on the packet is swapped to one that R6 understands to mean R2 and finally the label that R3 understands to mean R6 is used pushed on the packet. R6 as a penultimate router does PHP and R4 receives a labeled packet for R2.

This describes basically how Remote LFA can be used to provide link protection. Like LFA, Remote LFA is not guaranteed to find link-protecting alternates in a topology but it does significantly improve the coverage compared to LFA. Additional computation can be done so that Remote LFA finds node-protecting alternates when available.

The second tunneling mechanism: MPLS RSVP-TE-Fast Reroute can provide guaranteed protection for the links, nodes and SRLG failures. When used for local repair, an LSP can be created to protect against a particular link or node failing; each LSP requires a CSPF at the PLR.

- For example, R1 could have an LSP to protect against link R1-R2 failing; that LSP would be routed R1-R3-R5-R6-R4-R2. This LSP can be used as an alternate. Just as with any tunneling mechanism, targeted LDP sessions are needed to learn the labels protect the LDP traffic.

Since failure is local, as soon as it detects, alternate path can be started to use. Assume there is a LSP between R1 to R4. Since MPLS TE LSPs use by default shortest IGP path, R1-R2-R4 LSP is established.

If R1-R2 link will be protected, then backup tunnel is configured through the nodes R1-R3-R5-R6-R4-R2.

To reach the same destination behind R4, traffic flow would be R1-R3-R5-R6-R4-R2-R4. There is obvious hair pinning. Destination is R4 but since the backup LSP has to be terminated on R2 (It is link protection so next-hop tunnel is configured), traffic comes to R2 by passing through R4 and then from R2, back to R4.

This is well-known and common problem in the MPLS TE-FRR networks.

It appears unnecessarily with fast-reroute when the repair end-point is pinned to the next-hop (for link protection) or next-next-hop (for node protection).

Lastly, the third tunneling mechanism is **Not-Via** that can also guarantee protection for link, node, and SRLG failures. To accomplish this, each router is given additional IP addresses with extra semantics.

- For instance, R2 would have an address that means "R2 but not via R1-R2". To find the next-hop for "R2 but not via R1-R2", each router would remove R1-R2 from the network graph and then compute an SPF. The computation can be optimized with ISPF, but many ISPFs can be needed (per failure-point).

The alternate from R1 to R2 would thus involve tunneling the packet by adding a header that had a destination address of "R2 but not via R1-R2". The path from R1 to "R2 but not via R1-R2" is R1-R3-R5-R6-R4-R2. Because of the special semantics of the Not-Via address, R3 knows that it shouldn't use R1-R2 link to reach R2 and it sends the packets to R5.

MPLS TE FRR vs. IP FRR Mechanisms Comparison

Below table summarizes the similarities and the differences of the MPLS Traffic Engineering FRR (Fast Reroute) vs. IP FRR technologies in great detail. Network designers should know the pros and cons of the technologies, protocol alternatives and their capabilities from the design point of view.

Design Requirement	IP FRR	MPLS TE FRR
Scalability	More Scalable	Less Scalable, Uses RSVP for label distribution and tunnel creation, RSVP is soft state and refreshing the tunnel state is resource intensive
Working on Full Mesh	Works very well since IP FRR mechanisms need topology to be highly meshed to find an alternate path	Works very well because if the constraints are met TE FRR can find an alternate path in any topology
Working on a Ring Topology	Works very bad, it requires tunnelign mechanisms such as GRE or MPLS to find a node which will not send the traffic back	It already uses tunnel so can protect link, node or entire path in ring topology as well
Working on a Square Topology	Worst topology for IP FRR mechanisms since to find a node which won't send the traffic back requires extra processing	Finding an alternate tunnel is same as the other topologies
Suitable on Wide Area Networks	Yes	Yes
Standard Protocol	LFA,Rlfa,TI-LFA Cisco Proprietary	Yes IETF Standard
Stuff Experince	Not well known	It has been out there quite some time and deployed on many network, it is known

Design Requirement	IP FRR	MPLS TE FRR
Link Protection	Yes	Yes
Node Protection	Yes	Yes
Path Protection	No	Yes
Complexity	Easy	Complex
SRLG Protection	No	Yes
Maturity	Very new technology, not commonly used by the industry	Very old technology, used in many ISP, VPN-SP, Mobile SP and some large Enterprise networks for years
Control Plane Protocols	IP, It uses IPv4 or IPv6 routing control plane only for it's operation	IPv4 routing control plane and RSVP-TE is used as a control plane
Resource Requirement	Minimum	Too much
IPv6 Support	Yes	No
Coverage	Generally bad. If the topology highly meshed it is good, otherwise finding a repair/alternate path is very hard, link metrics should be arranged very carefully	It can cover every topology, ring,square,partial-mesh, full-mesh can be covered %100
Load Balancing over the backup path	If there are multiple repair/backup node, traffic can be shared between them	If there are multiple repair/backup node, multiple tunnels need to be created for load sharing
Training Cost	Cheap	Moderate
Troubleshooting	Easy	Hard

MPLS

Design Requirement	IP FRR	MPLS TE FRR
Routing Loop	Finds a node which won't send the traffic back via Reverse SPF. Reverse SPF allows the node to calculate the SPF for its neighbor point of view, same concept is used in BGP Optimal Route Reflector placement as well	It uses MPLS in the dataplane, receives a label over the protection tunnel. Creating a loop in MPLS is almost impossible

MPLS TE FRR vs. IP FRR Comparison

MPLS VPN and Other VPN Technologies Case Study

Enterprise Company has six datacenters. Between the datacenter they have non-IP clustering heartbeat traffic. They don't want to implement a vendor-specific solution between the datacenters

Their service provider is able to provide MPLS services.

Question 1:

Which datacenter interconnect solution is most appropriate for this company and why?

A. OTV

B. LISP

C. EoMPLS

D. TRILL

E. Fabricpath

F. VPLS

Answer 1:

The company is looking for a standard-based Layer 2 DCI solution. We know that they are looking for Layer 2 extension since they have applications that require non-IP heartbeat.

Since OTV and FabricPath are Cisco-specific solutions, they cannot be used. Also, FabricPath is not recommended for use as a DCI solution.

LISP is not a L2 extension protocol.

EoMPLS could be used, but since company has a lot of datacenters, it is not scalable.

TRILL is not recommended as a DCI solution

The best option for the given parameters is VPLS.

Question 2: The company sent their topology as it is shown below. Is there a solution to minimize the effect of specific VLANs in case their DC interconnect switch and the service provider link goes down?

If the requirement is minimum impact for the specific VLANs, we need flow-based load-balancing. Since the same VLAN with different flows can be carried over both links with flow-based load-balancing, in case one link in the bundle fails, some flows are affected but not the entire VLAN. This minimizes the effect of the specific VLANs in case of a link failure.

Unfortunately, VPLS cannot provide flow-based load-balancing, since MAC address learning is done through data plane. MAC addresses are advertised through control plane only via E-VPN technology over the BGP and only E-VPN can provide flow-based load-balancing among all the Datacenter Interconnect technologies including OTV, EoMPLS, STP, FabricPath, Trill, etc.

MPLS REVIEW QUESTIONS

Question 1:

What was the initial purpose of MPLS?

A. To avoid IP destination-based lookup and increase the performance of the routers

B. MPLS VPNs

C. MPLS Traffic Engineering

D. Alternative to the link state routing protocols

E. Virtualization

Answer 1:

MPLS VPNs and the MPLS Traffic Engineering are the applications of MPLS. They were not the initial purpose of MPLS.

By the time these capabilities are invented and used in MPLS.

MPLS is an encapsulation/tunneling mechanism. It is not a routing protocol. That's why it is not an alternative to the routing protocols.

MPLS provides virtualization with the MPLS VPNs but MPLS VPNs are not the initial purpose of inventing the MPLS.

Initial purpose of the MPLS was to avoid IP destination-based lookup and increase the performance of the routers. Thus the correct answer of this question is ' A '.

Question 2 :

Which of the options below are the characteristics of MPLS Layer 2 VPN service?

A. MPLS Layer 2 VPN allows carrying of Layer 2 information over service provider backbone.

B. Layer 2 VPN can provide point-to-point type of connectivity between customer sites.

C. It is used to carry Layer 3 routing information of the customers over the service providers.

D. It is used for datacenter interconnect.

E. Layer 2 VPN can provide point-to-multi- point type of connectivity between customer sites.

Answer 2:

MPLS Layer 2 VPNs doesn't carry layer 3 routing between the customer sites. All the other options are correct for MPLS Layer 2 VPN service.

Question 3 :

Which of the below statements describe MPLS Layer 3 VPN service?

A. Service Provider network is transparent to routing of the customer

B. It offloads routing between sites of the customer to the Service Provider

C. It improves network convergence time

D. OSPF is most common routing protocol between customer and the Service Provider

Answer 3:

MPLS Layer 3 VPN is a peer-to-peer service. Customer and the Service Provider are the routing peers. Service Provider controls the WAN routing of the customer. Thus SP network is not transparent to routing of the customer. Customer routing is offloaded to the Service Provider in MPLS Layer 3 VPN. Thus the correct answer of this question is ' B'.

Network convergence time is not improved with MPLS Layer 3 VPN. In fact, convergence is much better with **MPLS Layer 2 VPN.**

The Service Providers can support OSPF as a PE-CE routing protocol but it is not the most common protocol. In fast Static Routing and the BGP is the most common routing protocols with MPLS Layer 3 VPN service.

Question 4 :

Enterprise Company is using MPLS Layer 3 VPN for their Wide Area Network connections.

Their IGP protocol is EIGRP.

Service Provider's of the company is using IS-IS as an internal infrastructure IGP in their backbone and LDP for the label distribution.

Which protocols/technologies should be used on Point A, B and C in the below topology?

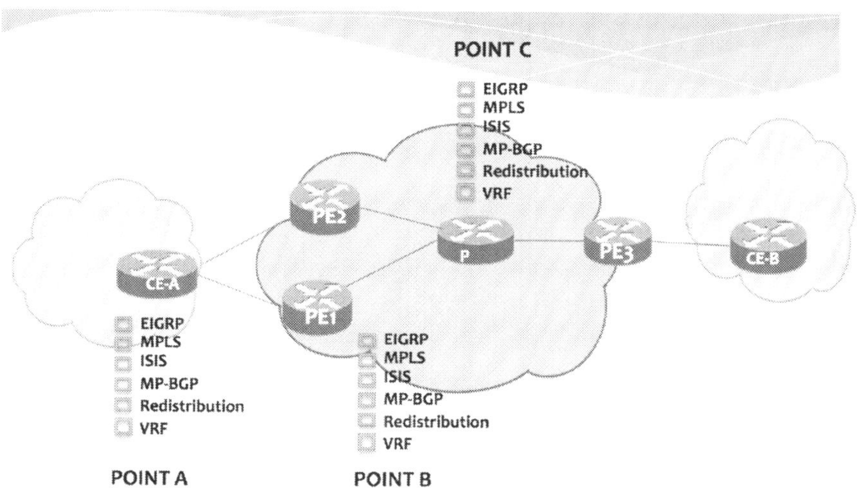

Answer 4:

Correct answer is Point A: EIGRP, Point B: EIGRP+MPLS+IS-IS+MP-BGP+Redistribution+VRF, Point C: MPLS+IS-IS.

PE router has to support customer routing as well as infrastructure routing. Customer routing protocol for this question is EIGRP. Service Provider is using IS-IS.

That's why on the PE and P devices IS-IS has to be enabled.

Also on the PE, EIGRP should run as well. VRF has to be enabled on the PE and redistribution from EIGRP into IS-IS and IS-IS into EIGRP is necessary. MPLS has to be enabled on both PE and P devices.

MP-BGP is only necessary on the PE devices. MPLS VPN removed the need of BGP in the core.

Question 5 :

Which below option depicts Inter-AS MPLS VPNs Option B deployment?

A

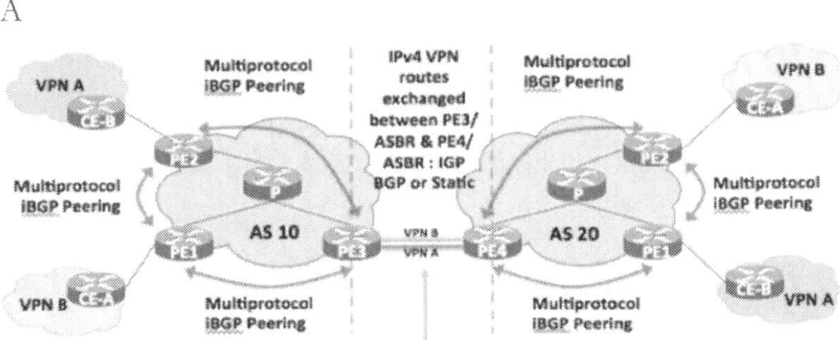

Multiprotocol iBGP Peering
IPv4 VPN routes exchanged between PE3/ ASBR & PE4/ ASBR : IGP BGP or Static
Multiprotocol iBGP Peering
VPN A
CE-B
PE2
P
PE1
AS 10
PE3
VPN B
VPN A
PE4
AS 20
VPN B
CE-A
PE2
Multiprotocol iBGP Peering
Multiprotocol iBGP Peering
VPN B
CE-A
Multiprotocol iBGP Peering
Multiprotocol iBGP Peering
CE-B
VPN A

B

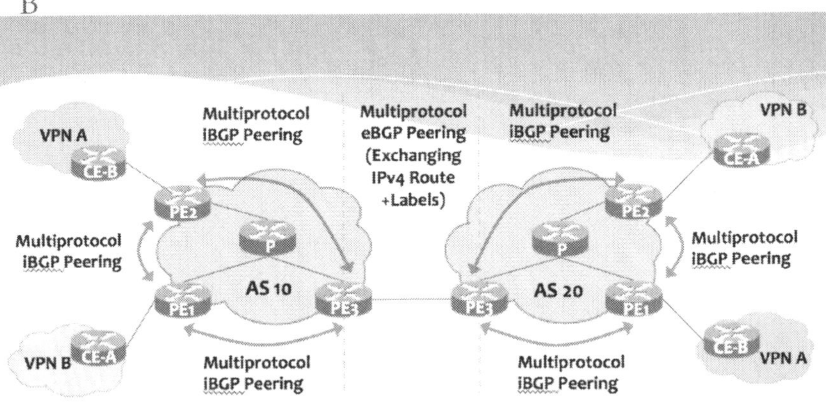

Multiprotocol iBGP Peering
Multiprotocol eBGP Peering (Exchanging IPv4 Route +Labels)
Multiprotocol iBGP Peering
VPN A
CE-B
PE2
Multiprotocol iBGP Peering
P
AS 10
PE1
PE3
VPN B
CE-A
Multiprotocol iBGP Peering
VPN B
CE-A
PE2
Multiprotocol iBGP Peering
AS 20
PE3
PE1
CE-B
VPN A
Multiprotocol iBGP Peering

C.

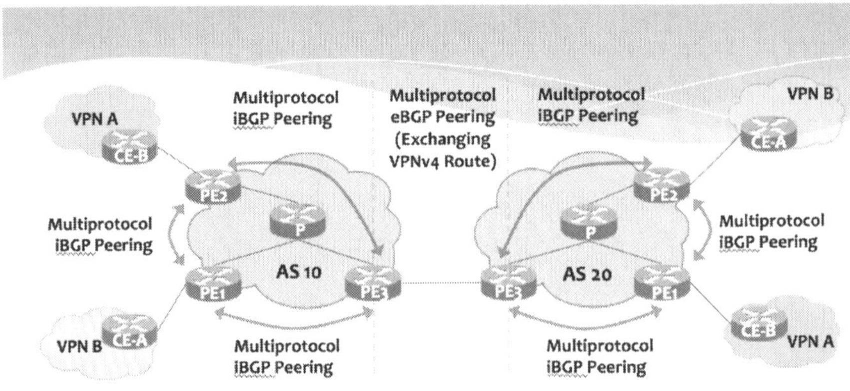

Multiprotocol iBGP Peering
Multiprotocol eBGP Peering (Exchanging VPNv4 Route)
Multiprotocol iBGP Peering
VPN A
CE-B
PE2
Multiprotocol iBGP Peering
P
AS 10
PE1
PE3
VPN B
CE-A
Multiprotocol iBGP Peering
VPN B
CE-A
PE2
Multiprotocol iBGP Peering
AS 20
PE3
PE1
CE-B
VPN A
Multiprotocol iBGP Peering

D.

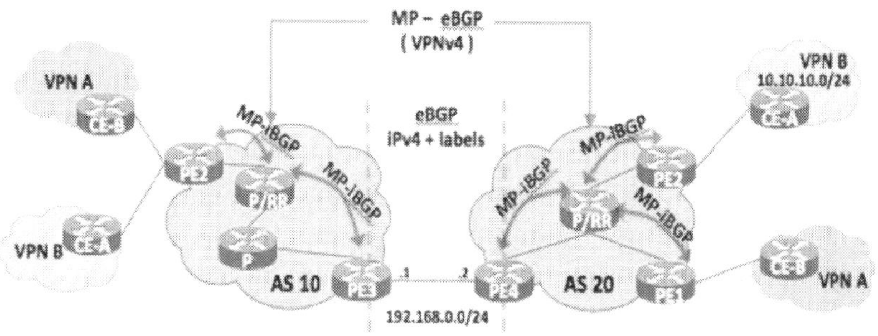

Answer 5:

Picture A shows Inter-AS MPLS VPN Option A that is back-to-back VRF option.

Picture B is very close to Inter-AS MPLS VPN Option B, but it is not correct since ASBRs between two AS in Option B have VPN connection.

Picture B shows IPV4 +LABEL, there is no such an option in Inter-AS MPLS VPNs

Picture C shows Inter-AS MPLS VPN Option B. Thus the correct answer of this question is ' C'.

Picture D shows Inter-AS MPLS VPN Option C.

Question 6 :

Service Provider Company due to their customer growth, re-evaluating their addressing plans. They want to ensure that their Enterprise MPLS Layer 3 VPN customer address space don't overlap on their PE device.

Which below option SP Company should use to avoid overlapping address space from the customers?

A. SP should do NAT on the PE devices

B. SP should assign different VRF names per customer on the PE devices

C. SP should assign different/unique RD value on the PE devices per customer

D. SP should assign different/unique RT value on the PE devices per customer

Answer 6:

As a network designer always you should look for the most easiest and elegance option.

NAT could be an option to avoid overlapping address space if this is the requirement but it would be too complex.

Can you achieve the same result with any alternative technology? You should always ask yourself this question.

Per customer, assigning a unique/different RD values create different VPN prefixes even the customer IP addresses are the same. So you can avoid overlapping address space issue by using different RD values on the PE devices.

Correct answer of this question is Option C.

Question 7 :

Enterprise Company has 6 datacenters. Between the datacenters, they have non-IP clustering heartbeat traffic. They are looking scalable solution, which will allow their future growth.

They don't want to implement any vendor specific solution between the datacenters.

Their Service Provider is able to provide MPLS services.

Which Datacenter Interconnect solution is most appropriate for this company?

A. OTV

B. LISP

C. EoMPLS

D. TRILL

E. FabricPath

F. VPLS

Answer 7:

Company is looking for standard based Layer 2 DCI (Datacenter Interconnect) solution.

We understand that they are looking for Layer 2 extension since they have an applications which requires non-IP heartbeat traffic.

Since OTV and Fabricpath Cisco specific solutions, they cannot be chosen based on the given requirements. Also there are some scalability limits for OTV so it shouldn't be chosen in any decent DCI deployment. Also Fabricpath is not a recommended DCI solution due to many reasons.

LISP is not a L2 extension protocol . Although there are some attempts to provide Layer 2 in LISP, there is no standard for that.

EoMPLS (Ethernet over MPLS) could be used but since company has a lot of datacenters, it is not scalable solution. And in the requirement of the question, it is given that Company is looking for scalable solution.

TRILL is not a recommended DCI solution as well. Inside the datacenter it can be used as one of the Fabric technologies but not for multiple datacenter interconnect.

Best option based on the given requirement is VPLS. It is standard based, used by many companies around the world, proven to scale and provides all the requirements in the question.

Question 8 :

Which below option is correct for Rosen GRE Multicast in MPLS Layer 3 VPN service?

A. Multicast traffic is carried over GRE tunnels

B. Unicast Traffic is carried over GRE tunnels

C. LDP is used for control plane for Rosen GRE in the Service Provider network

D. Multicast Traffic is carried over LDP LSP

E. GRE tunnels are created between the customer sites.

Answer 8:

In Rosen GRE Multicast approach, GRE tunnels are created in the Service Provider network. Not in the customer network. Thus Answer E is incorrect.

Multicast traffic of the customer is carried over GRE tunnels of the Service Provider. LDP is not used for Multicast control plane.

Unicast transport/tunnel LSP can be used for Unicast but not for Multicast. Thus the correct answer of this question is ' A'.

Question 9 :

Fictitious Service Provider Company runs MPLS Traffic Engineering on their network. They protect both MPLS Layer 2 and Layer 3 VPN service customers with MPLS Traffic Engineering Fast Reroute.

Company has chosen to deploy local protection rather than Path protection since they know that local protection can provide better fast reroute time in case of failure.

They deployed full mesh link and node protection LSPs.

Which one of the below failure scenarios Service Provider Company can cover?

A. PE-CE link failure

B. CE node failure

C. PE node failure

D. P node failure

E. P to P link failure

F. PE to P link failure

Answer 9:

In the question, it is given that company is doing MPLS Traffic Engineering Local protection. As it is explained in the MPLS chapter, two of the Local protection mechanisms are Link and Node protection.

With Link and Node protection, edge device failure and edge link failures cannot be protected. This failure could be covered with BGP PIC Edge feature but question is specifically asking about MPLS Traffic Engineering link and node protection.

P node failure, PE to P link and P-to-P link failure scenarios can be protected with TE FRR backup LSPs since none of them are the edge failure case.

Question 10:

Which of the options below are used in the MPLS header?

A. 20 bits MPLS label space.

B. Link cost

C. 12 bits TTL field.

D. 3 bits EXP field for the QoS.

E. Protocol number

Answer 10:

Link cost and protocol number is not in the MPLS header.

There are MPLS Label, TTL and the EXP fields in the MPLS header.

Label field is 20 bits, EXP is 3 bits and TTL is 8 bits long.

But in the question TTL field is shown as 12 bits in Option C. Thus that is wrong.

Correct answer of this question is A and D.

Question 11:

What are the characteristics of the below topology? (Choose all that apply)

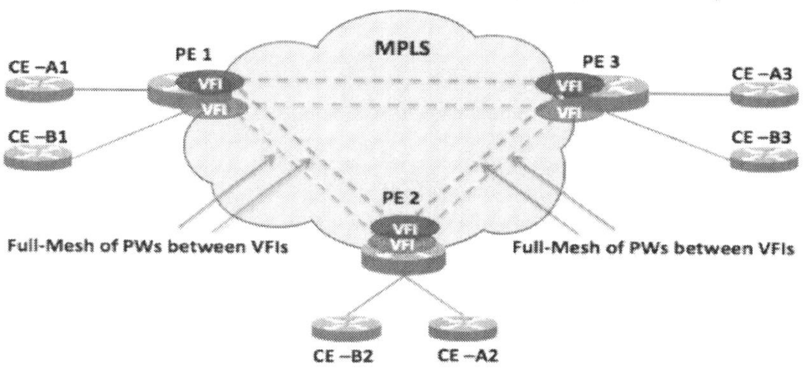

A. It doesn't support flow based load balancing

B. There is no spanning tree in the network core

C. Split horizon is enabled in the network core

D. D. It advertises the MAC Addresses through BGP control plane

E. MAC Address information is learned through dataplane

F. It requires full-mesh point to point PW between the VPN

sites

G. IS-IS is used to advertise MAC addresses between the sites

Answer 11:

In order to give correct answer to this question, you should understand the topology first. In the picture, VPLS architecture is shown.

VPLS uses data plane learning. MAC Address information from the customer site is learned through data plane. There is no MAC address advertisement through the control plane. EVPN does that though.

Also in the network core, MAC addresses are learned through data plane. Routing protocols; BGP or IS-IS are not used to advertise MAC address information. Spanning tree is not used in the network core. Split horizon is enabled in the network core. If the traffic is received from the PW, it is not sent back to another PW since full-mesh point-to-point PW has to be enabled between the VPN Sites.

VPLS doesn't support flow based load balancing. EVPN does.

Thus the correct answer of this question is A, B, C, E and F.

Question 12:

When designing an IS-IS network with MPLS, when is route leaking required from Level 2 to Level 1 sub domain?

A. If PE loopback will be carried in BGP

B. If PE devices in the L1 sub domain

C. If there is more than one L1-L2 router

D. If there are low end devices in the L1 sub domain

Answer 12:

When designing an IS-IS network, the problem with MPLS is, PE devices loopback IP addresses are not sent into IS-IS L1 domain.

In IS-IS L1 domain, internal routers only receive ATT (Attached) bit from the L1-L2 router. This bit is used for default route purpose.

In order to have MPLS Layer 3 VPN, PE devices should be able to reach each other and MPLS LDP LSP should be setup end to end.

If the PE loopback is not sent, end-to-end LSP cannot be setup. Answer of this question is ' B'.

If there is more than one L1-L2 router, still only default route is sent into L1 subdomain/area.

If PE loopback will be carried in BGP, which is called BGP + Label or BGP LU (Label Unicast) then there is no need for route leaking, but since the question is asking when it is required, answer is ' B'.

Question 13:

Which option below can be used as a PE-CE routing protocol in MPLS Layer 3 VPN? (Choose all that apply).

A. IS-IS

B. BGP

C. PIM

D. HSRP

E. OSPF

F. Static Route

Answer 13:

PIM and HSRP are not routing protocols. They cannot be used as PE-CE routing protocol in the context of MPLS Layer 3 VPNS.

OSPF, IS-IS, RIP, EIGRP, BGP and static routing, all of them are supported as MPLS VPN PE-CE routing protocol in theory. In practice, most of the Service Providers only provide Static Routing and BGP.

But in the question, it says, which protocols can be used !

Thus the correct answer of this question is 'A', 'B', 'E', and 'F'.

Question 14:

In an MPLS VPN, which below option is correct if the unique/ different RD and same RT is configured on the PE devices for a particular VPN?

A. Routes are rejected by the remote PEs.

B. Routes are accepted by the remote PEs and doesn't consume extra resources

C. Routes are accepted by the remote PEs and consume extra resources

D. They cannot be send from the Local PE since RD and RT should be the same across PE devices in a particular VPN

Answer 14:

For a particular VPN different RD and RT values can be configured. Local PEs advertise the routes and remote PEs accept these routes.

But the routes consume extra resources on the PEs since they are different VPN prefixes. When RD values append to the IP prefixes, VPN prefix is created. RD value is used to create different VPN prefixes in an MPLS VPN environment. Thus the correct answer of this question is ' C'.

Question 15:

What is the reason of using unique/different RD per VRF per PE in an MPLS VPN environment?

A. It is not good practice to use unique RD per VRF per PE.

B. It is used to send different VPN prefix to the VPN RR

C. It is used to send same VPN prefix to the VPN RR

D. It is used for scalability purpose

Answer 15:

Unique RD is a common approach in MPLS VPN environment.

It is a best practice because with unique RD per VRF per PE, VPN RR (Route Reflector) can receive more than one BGP next hops for a given VPN site from the local PEs and the remote PEs can receive more than one best path from the VPN RR.

These paths can be used for Hot Potato (Optimal routing), fast reroute and the Multipath purposes.

Question 16:

European Service Provider Company recently acquired smaller Service provider in Dubai. They want to merge two MPLS VPN via the Internet.

They want solution to be deployed very quickly so they can start utilizing end-to-end MPLS service for their customer.

Which below technologies can satisfy all the given requirements above?

A. MPLS over GETVPN

B. MPLS over GRE

C. MPLS VPWS

D. MPLS VPLS

E. MPLS over L2TPv3

F. MPLS over IPv6

Answer 16:

Important two points in this question are, solution should be over Internet and should be deployed quickly.

GETVPN cannot run over Internet due to IP Header Preservation. MPLS over GETVPN cannot be an answer.

IPv6 is not a tunneling mechanism, which MPLS can run over. Thus MPLS over IPv6 is not an answer.

VPWS and WPLS could be setup if between two service providers deploy long haul link between their core devices, but this is not an Internet based solution and requires too much time for provision.

Only remaining solution, which can run over Internet and quickly deployable are MPLS over GRE and MPLS over L2TPv3.

Question 17

What are the two possible options to create MPLS Layer 2 **VPN pseudowire?**

A. Martini Draft, LDP signalled pseudowires

B. Segment Routing

C. BGP EVPN

D. Rosen GRE Draft

E. Kompella Draft, BGP signalled pseudowires

Answer 17:

Two different methods to create MPLS Layer 2 VPNs are Kompella and Martini methods.

As it is explained in the MPLS chapter, Kompella method uses BGP for psedowire signaling and LDP for transport LSP. Martini method uses LDP for both pseudowire signaling and transport LSP.

Rosen GRE is a Multicast application on MPLS VPN network and not used for Layer 2 VPN.

BGP EVPN is used to advertise MAC address information of the customer between the PEs, so it provides MPLS Layer 2 VPN as well. But since question is asking MPLS Layer 2 VPN pseudowire creation and since there is no pseudowire in BGP EVPN, this option is wrong.

Correct answer of this question is A and E.

Question 18:

Which below options are correct for MPLS TP (MPLS Transport Profile) as a transport mechanism? (Choose all that apply)

A. MPLS TP requires routing control plane

B. MPLS TP requires Penultimate Hop Popping

C. MPLS TP is a newer packet transport mechanism which replaces SONET/SDH

D. MPLS TP brings extra OAM capability to MPLS OAM.

E. MPLS TP benefits from ECMP (Equal Cost Multi Path) for better link utilization

F. MPLS TP uses Label 13 (GAL) for OAM purpose

Answer 18:

MPLS TP as it is explained in the MPLS chapter is a newer packet transport mechanism that replaces SONET/SDH. Today there are many discussion between MPLS TP and the Carrier Ethernet in the SP access domain.

MPLS TP doesn't use PHP, ECMP and the routing control plane. Thus, 'A', ' B' and ' E' are the wrong answers.

One of the most important reasons to deploy MPLS TP is excellent OAM capability. It uses IANA assigned Label 13 for OAM operations.

Question 19:

Enterprise Company receives an MPLS Layer 2 VPN service from the Service Provider. Enterprise topology is Hub and Spoke.

With which devices do the Enterprise spoke routes form an IGP adjacency?

A. Hub CE Routers

B. Other Spoke CE routers

C. Hub PE routers

D. Spoke PE routers

Answer 19:

Question is looking whether you know the MPLS Layer 2 VPN behavior. In an MPLS Layer 2 VPN, CE routers form an IGP adjacency with each other. Not with the PE routers.

Thus option C and D is wrong.

Also since in the question, it is given that The Company's topology is Hub and Spoke, spoke shouldn't form and IGP adjacency with each other.

That's why; the answer of this question is ' A', Hub CE routers.

Question 20:

Which of the below options are the results of having MPLS in the network? (Choose all that apply)

A. BGP Free Core

B. Hiding service specific information (customer prefixes, etc.) from the core

C. More scalable network

D. Faster convergence

E. Better security

Answer 17:

MPLS removes the need of BGP in the core. P devices don't know the customer information.

They don't keep layer 2 or layer 3 information of the customer. This provides scalability for the core but it is not enough to say that overall scalability of the network increases with MPLS.

If question would say, scalability of the core it could be correct.

MPLS doesn't bring security by default. If security is needed then IPSEC should run on top of that. Best IPSEC solution for the MPLS VPNs is GETVPN since it provides excellent scalability.

Without MPLS, network could convergence fast as well. MPLS TE FRR is a fast reroute mechanism, which can provide sub 200msec data plane convergence for the MPLS encapsulated traffic.

Same data plane fast reroute convergence can be provided with IP FRR mechanisms such as LFA, Remote LFA or Topology Independent LFA.

Thus the correct answer of this question is A, B and C.

Question 21:

If customer is looking to carry Layer 2 traffic with the encryption, which below options can be chosen?

A. VPLS

B. EoMPLS

C. GET VPN

D. MACsec 802.1AE

E. IPSEC

F. L2tpv3

Answer 21:

Question is looking for a technology, which provides Layer 2 VPN and encryption.

VPLS, EoMPLS and L2TPv3 is used to provide Layer 2 VPN service across Layer 3 infrastructure.

VPLS and EoMPLS does this with MPLS, L2TPv3 doesn't require MPLS but accomplished it over IP.

But none of them support encryption.

Only the correct answer of this question is MACsec, which is ' D'.

Question 22:

Which of the below options can be used to extend VRFs across a Campus network IF there are not much VRFs (Choose all that apply)

A. 802.1q Trunk
B. GRE tunnels
C. CDP
D. RSVP-TE
E. LDP LSPs

Answer 22:

If there are not much VRF, there is no scalability concern. LDP LSPs could be setup to carry if there are too many VRFs.

Since this is given in the question as a requirement, best and easiest options are 802.1q trunks and GRE tunnels to carry VRF across a campus network.

Question 23:

Which of the below options are correct for the Inter-AS MPLS VPN Option A?

A. It provides the most flexible QoS deployment compared to other Inter-AS MPLS VPN options.
B. It is least secure Inter-AS option.

C. It is most scalable Inter-AS option.

D. It requires MPLS between the Autonomous Systems.

E. BGP+Label (RFC3107) is used between two Autonomous Systems.

Answer 23:

Inter-AS Option A provides most flexible QoS deployment since there are separate interfaces per customer. It is the most secure VPN option since there is no information sharing between Autonomous Systems.

It is least scalable VPN option since requires per customer configuration and ASBRs keep too much information compare to other Inter-AS VPN options.

Inter-AS MPLS VPN Options comparison charts provided too much information on pros and cons of each of the method in the MPLS Chapter.

It doesn't require MPLS between the Autonomous Systems and BGP + Label is not required as well.

Correct answer of this question is ' A'.

Question 23:

Enterprise Company is using OSPF on their network and has Frame Relay transport. They want to receive MPLS VPN service as well and continue with OSPF as a PE-CE protocol. They have received a good SLA for the MPLS VPN service from the Service Provider thus they want to use for their all traffic MPLS VPN link.

Which below feature MPLS VPN Service Provider should enable to ensure in steady state always MPLS VPN link is used?

A. OSPF Super backbone

B. OSPF Sham link

C. OSPF Virtual link

D. MP-BGP (Multi Protocol BGP)

E. Multi area OSPF

Answer 24:

As it is explained in the MPLS Chapter, when OSPF is used as a PE-CE routing protocol, if there are backdoor link, backdoor link can be used if Service Provider doesn't setup OSPF sham link.

When OSPF is used as a PE-CE protocol, service provider backbone is called Super backbone and it is unrelated with the question. Only the way of ensuring MPLS VPN link to be used as a primary link is OSPF Sham link.

Question 25:

Which of the terms below are used to define a label that provides reachability from one PE to another PE in MPLS networks? (Choose all that apply)

A. Topmost Label

B. Transport Label

C. Outer Label

D. VC Label

E. VPN Label

F. Tunnel Label

Answer 25:

Topmost label, Transport label, Outer label and Tunnel label are used to define end-to-end LSP between the PE devices.

They can be used interchangeably since they define the same thing.

With this reachability MPLS Layer 2 and Layer 3 VPN, MPLS Traffic Engineering tunnels are created.

Question 26:

Which below attributes are carried in link state protocol messages in MPLS Traffic Engineering for constrained based path computation? (Choose all that apply).

A. Link bandwidth

B. Link delay

C. Link utilization

D. Link jitter

E. Link affinity/color

Answer 26:

For constrained based computation purpose, link reserved bandwidth, unreserved, used and unused bandwidth are carried in the protocol messages. OSPF and IS-IS carries this information. OSPF does this with Opaque LSAs; IS-IS carries with TLV 22, 135.

Link delay and jitter information is not carried. Link affinity (A.K.A coloring) information is carried for Shared Risk Link Group purpose. Links which use same fiber conduit, same transport equipment or even same building can be avoided and disjoint LSPs can be setup.

Link utilization is the dataplane information and it cannot be carry. Routers can act locally and change the LSP status if the utilization increases on the link, by configuring ' Auto-bandwidth ' feature but link utilization information is not carried between the devices.

Thus the answer of this question is ' A' and ' E'.

Question 27:

Which below options provide Control Plane MAC address advertisement for MPLS Layer 2 VPNs?

A. EVPN

B. VPLS

C. EoMPLS

D. BGP L3VPN

E. PBB EVPN

F. VXLAN EVPN

Answer 27:

Only EVPN provides Layer 2 MAC advertisement through control plane. VPLS does Layer 2 VPN through dataplane.

BGP L3 VPN is used for Layer 3 prefixes not for the MAC addresses.

EVPN can use different dataplane for scalability purposes. Common ones are PBB EVPN and VXLAN EVPN.

Thus the correct answer of this question is A, E and F.

Question 28:

What are the requirements to run MPLS Traffic Engineering in the network with constraint based SPF?

A. Extensions to routing protocols

B. RSVP

C. LDP

D. D. BFD

E. BGP

Answer 28:

MPLS Traffic Engineering can be enabled either in a distributed or centralized manner.

If TE LSPs will be computed at the centralize location with the offline MPLS TE tools, link state routing protocols are not required. CSPF is not used as well.

If there is no offline tool to compute the MPLS TE topology, routers should run link state routing protocols and CSPF (Constraint based SPF) should be enabled.

CSPF can access to the TED (Traffic Engineering Database) with the help of routing protocol extensions.

Also RSVP has to be enabled on the every link which MPLS TE are required.

Since in the question, it is said that it will be used with constraint based SPF, we need routing protocol extensions and only OSPF and IS-IS can provide it.

LDP, BGP or BFD is not required to run MPLS TE, BFD can help fast failure detection though.

Correct answer of this question is A and B.

Question 29:

Service Provider creates a network design that runs MPLS in its WAN backbone, using IS-IS as the infrastructure IGP routing protocol.

What would be two effects of additionally implementing MPLS-TE? (Choose all that apply)

A. For the sub second convergence MPLS TE FRR is required

B. MPLS Traffic Engineering and IS-IS cannot be used together

C. MPLS Traffic Engineering overcome the problems in Multi Level IS-IS design

D. MPLS Traffic Engineering is required to create backup path independently from the IS-IS

E. To route different MPLS QoS classes through different path, MPLS Traffic Engineering is required

Answer 29:

For the sub second convergence MPLS Traffic Engineering is not required if the IGP protocol is IS-IS. IS-IS can be tuned as it is shown in the IS-IS chapter to convergence in sub second. Option A is incorrect.

MPLS Traffic Engineering works best with IS-IS and OSPF, thus Option B is incorrect.

MPLS Traffic Engineering doesn't solve the Multi Level IS-IS traffic engineering issue. Actually it creates.

Because; MPLS TE requires topology information. But in Multi Level IS-IS design, topology information is not sent between Levels.

Thus Option C is incorrect as well.

MPLS Traffic Engineering allows backup path to be used. This is explained with the Fish diagram in MPLS Chapter.

Also different MPLS QoS classes can be routed through different paths with MPLS Traffic Engineering at the Headend router.

The correct answer of this question is D and E.

Question 30:

Enterprise Company wants to upgrade their legacy Frame Relay WAN circuits to MPLS. Based on the below migration steps, can you choose the best option for the smooth migration?

Choose a transit site for the communication between migrated and non-migrated site.
Establish a new circuit at the transit site
Establish a new circuit at the remote site
Establish a BGP over the MPLS circuit
Arrange the routing protocol metric to choose MPLS over Frame Relay
Remove the old Frame Relay circuit from the remote site
Enable Quality of Service and Monitoring for the new MPLS connection
Remove the old Frame Relay circuit from the transit site

Answer 30:

In the migration questions, first step should be choosing the transit site. Some amount of time, any particular site will have both Frame Relay and MPLS VPN connections.

Second step should be arranging a new circuit at the transit site and configure the required protocol at the transit site.

After that remote site circuit one by one can be enabled and their configuration can be done. MPLS service is preferred over legacy service. This site reaches to the sites that have not been converged, through the transit site.

QoS and security operation is done after routing protocol configuration at the remote site.

When one site is finished, legacy circuit is removed and next remote site provisioning starts.

When all the remote sites are migrated to the MPLS, Transit site legacy circuit is removed as well.

Thus the correct order of operation of this question should be as below.

- Choose a transit site for the communication between migrated and non-migrated site
- Establish a new circuit at the transit site
- Establish a new circuit at the remote site
- Establish a BGP over the new circuit
- Arrange the routing protocol metric to choose MPLS over Frame Relay
- Enable QoS and monitoring for the new MPLS connection
- Remove the Frame Relay circuit from the remote site
- Remove the Frame Relay circuit from the transit site

MPLS FURTHER STUDY RESOURCES

Books

Guichard, J. (2005). *Definitive MPLS Network Designs*, Cisco Press.
Minei, I. (2011). *MPLS-Enabled Applications: Emerging Developments and New Technologies*, Wiley.

Videos

Ciscolive Session-BRKRST-2021 Ciscolive Session – BRKMPL-2100
https://www.youtube.com/watch?v=DcBtot5u_Dk
https://www.nanog.org/meetings/nanog37/presentations/mpls.mp4
https://www.youtube.com/watch?v=p_Wmtyh4kS0
https://www.nanog.org/meetings/nanog33/presentations/l2-vpn.mp4

Articles

http://orhanergun.net/2015/02/carrier-supporting-carrier-csc
http://www.cisco.com/c/en/us/td/docs/solutions/Enterprise
http://orhanergun.net/2015/06/advanced-carrier-supporting-carrier-design/
http://d2zmdbbm9feqrf.cloudfront.net/2013/usa/pdf/BRKMPL-2100.pdf

Chapter 12

CCDE PRACTICAL SCENARIO

SpeedNet Telecom

This is a Cisco CCDE Practical exam demo scenario. There are 30 questions in this scenario. In the real exam, 25 to 35 questions are asked generally. You will have two hours and you cannot go back to previous question when you select your answer in the real exam.

Some questions are single choice, some of them Multiple choice. For the multiple-choice questions, partial scoring applies in the real exam.

Passing score is 80 in the CCDE Practical exam.

Throughout this scenario, you will receive multiple emails, similar to real exam.

Emails will provide extra bit of information and will redirect you to new set of problems. The purpose of this demo to show you what kind of questions you may encounter in the CCDE Practical exam, how you should approach the questions and how should be your design mindset.

Background Documentation

SpeedNet Background Information

SpeedNet Telecom is a US Service Provider Company, which was founded in 1990. Company started their business with the Residential Wire line Dial up customers. They had Metropolitan Wireless infrastructure in Rural Areas in the beginning. When the Broadband become mainstream, they started to deploy DSLAMs in every major cities throughout U.S

Beginning of 2000, SpeedNet started to deliver Metro Ethernet service as well. They deployed 1000 CPE devices throughout U.S and started to provide MPLS VPN Services for the Business Customers. They upgraded their Core backbone uplinks two times in the past. Although inside the POPs they have 10Gbps and 40Gbps uplinks, their all POPs are connected through minimum 2x10Gbps.

Today SpeedNet is serving around 6.5 Million customers including more than 5.5 Million Residential Broadband customers, L2 and L3 VPN Services, some Rural Wireless deployments and so on.

Their customer growth forecast is 30% year-to-year basis for the next 5-6 years. All the forecasts had been successful for far.

Their Internal IPv4 Addressing scheme as below:

For Internal purposes they are using 10.0.0.0/8 block:

/16 per Data Center

/16 per Region

/31 for point to point links

/32 for the Loopbacks

They don't currently have IPv6 in their network due to lack of demand from their customers. SpeedNet haven't implemented QoS on their network since they rely on 50% rule on their core network. So if any of the redundant links fail, remaining link doesn't become congested. When the overall bandwidth requirement exceeds 50% of the link capacity, they upgrade the link capacity.

Their IGP is flat ISIS L1. They are running BGP as external protocol and they are also providing BGP as a PE-CE protocol to their MPLS L3 VPN customer due to the corporate network security policy and the operational challenges with the other protocols.

Services provided to clients:

Residential Internet Access

L3VPN for Business Customers

L2VPN VPLS for Business Customers

L2VPN VPWS for Business Customers

MPLS NNI (Inter-AS Connections with some providers)

Metropolitan Wireless

SpeedNet is using a TCP based home built application, as their CRM.

It is very sensitive to any kind of delay and drops.

There's also a billing system that primarily using IPFIX to communicate with networking HW and their Corporate File Exchange protocol is NFS.

SpeedNet doesn't have currently Multicast on their network but their all Layer 2 switches support IGMP Snooping and MLD, and their routers support all Multicast Routing protocols.

SpeedNet is internally using Voice over IP and the video conferencing. They are utilizing FTP heavily for their HR applications specifically. They are using an entertaining application but they don't want these applications to consume more bandwidth.

Hypercom Background Information

Hypercom is another U.S based Service Provider Company which has much smaller network and customer reach compare to SpeedNet.

Hypercom have started also by providing Dial up Internet Access for the Residential home users back in early 2000. They quickly upgraded their residential broadband customers over DSLAM and recently they replaced their all DSLAM access nodes with GPON.

Two retired Network Engineers founded Hypercom and today they have over a million customers. Hypercom acquired three smaller Service providers in the different parts of US. As there might be in any merger and acquisition, there was some IP addressing overlap between the POPs in Raleigh and Austin but they have been able to fix it.

Full mesh GRE tunnels connect all these smaller SPs, which Hypercom acquired, over the Internet.

Hypercom is using single area OSPF in their network. Their network is very stable and they don't have any resource issue with their routers. They don't have any plan to design a multi area OSPF.

They did an IPv6 readiness assessment last year and checked whether all their IPv4 features are supported with IPv6 software and hardware and their networking and applications team are totally ready for IPv6.

So far Hypercom was providing only the Internet service to their residential broadband customers.

Core and DC Topologies

SpeedNet Core Diagram and Services Topology

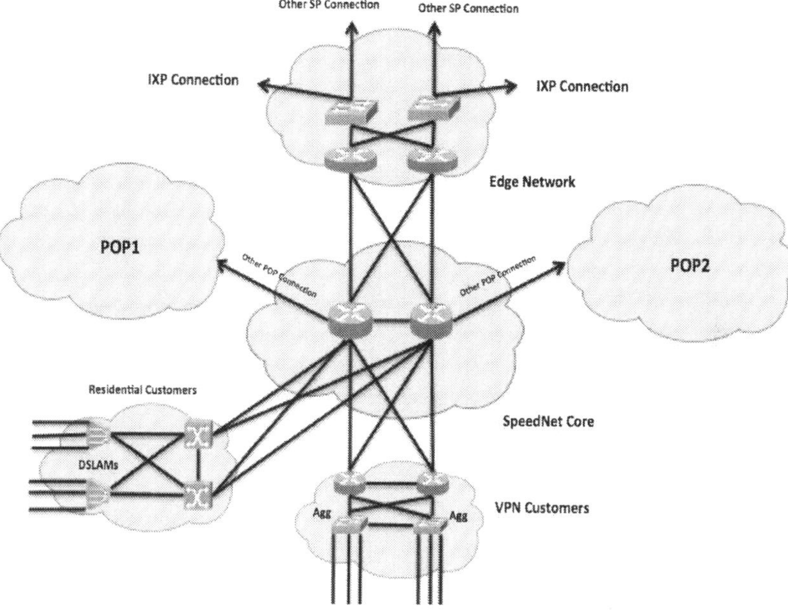

SpeedNet Telecom Core Network Diagram

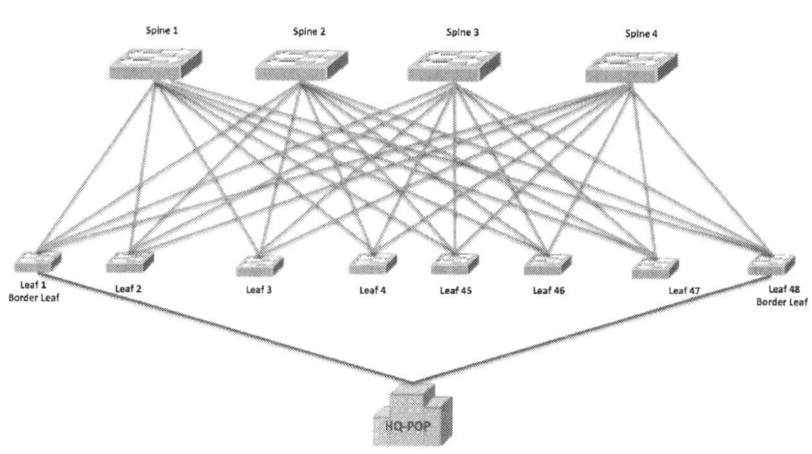

Hypercom Datacenter Diagram

SpeedNet Telecom Datacenter Topology

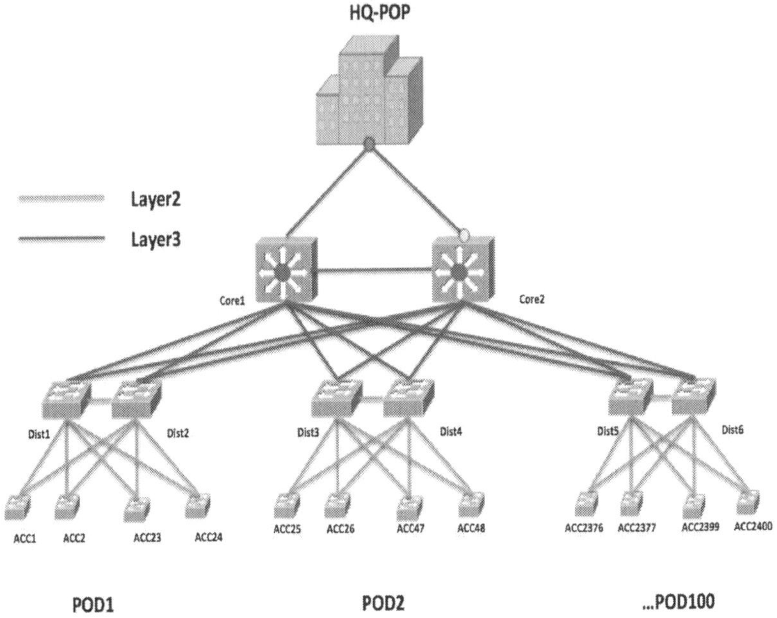

HQ-POP

Layer2

Layer3

Core1

Core2

Dist1

Dist2

Dist3

Dist4

Dist5

Dist6

ACC1 ACC2 ACC23 ACC24

ACC25 ACC26 ACC47 ACC48

ACC2376 ACC2377 ACC2399 ACC2400

POD1

POD2

...POD100

Email 1

As we have mentioned previously, Hypercom made three acquisitions few years ago. Unfortunately, they could not keep their promises to main investors so they have just sold the company to SpeedNet. Two network will be merged but first thing to do is analyzing which kind of information we are still missing before we proceed with merging both SpeedNet and Hypercom networks.

There may not need for some POP and Datacenters when merge of two networks are completed because Hypercom POP and DC operational costs are too low compare to SpeedNet.

Main concern and top priority is that merged network should be able to provide all of current SpeedNet MPLS customers.

1. **What information do you need from SpeedNet to start merging the two networks? (Choose Two)**

A. IPv4 addressing scheme
B. IGP routing information
C. BGP architecture
D. POP Architecture
E. Backbone speed
F. QoS information
G. MPLS Services Support

Answer 1:

IP address information is already provided in the background documentation that's why you shouldn't ask it again.

In the CCDE exam, if information is provided already, you can't ask it again. This is an **analyzing the design** type question.

IGP routing is given as IS-IS Flat Level 1 design, so you don't need to ask it again as well.

You don't know whether SpeedNet is using single AS or multiple ASes such as confederation, we need more information on this, that's why BGP architecture should be learned.

POP architecture should be provided as well, so if we need to remove some POPs we can plan accordingly.

Backbone speed of SpeedNet is already provided. QoS information is provided as well and also you wouldn't need it in order to start merging the two networks

It is already given that SpeedNet is providing MPLS VPN to their customers.

That's why, you should learn BGP and POP architectures, and answer is C and D.

Also please note that, if you need to ask two items, as it is in this question, you will be told that choose two in the real exam. If you would need to choose three, they would tell you, choose three in the question.

2. **What information do you need from Hypercom to start merging design? (Choose Three)**

A. IPv4 addressing scheme

B. IGP routing information

C. BGP architecture

D. POP Architecture

E. QoS information

F. MPLS Services support

Answer 2:

IPv4 Addressing scheme of Hypercom is not provided, in order to understand whether there is conflict for the merged network, we need to learn IP addressing of Hypercom.

IGP routing information was provided so you cannot ask it again.

BGP architecture should be learned as well. We don't know how their Internal and External BGP is setup. Do they have full mesh IBGP, Route Reflector design or Confederation?

POP architecture should be learned as well. How their POP location is connected to the DCs and DC to the core network and so on.

QoS information can be asked if needed later on, it is not needed to start merging design. We know that they don't support MPLS services from the background information.

You cannot ask since it is already known.

Answer of this question is A, C and D.

Email 2

This is some of the information we have been able to get for you:

- SpeedNet BGP architecture is single AS in their network. Each POP location has separate BGP RR for Internet and VPN services.
- We decided to continue with the existing POPs and DCs for now. In the future we can reevaluate but currently we will not redesign any physical location.

Hypercom backbone uplink between the POPs is 2x10G links. They are considering to connect the POPs via direct links since there is too much overhead with GRE tunnels and they don't want to see GRE tunnels on their network.

- Hypercom is using 10.10.0.0/16, 10.0.0.0/16, 172.16.0.0/18 and 172.22.0.0/16 IP addressing blocks
- Hypercom has currently full mesh IBGP peering at the moment.

3. One of our new network architects was concerned about current IS-IS in SpeedNet. He thinks that we might be facing some issues while merging SpeedNet and Hypercom networks together. Is there any problem with the current ISIS design?

A. YES

B. NO

Answer 3:

There is no known problem with the current IS-IS design. Detailed answer will be provided in the subsequent answers.

4. What might be the concern of the SpeedNet for their IS-IS?

A. Migration from IS-IS L1 to Multiple flooding domains is hard

B. IS-IS L1 does not support traffic engineering

C. Redistribution is not possible to ISIS L1

D. ISIS L1 is not a scalable solution

Answer 4:

Flat IS-IS L1 is not the different from the scalability point of view from the IS-IS L2, that's why Option D is not correct.

Redistribution is possible into IS-IS L1 domains, this is not correct either.

IS-IS L1 provides Traffic Engineering and so far there is no requirement for MPLS Traffic Engineering. It is not the feature that every network should have also. Thus Option B is not correct answer either.

Option A is definitely correct; in general it is hard to migrate from flat IS-IS L1 design to multiple flooding domains such as L1 in the POP, L2 in the Core. Answer of this question is Option A.

But this is not a realistic concern in the current situation since we don't know whether merged network will have problem with the scalability. If scalability and manageability is okay for the customer, IGP can be migrated to either different one or to the multiple levels one.

5. Should they migrate the IGP protocols to run a common IGP for the merged network?

A. Yes

B. No

Answer 5:

There is no need currently. SpeedNet's main concern and top priority is to extend their MPLS services as it is given in the initial background information.

Providing an Inter-AS MPLS VPN services don't require to use common IGP, although using common IGP would provide additional benefits; especially in the MPLS network. But this can be decided after the first phase of merge; right now there is no need.

6. WHAT CAN BE THE PROBLEM IF HYPERCOM WANTS TO DEPLOY BGP ROUTE REFLECTOR BASED ON THEIR CURRENT BGP DESIGN? (CHOOSE TWO)

A. They would loose path visibility

B. There is no problem, it is same as running full mesh

C. BGP RR always bring benefits to BGP design

D. BGP RR puts additional load into the control plane

E. BGP RR can cause suboptimal routing

Answer 6:

Classical problem of BGP Route Reflector is path visibility. If you have more than one exit point from the domain for the same prefix, BGP RR selects the best path from its point of view and sends all the BGP RR clients.

That's why Option A is one of the correct answers. Less number of total path means might cause sub optimal routing from some BGP RR clients. Thus Option E is the other correct answer.

BGP RR doesn't put additional burden into the control plane. It actually removes the load from the full-mesh IBGP design.

BGP Route Reflector placement, best practices and the design recommendations were explained in the BGP Chapter of the book.

That's why answer of this question is A and E.

7. WHICH BELOW METHODS CAN BE USED TO ELIMINATE THE POSSIBLE PATH VISIBILITY PROBLEM OF BGP ROUTE REFLECTOR? (CHOOSE ALL THAT APPLY)

A. Using BGP Add-Path

B. BGP Shadow Sessions

C. Not using BGP Route Reflector

D. Using full-mesh and BGP Route Reflector in the same network

E. BGP Shadow Route Reflectors

F. BGP Best External

G. BGP PIC-Prefix Independent Convergence

Answer 7:

Except BGP PIC, all the option is used to send more than one BGP path to the BGP speaker. In order BGP PIC to function properly, one of the above options is used.

In the exam they don't ask as ' Choose All that apply ' but instead, they ask as ' Choose Two ', ' Choose Three ' and so on. Number of options that they want will be given.

Additional information: In the MPLS VPN network, using unique RD per PE provides same functionality. That's why to send more than one path for a given customer prefix, unique RD per PE is the best option in MPLS VPN network.

Email 3

One of our customers asked us about the best way to provide connectivity between their HQs and the remote sites. Could you help us out?

8. Please fill in the table below

	Multicast support over Internet	Multicast replication at Hub/WAN	Topology P2P/P2MP /MP2MP	Overlay/Underlay Routing	Redundancy	Runs over Internet/Private WAN
DMVPN						
GETVPN						
mGRE						
P2P IPSec						
GRE						

Answer 8:

In the exam, you will not fill the blank. But they may provide you an already filled table and you choose the correct option or you may select the correct option from the drop-down menu.

	Multicast support over Internet	Multicast replication at Hub/WAN	Topology P2P/P2MP /MP2MP	Overlay/Underlay Routing	Redundancy	Runs over Internet/Private WAN
DMVPN	Yes	Yes	MP2MP	Underlay all, Overlay all except is-is	Yes	Any
GETVPN	No	No	MP2MP	Underlay all, overlay is none, since there is no tunnel	Yes	Private WAN
mGRE	Yes	Yes	MP2MP	Underlay all, Overlay all	Yes	Any
P2P IPSec	No	Multicast is not Supported	P2P	Underlay all, overlay only unicast	Yes	Any
GRE	Yes	Yes	P2P	Underlay all, Overlay all	Yes	Any

9- What is the best solution for VPN security with minimal OpEx?

A. GETVPN

B. DMVPN

C. mGRE

D. P2P IPSec

Answer 9:

GETVPN provides minimum OPEX. More information is available in the online classes.

Email 4

Top management and company owners have been pushing to come up with new backbone design as soon as possible. They wanted new backbone network to be simple and flexible, efficient and be able to handle any single point of failure at POPs connecting to Data Centers.

After merging both SpeedNet and Hypercom we have started experiencing bandwidth utilization problems. Between different region the traffic flow always follow the shortest IGP path. Please can you help us to start sending traffic over all the available paths?

10- Which below option would be the best short-term solution in this case?

A. Use MPLS Traffic Engineering- Tactical Approach and distribute the traffic between the regions based on bandwidth constraint

B. Use static routes and GRE tunnels and optimize traffic flow

C. Implement DiffServ QoS all over the backbone network

D. Implement DiffServ QoS at places of traffic congestion

E. Redesign Backbone network and add few more inter-POP links

F. Use MPLS Traffic Engineering Strategic Approach

Answer 10:

Using tactial MPLS traffic engineering. Their problem is Routing metric. They cannot use their free capacity. Because IGP routing protocols chooses the shortest path.

You don't need QoS, GRE tunnel or PBR and so on. If IGP metric is carefully chosen and still there are links, which are not used, MPLS Traffic Engineering allows you to utilize the available bandwidth efficiently.

Strategic and the tactical MPLS Traffic Engineering approaches was explained in the MPLS chapter in detail.

11. WHAT ABOUT PERMANENT SOLUTION?

A. Use MPLS Traffic Engineering Strategic Approach
B. Use static routes and GRE tunnels and optimize traffic flow
C. Implement DiffServ QoS all over the backbone network
D. Implement DiffServ QoS at places of traffic congestion
E. Redesign Backbone network and add few more inter-POP links
F. Use MPLS Traffic Engineering- Tactical Approach and distribute the traffic between the regions based on bandwidth constraint

Answer 11:

Using Strategic MPLS Traffic engineering. Since it seems that they cannot use their available uplinks because IGP is only utilizing Shortest Path, Strategic MPLS Traffic Engineering helps them in the long term to provide guaranteed services and better capacity usage.

Details of the Strategic and Tactical MPLS Traffic Engineering approaches were provided in the MPLS chapter of the book.

In order to understand why Tactical MPLS Traffic Engineering has been chosen as short term and Strategic MPLS Traffic Engineering for the long term solution, please read MPLS Traffic Engineering section of MPLS chapter.

Email 5

It seems that MPLS Traffic Engineering Strategic Approach can provide us a better capacity management. Can you help us to setup MPLS Traffic Engineering on our network?

Also we will have series of questions for you regarding MPLS Traffic Engineering. We have been also told to provide QoS all across the new network within the next couple of months. We need your expert recommendations.

12. Which features need to be enabled in order for MPLS TE to function properly? (Choose Four)

A. LDP

B. RSVP

C. MP-BGP

D. Unidirectional tunnel headend

E. Unidirectional tunnel tailend

F. Bidirectional tunnel headend and tailend

G. IGP TE (TED)

H. VRF

I. Send-Label

Answer 12:

LDP, MP-BGP, VRF and Send-label (BGP + Label/RFC 3107) are not required for MPLS Traffic Engineering.

MPLS TE tunnels are unidirectional tunnel. If traffic will be placed in MPLS TE tunnels, unidirectional tunnels should be created in two directions.

Answer of this question is option B, D, E, G.

Please refer MPLS Traffic Engineering section of MPLS chapter for detail.

Email 6

We created an MPLS tunnels, RSVP and other necessary extensions are in place but unfortunately our traffic doesn't go through the TE tunnels.

Once you help to get the traffic into the MPLS TE tunnels one little thing will left.

We still need to enable DiffServ QoS throughout our new network. One of our engineers told us that it is not possible to run both IntServ and DiffServ QoS. As a company policy, we allow YouTube and Gaming applications but we prefer to limit this traffic on our network. Yes productivity is good but we are selling our bandwidth capacity as you know!.

13 Why do you think SpeedNet cannot send traffic into the MPLS TE tunnels although everything is set?

A. Multicast traffic can pass but unicast traffic might have an issue

B. Routing table should point to the tunnel interface for the TE destination prefixes

C. TE tunnel links must be advertised into the IGP protocol

D. SpeedNet probably didn't create reverse unidirectional tunnel

Answer 13:

If Multicast is setup in the network and unicast traffic would pass over the TE tunnels, Multicast could follow it. But SpeedNet doesn't say that they have a problem with Multicast, actually they didn't say anything about Multicast yet.

TE tunnels don't need to be advertised as a link into the routing protocol in order to IGP take MPLS TE link in the SPF calculation. This is done through forwarding adjacency and could be one of the solutions for the problem of putting traffic into the MPLS TE tunnel but since the Option C says that ' TE tunnel links must be advertised into the IGP protocol' this statement is wrong.

SpeedNet even doesn't create reverse uni-directional tunnel, traffic would follow the MPLS TE tunnel in one direction. Return traffic could follow the IGP shortest path. SpeedNet cannot place the traffic into the TE tunnel at all; nothing is said about one direction.

That's why the answer is Option B. Routing table should show that the destination behind the MPLS TE tail- end should be seen from the tunnel interface. This can be done via many methods. (Static route, PBR, CBTS, Auto Route, Forwarding Adjacency)

Thus, Option B is the correct answer.

14. Is it possible and recommend to run IntServ and DiffServ QoS in the same network?

A. Yes, it's possible but its not a good idea to run both IntServ and DiffServ in the same network

B. No, there's no specific restrictions and they can both run in the same network

Answer 14:

Answer is Option A. It is possible but since both are two different approaches for QoS design as they were explained in the QoS chapter of the book, they shouldn't be used on the same network together.

15. We are considering several QoS models. Which one is the best fit for us?

A. 1 PQ, 3 BQ

B. 1 PQ, 4 BQ

C. 3BQ

D. 5BQ

E. 3PQ, 1BQ

Answer 15:

SpeedNet was provided their application profile in the background document as well as in Email 6. Based on the given information of course:

Voice and Video conferencing should go to the PQ, SAP and HR applications are business critical, thus they should be placed into the same queue but separate than bulk traffic.

NFS and FTP are the bulk traffic; we can place them into the same queue. But different bandwidth queue than business critical traffic.

Since Company is allowing gaming/entertaining application, which should go to the scavenger queue, and the rest of the traffic should go to the best effort.

That's why we need 1 PQ and 4 BQ.

EMAIL 7

All our users have a problem accessing to cloud gaming application we have deployed recently and it looks like the somewhere in our network, but we are not sure where. We need your help to identify the problem!

16. WHICH PART OF THE NETWORK SHOULD WE FOCUS ON?

A. Place the monitoring probes closer to application

B. Place the monitoring probes closer to end users

C. Place the probes closer to both end users and application

D. Place the probes at all the POPs

E. Place the probes everywhere in the network

Answer 16:

Answer is closer to the application since all the users have a problem at the same time, so the problem should be with the application.

All the traffic should come through those nodes, which the probe is running. Correct answer is Option A.

Email 8

Since we have done merging, we have lots of requests from the SpeedNet customers to extend their current VPN networks to different locations where Hypercom have presence. SpeedNet wants to have separation of their core network task from the Inter domain task, that's why they implemented a new ASBR routers but Hypercom is okay with the existing routers for new inter domain communication.

17. Which below option would you suggest to implement in order to extend your VPNs to Hypercom backbone?

A. Inter-AS Option A

B. Inter-AS Option B

C. Inter-AS Option C

D. Redistributing the prefixes of two networks to each other

Answer 17:

Since there is overlapping IP addresses between SpeedNet and Hypercom that's why we cannot leak the internal prefixes, so Option C cannot be chosen.

Option A cannot be chosen either since it is stated in the email that lots of request is coming for the Inter-AS service.

Very detailed explanation for the Inter-AS MPLS VPNs have been provided in the MPLS Chapter of the book.

Answer is Option B.

18. **What is the main reason to implement it?**

A. It is the most secure option among the others

B. It fits SpeedNet scalability needs

C. It is the easiest option to configure

D. It provides end-to-end LSP

Answer 18:

It fits SpeedNet scalability needs. It is not the most secure option. Inter-AS Option A is the most secure Inter-AS MPLS VPN solution.

It is not the easiest to configure, Inter-AS Option A is the easiest one but when the number of Inter-AS MPLS customer grows, it doesn't scale.

Inter-AS MPLS Option B doesn't provide end-to-end LSP, only Inter-AS Option C does.

Answer is B.

19. **Please check the right boxes to implement Inter-AS Option B between the SpeedNet and Hypercom networks**

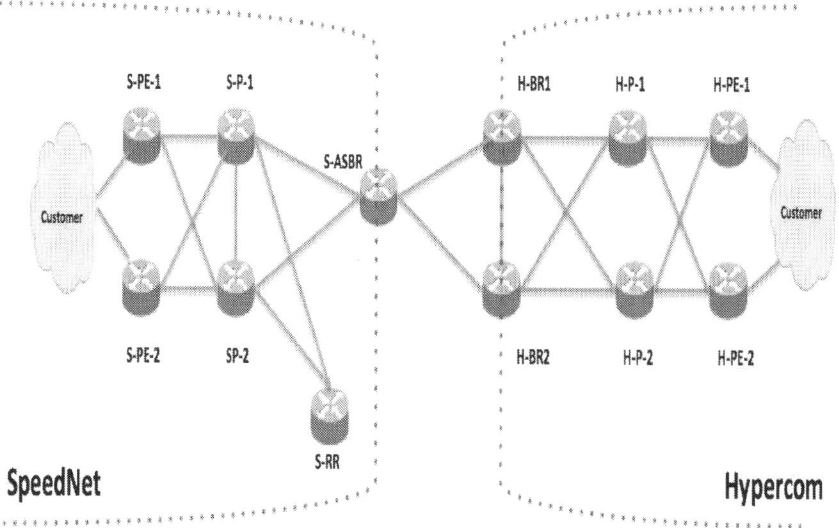

Protocols	S-PE-1	S-RR	H-S-ASBR	H-BR-1	H-P-1
VRF					
MP-IBGP					
MP-EBGP					
Infrastructure IGP					
Customer IGP					
Send Label					
MPLS					

Answer 19:

Answer should be as below. Please note that there is no Customer IGP on the PE devices since in the scenario you are told that as the company policy they just want to provide BGP as a PE-CE protocol.

Also there is no send-label in Inter-AS Option B and Route Reflector doesn't have to run MPLS when they are not used as inbound RR.

Protocols	S-PE-1	S-RR	H-S-ASBR	H-BR-1	H-P-1
VRF	*				
MP-IBGP	*	*	*	*	
MP-EBGP	*		*	*	
Infrastructure IGP	*	*	*	*	*
Customer IGP					
Send Label					
MPLS	*		*	*	*

EMAIL 9

One of our lead architect came up with new IP addressing scheme that new network is going to migrate to within the next 6 months. And Hypercom Full Mesh IBGP is migrated to Route Reflector topology. RRs will be placed in the centralized location, they will not be used as inline RR.

It gives us opportunity to use Inter-AS Option C.

20. PLEASE CHECK THE RIGHT BOXES TO IMPLEMENT INTER-AS OPTION C.

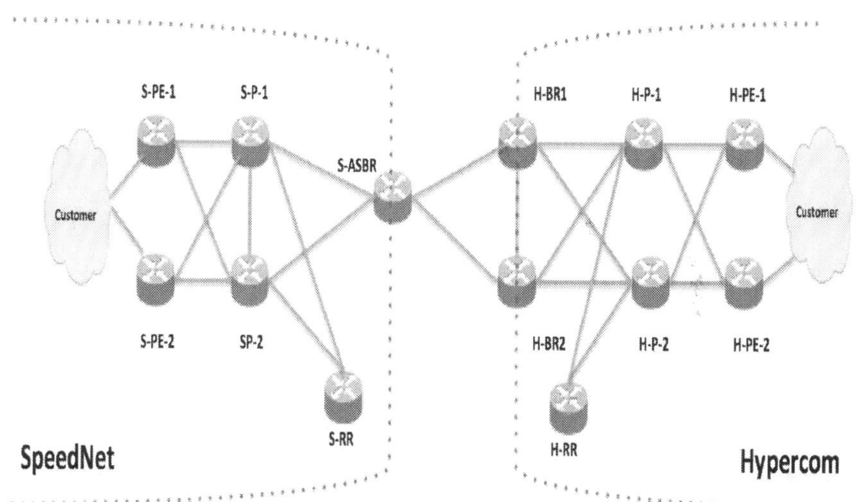

Protocols	S-PE-1	H-RR	S-RR	S-ASBR	H-BR-1	H-P-1
VRF						
MP-IBGP						
MP-EBGP						
Infrastructure IGP						
Customer IGP						
Send Label						
MPLS						

Answer 20:

Answer should be as below. Please note that there is no Customer IGP on the PE devices since in the scenario you are told that as the company policy they just want to provide BGP as a PE-CE protocol.

H-RR is added in the Hypercom network since in the last email it is told that they migrate to BGP RR design from the full-mesh IBGP.

In Inter-AS Option C, there is MP-EBGP session between the RR, BGP+Label between ASBR and the BRs.

Also there is send-label in Inter-AS Option C and Route Reflector doesn't have to run MPLS when they are not used as inbound RR.

Protocols	S-PE-1	H-RR	S-RR	S-ASBR	H-BR-1	H-P-1
VRF	*					
MP-IBGP	*	*	*	*	*	
MP-EBGP	*	*	*	*	*	
Infrastructure IGP	*	*	*	*	*	*
Customer IGP						
Send Label						
MPLS	*			*	*	*

21. What is the main benefit of implementing Inter-AS Option-C between SpeedNet and Hypercom?

A. The only option with the support of 6vPE

B. Better scalability compared to Inter-AS Option B

C. The easiest Inter-AS Option to implement

D. More secure compare to Inter AS Option B

Answer 21:

It is not the only option, which can support 6VPE. It is not the easiest way to deploy Inter-AS MPLS service.

Option A is the easiest as it is explained before. It is not the most secure Inter-AS MPLS VPN solution. Option A is the most secure one.

Correct answer is B.

Email 10

Hi Mr. Designer,

As you know we have MPLS Layer 3 VPN, Internet, Point to point MPLS VPN and VPLS customers. Especially for the VPLS customers, when we want to add a new site to the current VPLS of the customers, it is operationally very hard for us to touch every PE of the customer.

We afraid that this will be a bigger problem for the merged network since we want to span the VPLS and our other services throughout the merged network. But especially for the VPLS issue, we want to have an immediate solution.

Please note that we have an LDP-based VPLS in our network and the Hypercom network doesn't have VPLS at all currently.

Can you help us to fix our operational problem?

22. Which below option is defined the SpeedNet's operational problem?

A. Their network engineers don't have a capability to manage merged network

B. Their existing gear don't have a capability to keep the state of merged network

C. They want to reduce the operational touch point for the existing services, especially VPLS

D. They don't know whether VPLS service can be extended over the Inter-AS links

Answer 22:

As it is given in the email, SpeedNet wants to reduce the operational touch point for the existing services, especially VPLS.

In the CCDE Practical exam, most important thing is to answer the question based on the given requirements. Requirements are given in the initial background documentations and in the emails.

Answer is Option C.

23. What would be your solution for their VPLS service?

A. Use H-VPLS

B. Use A-VPLS

C. Replace VPLS with EVPN

D. Replace VPLS with PBB-EVPN

E. Use BGP AD for their VPLS solution

Answer 23:

Replacing VPLS with EVPN or PBB-EVPN is not an option since they want immediate solution and we are don't know whether their devices support EVPN or PBB-EVPN.

BGP Auto Discovery reduces their operational tasks by advertising the VPLS membership information. And we know that BGP is already used on their networks.

Answer is Option E.

24 If SpeedNet would request to have the most granular QoS support for their Inter-AS VPLS service, which below option you would recommend?

A. Inter-AS Option A

B. VPLS cannot be extended over Inter-AS

C. Inter-AS Option B

D. Inter-AS Option C

E. Inter-AS Option AB

Answer 24:

Most granular QoS is achieved with Inter-AS Option A since there is separate physical or logical link per customer VPN. With the other option, same link(s) is used for all the Inter-AS customers.

Answer is Inter-AS Option A.

Would you recommend SpeedNet to deploy BGP-VPLS on the Hypercom network?

A. Yes

B. No

Answer 25: Correct answer is Option A, Yes. It fits all their requirements, which are given in the Email 10.

26. Is there any problem for LDP and BGP based VPLS to support end-to-end VPLS?

A. Yes

B. No

Answer 26:

Correct answer is No.

With adding interconnect nodes between the LDP-VPLS and BGP-VPLS domains, end-to-end VPLS service is created.

Email 11

One of our customers is asking whether we can provide IPv6 L3 VPN services for them. We have not been thinking about it, but as our assessment all our networking nodes support IPv6

27. Which technology will help SpeedNet to meet the requirements above?

A. 6PE

B. DMVPN

C. 6vPE

D. NAT64

E. NAT46

Answer 27:

Correct answer is 6VPE, Option C. All the details of the IPv6 transition mechanisms have been provided in the IPv6 chapter of the book. 6VPE is the best solution for the VPNs on the MPLS backbones.

If Internet reachability would be asked over MPLS backbone 6VPE would be the solution.

28. Which additional technology/protocol is needed as an underlay transport to support 6VPE service for SpeedNet?

A. IPv6 LDP in the core

B. IPV6 IGP in the core

C. IPv6 RSVP-TE

D. Both IPv6 IGP and LDP

E. IPv4 transport is enough for 6VPE

Answer 28:

Correct answer is Option E. IPv4 transport is used to create 6VPE. LDPv6 or IPv6 transports are not needed.

EMAIL 12

In the future, we are planning to expand to EMEA region. Our management has found one of the small local service providers in UK that they are going to acquire within the next several months. We are looking for a cost effective short-term solution for acquisition to extend MPLS VPN services between the two networks.

We also need a good design and migration plan for a long-term solution if this acquisition goes well. We don't have a budget issue for long haul links. As we are planning to provide different value added services for our customers, both short-term and long-term solutions must support end-to-end QoS and Multicast.

29. What is the fastest short-term solution to connect current SpeedNet network and a new one in the UK?

A. Use L2VPN from another MPLS Service Provider to connect current SpeedNet network and a new one with MPLS and QoS over that L2VPN

B. Use L3VPN from another MPLS Service Provider to connect current SpeedNet network and a new one with MPLS and QoS over that L3VPN

C. Build GRE tunnels over Internet and run MPLS and the necessary services on top of it

D. Order dedicated circuits

Answer 29:

Answer is Option C. It is the fastest solution to extend their VPNs, although there might be a lot of problem with GRE tunnels.

30. What would be the problem with this short-term solution? (Choose Three)

A. It is not reliable and there is no SLA guarantee

B. It is not secure

C. QoS is not under control of SpeedNet
D. For each customers require separate overlays
E. Multicast routing is not supported with it
F. All of the above

Answer 30:

It doesn't require separate overlay tunnels per customer.

Multicast routing is supported over GRE tunnels. But it is not secure since it is over the Public Internet. IPSEC can run on top of that but it was not mentioned in the question.

It is not reliable and there is no SLA since the Internet is best effort.

QoS is not under control of the SpeedNet because of the above reason, Internet is best effort and if there is any congestion throughout the path, there is no SLA for QoS.

Correct answer, Option A, B and C.

Chapter 13
CCDE PRACTICAL SCENARIO
MAG Energy

This is a Cisco CCDE Practical exam demo scenario. There are 23 questions in this scenario. In the real exam, 25 to 35 questions are asked generally. You will have two hours and you cannot go back to

previous question when you select your answer in the real exam.

Some questions are single choice, some of them Multiple choice. For the multiple-choice questions, partial scoring applies in the real exam.

Passing score is 80 in the CCDE Practical exam.

Throughout this scenario, you will receive multiple emails, similar to real exam.

Emails will provide extra bit of information and will redirect you to new set of problems. The purpose of this demo to show you what kind of questions you may encounter in the CCDE Practical exam, how you should approach the questions and how should be your design mindset.

Document 1

Company Profile:

MAG Energy (MAG-E) is an energy broker and middleman between Energy Providers and their customers located in the United States. MAG-E has been in business for just over 10 years. The company and its network were built organically, only as the needs of the business increased. Historically, the primary source of revenue has been deploying Site Devices at customer locations. While this primary method has been effective over the years, it has not been efficient from both a monetary and time to deployment standpoint. For the short term, MAG-E has purchased a manufacturing plant in Boise Idaho to bring all Site Device manufacturing in house to significantly reduce the overall cost of each Site Device. As for the long term, the Executive team is currently researching different SaaS solutions that would replace the current Site Device model.

Power Usage / Reduction Event Process:

MAG-E is a middleman between Energy Providers and the Enterprise Customers of the Energy Provider. For example, the energy provider would first work with MAG-E to negotiate a contract for power reduction in the energy provider's area of responsibility. Once the contract is finalized, MAG-E works with Enterprise customers of the energy provider to negotiate a child contract for a reduction in power usage. Common Enterprise customers are grocery stores, pharmacies, retail stores, farms and silos, and factories.

An Event is when the energy provider has a high amount of power usage that they cannot maintain. When this occurs, the energy provider will initiate the Event by calling the Support Line at MAG-E, which starts the internal process within MAG-E to engage all child contracts to comply with the reduction in power. Traditionally, these Events happen more in the summer seasons when the temperatures are very high which causes a high power usage state with all of the Air Conditioners being turned on.

Some Event responses are automatic with the deployed Site Device turning a system off and on as needed while other Event responses are manual, requiring MAG-E to contact the child customer to manually lower their power usage by shutting equipment down.

Site Profiles:

MAG-E currently has two Data Centers, one located in Boston, MA and the other located in Dallas, TX. The primary DC in Boston has 2000 servers, while the Dallas DC has 1400 servers. MAG-E is headquartered out of Boston, MA. In Boston there is an Event Support Center staffed with 500 users that process all of the Events placed by the Energy Providers. In addition to the Event Support Center Staff, the Boston location has 3000 more employees. In Boise Idaho, there is the newly acquired manufacturing plant that consists of 1000 employees and another separate legacy remote office that consists of 50 employees. The rest of the US network consists of 57 office locations that range from five users to one hundred users.

Site Devices:

MAG-E's innovative Site Devices have been the bread and butter for their business since the beginning. Over the years, there have been 3 different Site Device model series; the S, X, and E. The S series was the pioneer of Site Devices but were limited in functionality as they could only push data back to the servers in Boston and Dallas. The S series also lacked common security best practices such as SSH support and AES support. The second generation of Site Devices was the X model series. With the X series, some significant improvements were implemented. The majority of these improvements was around security of the Site Device and the Energy data, by integrating AES and SSH support. MAG-E wanted to significantly improve data efficiency that the current Site Device series lacked by implementing a data pull operation. This last and final series of Site Devices was the E series. The E Series has now become the Spearhead of the business. The E series was developed with both a push and pull data method that could function independently and concurrently. MAG-E has a total of ~2,000 Site Devices deployed today.

S Series	Deployed	X Series	Deployed	E Series	Deployed
S1	402	X1	53	E1	131
S2	238	X2	18	E2	106
S3	157	X3	102	E3	23
S4	318	X4	378	E4	53

MAG-E's Network:

MAG-E's US WAN currently uses a single MPLS L3VPN provider network from Level 3. The two data centers have two routers connecting to the MPLS L3VPN network over 200mb/s Ethernet circuits. The headquarter location also has two routers connecting to the MPLS L3VPN network but over 50mb/s Ethernet circuits. All other office locations have a single router with a single connection to the MPLS L3VPN network with bandwidth ranging from 1.5mb/s to 50mb/s, depending on the needs of the office locations. The manufacture plant in Boise, Idaho was brought into the MPLS L3VPN network over a single 10mb/s Ethernet circuit. There are two Level 3 Gigabit Ethernet Circuits connecting the two data centers together and there is a single 10GB dark fiber connection between the Boson data center and the Boston headquarters.

Site Device connectivity is terminated in MAG-E's production DMZ. The most popular termination method currently implemented is via private cellular networks. All private cellular networks being used have a dedicated hub router in the production DMZ where all traffic for that cellular provider is provided. For this termination method, a dedicated router with a 3G/4G card is deployed alongside the Site Device.

The next termination method is via site to site VPNs between a dedicated firewall cluster in the production DMZ and customer firewalls. This termination is primary used for customers that have a significant number of Site Devices.

The final termination method is via the Internet where a Site Device is deployed and given a static public address from the customer's network to then connect back to the servers in MAG-E's data centers.

A single EIGRP process is configured throughout MAG-E's network to handle all of the internal routing.

Applications:

MAG-E has a number of production and corporate applications:

Production Applications:

- •MAG-E Energy Intel (MAG-E-EI) – MAG-E-EI is a Web based dashboard to display all customer energy information, reports, usage, billing, and savings data in real time. This application is the primary resource for the Energy Providers and the Enterprise Customers of the Energy Providers.

- •MAG-E Ordering System (MAG-E-OS) – MAG-E-OS is an internal only application for MAG-E's sales departments to put in new orders and track already placed orders. The front end of MAG-E-OS is a Web based portal for easy access, while the backend is a SQL database.

- •MAG-E Data Feeds (MAG-E-DF) – MAG-E-DF differ depending on the Site Device data method (push or pull). Site Devices will either push (UDP) data to the backend servers or the servers will periodically pull (TCP) data from the site devices. The Site Devices do have a local buffer that can store 12 hours of data in a failure situation. After 12 hours, the Site Device starts to overwrite the oldest data in its buffer. With all Site Device Series, data feed traffic is a custom XMPP packet over ports 5002 (push) and 5502 (pull).

- MAG-E Event Tracking Center (MAG-E-ETC) – MAG-E-ETC is the heart and the brain behind the Event Support Center. This web based application tracks all Events as they are happening. In addition to the live tracking of Events, this application also sends instructions to Site Devices during Events to automatically turn systems off and on. For the manual Site Devices, this system will alert the operator to call the Enterprise Customer as they are not setup for automatic Event instructions. The protocol between the application and the site devices is also using XMPP over TCP port 9002.

Corporate Applications:

- MAG-E currently runs VoIP, IM, Video, and Email internally. These applications are used by all employees of MAG-E but VoIP is specifically critical to the Event Support Center Staff as they cannot act on an Event if they cannot call an Enterprise Customer.

Diagram 1

MAG-E WAN Diagram

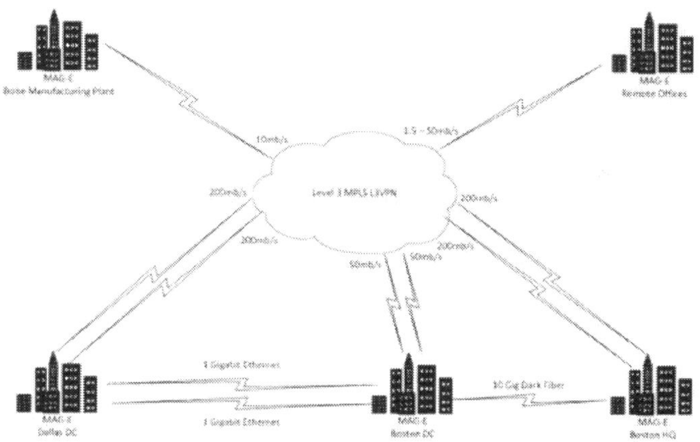

Diagram 2

MAG-E Site Device Termination Internet Option

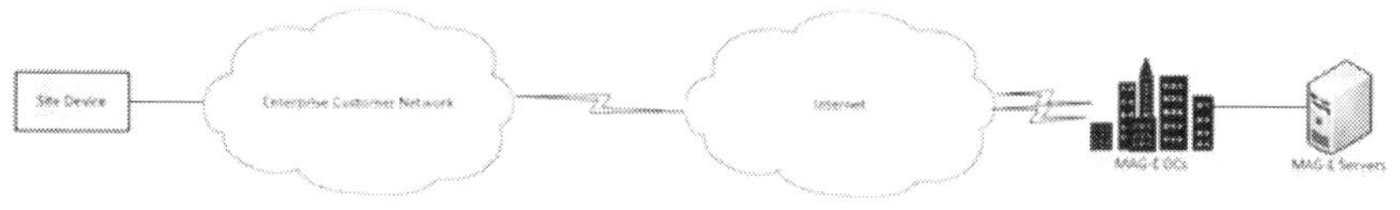

- Site Device will either have a static public address or it will be statically translated to one in the customers network
- The Server needs to access the Site Device over this IP address

Diagram 3

MAG-E Site Device Termination Site to Site IPSEC VPN Option

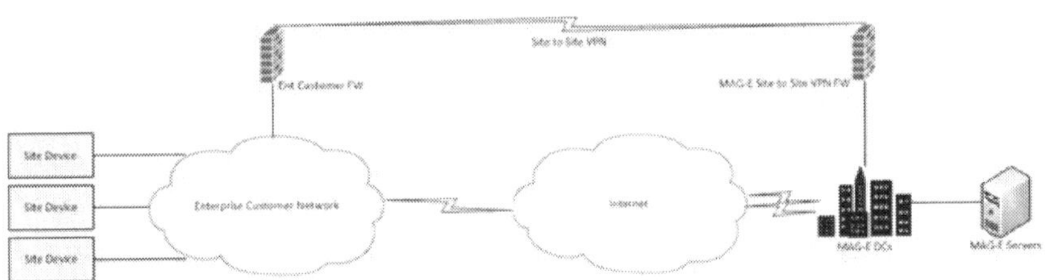

Diagram 4

MAG-E Site Device Termination Private Cellular Network Option

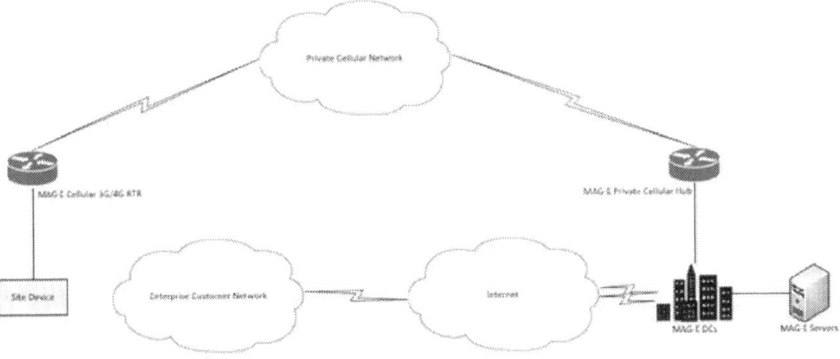

Document 2

From: bob_murphy@mag-e.com

To: Network_Designer

Subject: SAAS Acquisition & Immediate need!

Designer,

The Board will be finalizing the Acquisition of Canada Energy (CAN-ENG) by the end of the week. I need you to clear your schedule ASAP as this is going to be a huge project which I am going to need some significant help. From the little information I have been given today, CAN-ENG has 2,000 employees geographically dispersed across Canada in 37 office locations. CAN-ENG has one data center located in Vancouver and one headquarters located in Montreal. CAN-ENG's Energy Eye,

SAAS application, lives in Vancouver. For the short term, we will be setting up Site to Site VPNs between MAG-E's Boston HQ and CAN-ENG's Montreal HQ, and between MAG-E's Dallas DC and CAN-ENG's Vancouver DC. I'm looking to you to design a long term solution.

The board wants CAN-ENG integrated ASAP so that all MAG-E and CAN-ENG applications can be used from all locations.

In addition to the above, we have an immediate need to develop a new Site Device termination solution. In the past, you've heard me complain about this customer before, and this request is no different. To say it nicely, this Enterprise Customer is a primadonna but we have to play nice because this is a 50 Million dollar contract for us. This customer will not use NAT/PAT or static IP Addresses. They will not change their subnets or configure any VPNs on their hardware. We need you to design a solution that meets these needs and also keeps the Site Devices secure. We need to keep future scalability in mind. Cost shouldn't be a concern but let's not go hog wild now.

Good luck Designer, I know you will do us proud!

Dr. Bob Murphy

VP of Network Infrastructure, MAG-E

Diagram 5

MAG-E and CAN-ENG Site to Site IPSEC VPN

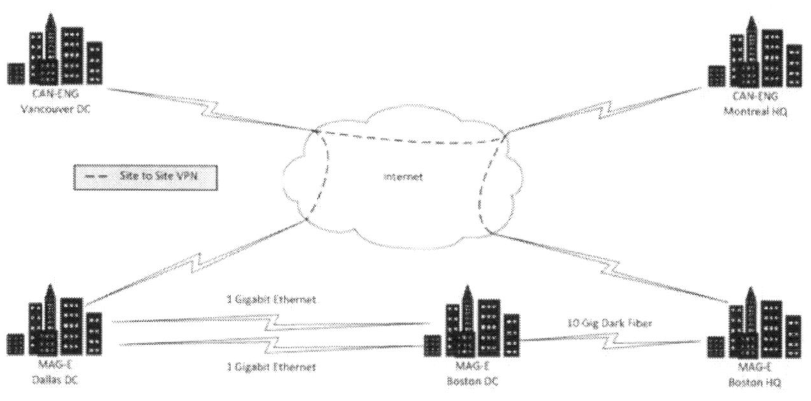

Question 1)

What is the most important design issue with the short term integration plan between MAG-E and CAN-ENG (Choose 1)?

A. A) There is no design issue and this design is a good long term solution

B. B) This design does not follow redundancy/resiliency best practices

C. C) There are a number of bandwidth saturation issues with the different circuits

D. D) There is no guaranty that all applications from both companies will properly function

E. E) This design does not meet the time requirement the customer is requiring

Question 2

Which of the following items will you need from MAG-E to create a successful network design for the new Site Device termination solution (Choose 3)?

A. Network Security Policy

B. IP Addressing Scheme

C. Expected Growth Increase

D. Network Utilization Reports

E. Memory/CPU Utilization Reports

Question 3

If you requested IP Addressing Scheme, which is the best reason to request IP Addressing Scheme (choose 1)?

A. Route summarization

B. IP address scaling

C. Customer needing to change subnets

D. IP address overlap

E. I did not request IP Addressing Scheme

Question 4

What information is needed to properly design the CAN-ENG

Energy Eye integration with MAG-E (Choose 1)?

A. QoS values for application traffic
B. Encryption requirements
C. Application IP address
D. CAN-ENG's Routing protocol

Document 3

From: bob_murphy@mag-e.com
To: Network_Designer
Subject: New Network Security Policy – Encryption Requirements

Designer,

We at MAG-E have recently updated our Network Security policy per the recent Government regulations placed on Energy Data. All data on the wire must be encrypted no matter if it's our own wire, leased wire, or over the internet. We are highly out of compliance with this on our current MPLS L3VPN Cloud and could use some assistance with migrating to a new design that will comply with this new policy. In addition to that, CAN-ENG is also not in compliance with this security policy.

Dr. Bob Murphy
VP of Network Infrastructure, MAG-E

Question 5

Which of the following proposed network solution will meet MAG-E's new encryption requirements for the new Site Device Termination solution? (Choose all that apply)?

A. DMVPN
B. GETVPN

C. Full Mesh of IPSEC VPNs

D. Hub and Spoke IPSEC VPNs

E. VPLS

Question 6

Which of the following proposed network solution will meet all MAG-E's requirements for the new Site Device Termination solution (Choose 1)?

A. DMVPN

B. GETVPN

C. Full Mesh IPSEC VPNs

D. Hub and Spoke IPSEC VPNs

E. VPLS

Question 7a

If you selected DMVPN, which option below is the best reason why (Choose 1)?

A. Running EIGRP is needed on hub and spoke networks

B. A solution that supports encryption is needed per the new security policy implemented.

C. A solution that is highly scalable is needed per the requirements.

D. I did not selected this option

Question 7b

If you selected GETVPN, which option below is the best reason why (Choose 1)?

A. Running EIGRP is needed on hub and spoke networks

B. A solution that supports encryption is needed per the new security policy implemented.

C. A solution that is highly scalable is needed per the requirements.
D. I did not selected this option

Question 7c

If you selected Full Mesh IPSEC VPNs, which option below is the best reason why (Choose 1)?

Running EIGRP is needed on hub and spoke networks

A solution that supports encryption is needed per the new security policy implemented.

A solution that is highly scalable is needed per the requirements.

I did not selected this option

Question 7d

If you selected Hub and Spoke IPSEC VPNs, which option below is the best reason why (Choose 1)?

A. Running EIGRP is needed on hub and spoke networks
B. A solution that supports encryption is needed per the new security policy implemented.
C. A solution that is highly scalable is needed per the requirements.
D. I did not selected this option

Question 7e

If you selected VPLS, which option below is the best reason why (Choose 1)?

A. Running EIGRP is needed on hub and spoke networks
B. A solution that supports encryption is needed per the new security policy implemented.
C. A solution that is highly scalable is needed per the requirements.

D. I did not selected this option

Document 4

From: bob_murphy@mag-e.com

To: Network_Designer

Subject: New Site Device Termination Solution

Designer,

As you have seen with our network in the past, we use RFC 1918 addressing. Our Boston data center uses 10.0.0.0/11, and our Dallas data center uses 10.120.0.0/11. All of our remote office locations currently fit in the 172.16.0.0/12 block in different /22 increments. The 192.168.50.0/24 and 192.168.51.0/24 are reserved networks for our Production DMZ and are used for translating overlapping customer subnets in regards to deployed Site Devices. If there isn't a subnet overlap with a customer's network, then we just dynamically route for the customer's network in our own network. As you can imagine, this leads to a lot of random networks in our routing table that are not our networks but we do need to access them to connect to the Site Devices at the customer locations. Our applications use the following IP addresses:

	MAG-E App	Boston	Dallas
MAG-E-EI	10.1.1.200	10.121.1.200	
MAG-E-OS	10.1.10.50	10.121.10.50	
MAG-E-DF	10.1.57.23	10.121.57.23	
MAG-E-ETC	10.2.0.18	10.122.0.18	

The business is looking at this new Site Device Termination Solution as the last iteration of deploying additional equipment at customer locations other than a Site Device. There will be some growth with the total number of Site Devices over the next few years. The customer would also like direct spoke to spoke connectivity if that is even possible these days.

Time Projected

Device Count	
Today	1,979
3 yrs	2,714
5 yrs	3,418
7 yrs	3,827
10 yrs	4,285

CAN-ENG also uses RFC-1918 private addresses internally. For Vancouver they use 10.2.0.0/16. The CAN-ENG Energy Eye SAAS application resides in Vancouver and it is currently using IP address 10.2.0.100. In Montreal they are using 192.168.200.0/22 and for all other locations the subnets fall within the 10.57.0.0/16 summary range. CAN-ENG is currently using OSPF in a single area 0 as its routing protocol.

I have no Network, CPU or memory utilization reports that would be of importance.

Dr. Bob Murphy

VP of Network Infrastructure, MAG-E

Question 8

Based on the new requirements which solution should MAG-E implement for the New Site Device Termination Solution?

A. GETVPN

B. DMVPN

Question 9a

Why is GETVPN the best option?

A. It fulfills the encryption requirement

B. It fulfills the spoke to spoke traffic pattern requirement

Question 9b

Why is DMVPN the best option?

A. It fulfills the encryption requirement

B. It fulfills the spoke to spoke traffic pattern requirement

DOCUMENT 5

From: bob_murphy@mag-e.com

To: Network_Designer

Subject: New Site Device Termination Solution # 2

Designer,

Thank you for your help thus far. I know it's been a rocky road and I can definitely promise you it's only going to get rockier. As for the New Site Device Termination Solution that you have been working on in your sleep, we are going to implement DMVPN but I still need your help selecting which DMVPN design to implement.

Dr. Bob Murphy

VP of Network Infrastructure, MAG-E

Question 10

Which DMVPN phase and routing protocol combination can meet the requirements (Check all that apply)?

	EIGRP	OSPF	BGP	RIP	ISIS
DMVPN Phase 1					
DMVPN Phase 2					
DMVPN Phase 3					

Question 11

Which DMVPN implementation is the best design given the requirements (Choose 1)?

A. DMVPN Phase 3 with EIGRP

B. DMVPN Phase 2 with OSPF

C. DMVPN Phase 1 with BGP

D. DMVPN Phase 1 with EIGRP

E. DMVPN Phase 3 with ISIS

F. DMVPN Phase 2 with RIP

Question 12

Please place the following implementation tasks regarding the new Site Device Termination solution in the correct order.

A. Protect the mGRE tunnel with IPSEC

B. Configure DMVPN on the spoke routers

C. Configure EIGRP routing between DMVPN mGRE Tunnels

D. Deploy new spoke routers at Site Device Locations

E. Deploy new hub routers at Dallas and Boston DCs

F. Create FVRF on hub routers

G. Configure DMVPN on the hub routers

H. Create FVRF on spoke routers

Question 13

Which of the following information is needed to create a valid network design for the merger of between MAG-E and CAN-ENG (Choose 3)?

A. MAG-E QoS information

B. CAN-ENG QoS information

C. MAG-E Subnet information

D. CAN-ENG Subnet information

E. MAG-E WAN Network Diagram

F. CAN-ENG WAN Network Diagram

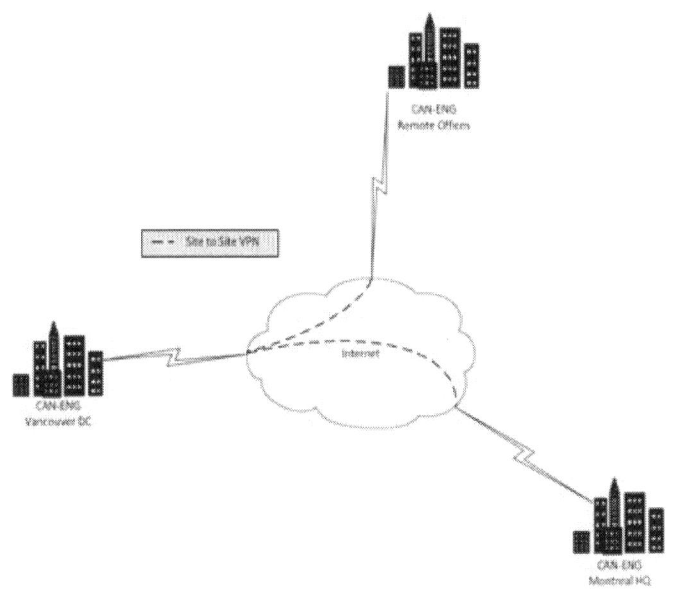

Diagram 6

CAN-ENG WAN Site to Site IPSEC VPN Diagram

Question 14

mary concern if CAN-ENG were to continue with a hub and spoke of IPSEC Tunnels over the internet for its WAN connectivity (Choose 1)?

A. Over Subscription of Circuits

B. Performance of applications

C. Security of energy data

D. Control Plane instability

Question 15

If we were to replace the hub and spoke IPSEC Tunnels that CAN-ENG is using with another technology which technologies below best meet the requirements (Choose 2)?

A. Provision a second MPLS L3VPN network for all Canada location and bridge both MPLS L3VPNs together at the DCs.

B. Implement VPLS to replace the current WAN

C. Deploy a hub and spoke network of L2TPv3 connections

D. Implement LISP to replace the current WAN

E. Add the CON-ENG network into the current MPLS L3 VPN network

Document 6

From: bob_murphy@mag-e.com

To: Network_Designer

Subject: QoS Design

Designer,

Surprisingly, neither company has implemented much QoS as of yet. The only QoS that is implemented is in the MAG-E network for Voice and Video related traffic. All Voice and Video is configured with the EF DSCP value and placed in a LLQ with 33% of the bandwidth. The rest of the applications in both companies are configured for Best Effort.

This is a fairly big issue so I would like to make sure we implement a valid QoS design ASAP. I would like to keep our Queue count simple with only 4 queues: Realtime (EF), Control (CS3), Transactional Data (AF21), and Best Effort (DF) but still manage to include all of the different applications that both companies have.

Regarding the CAN-ENG WAN discussion we had earlier, we have decided to move CAN-ENG from Site to site VPNs to our current MPLS L3VPN. We need to make sure this migration goes over very smoothly and with very little interruption. During this migration we would also like to remove any single points of failures in the DC and HQ locations for the CAN-ENG network.

Dr. Bob Murphy
VP of Network Infrastructure, MAG-E

Question 16

Before we go any further, I need help determining all of the QoS related information for the following application QoS matrix. Please check each box that applies for each application, for the DSCP field please place the DSCP value needed for that application in this design?

	Voice	Video	CAN-ENG Energy Eye	MAG-E-DF	MAG-E-ETC	MAG-E-EI	MAG-E-OS	IM (CHAT)	Network Control	Email	All other traffic
CBWFQ											
WRED											
LLQ											
DSCP											

Question 17

Which of the following CAN-ENG MPLS L3VPN designs meets the requirements (Choose 1)?

A. Diagram A

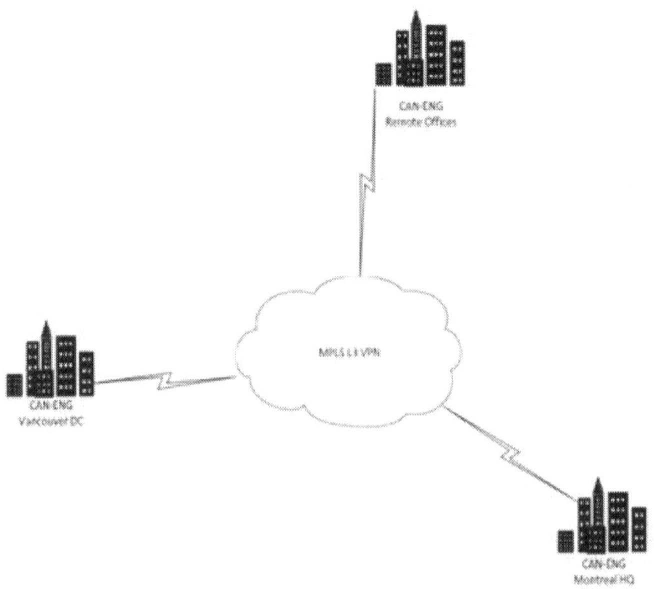

B. Diagram B

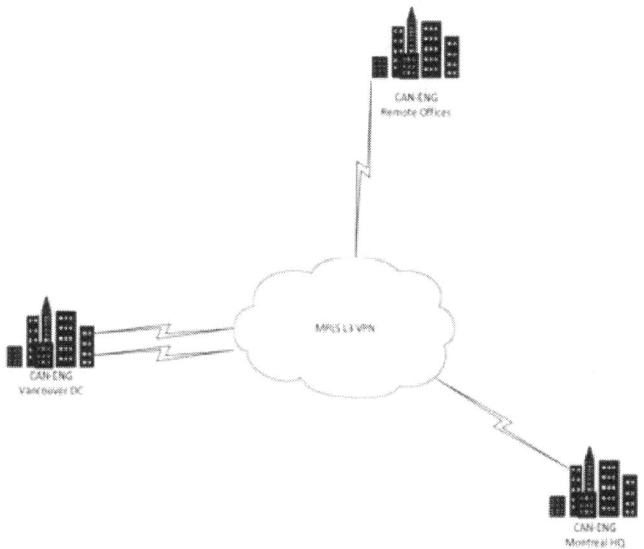

C. Diagram C

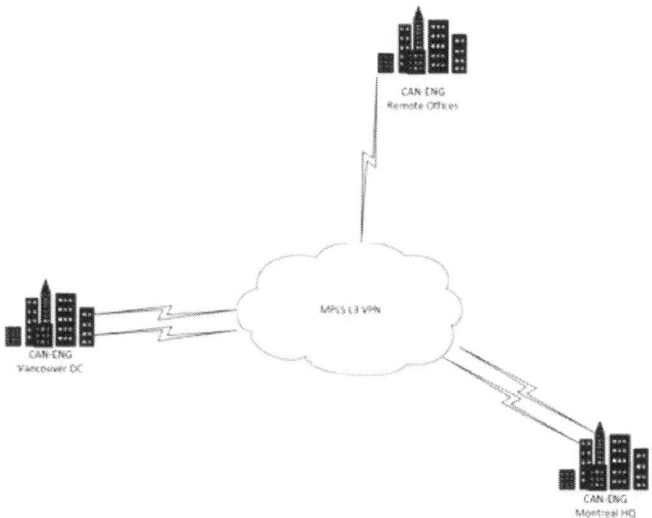

D. Diagram D

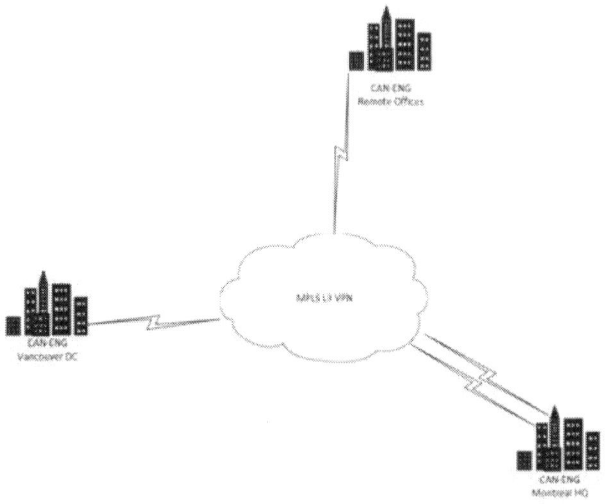

Question 18

Place the following tasks in the order that they should occur to properly migrate the CAN-ENG WAN to MPLS L3VPN.

A. Configure PE-CE routing protocol at DC and HQ, and redistribute
B. Deploy new WAN router at DC and HQ
C. Decommission all Site to Site VPNs
D. Provision and connect new MPLS L3VPN circuits at each location
E. Configure PE-CE routing protocol at each remote location, and redistribute
F. Deploy new WAN router at each remote location
G. Deploy QoS design on all WAN routers.

Document 7

From: bob_murphy@mag-e.com

To: Network_Designer

Subject: WAN Migration Complete

Designer,

The WAN Migration is completed! We do have one major issue that needs to be addressed. We can no longer access the MAG-E-ETC resource from anywhere in the network. We need this resolved before Monday morning or somethings going to hit the fan if you can smell what I am cooking?!?!

In addition to the above, we just got hit with a nasty data privacy lawsuit. We were unaware of some of the new Data separation requirements between Energy Data, Finance Data, and HR Data. As you know, we do not currently segregate our data at all, everyone can access everything. Well these suit and tie nutcases just determined that we cannot continue like this so we need to come up with a solution that allows full separation of data between departments, customers and site devices across all office locations. Keep in mind that most office locations have a small number of people from each department in the office. Each department needs to collaborate, within the department, across different offices at any given time. We would prefer that their traffic would take the most direct path to each other that is possible.

Dr. Bob Murphy

VP of Network Infrastructure, MAG-E

Question 19

What is the best possible reason why the MAG-E-ETC application is no longer accessible throughout the network?

A. Duplicate IP addresses with the Energy Eye Application in CAN-ENG

B. Traffic is no longer allowed via an infrastructure ACL on the core

C. Missing a dynamic route for the MAG-E-ETC subnet

D. Subnet overlap

E. There is a route redistribution issues between EIGRP in MAG-E and OSPF in CAN-ENG.

Question 20

What solution below would be the quickest way to resolve the issue with the MAG-E-ETC application?

A. Advertise a host route for 10.2.0.100

B. Configure NAT for 10.2.0.0/16 to an unused /16 subnet

C. Configure NAT for 10.0.0.0/11 to an unused /11 subnet

D. Advertise a host route for 10.2.0.18

E. Change the IP address of the MAG-E-ETC to another IP in the 10.0.0.0/11 range.

Question 21

What solution below would be the most efficient way to resolve the issue with the MAG-E-ETC application?

A. Advertise a host route for 10.2.0.100

B. Configure NAT for 10.2.0.0/16 to an unused /16 subnet

C. Configure NAT for 10.0.0.0/11 to an unused /11 subnet

D. Advertise a host route for 10.2.0.18

E. Change the IP address of the MAG-E-ETC to another IP in the 10.0.0.0/11 range.

Question 22

Which solutions below are capable of meeting the Data separation requirements, assuming that each option below also includes VRF-Lite (Choose all that apply)?

A. L2TPv3

B. VPLS

C. MPLSoDMVPN

D. GETVPN

E. VXLAN

Question 23

Which solution below meets all of the requirements, assuming that each option below also includes VRF-Lite (Choose 1)?

A. L2TPv3

B. VPLS

C. MPLSoDMVPN

D. GETVPN

E. VXLAN

CCDE PRACTICAL SCENARIO

MAG ENERGY DETAILED ANSWERS

Question 1

What is the most important design issue with the short-term integration plan between MAG-E and CAN-ENG (Choose 1)?

A. There is no design issue and this design is a good long term solution

B. This design does not follow redundancy/resiliency best practices

C. There are a number of bandwidth saturation issues with the different circuits

D. There is no guaranty that all applications from both companies will properly function

Detailed Answer Breakdown:

A. Initial thought: if there is no design issue then why would we be involved to begin with? Let's forget that comment for a minute and look at the other options below.

B. While this might be true from a best practice perspective, there is nothing in the background information to link us to this requirement. If there are no other better options in the question then it might be a good choice to follow best practices as long as no other requirement is inversely affected by doing so.

C. While using IPSec Site to Site VPNs over the Internet could be a bandwidth concern, we have no background information yet regarding the bandwidth or circuit speeds. We also have no information regarding any underlying bandwidth or circuit issues so this option would be incorrect.

D. Of the options for this question, this is the best option as the customer is currently running VoIP and Video. It is also stated in Document 2 that the board wants all MAG-E and CAN-ENG applications to be used from all locations. This line doesn't specifically come out and state VoIP and Video, but it is an application and is included in this statement. This is the correct answer.

E. This is a distractor / obvious wrong answer as the scenario has already stated that this is a short-term solution. This is an incorrect answer.

Question 2

Which of the following items will you need from MAG-E to create a successful network design for the new Site Device termination solution (Choose 3)?

A. Network Security Policy

B. IP Addressing Scheme

C. Expected Growth Increase

D. Network Utilization Reports

E. Memory/CPU Utilization Reports

Detailed Answer Breakdown:

A. To determine a successful network design for the new Site Device termination solution, we would definitely want to know what the security policy is for MAG-E/CAN-ENG. This will determine if we need to have encryption, or if there is any reason why we cannot deploy a specific tunneling technology. This is one of the correct options

B. IP Addressing Scheme would not normally be an intuitive choice for this question but there is a requirement that we must meet for the new Site Device termination solution in Document 2, "This customer will not use NAT/PAT or static IP Addresses". From this requirement we must understand that we will end up routing in some fashion for the customer's networks and overlapping IP Addresses between the customer's network and our network will break functionality and requirements. Of course we should keep in mind that even though the customer is not willing to translate addresses, we could still translate addresses on our site if there is an overlapping IP Subnet Scheme, but we need to know this before designing a solution. This is one of the correct options.

C. When developing a design and a solution, we really should know the grown expectation of the environment in question. In this specific case, we really need to know how many Site devices will be used at initial deployment and how many will be expected over the next 2 – 5 years. These numbers will determine if a solution like DMVPN, Full Mesh GRE Tunnels, MPLS, MPLSoDMVPN, etc.... are even options or not. This is one of the correct options.

D. So far in this scenario there is no real push for resource problems that would require asking for any Utilization/Memory/CPU reports. This is an incorrect option.

E. So far in this scenario there is no real push for resource problems that would require asking for any Utilization/Memory/CPU reports. This is an incorrect option.

Question 3

If you requested IP Addressing Scheme, which is the best reason to request IP Addressing Scheme (choose 1)?

A. Route summarization

B. IP address scaling

C. Customer needing to change subnets

D. IP address overlap

E. I did not request IP Addressing Scheme

Detailed Answer Breakdown:

A. We haven't really discussed routing at all in the scenario except for a brief mention of EIGRP as the IGP in the MAG-E network. In addition, Route summarization wouldn't be a direct reason why we would have chosen IP Addressing Scheme in the previous question. This is an incorrect option.

B. While Scalability of IP Addresses is a good design element, this is an incorrect option for this question as there is a better choice.

C. This is actually a customer requirement in Document 2, "They will not change their subnets…". Selecting this answer would violate this requirement that the customer currently has. This is an incorrect option.

D. Overlapping subnets, or IP Address overlap, is the best option for this question as the customer specifically stated they will not change their subnets.

E. If you didn't choose IP Addressing Scheme in the previous question, you might have thought this was the correct answer but this should have made you think about why it would be important enough to choose IP Addressing Scheme. Even if you got the previous question incorrect you still could have gotten this question correct. With that stated, this is an incorrect option.

Question 4

What information is needed to properly design the CAN-ENG Energy Eye integration with MAG-E (Choose 1)?

A. QoS values for application traffic

B. Encryption requirements

C. Application IP address

D. CAN-ENG's Routing protocol

Detailed Answer Breakdown:

A. Determining / finding out the QoS values for all application traffic is an important requirement for the overall design between MAG-E and CAN-ENG but specifically to the merger, it is a less priority option that option C. This is an incorrect option.

B. The Encryption requirements are an important requirement for the overall design between MAG-E and CAN-ENG but specifically to the merger, the initial priority is option C. This is an incorrect option.

C. This question was done in this order to make the test taker second guess themselves. This question, while a similar answer as the previous questions, is for a different reason. Knowing the Application IP addresses is extremely important for a merger / acquisition design as there might be overlapping IP Addresses / overlapping subnets during the merger of the two networks into one. This is the correct option.

D. CAN-ENG's routing protocol is not necessarily information we need specifically for the Energy Eye application. This is an incorrect answer.

Question 5

Which of the following proposed network solution will meet MAG-E's new encryption requirements for the new Site Device Termination solution? (Choose all that apply)?

A. DMVPN

B. GETVPN

C. Full Mesh of IPSEC VPNs

D. Hub and Spoke IPSEC VPNs

A. VPLS

Detailed Answer Breakdown:

A. Yes DMVPN supports the new Encryption requirements in the new Network Security Policy in Document 3. This is a correct option.

B. Yes GETVPN supports the new Encryption requirements in the new Network Security Policy in Document 3. This is a correct option.

C. Yes Full Mesh IPSEC VPNs supports the new Encryption requirements in the new Network Security Policy in Document 3. This is a correct option.

D. Yes Hub and Spoke IPSEC VPNs supports the new Encryption requirements in the new Network Security Policy in Document 3. This is a correct option.

E. VPLS does not support the new Encryption requirements in the new Network Security Policy in Document 3. This is an incorrect answer.

Question 6

Which of the following proposed network solution will meet all MAG-E's current requirements for the new Site Device Termination solution (Choose 1)?

A. DMVPN

B. GETVPN

C. Full Mesh IPSEC VPNs

D. Hub and Spoke IPSEC VPNs

E. VPLS

Detailed Answer Breakdown:

A. DMVPN does meet all of MAG-E's requirements for the new Site Device Termination solution. It meets the Security requirement and the scalability requirement. This is a correct option.

B. GETVPN does meet all of MAG-E's requirements for the new Site Device Termination solution. It meets the Security requirement and the scalability requirement. This is a correct option.

C. The Full Mesh IPSEC VPNs solution does not meet the scalability requirement from Document 2, "We need to keep future scalability in mind". This is an incorrect option.

D. The Hub and Spoke IPSEC VPNs solution does not meet the scalability requirement from Document 2, "We need to keep future scalability in mind". This is an incorrect option.

E. VPLS does not support the new Encryption requirements in the new Network Security Policy in Document 3. This is an incorrect answer.

Question 7a

A. If you selected DMVPN, which option below is the best reason why (Choose 1)?

B. Running EIGRP is needed on hub and spoke networks

C. A solution that supports encryption is needed per the new security policy implemented.

D. A solution that is highly scalable is needed per the requirements.

E. I did not selected this option

Detailed Answer Breakdown:

EIGRP is not a deciding factor to run DMVPN for this solution. This is an incorrect option.

A. While encryption is a requirement and DMVPN supports it, it is not the best option given. All other options in question 6 support Encryption so we need to compare something else here instead of encryption. This is an incorrect option.

B. Scalability of the solution is the determining factor here that rules out some of these options. This is the correct option.

C. This is an incorrect option.

Question 7b

If you selected GETVPN, which option below is the best reason why (Choose 1)?

A. Running EIGRP is needed on hub and spoke networks

B. A solution that supports encryption is needed per the new security policy implemented.

C. A solution that is highly scalable is needed per the requirements.

D. I did not selected this option

Detailed Answer Breakdown:

A. EIGRP is not a deciding factor to run GETVPN for this solution. This is an incorrect option.

B. While encryption is a requirement and GETVPN supports it, it is not the best option given. All other options in question 6 support Encryption so we need to compare something else here instead of encryption. This is an incorrect option.

C. Scalability of the solution is the determining factor here that rules out some of these options. This is the correct option.

D. This is an incorrect option.

Question 7c)

If you selected Full Mesh IPSEC VPNs, which option below is the best reason why (Choose 1)?

A. Running EIGRP is needed on hub and spoke networks

B. A solution that supports encryption is needed per the new security policy implemented.

C. A solution that is highly scalable is needed per the requirements.

D. I did not selected this option

Detailed Answer Breakdown:

A. This is an incorrect option.

B. This is an incorrect option.

C. This is an incorrect option.

D. This is an incorrect option.

Question 7d

If you selected Hub and Spoke IPSEC VPNs, which option below is the best reason why (Choose 1)?

A. Running EIGRP is needed on hub and spoke networks

B. A solution that supports encryption is needed per the new security policy implemented.

C. A solution that is highly scalable is needed per the requirements.

D.) I did not selected this option

Detailed Answer Breakdown:

A. This is an incorrect option.

B. This is an incorrect option.

C. This is an incorrect option.

D. This is an incorrect option.

Question 7e

If you selected VPLS, which option below is the best reason why (Choose 1)?

A. Running EIGRP is needed on hub and spoke networks

B. A solution that supports encryption is needed per the new security policy implemented.

C. A solution that is highly scalable is needed per the requirements.

D. I did not selected this option

Detailed Answer Breakdown:

A. This is an incorrect option.

B. This is an incorrect option.

C. This is an incorrect option.

D. This is an incorrect option.

Question 8

Based on the new requirements which solution should MAG-E implement for the New Site Device Termination Solution?

A. GETVPN

B. DMVPN

Detailed Answer Breakdown:

A. GETVPN is an incorrect answer because it does not support the Spoke-to-Spoke traffic pattern requirement in Document 4. This is an incorrect option.

B. DMVPN is the correct answer because it does supports the Spoke-to-Spoke traffic pattern requirement in Document 4. This is the correct option.

Question 9a

Why is GETVPN the best option?

A. It fulfills the encryption requirement

B. It fulfills the spoke to spoke traffic pattern requirement

Detailed Answer Breakdown:

A. There is no correct answer for this branching path.

B. There is no correct answer for this branching path.

Question 9b)

Why is DMVPN the best option?

A. It fulfills the encryption requirement

B. It fulfills the spoke to spoke traffic pattern requirement

Detailed Answer Breakdown:

A. This is not the correct reason why we are choosing DMVPN over GETVPN. They both support the encryption requirement. This is an incorrect option.

B. This is the correct reason why we are choosing DMVPN over GETVPN because of the requirement for a Spoke-to-Spoke traffic pattern. This is the correct option.

Question 10)

Which DMVPN phase and routing protocol combination can meet the requirements (Check all that apply)?

Detailed Answer Breakdown:

	EIGRP	OSPF	BGP	RIP	ISIS
DMVPN Phase 1					
DMVPN Phase 2					
DMVPN Phase 3	X		X		

Question 11)

Which DMVPN implementation is the best design given the requirements (Choose 1)?

A. DMVPN Phase 3 with EIGRP

B. DMVPN Phase 2 with OSPF

C. DMVPN Phase 1 with BGP

D. DMVPN Phase 1 with EIGRP

E. DMVPN Phase 3 with ISIS

F. DMVPN Phase 2 with RIP

Detailed Answer Breakdown:

A. DMVPN Phase 3 with EIGRP is the best option shown. There may be some scaling issues once it starts to get into higher number of EIGRP neighbors but we need to Spoke-to-Spoke tunnels to support the customer requirements. This is the correct option.

B. DMVPN Phase 2 is ruled out with any routing protocol because we would need to implement some sort of summarization to reduce the number of routes being advertised and we cannot do this in DMVPN Phase 2. With DMVPN Phase 2, all spokes must learn all routes. This is an incorrect option.

C. DMVPN Phase 1 is ruled out with any routing protocol because we need spoke-to-spoke tunnels and DMVPN Phase 1 does not support this. This is not a correct answer.

D. DMVPN Phase 1 is ruled out with any routing protocol because we need spoke-to-spoke tunnels and DMVPN Phase 1 does not support this. This is an incorrect option.

E. ISIS is not supported over DMVPN because it's not an IP protocol. This is an incorrect option.

F. DMVPN Phase 2 is ruled out with any routing protocol because we would need to implement some sort of summarization to reduce the number of routes being advertised and we cannot do this in DMVPN Phase 2. With DMVPN Phase 2, all spokes must learn all routes. This is an incorrect option.

Question 12

Please place the following implementation tasks regarding the new Site Device Termination solution in the correct order.

A. Protect the mGRE tunnel with IPSEC
B. Configure DMVPN on the spoke routers
C. Configure EIGRP routing between DMVPN mGRE Tunnels
D. Deploy new spoke routers at Site Device Locations
E. Deploy new hub routers at Dallas and Boston DCs
F. Create FVRF on hub routers
G. Configure DMVPN on the hub routers
H. Create FVRF on spoke routers

DETAILED ANSWER BREAKDOWN:

A. The tasks (E,F,G) have to happen in that order.
B. The tasks (D,H,B) have to happen in that order.
C. The above two groupings of tasks can happen in any order between the two groupings, for example: (E,F,G)/(D,H,B) or (D,H,B)/ (E,F,G).
D. Finally C/A can happen in any order but have to be after the above two groups, for example: (E,F,G)/(D,H,B), C/A

Question 13

Which of the following information is needed to create a valid network design for the merger of between MAG-E and CAN-ENG (Choose 3)?

A. MAG-E QoS information
B. CAN-ENG QoS information
C. MAG-E Subnet information
D. CAN-ENG Subnet information
E. MAG-E WAN Network Diagram
F. CAN-ENG WAN Network Diagram

Detailed Answer Breakdown:

A. QoS for MAG-E's applications is needed to verify interoperability and end user expected performance for said applications. We can determine what VoIP and Video would be but the other applications that MAG-E has we have no way to determine without the customer telling us. This is a correct option.

B. QoS for CAN-ENG's Energy Eye application is needed to verify interoperability and end user expected performance between MAG-E and CAN-ENG. We can determine what VoIP and Video would be but regarding Energy Eye we have no way to determine without the customer telling us. This is a correct option.

C. We have already been given MAG-E's subnet information so there is no need for us to ask for it. This is an incorrect option.

D. We have already been given CAN-ENG's subnet information so there is no need for us to ask for it. This is an incorrect option.

E. We have already been given MAG-E's WAN Network Diagram so there is no need for us to ask for it. This is an incorrect option.

F. To successfully develop a network design we need to have the CAN-ENG WAN Network Diagram. Without the CAN-ENG WAN Network Diagram, we would have no information on how the CAN-ENG network is setup currently to then come up with a new design to merge the two environments. This is a correct option.

Question 14

What would be a primary concern if CAN-ENG were to continue with a hub and spoke of IPSEC Tunnels over the Internet for its WAN connectivity (Choose 1)?

A. Over Subscription of Circuits

B. Performance of applications

C. Security of energy data

D. Control Plane instability

Detailed Answer Breakdown:

A. While over subscription of circuits could very well be an issue in some cases, we still do not know the current utilization of CAN-ENG WAN circuits. Nothing in the information given so far has mentioned anything to this being an issue. This is an incorrect option.

B. The key to this question is that the Site-to-Site IPSEC VPNs are going over the internet which has no form of traffic guarantee. Because MAG-E is running VoIP and Video, and CAN-ENG will be running both of these along with all of the MAG-E applications, we need to care about the performance of the applications going across these Site to Site IPSEC Tunnels. There are a number of better solutions that can handle different forms of traffic guarantee. This is the correct option.

C. CAN-ENG is already running hub and spoke IPSEC Tunnels, which would provide an encryption layer over the transport path, thus securing any traffic between the different sites, including Energy Data. This is an incorrect option.

D. The current number of remote office sites for CAN-ENG is only 37. (Found in Document 2). In a bigger network that would have thousands of offices I would think Control Plane instability would be extremely important but for only 37 remote offices, this isn't a huge number of sites. This is an incorrect option.

	Voice	Video	CAN-ENG Energy Eye	MAG-E-DF	MAG-E-ETC	MAG-E-EI	MAG-E-DS	IM (CHAT)	Network Control	Email	All other traffic
CBWFQ			X		X	X	X	X		X	
WRED			X	X	X	X	X	X		X	X
LLQ	X	X									
DSCP	EF	EF	AF21	DF	AF21	AF21	AF21	AF21	CS3	DF	DF

Question 15

If we were to replace the hub and spoke IPSEC Tunnels that CAN-ENG is using with another technology which technologies below best meet the requirements (Choose 2)?

A. Provision a second MPLS L3VPN network for all Canada location and bridge both MPLS L3VPNs together at the DCs.

B. Implement VPLS to replace the current WAN

C. Deploy a hub and spoke network of L2TPv3 connections

D. Implement LISP to replace the current WAN

E. Add the CON-ENG network into the current MPLS L3 VPN network

Detailed Answer Breakdown:

A. Deploying a dedicated MPLS L3VPN WAN solution in Canada is a valid option that meets all of the requirements that both MAG-E and CAN-ENG have. This solution would cost a lot more money than what is currently being spent on the single MPLS L3VPN in the United States. If you recall from Document 2, we were given some leniency on the overall cost of the solution. In addition to that, this is the same technology that is already implemented within MAG-E so there will be some similarity for management and troubleshooting. This is one of the correct options.

B. VPLS solutions have less scalability than an MPLS L3VPN option. In this scenario there is also an issue with lack of staff knowledge on VPLS, so I wouldn't implement VPLS here unless the MPLS L3VPN options broke a requirement in some fashion. This is an incorrect option.

C. Hub and Spoke L2TPv3 would meet some of the requirements but not spoke-to-spoke connectivity or the scalability level that MAG-E has required. This solution would also have a high OPEX cost that wouldn't be manageable. This is an incorrect option.

D. LISP is a very specific and special technology. I would rule out LISP based on the fact that it's not currently implemented in either network MAG-E or CAN-ENG. Thus, the support staff would need time to ramp up on the technology before they would be proficient in it, which could lead to an increase in OPEX and a delay in deploying a solution. This is an incorrect option.

E. Connecting CON-ENG locations into the current MPLS L3 VPN network sounds like a good option if it is available in Canada. This is traditionally much cheaper than option A, two different MPLS providers, but also has limited resiliency. Sticking with MPLS L3VPN would be a good from a staff knowledge point of view since current engineers are familiar with it. This is a correct option.

Question 16

Before we go any further, I need help determining all of the QoS related information for the following application QoS matrix. Please check each box that applies for each application, for the DSCP field please place the DSCP value needed for that application in this design?

Detailed Answer Breakdown:

	Voice	Video	CAN-ENG Energy Eye	MAG-E-DF	MAG-E-ETC	MAG-E-EI	MAG-E-OS	IM (CHAT)	Network Control	Email	All other traffic
CBWFQ			X		X	X	X	X		X	
WRED			X	X	X	X	X	X		X	X
LLQ	X	X									
DSCP	EF	EF	AF21	DF	AF21	AF21	AF21	AF21	CS3	DF	DF

Question 17

Which of the following CAN-ENG MPLS L3VPN designs meets the requirements (Choose 1)?

A. Diagram A

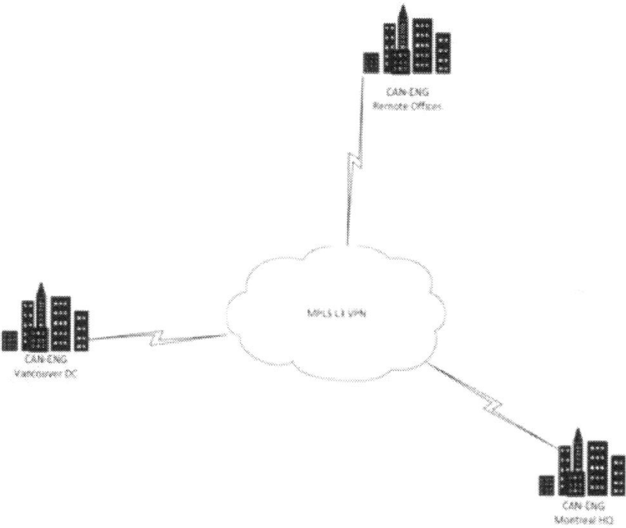

B. Diagram B

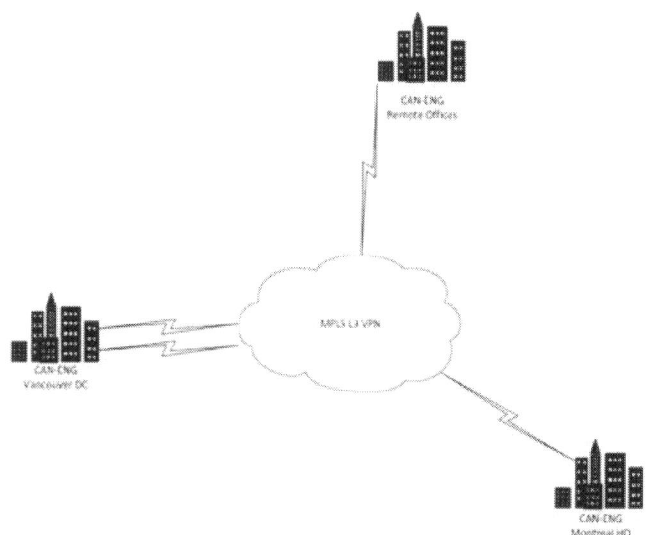

C. Diagram C

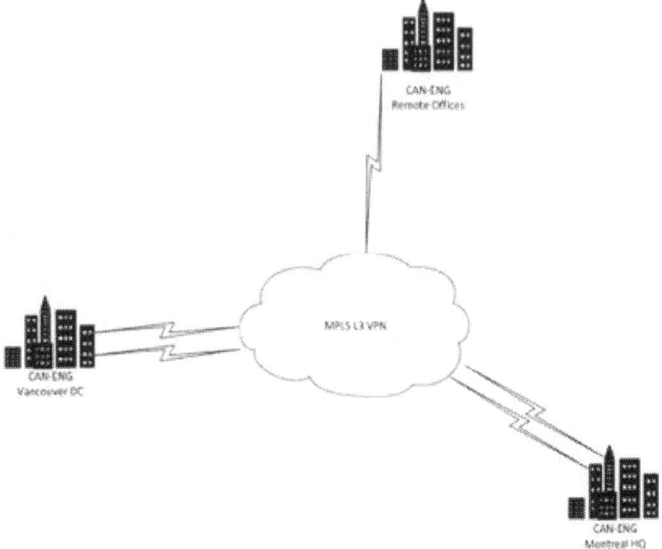

D. Diagram D

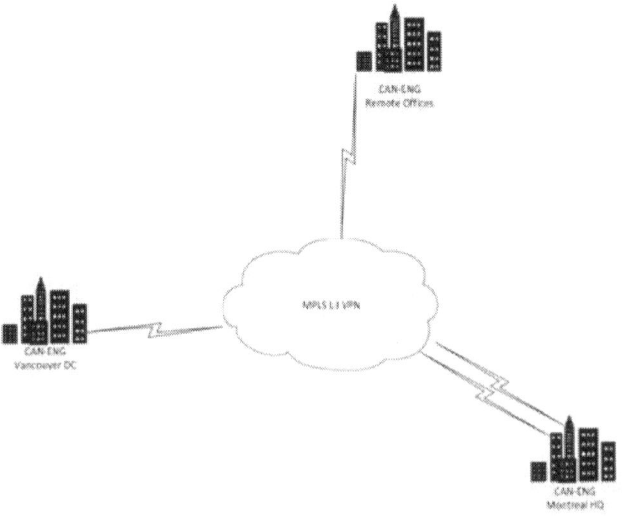

Detailed Answer Breakdown:

For this question you had to find the requirement in Document 6,

"During this migration we would also like to remove any single points of failures in the DC and HQ locations for the CAN-ENG network"

If you happened to miss this requirement it would have made answering this question correctly, very hard.

A. This option has single points of failure in both the DC and HQ locations.
B. This option has a single point of failure in the HQ location.
C. This is the correct option as it does not have any single points of failure in the DC or HQ locations.
D. This option has a single point of failure in the DC location.

Question 18

Place the following tasks in the order that they should occur to properly migrate the CAN-ENG WAN to MPLS L3VPN.

A. Configure PE-CE routing protocol at DC and HQ, and redistribute
B. Deploy new WAN router at DC and HQ
C. Decommission all Site to Site VPNs
D. Provision and connect new MPLS L3VPN circuits at each location
E. Configure PE-CE routing protocol at each remote location, and redistribute
F. Deploy new WAN router at each remote location
G. Deploy QoS design on all WAN routers.

Detailed Answer Breakdown:

A. The tasks (B, A) have to happen in that order.
B. The tasks (F, E) have to happen in that order.

C. The above two groupings of tasks can happen in any order between the two groupings, for example: (B,A)/(F,E) or (F,E)/(B,A).

D. Finally D,G, and C have to be in this order after the above two groups, for example: (B,A)/(F,E) D , G ,C or (F,E)/(B,A) D , G ,C

Question 19

What is the best possible reason why the MAG-E-ETC application is no longer accessible throughout the network?

A. Duplicate IP addresses with the Energy Eye Application in CAN-ENG

B. Traffic is no longer allowed via an infrastructure ACL on the core

C. Missing a dynamic route for the MAG-E-ETC subnet

D. Subnet overlap

E. There is a route redistribution issues between EIGRP in MAG-E and OSPF in CAN-ENG.

Detailed Answer Breakdown:

A. It's meant to look like there might be a duplicate address between MAG-E and CAN-ENG but in reality there isn't. This is an incorrect option.

B. An infrastructure ACL has never been discussed and thus this option should be ruled out just because of this. This is an incorrect option.

C. If the network was missing the route for MAG-E-ETC subnet then a lot of other applications would not be functional. This is an incorrect option.

D. Subnet overlap between MAG-E and CAN-ENG is the reason the MAG-E-ETC application is no longer accessible. The CAN-ENG network has a longer match route in its routing table that is blackholing all traffic destined to MAG-

ETC to somewhere in CAN-ENG's Data Center. This is the correct option.

E. This option looks promising but if we were to draw a new WAN diagram including both MAG-E and CAN-ENG remote offices, we would quickly realize that MAG-E and CAN-ENG's IGPs never touch. The sites connect into the MPLS L3VPN provider before routing to each other. In Summary, there is no redistribution between EIGRP and OSPF between these two merged companies. This is an incorrect answer.

Question 20

What solution below would be the quickest way to resolve the issue with the MAG-E-ETC application?

A. Advertise a host route for 10.2.0.100

B. Configure NAT for 10.2.0.0/16 to an unused /16 subnet

C. Configure NAT for 10.0.0.0/11 to an unused /11 subnet

D. Advertise a host route for 10.2.0.18

E. Change the IP address of the MAG-E-ETC to another IP in the 10.0.0.0/11 range.

Detailed Answer Breakdown:

A. Advertising a host route for 10.2.0.100 would have no effect on MAG-E-ETC. This IP address is the IP for CAN-ENG Energy Eye SaaS application. Implementing this would not break the Energy Eye application but it would not resolve the current issue with MAG-E-ETC. This is an incorrect option.

B. Configuring NAT for 10.2.0.0/16 would be a good choice but it will take some time to complete. This would be more of a long-term solution than a quick solution to resolve the issue right now. This is an incorrect option.

C. Configuring NAT for 10.0.0.0/11 would not be a good choice, as it will affect every application within MAG-E's network. It would eventually resolve the issue with MAG-

E-ETC but it would cause issues with the other applications that MAG-E hosts. This is an incorrect option.

D.

E. This is the best short-term option to resolve the current routing issue with MAG-E-ETC. By advertising a host route for 10.2.0.18, it will allow all traffic to MAG-E-ETC take presentence over the summary route from CAN-ENG. This is the correct option.

F. Changing the IP address of the MAG-E-ETC application would not be a good idea as the customer would have to repoint all site devices to the new IP Address and this would require physically touching each site device, which would take a very long time and would cost a lot of money. This is an incorrect option.

Question 21

What solution below would be the most efficient way to resolve the issue with the MAG-E-ETC application?

A. Advertise a host route for 10.2.0.100

B. Configure NAT for 10.2.0.0/16 to an unused /16 subnet

C. Configure NAT for 10.0.0.0/11 to an unused /11 subnet

D. Advertise a host route for 10.2.0.18

E. Change the IP address of the MAG-E-ETC to another IP in the 10.0.0.0/11 range.

Detailed Answer Breakdown:

A. Advertising a host route for 10.2.0.100 would have no effect on MAG-E-ETC. This IP address is the IP for CAN-ENG Energy Eye SaaS application. Implementing this would not break the Energy Eye application but it would not resolve the current issue with MAG-E-ETC. This is an incorrect option.

B. Configuring NAT for 10.2.0.0/16 would be a good choice but it will take some time to complete. This would be more of a long-term solution than a quick solution to resolve the issue right now. From a NAT solution design perspective we would want to minimize the impact to as little as possible within the network. In this case, we would only be impacting the Energy Eye application and all of the MAG-E applications would continue to be working as expected. This is the correct option.

C. Configuring NAT for 10.0.0.0/11 would not be a good choice as it will affect every application within MAG-E's network. It would eventually resolve the issue with MAG-E-ETC but it would cause issues with the other applications that MAG-E hosts. This is an incorrect option.

D. This is the best short-term option to resolve the current routing issue with MAG-E-ETC. By advertising a host route for 10.2.0.18, it will allow all traffic to MAG-E-ETC take presentence over the summary route from CAN-ENG. This was the short term / quickest option but is not a longer-term solution. This is an incorrect option.

E. Changing the IP address of the MAG-E-ETC application would not be a good idea as the customer would have to repoint all site devices to the new IP Address and this would require physically touching each site device, which would take a very long time and would cost a lot of money. This is an incorrect option.

Question 22

A. Which solutions below are capable of meeting the Data separation requirements, assuming that each option below also includes VRF-Lite (Choose all that apply)?

B. L2TPv3

C. VPLS

D. MPLSoDMVPN

E. GETVPN

F. VXLAN

Detailed Answer Breakdown:

All of the above options with VRF-Lite would meet the new Data separation requirements that have been added in Document 7. Some will be very difficult to implement and manage, while others would be unable to scale with the other requirements in the scenario. For example, with VXLAN and VRF-Lite, we would need to do manually mappings between the VTEPs and the VRF's in question.

Question 23

Which solution below meets all of the requirements, assuming that each option below also includes VRF-Lite (Choose 1)?

A. L2TPv3

B. VPLS

C. MPLSoDMVPN

D. GETVPN

E. VXLAN

Detailed Answer Breakdown:

A. L2TPv3 & VRF-Lite does not meet the scalability or the spoke to spoke traffic pattern requirements that have been discussed throughout the scenario. This is an incorrect option.

B. VPLS & VRF-Lite does not meet the scalability or the Encryption requirements that have been discussed throughout the scenario. VPLS would also require the staff to learn and manage a new technology that they wouldn't normally need to know about. This is an incorrect option.

C. MPLSoDMVPN & VRF-Lite does meet all of the requirements within the scenario. This option is the only option that meets the most direct path, Spoke to Spoke, for a single department to collaborate together across geographically separated offices. This option also ensures that all Department specific traffic is secured in its own VRF and VPN with MPLS and VRF-Lite. This is the correct option.

D. GETVPN & VRF-Lite does not meet the requirement of traffic traversing over the Internet (Site Devices). GETVPN does not work over the Internet and thus will not work as a solution. This is an incorrect option.

E. VXLAN & VRF-Lite does not meet the scalability requirements within the scenario. Having to manually create VTEP and VRF mappings on devices will be tedious and confusion to manage / maintain. This solution also requires a good amount of staff knowledge with VXLAN, which is a new technology that can be complex. This is an incorrect option.

APPENDIX
NETWORK COMPLEXITY

Network complexity plays a very important role during network design. Every network designer tries to find the simplest design.

Although there is no standard definition for the network complexity yet, there are many subjective definitions.

In today network designs decisions are taken based on an estimation of network complexity rather than absolute, solid answer.

If you are designing a network, probably you heard many times a KISS (Keep it simple and stupid) principle.

We said that during a network design you should follow this principle. As you will see later in this topic, if you want to have robust network you need some amount of complexity.

People refuse to have network complexity and believe that network complexity is bad. But this is wrong!

Every network needs complexity and network complexity is good!

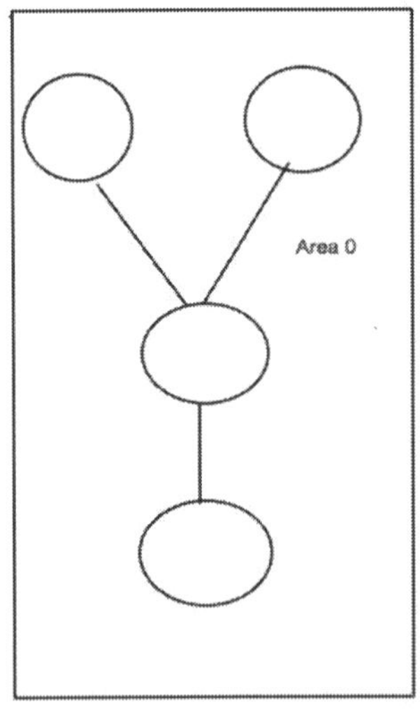

a

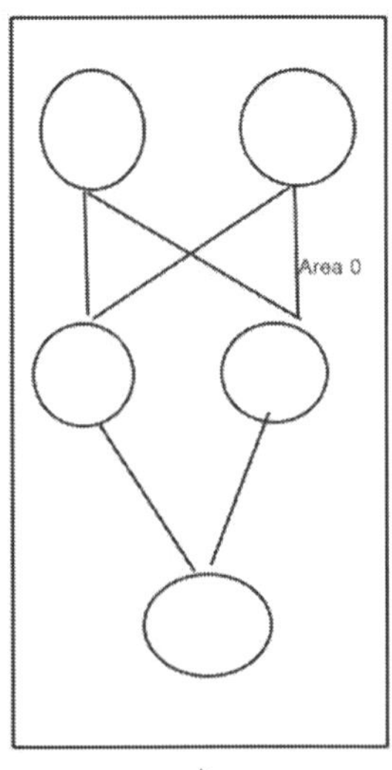

b

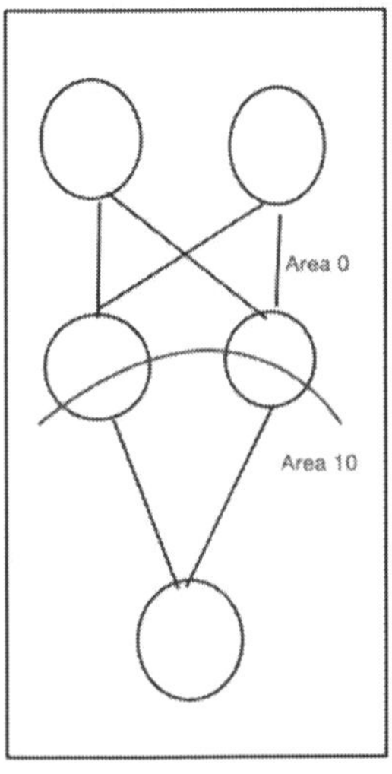

c

In the figure above, the router in the middle is connected to the edge router. Obviously it is not redundant. If we want to design resilient network, we add second router (figure-b), which creates network complexity but provides resiliency through redundancy.

In order to provide resiliency we needed a complexity. But this is a necessary complexity. There is an unnecessary complexity, which we need to separate from the necessary one as I depicted above.

Simple example for the unnecessary complexity is adding a 3 OSPF ABR in the picture-1.

Assume that we are running flat OSPF network as in the picture a and b, state information is kept exactly identical on every node in the domain.

Through layering, complexity can be decreased. In the figure-c, there is an area routing, so multiple area is created to allow summarization of reachability information. Thus state in the devices can be kept smaller so limiting the control plane state might reduce complexity.

But there are tradeoffs here. In order to reduce the control plane states on those devices, summarization needs to be configured on the ABRs, which increases configuration and management complexity.

Although this task can be automated through management systems, someone needs to operate the management systems, so management complexity is not avoided but shifted from operators to management systems.

In this example, placing a second router and then creating multiple OSPF areas allow us to achieve many network design goal.

Resiliency (through redundancy, scaling through layering/hierarchy). These are the parameters of robustness.

John Doyle who is a lead scientist of the Network complexity area states that;

Reliability is robustness to component failures.

Efficiency is robustness to resource scarcity.

Scalability is robustness to changes to the size and complexity of the system as whole.

Modularity is robustness to structure component rearrangements

Evolvability is robustness of lineages to changes on longtime scales.

Robust Yet Fragile is very important paradigm and helps us to understand the network complexity.

A system can have a property that is robust to one set of perturbations and yet fragile for a different property and/or perturbation.

Internet is a good example for robust yet fragile paradigm. It is robust to single component failure but fragile for a targeted attack.

Network design follows Robust Yet Fragile paradigm. Because RYF touches on the fact that all network designs make a tradeoffs between different design goals.

In the picture-1, creating multiple OSPF areas provides scalability through summarization/aggregation but it is fragile because creates a chance for a suboptimal routing.

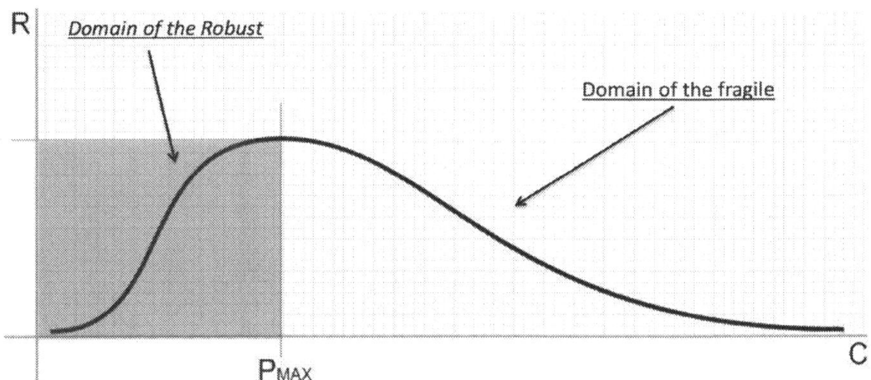

Look at the above figure. We should be in the domain of the Robust and tried to find Pmax. Robustness definitely needs a complexity (at least some) thus NETWORK COMPLEXITY IS GOOD.

What are the elements of the networks?

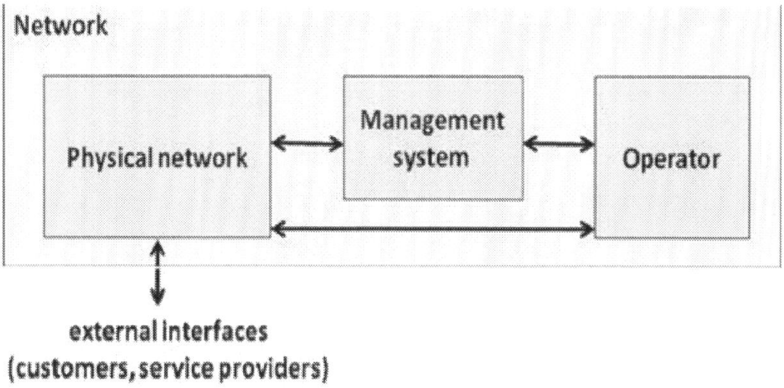

Network

Physical network

Management system

Operator

external interfaces (customers, service providers)

Networks have physical elements, external systems, management systems and operator.

Complexity is found in each sub component of these elements.

Let me explain the network elements in detail :

The physical network contains:

- Network devices, such as routers, switches, optical equipment, etc. This includes components in those devices, such as CPUs, memory, ASICs, etc.
- Links between devices.
- External links, to customers and other service providers.
- Support hardware, such as power supplies, heating, cooling, etc.
- Operating systems.
- Device configurations.
- Network state tables, such as routing tables, ARP tables, etc.

The management system consists of:

- Hardware used for the management systems, and the network connecting them.
- Operating systems of these management systems
- Software for management, provisioning, etc.
- Operational procedures.

he operator is an abstract notion for the combined knowledge required to operate the network. Complexity is in each subcomponent of these three elements. And to understand overall network complexity, we should look at combination of all the subcomponents.

For example, ASICs of one switch can contain 10 million logic gates but in different switch might have 100 million logic gates in ASIC on the line card.

Or in one software might have 1000 of features, but another software might have 10000 of features. When the features increase on the software the chance of problems in the code increases due to increasing complexity.

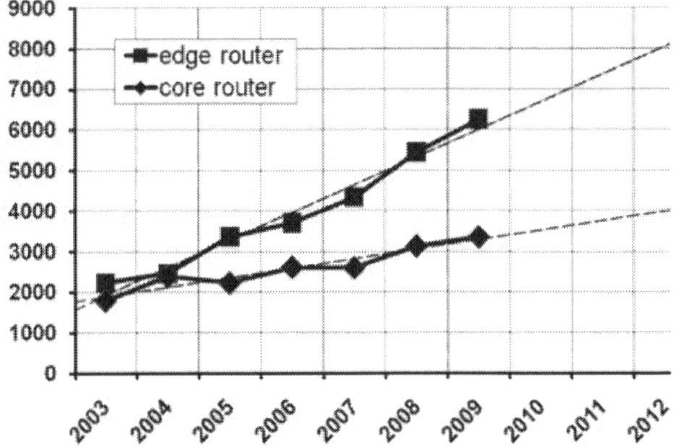

Figure 1: Configuration size (lines) of two typical routers at a tier-2 service provider.

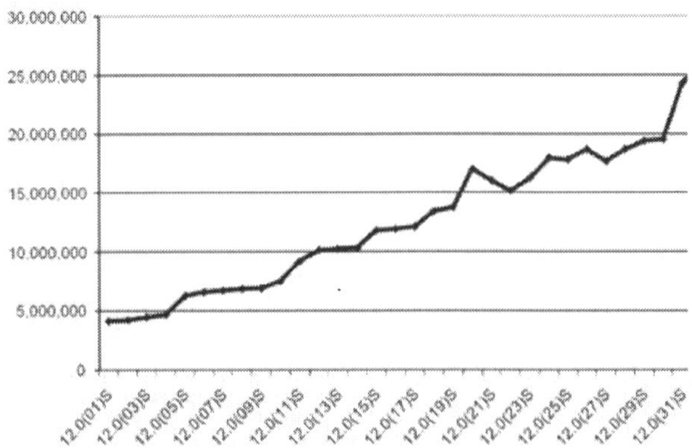

Figure 2: Increase of code size of Internet routers. (Example: Size of binary (bytes), Cisco 12.0S train)

In the picture above figure-1 configuration size on the routers in Tier-2 Service provider .In the figure-2 size of code is shown on the routers.

As you can see, things tend to grow, not shrink!

Increasing line of configuration or size of code comes with a cost of complexity. More features in the software, more configuration on the devices by the time.

Vendor vulnerability announcements increase every period/year due to added features.

How many people know or can remember about all the config on the router from top to bottom.

Entire configuration on the router is managed by the different set of people in the companies!

By the way I should say that having a different configuration on the 10 interface of a router is more complex than having same configuration on the 1000 interface on that router. This is known as modularity and repeatable configuration and deployments are good.

How do you understand whether the network is complex?

Many protocols and features: Networks run many protocols and have processes for their operation.

These protocol interactions create a complexity in your networks.

Example for this, you run OSPF or IS-IS as a link state protocols and for the fast reroute you might be running MPLS TE-FRR. To be able to provide it, you need to run not only OSPF or IS-IS but also RSVP and most probably LDP as well.

It is of course relative but BGP is not a complex protocol for me and probably for those who read this article up to here. But policy interaction between BGP peers create BGP wedgies(RFC 4264) and policy violations due to data plane vs. control plane mismatch.

So the complexity here comes from conflicting policy configuration used on two different Autonomous Systems although you understand many thing about BGP.(Small amount of input (policy in BGP) creates large amount of output in complex networks)

Unpredictable: In a complex network, effect of a local change would be an unpredictable on the global network.

Don't you have a configuration on your routers or firewall, which even you don't know why they are there but you can't touch them since you cannot predict what, can happen if you remove them.

Predictability is critical for the security.

Fragility: In a complex networks, change in one piece of the network can break the entire system.

I think layering is a nice example to explain fragility. I use layering term for the underlay and overlay networks here.

In an MPLS networks, you run routing protocol to create a topology and run MPLS control and data plane for the services. Overlay network should follow the underlay network.

Overlay is LDP and underlay is IGP. If failure happens in the network, due to protocol convergence timing, blackhole occur. In order to solve this issue, either you enable LDP session protection or LDP-IGP synchronization.

Protocol interactions are the source of complexity, it creates fragility and to make the network more robust you add new set of features (in this example LDP-IGP Synchronization or Session protection). Added each feature increases the overall complexity.

Expertise : If some of the failures in your network require the top experts involvement to resolve the issue, most probably your network is complex.

Ideally the front line/layer 1 or 2 engineers should resolve many of the issues.

We can visualize network complexity as a cube. It is shown in the below picture.

The overall complexity of a network is composed of three vectors: the complexity of the physical network, of the network management, and of the human operator. The volume of the cube represents the complexity of the overall network.

Most of the networks including Enterprises and Service providers had a second complexity model, which is shown below, in the beginning of the Internet. Small physical network, less network management but mostly operated by humans.

Large service providers today attempt to lower the dependencies of human operators, and instead use sophisticated management systems. An example complexity cube could look like illustrated in the first figure. Overall complexity of today's networks, illustrated by the volume of the cube, has increased over the years.

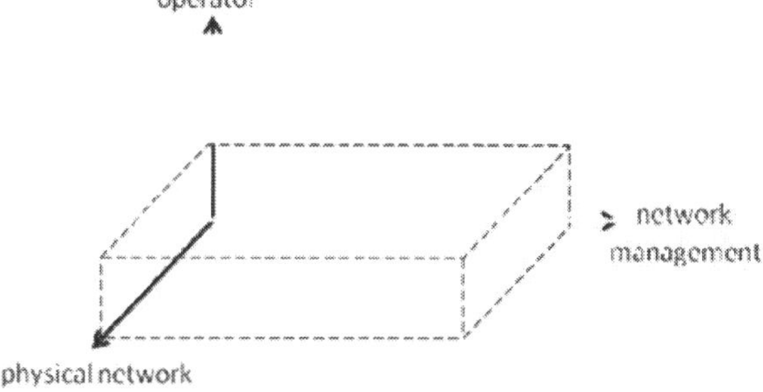

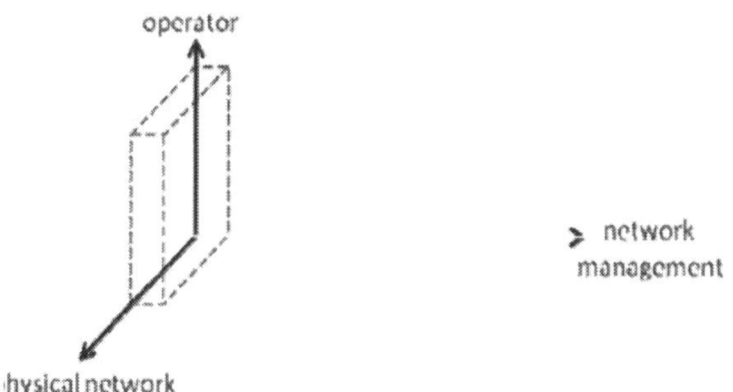

Today with the SDN idea, we target to remove the complexity from the operator and shifting to network management systems. Also centralizing control plane to the logically centralized but physically still distributed place.

This is not a totally bad idea in my opinion since it provides a coherency.

We don't configure the networks, we configure the routers !

We try to configure the many routers, switches etc. and wait the result to be a coherent. But at the end we face all kind of loops, micro loops, broadcast storms, routing churns, and policy violations.

Network management systems reduce the effect of those by knowing the entire topology, intend of the policy and configure the results to entire network.

I mentioned above that network design is about making tradeoffs between different design goals.

Network complexity research group published a draft and covered some of the design goals, of course these are not the full list but it is a good start.

- Cost: How much does the network cost to build (capex) and run
- (opex)
- Bandwidth / delay / jitter: Traffic characteristics between two points (average, max)
- Configuration complexity: How hard to configure and maintain the configuration
- Susceptibility to Denial-of-Service: How easy is it to attack the service
- Security (confidentiality / integrity): How easy is it to sniff /modify / insert the data flow
- Scalability: To what size can I grow the network / service
- Extensibility: Can I use the network for other services in the future?
- Ease of troubleshooting: How hard is it to find and correct problems?
- Predictability: If I change a parameter, what will happen?
- Clean failure: When a problem arises, does the root cause lead to
- Deterministic failure

We should add resiliency and fast convergence into the list.

But don't forget that your network don't have to provide all these design goals.

For example my home network consist of wireless modem, which has one Ethernet port. It is not scalable but very cost effective.

Cost vs. Scalability is the tradeoff here.

I don't need scalable network in my home if I need it obviously it will cost me more.

Or scalability requirement of your company network is not the same as Amazon probably. But to have Amazon scale network, you need to invest.

CONCLUSIONS:

- If you need robust network, you need some amount of complexity.
- You should separate necessary complexity from an unnecessary complexity. If you need redundancy dual redundancy is generally good and enough. You can unnecessarily make it complex by adding third level of redundancy.
- You can come up with many valid network design for the given requirements, eliminate the ones, which have unnecessary complexity.
- We don't have numeric number for the network complexity, for example you can't say that out of 10, my network complexity is 6 and if I add or remove this feature,protocol,link etc. I can reduce it to 5. We are seeking to find a way to have these numbers.
- Network design is about managing the tradeoffs between different design goals.
- Not all network design has to be scalable, fast convergence, maximum resiliency characteristics and so on.
- Complexity can be shifted between physical network, operators and network management systems and overall complexity is reduced by taking the human factor away. Complexity cube is a good idea to understand this.SDN helps to reduce overall network complexity by taking some responsibility from the human operators.
- Network design follows Robust Yet Fragile paradigm. Robustness requires complexity.
- Don't try the fancy,bleeding edge technologies just to show that you are smart !
- System complexity is not the same as network complexity. System complexity should be thought as the combination of the edges (hosts,servers,virtual servers etc) and the network core.

SEGMENT ROUTING

Segment routing refers to a source routing mechanism that provides Traffic Engineering, Fast Reroute, and MPLS VPNS without LDP or RSVP-TE.

As you are reading this post, you will learn everything about segment routing. With some extension to the existing protocols, this source routing mechanism will assist you to solve all the complex problems related to Traffic Engineering, Fast Reroute, and MPLS VPNS.

With RSVP-TE, you can use MPLS to create BGP free core, VPN services (layer 2 and layer 3), and traffic engineering capability.

What is Segment Routing ?

Segment Routing is one of the ways of implementing source routing mechanism.

I implore you not to confuse source routing with policy based routing (PBR), they are totally different.

With Segment routing, end-to-end path is pushed to the ingress node and the subsequent nodes just apply the instructions. With PBR, if path will be different than the routing table, each and every node as hop by hop fashion should be configured.

Segment routing can be compared with the MPLS Traffic Engineering since both protocols can route the traffic explicitly.

While the source is an edge node, it can be a server, a top of rack switch, a virtual switch, or an edge router. Source allows service chaining, and its entire path can be exposed to ingress/head end router.

What does segment means ?

Segment is the component path that allows the packets to travel, a task specified by the user.

For instance, you could direct a component travelling from firewall X to go to router A, and then to router B. Yes, you can do that.

In fact, service chaining can be achieved with Segment Routing.

Even though Segment Routing uses IP control plane, it employs MPLS data plane in its operation. Segment ID is equivalent to MPLS label, and segment list is exposed to label stack.

Some extensions of OSPF and IS-IS are necessary for the Segment Routing because segment/label moves within the link state IGP protocol messages.

To understand how Segment Routing functions, you need to understand MPLS VPN operation.

MPLS VPN Operation

If you know everything about MPLS VPN operation already, you can skip this section.

The below diagram depicts the MPLS VPN operation.

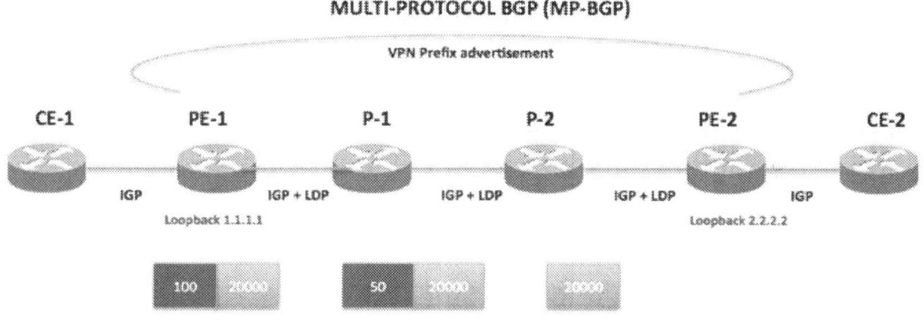

MPLS VPN Label Operation (Control and Dataplane)

The diagram above has two labels: core label, also known as transport, tunnel or topmost label. In MPLS layer 2 or layer 3 VPN operations, the topmost label moves from PE1 loopback to PE2 loopback. While the topmost label provides an edge-to-edge reachability, LDP, RSV, or BGP allows core/transport label.

In the context of MPLS VPN, LDP is the most commonly used label distribution protocol.

If you want to use MPLS Traffic Engineering architecture, then you need to enable RSVP-TE for label distribution. And of course, LDP and RSVP can coexist in the network.

VPN label is provided by BGP, specifically Multi-protocol BGP.

PE routers change BGP next hop as their loopback addresses to the VPN prefixes. Also, core/transport label is used to reach the BGP next hop.

PE1 pushes two labels: the red label and the blue label. Sent by P1 to PE1 via LDP, red label – which is the core/transport label – is changed at every hop.

The red label is removed at P2 if PE2 sends an implicit null label, a process known as PHP (Penultimate hop popping).

The blue label is the VPN label sent by PE2 to PE1 through MP-BGP session.

Next, I will explain MPLS VPN operations with Segment Routing.

MPLS VPN with Segment Routing

If similar operation is done with Segment Routing, the red label is sent from PE2 to all the routers within the IGP domain via link state protocols (OSPF or IS-IS), not within the LDP label messages (see picture below).

Node segment ID, also known as prefix segment ID, is used for specifying the loopback interface of Segment Routing enabled device.

Within the loopback interface, Segment Routing is enabled; because of that, Node/Prefix Segment identifier is assigned to such loopback interface. Throughout this post, I will use the SID abbreviation for Segment ID.

Node/Prefix SID is sent via either IS-IS or OSPF LSP and LSAs.

All the Segment Routing enabled routers receive and learn Node/ Prefix SID from one another.

To assist you to understand this topic, I will explain MPLS Layer 3 VPN operation as well as segment routing.

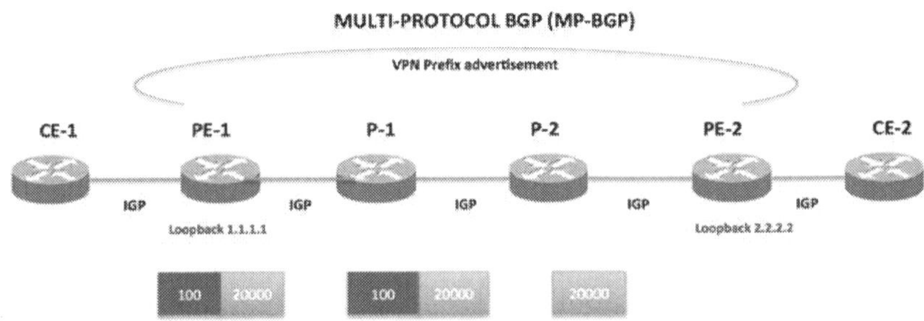

Segment Routing Label Operation (Control and Dataplane)

As you must have observed, there is no LDP in the above diagram. Label 100 is advertised with the IGP protocol (Not via LDP or RSVP), and all the routers use identical label.

Unlike LDP, label 100 does not change hop by hop.

Through MP-BGP, PE1 still receives a VPN label for the CE2 prefixes.

BGP next hop is PE2 loopback. PE2 loopback uses label 100 in the IS-IS sub-TLV or OSPF Opaque LSA.

PE1 assumes label 100 as a core / transport label, and so too does the outer label consider label 2000 the inner VPN label.

P1 does not change the core/transport label; rather, it sends the packet to the P2.

If P2 receives an implicit null label from PE2, P2 does PHP (Penultimate Hop Popping). In sum, only the VPN label is sent to the PE2.

Without using LDP but by using IGP, MPLS VPN service is provided. Segment Routing does not require LDP for the transport tunnel because it uses IGP for the label advertisement.

Please note that Segment Routing eliminates to use LDP only for the transport label operation.

If you setup MPLS layer 2 VPN for the PW label, you will use either LDP or BGP because Segment Routing does not provide such capability.

PW (Pseudowire) can be signaled via LDP or RSVP. LDP signaled pseudowire is also known as Martini pseudowire, while BGP signaled pseudowire is also known as Kompella pseudowire.

So, if you provide layer 2 VPN service with Segment Routing, you will notice two labels: transport label provided by the IGP to reach the correct PE; and LDP or BGP assigned label for the end customer AC (Attachment circuit) identification in the remote PE.

MPLS is very powerful with its applications.

MPLS layer 2 VPNs (VPWS, VPLS, and VPMS), MPLS Layer 3 VPNs, and MPLS Traffic Engineering are the most common applications of IP/MPLS networks.

MPLS Traffic Engineering is used in large enterprise networks, especially in Service Provider and Web OTT.

More importantly, you can use all the MPLS applications with Segment Routing.

Source routing is not a new topic but Cisco's Segment Routing brought some enhancements to the Source Routing paradigm and IETF SPRING Working group published several draft (there is even an RFC for the problem statement) for the Segment Routing.

Resource consumption such as the CPU and Memory can be reduced with Segment Routing greatly.

If you have 100 Edge Routers in your network and if you enable MPLS Traffic Edge to Edge, you would have 100×99/2 = 4950 LSP states on your Midpoint LSR. This is prevalent in many MPLS TE enabled network. If you enable Segment Routing and if you evaluate the same midpoint case (since you assign a Prefix/Node SID for every Edge router), Midpoint LSR would have 110 entries instead of 4500 entries.

In Segment Routing, segment list can easily get big if you use explicit routing for the purpose of OAM. If you do that, you may end up with 7-8 segments. In that case, hardware support should be verified.

Cisco claims that they have performed the tests on a number of service provider networks and that their findings show that two or three segments would be enough for the most explicit path scenarios.

Segment Routing Conclusion:

- You can use Segment Routing to provide MPLS VPN service without using LDP for the transport label distribution.
- Segment Routing reduces memory and CPU requirements in the network.
- Segment Routing is totally different technology than PBR (Policy Based Routing).
- Segment Routing requires OSPF or IS-IS and sends MPLS labels within these protocols update packets.
- Segment Routing provides Traffic Engineering without having soft state RSVP-TE protocol on your network. Soft state protocols require a lot of processing power. Although Segment Routing does not have permission control, you can use routers to specify, for instance, 50Mbs LSP path for traffic A and 30 Mbps for traffic B using centralized controller, a process that allows you to use traffic engineering.
- Segment Routing provides Fast Reroute without RSVP-TE, and you do not need to have thousands of forwarding state in the network, as it uses IP FRR technology, specifically Topology Independent LFA. (TI-LFA)

- Segment Routing has many use cases. Segment routing can be used together with MPLS VPN, Traffic Engineering, and Fast Reroute even though Dual Plane topologies are other use cases for the operators.
- With Traffic Engineering, you can have ECMP capability, a task that is very difficult to achieve with MPLS Traffic Engineering (You need to create multiple parallel LSPs).
- There are other use cases such as Egress peering engineering. Today, this can be achieved by the complex BGP policy or LISP. Segment routing is another way of doing BGP Egress peer engineering (BGP EPE).
- Major vendors – including Alcatel, Ericson, and Juniper – support segment Routing.
- If you have devices not supported Segment Routing but only LDP, you can use Segment Routing to interwork with the LDP enabled devices. Segment Routing Mapping Server provides interworking functionality.
- Segment Routing with the help of controller such as PCE (Path Computation Element) can be used for Centralized Traffic Engineering, which provides better Global Path Optimization, and enhanced services such as bandwidth calendaring and complete disjoint paths. Although these features are not done only by Segment Routing (MPLS TE with centralized controller provides the similar functionalities), Segment Routing LSPs can be signaled or instantiated via the controller as well.

CARRIER ETHERNET

Carrier Ethernet is an attempt to expand Ethernet beyond the borders of Local Area Network (LAN), into the Wide Area Networks (WAN).

With Carrier Ethernet, customer sites are connected through the Wide Area Network. Carriers have connected the customers with ATM (Asynchronous Transfer Mode) and Frame Relay interfaces in the past. (User to Network Interface/UNI).

Carrier Ethernet is not about the Ethernet within the Local Area Networks.

Driver of Carrier Ethernet is; since Ethernet is the de-facto protocol on the Local Area Network, why not to use Ethernet everywhere, and not only within LAN. When any other Wide Area Network protocol is used such as ATM, customer Ethernet frame is encapsulated into another protocol.

This reduces the overall efficiency of customer service, consumes more network bandwidth, makes troubleshooting harder and many other drawbacks.

Carrier Ethernet is also known as Carrier Class Ethernet and Carrier Grade Ethernet.

Another reason for Carrier Ethernet is; Ethernet interfaces and the devices are cheaper compare to the other technologies. This results cheaper service to the customers.

CARRIER ETHERNET REQUIREMENTS

Traditional Ethernet lacks many features, which are required to transport critical services, time sensitive applications and voice services.

These are:

- Traffic Engineering
- Bandwidth Guarantee
- Quality of Service
- OAM
- Decoupling of Providing and Customer Networks
- Resilience, High Availability, Fast Convergence

Metro Ethernet Forum (MEF) is a standard body, which defines the Carrier Ethernet, its services and all the extensions.

CARRIER ETHERNET SERVICE TYPES

MEF has been defined three service types for Carrier Ethernet:

- E-LINE (Point-to-Point)
- E-LAN (Multipoint-to-Multipoint)
- E-TREE (Hub and Spoke)

E-LINE, E-LAN and E-TREE are the MEF terms. They are used as below in the IETF standards. They are exactly the same things.

- E-LINE = VPWS
- E-LAN = VPLS
- E-TREE = VPMS

Very important point in Carrier Ethernet is Service Provider transport protocol doesn't have to be Ethernet. If it is Ethernet, then the solution is called Carrier Ethernet Transport.

So in this case, Customer's Ethernet frame is carried over Provider's Ethernet infrastructure with the Resiliency, OAM, Bandwidth guarantee, Traffic Engineering, QoS and other Carrier Ethernet feature supports.

ETHERNET over NON-ETHERNET TRANSPORT

As it is stated above, Customer Ethernet service can be carried over Non-Ethernet Service Provider transport infrastructure, so different technologies can be used. These are:

- SONET/SDH
- Ethernet over MPLS (E-LINE, E-LAN , E-TREE)
- MPLS-TP (MPLS Transport Profile)
- PBB-TE (Provider Backbone Bridge - Traffic Engineering)
- Synchronous Ethernet
- OTN (Optical Transport Network)

This is not the full list but the common ones. Still many networks use

SONET/SDH as a transport mechanism.

Recently there are many debates in the Carrier community around MPLS-TP, OTN and Ethernet.

Carrier Ethernet and the transport technologies are still evolving. Some standards are completed and others are still being developed.

Made in the USA
Middletown, DE
22 November 2016